3/2000    $30⁰⁰

D1558833

*Abraham Hammatt. 1854.*

# THE HAMMATT PAPERS

## EARLY INHABITANTS OF IPSWICH, MASSACHUSETTS, 1633-1700

BY ABRAHAM HAMMATT

*Indexed by Robert Barnes*

*Baltimore*
GENEALOGICAL PUBLISHING CO., INC.

Originally published in seven parts
Ipswich, Massachusetts, 1880-1899
Reprinted, seven parts in one,
With an added Index
Genealogical Publishing Co., Inc.
Baltimore, 1980, 1991
Library of Congress Catalogue Card Number 80-65361
International Standard Book Number 0-8063-0889-3
Made in the United States of America

# PREFATORY NOTE.

THIS edition of Mr. Hammatt's Papers is printed from his MSS as he left them. He confined his labors chiefly to the Inhabitants of Ipswich between the years 1633 and 1700.

Since his death—twenty-six years ago—many facts concerning Early Ipswich have been unfolded by historical research and publications; and it is hoped that the printing of these pages will develope an interest in our ancestors, so true and so deep and so abiding, that the result will be the continuation of the work to 1800, with the addition of all the more recently discovered facts, and thus make Mr. Hammatt's inestimable labor to be of increased interest and value.

# ABRAHAM HAMMATT.

The Historical and Genealogical Register recorded the death of Mr. Hammatt as follows:

Abraham Hammatt, Ipswich, died 9 August, 1854, æ 74. Mr. Hammatt was a true Antiquary and remarkably accurate Genealogist. The New England Historical and Genealogical Society, of which he was a member, have sustained a severe loss in his death.

A newspaper printed in Bath, Me., paid a just tribute to his memory :—

Died at Ipswich, Mass., August 9, 1854, Mr. Abraham Hammatt. He had been for more than thirty years an inhabitant of our city, [Bath, Me.,] and was so well known among us as a gentleman, and as accomplished in the *belles lettres* and mathematical departments of learning, besides being a very able mechanic, that it may not be deemed presumption to respectfully notice his death.

He was a native of Plymouth, Mass., and of Pilgrim descent. " I have succeeded," he wrote, "in tracing my ancestry to six of the passengers in the May Flower and six who came in the Anne."

At an early age he went to learn the trade of a Rope Maker, and served out his time in Plymouth.

In the year 1800 he came to Bath, a stranger, with a letter of introdvction to the late Gen. King, who assisted him in setting up his business here.

He owned the old rope walk, which headed on Centre street. For years he carried on the business of rope making in Bath, which was not then as now : for early in this century there were no chain cables, all were made of hemp.

After years of industry in the pursuit of his business, Mr. Hammatt who was a bachelor, found himself in so easy circumstances as to be able to devote himself to literature and science, for which he had a fine taste, and equally fine talent. In a few years few men could be found of such varied learning. He was unquestionably the best scholar in Bath, not excepting the men of any of the learned professions.

During the first fifteen years of his residence in Bath, his society was courted by Gen. King, Gen. Wingate, Peleg Tallman, as well as by most of the learned professions, and this because he was a gentleman and man of science.

About eighteen years since, Mr. Hammatt left Bath and took up his permanent residence in Ipswich, Mass., where he married an accomplished widow, Mrs. Dodge. He carried with him and sustained there the same character and rank he held while an inhabitant of Bath.—*Bath, Me., August, 1854.*

Mr. Hammatt married Mrs. Lucy [Farley] Dodge, widow of Mr. William Dodge. She was a lady of queenly bearing, and by birth, marriage, and estate, held position in the cultivated rank of Ipswich society. She was the daughter of Maj. Robert and Susan [Kendall] Farley, and grand daughter of Gen. Michael and Elisabeth [Choate] Farley. Her father and grandfather were thorough patriots, both serving in the Revolution. It is said of her grandmother Farley, that when a regiment, expecting to meet the enemy were to be supplied with ammunition, which was in the garret of her house, she filled every man's powder horn with her own hands.

At his marriage Mr. Hammatt came to Ipswich to reside. His quiet and gentlemanly ways, his continuous interest in educational matters, won for him a general recognition and regard. He held the office of Feoffee of the Grammar School, and visiting committee of other schools. His presence was always welcome in the school room. Scores of Ipswich boys and girls, now in the midst of their days, have kindest memories of him.

In his pleasant and comfortable declining years, he prepared the following pages : " *The Early Inhabitants of Ipswich;*" and copied the Inscriptions in the ancient Burying Yard on High Street ; and wrote a History of the Grammar School, from its foundation, January 11-21, 1650-1, to its 200th Anniversary, 1851 ; at which time it was read by John Richards Baker, Esq.

He had begun the revision of his Manuscripts, apparently, and had proceeded about twelve pages, when this labor of his mind and hand ceased ; and in the satisfaction of a blameless and benevolent life, and in great quietness of spirit, he fell asleep.

Mrs. Hammatt, with true wisdom, donated his Papers to our Public Library, thus affording opportunity to all to gather such help from them as they afford.

Ipswich, *January, 1880.*

*Aprill 1th, 1633.* It is ordered, that noe pson wtsoeuer shall goe to plant or inhabitt att Aggawam, withoutt leave from the Court, except those that are already gone, vz : Mr. John Winthrop, Jun'r, Mr. Clerke, Robte Coles, Thomas Howlett, John Biggs, John Gage, Thomas Hardy, Willm Perkins, Mr. Thornedicke, Willm Srieant.

June 11, 1633. There is leave graunted to Tho : Sellen to plant att Aggawam.

5 August, 1634. It is ordered that Aggawam shalbe called Ipswitch.

At Ipsidge a plantation made upe this yeare. Mr. Ward P. Mr. Parker T.—*James Cudworth, 1634.*

ABBOTT, Nehemiah, son of George of Rowley, is mentioned in the will of his brother Thomas, Sept. 30, 1659. He was a commoner of Ipswich in 1664 and 1678. He married Dec. 19, 1659, Mary How, and had a daughter Mary, born Nov. 19, 1660, and another with the same name, Nov. 1, 1665, who died Dec. 12, 1668. With the the title of Deacon, he had a seat assigned to him "behind ye pulpit" in the Meeting House then recently built, Jan. 16, 1700. He died in 1706, leaving an only child, Nehemiah, who administered on his estate.

Nehemiah 2, son of Nehemiah 1, married Jan. 21, 1685, Remember Fisk, and had John born April 9, 1691, who died June 5, 1710. They had another son, Nehemiah, born Oct. 19, 1692.

Arthur 1, is the only person of the name of Abbott in a "list of those that by law are allowed to have their votes in Town affairs, voted to be recorded at the Town meeting, December the 2, 1679." He occupied a farm belonging to John Whipple Sept. 28, 1683. His wife was fined "10s & costs and fees," Sept..28, 1675, for "wearing silk." He married April 26, 1669, Elisabeth White, and had Arthur, born Oct. 1, 1670 ; Philip, born Aug. 30, 1672. He had a seat assigned to him on the same seat with the Deacon, behind the pulpit, in the new Meeting House, in 1700. He was commoner of Ipswich, 1708.

Arthur 2, son of Arthur 1, was a constable in 1729.

Philip 2, son of Arthur 1, with Mary his wife, had Arthur, born Feb. 3, 1693, and a daughter Frances, May 18, 1696.

Mary Abbot, widow, died Jan. 11, 1730.

ADDAMS, Robert, was an inhabitant of Ipswich in 1635, when he had a house lot granted him "in town, near ye river side." He probably removed from Ipswich soon afterwards.

Addams William, was a commoner of Ipswich in 1641. The inventory of his estate is dated, 1658, 24, (11.) He possessed a "Dwelling house and orchard together with six or seven acres of marsh near to Mr. William Paynes," appraised at £70. "Clear estate £278, 13, 7d." " Sixty acres or there abouts of land on the south side of the river by John Addams." He died Jan. 18, 1658. William, sen'r, and William, jun'r, are subscribers toward a compensation for Major Denison's military services in 1648. William, probably the junior, died in 1661.

John 1, lost a wife named Rebecca, who died Dec. 31, 1666, and another named Sarah, May 31, 1675. He married Doritha Dwitt May 8, 1677. He was a " Tythingman" in 1679. With the addition of "sen'r," he subscribes 10s towards the bell, 1699. He was a commoner in 1664 ; and the name of " Corp'l Jo : Addams," is on a "list of those that by law are allowed to have theer votes in Town affairs, Dec. 2, 1679." John, sen'r, and John, jun'r, together with Michael Farley have in 1697, the privilege granted to build a miil on their land. He had a son John, born March 11, 1667, and daughter Dorcas, Mch 16, 1678.

John 2, son of John 1, was born March 11, 1667, and married Hannah, daughter of Nathaniel Treadwell, May 22, 1690. They had a daughter Hannah, born April 25, 1691. He was a commoner in 1707.

Nathaniel, was born about 1641. He married June 30, 1668, Mercy Dickerson, and had :

> Thomas, born June 14, 1672,
> Mercy, born April 1, 1674, who died June 13 following ;
> William, born June 22, 1678,
> Marcie, born March 18, 1679,
> Nathaniel, born March 1, 1694,
> William, born Nov 26, 1696,
> Abigail, born Dec, 6, 1699.

He was a commoner in 1664, freeman May 27, 1674, and joined the church in full communion, August 12, 1674. His last wife was named Abigail, and was probably the mother of the three younger children. He died April 11, 1715. (See Epitaph 16.)

Adams, Simon, with Hannah his wife, had :

> Hannah, born Jan. 18, 1691,
> Simon, b Oct. 20, 1694, d of small pox, Dec. 24, 1721. (Epitaph)
> Daniel, born Nov. 26, 1697.

He died Oct. 17, 1723. Capt. Simon Stace by his will, dated Oct. 20, 1699, bequeaths property to his "cousin Simon Adams, and to Simon, eldest son of said Simon." Lt. John, Mr. Nathaniel, and Simon, had seats assigned to them in the Meeting House, January 16, 1700.

Thomas, probably son of Nathaniel, born March, 18, 1679, with Bethiah his wife, had :

> Bethiah, born Oct 21, 1694,
> Sarah, April 29, 1697,
> Thomas, August 31, 1699.

He was commoner, 1707.

Samuel, married Mehitable Norton, Dec. 20, 1664, and had :

Mehitable. born Oct. 27, 1665,
Mary, Oct. 20, 1667,
Samuel, Dec. 26, 1670,
William, Jan. 26, 1673,
Sarah, June 12, 1676.

He was a commoner, 1707.

Archelaus, was a soldier at York in Maine, in 1695.

" 1667, Nov. Jacob Addams and his wife upon their presentment for fornication, the sentence of the court is, they shall be severely whipt, unless they pay a fine of five pound."—*Essex County Records*.

ANDREWS, Robert 1, was admitted a freeman May 6, 1635, in which year he possessed a house lot on the south side of the river. He was licensed by the General Court to keep an ordinary, Sept. 3, 1635, and 1636 is allowed to sell wine by retail, "if he do not wittingly sell to such as abuse it by drunkeness."

Robert 2, probably son of Robert 1. died about 1675. His will dated December 6, 1673. was proved March 26, 1676. By it he directs his property to be divided between his mother and his brothers, John and Joseph. He bequeaths to "each of my brothers and sisters, twelve shillings a piece, and five pounds to Mary Towne." He appoints his "brother Samuel Symonds," executor.

Andrews, John, was a soldier in the war against the Pequott Indians in 1639, and had eight acres of land granted to him by the town for his services. With the title of "sen'r." he subscribes to the allowance to Major Denison for military services, 1648.

John 2, probably son of Robert 1, was an inhabitant of Ipswich in 1646, when he with others gives a day's work to carting binds, the rate toward the cart bridge, then just built where the Stone bridge now is. With the title of "jun'r," he subscribes towards Major Denison's allowance in 1648. He conveys to Mary Webster, widow, Nov, 30, 1646, "to the use of her and her children, all ye island lately in possession of George Carr, twenty acres more or less; bounded by the labor in vain creek west, Thomas Emersons farm south east; Thomas Boreman's farm on the north east, which said Island lyeth in the town of Ipswich." " Acknowledged 14 8mo. 1652." With Sarah his wife he conveys, November 14, 1659, to Mr, Richard Dumer of Ipswich, a house and four acres of land in the hill street (commonly called by the name of the white house.) Richard Wattles north west, street north east, Phillip Call south east, Henry Pinder south east, Widow Quilter south west, Mr. Ayres north west, said Richard

Wattles north east in part, land of Mr. William Norton east in part. February 7, 1659, they convey to William Fellows a farm on the south side of the river, bounded by a brook called Mile brook west; the lot of Mr. Saltonstall called the forty-acres north west; the common north east and south east: John Tuttle's south in part; a swamp called Walker's swamp south in part. He was a surveyor of highways in 1661.

John 3, with the title of ' Corp'l' was tythingman in 1697. He was lieut. of a company at Chebacco in 1683. He was imprisoned and fined £30 for opposing in town meeting the arbitrary measures of Sir Edmund Andros in 1687. His companions were John Appleton, Thomas French, John Wise, Robert Kinsman. and William Goodhue. His will was dated March 13, 1705, and proved May 17, 1709. He left a wife named Judith, and sons John the eldest, William the second, Thomas and Joseph ; a daughter Elisabeth, born March 7, 1684, wife of James Giddings. He appoints " William Giddinge of Jebacco Cordwinder," sole executor ; the will was witnessed by Nathaniel Goodhue, Job Giddings and Samuel Giddings.

William 4, son of John 3, married Margaret Woodward Oct. 21, 1672, and had :

William, born Oct. 22. 1674,
John, born Feb. 2, 1675,
Ezekiel, born June 1680,
Elisabeth, born Jan. 5, 1684, died Dec. 26, 1685.

Solomon, son of William and Margaret was born Aug. 8, 1699.

Thomas 4, son of John 3, married Mary Belcher Feb, 9, 1681.

John 4, son of John 3, was tythingman in 1697.

Joseph 4, son of John 3, married Sarah Ring, Feb. 16, 1680,—had,
Susannah, born Aug. 16, 1687,
John, born June 1, 1691,
Hannah, born July 3, 1694,
Dorothy, born Nov. 23, 1697.

ANNABLE, John, a tailor, was an inhabitant in 1647. The same name occurs as a contributor to Major Denison's allowance in 1648 ; and as one of the inhabitants who are entitled to shares in Plum Island, Castle Neck, &c., in 1664. Again in 1697, the name is among those who have horses that go on the common ; and in a list of commoners made March 9, 1707-8. Two persons are probably here designated ; father and son. John and Mary had children :
John, born Jan. 3, 1678,
Jacob, born Aug. 25, 1681,

Jacob, born Feb. 20, 1682,

Matthew, born Feb. 25, 1683,

Mary, born December 7, 1684.

Joseph and Mary had :

Elisabeth, born April 16, 1694,

Joseph, January 31, 1690.

In 1706 permission was granted to John and Matthew, with others, to raise a seat in the gallery of the meeting house. Robert was commoner, in 1707.

John, the first named, was a commoner in 1641, and died Oct. 8, 1664. He had :

Joseph, born Oct. 2, 1658,

Elizabeth, born April 17, 1661.

ANDERSON, John, was a soldier, and died probably in the army, in 1700. Daniel Ringe was appointed administrator on his effects, Nov. 20, of that year. His property was £3, 1, 5, wages received, and a like sum then due.

AYRES, John 1, was an inhabitant of Ipswich, 1648. He had :

Edward, born Feb. 12, 1658,

Mark, Dec. 14, 1661,

Nathaniel, July 6, 1664.

He was admitted a commoner March, 1667, and had privilege of commonage granted Feb. 1667. He removed to Quabog, afterwards Brookfield, about 1672. He had the title of Captain, and was killed by the Indians at Squakeag, now Northfield, in 1675. (*Felt.*) His wife Susanna, rendered an inventory of his estate, amounting to £195, 13, 6, to which she adds, " I have seven sons and one daughter."

John 2, son of John 1, married Mary Woodam, only child of John Woodam, before May 1678. They had :

Abigail, born May 14, 1680,

Ruth, Nov. 22, 1685, died the 24 of Dec. following.

He died about April, 1691, the 22d of which month Joseph, his brother, was appointed administrator on his estate.

Susanna Ayres, widow of John 1, possessed a house in Ipswich in 1678. John 1 occupied a farm belonging to Mr. Norton in 1664. The widow died February 8, 1682.

Thomas 2, son probably of John 1, married Hannah Erington, Mch. 21, 1677, and had had :

Thomas, born Jan 25, 1678,

Hannah, born Aug. 2, 1680,

Rebecca, born May 17, 1682,
Another daughter, June 14, 1686.
Joseph 2, probably son of John 1, married Sarah, daughter of John
Caldwell, June 9, 1684.   They had :
   Sarah, born Aug. 5, 1685,
   Elizabeth, born Jan. 28, 1687,
   John, Feb. 26, 1692,
   Benjamin, Sept. 13, 1696.
*Samuel 2, probably son of John 1, had :
   Samuel, born Sept. 14, 1658,
   John, born May 1661,
   Joseph, Oct. 9, 1664,
   Mary, June 22, 1667,
   John, March 16, 1678,
   William, Jan. 26, 1681.
He married Abigail Fellows, April 16, 1677.   He was commoner in
1664 and 1697 ; Tythingman in 1679.   His will is dated February · 3,
1696-7, proved March 29, 1697.   He bequeathes to his son Samuel,
" Homestead and six acres pasturage land at heart break hill, and a
three acre lot at Plum Island ;" "he to maintain his mother."   He
mentions a daughter Mary, and a grandchild Susanna Waite.   It is
probable that the Samuel who married Abigail Fellows was the son of
Samuel 2.   He mentions in his will that he "formerly gave to son
Joseph, land where his house stands."   He died Feb. 7, 1696.

ATTWOOD, Thomas, was a surveyor of highways in 1673.   He
died April 10, 1694.   By his will dated March 25, 1693-4 after legacies to his wife Elizabeth, his eldest son John, and his son Thomas,
directs that the residue of his property be divided equally among his
other seven children, being 5 sons and 2 daughters.   The inventory of
his property amounted to £267, 13, 5d.   His widow married John
West, Sept. 9, 1697.   Elisabeth West, late widow of Thomas Attwood, Sept. 5, 1698, exhibits a list of debts paid as ex'x of Thomas
Attwood.   She charges "for ye bringing up Elizabeth from her father's
decease to this day 4 years and 1-2 till six yr old ;" "bringing up
Francis for 5 yr old, 4 yr and 1-2 ;" "bringing up Joseph fr 3 yr old

---

* This Samuel Ayres was probably *not* a son of John 1.   There was
a Samuel *Arres*, servant, who came to New England with John and
Elizabeth Baker, 1637.   He was then 14 years of age.   (See Ancestry of Priscilla Baker.)   W. H. Whitmore, in his Genealogy of John
Ayres, does not include Samuel among the children of John.—*Printer*

when his father died 4 yr & 1-2." She had rights of commonage in 1697.

AVERYE, Avery, Averell, or Averill, William 1, had a house lot on the south side of the river in 1638, near where the meeting house now stands. He was commoner in 1641, subscriber to towards Major Denison's allowance in 1648. He died before May 20, 1653, at which time his widow possessed a house lot near John Woodam's land. His widow, Abigail Averill, died before March 27, 1655, under which date William, probably her son, presents an inventory of her estate. The effects with their appraised value are as follows:

| | | | |
|---|---|---|---|
| " House lot and house | £12 | 00 | 0 |
| The six acre lot at muddy river, | 4 | | |
| The pequitt lot 7 acres | 6 | | |
| 6 acres of meadow | 5 | | |
| A steer 4 year old | 5 | 10 | |
| A cow and heifer | 8 | 10 | |
| A year old steer anvantage | 2 | | |
| A year old haifer anvantage | 2 | | |
| A calf | 1 | 4 | |
| Total, | £47 | 4 | 11 |

William Averill 2, probably son of William 1, married Hannah Jackson, July 31, 1661, in which year he was surveyor of highways. He sold to John Woodam, Oct. 4, 1658, a six acre lot of land; he possessed a lot of land Aug. 30, 1655, the "corner of which came near the mill dam." He had a son William born May 1, 1662.

ARDWAY, see Ordway.

ARCHER, Henry possessed a houselot and probably a house on the 'highway leading from the High street to Bridge street,' Feb. 18, 1638. He was a free holder in 1648. May 10, 1649, he together with his wife Elizabeth, who died April 11, 1669, conveys to William Story, "a farm of ninety acres, granted unto him by the Town of Ipswich, beyond Chebacco falls. He was entitled to certain commoners rights in Plum Island, &c., as Mr. Symonds' farmer in 1664. He appears to have had a house and land in town in 1656; he had granted to him "an acre of land as a house lot and privilege of commonage," February, 1667.

ALLIN, Edward, married Sarah Kimball, Nov. 24, 1658. They

had : John, born August 9, 1659,
Sarah, July 4, 1661, died February 10, 1661,
Edward, May 1, 1662,
Sarah, March 1, 1664,
Elizabeth, December 20, 1666,
William, March 12, 1668,
Benjamin, September, 1673,
David, February 1, 1675,
Abigail, March 25, 1678.

In 1669 he was "too much rated," and the excess was ordered to be "allowed him next year."

" 1672. Agreed with Edward Allin to allow him four pounds for to keep John Osborne for a year, to find him meat drink and cloths, he to imploy for his own use what he can doe."—*Town Records*.

APPLETON, Samuel, was born at Little Waldingfield, or as it is now written, Waldringfield, in the shire of Suffolk, Eng., 1586. The family trace his descent through Thomas, William, Robert, Thomas, John and John, from John Appleton of Great Waldingfield, who died in 1436.

He came to Ipswich in 1635, and brought with him two sons : John 2, born about 1622, and Samuel 2, born about 1626. He was "admitted to the freeman's oath" at the general election in May, 1636.

He had large possessions in lands, of which a tract of about 600 acres lay bounded by the Ipswich River and the Mile Brook. A part of this land yet remains in the possessions of his descendants. The farms of Samuel and Timothy Appleton, and of Oliver Underhill have passed by inheritance from the first grantee to the present possessors. He also possessed lands on the north side of the river above the mill dam. His residence was, probably, near where the railroad station now is, on the right hand side of the road to Topsfield. This property on both sides of the road, remained in his family for several generations.

" 1641, December 3. Mr. Appleton hath promised the Town to have a malt house ready by the first of April next, and to malt such corn as shall be brought to him from the people of this town at such rates as shall be thought equal from time to time. And no man (except for himself) is to have any made elsewhere for the space of five years now next ensueing." (*T. R.*)

He died in June, 1670, at Rowley, where he was buried, and left two sons, John 2, and Samuel 2, before mentioned, and daughters :—
Sarah, wife of the Rev. Samuel Phillips of Rowley ; Judith, wife of Samuel Rogers, the son of the Rev. Nathaniel Rogers, m. April 8, 1657 ; and Martha, wife of Richard Jacobs.

John 2, son of Samuel 1, was born in England about 1662. He came with his father, and settled in Ipswich, 1635. He married in 1651, Priscilla, daughter of the Rev. Jessee Glover. She died Feb. 18, 1697. (See epitaph 4.) He died Nov. 4, 1699. (See epitaph 2.) His will is dated Feb. 16, 1697, two days before the decease of his wife, in which he says, " I have taken care for my beloved wife Priscilla, so she shall be provided for, in an obligation from my two sons, John and Samuel, dated 13th March, 1688." "The bond that my son John and Samuel gave me for the security of their sisters portions I have signed over to my son John Ex'r, to help him pay his sisters portions and other debts w'ch my son Samuel was to doe, he having his proportion of lands in consideration." Samuel had died previously, August 16, 1693.

Besides John 3, and Samuel 3 deceased, there was a son Jessee, or Jose, born March 77, 1660, who died April 11, 1660, and daughters, Elizabeth Dummer, wife of Richard Dummer, married November 2, 1673 ; Priscilla, born Dec. 25, 1657, wife of the Rev. Joseph Capen of Topsfield, and two younger daughters, Sarah Rogers, born Aug. 19, 1670, and Mary Thomas, born April 15, 1673.

He was selectman with the title of " Mr." 1661, Captain, 1677. He was captain of a troop, clerk of the courts. and county treasurer ; representative to the General Court 16 years, between 1656 and 1678. He was fined and imprisoned for opposing the arbitrary measures of Sir Edmund Andros, in 1687. (See Andrews John.) He subscribed £4, "for procuring of a bigger Bell for ye good of ye Town, of about 5 or six [hundred] weight." There were 53 subscribers for the object, who gave £50, 18s. The highest subscription was that of Jno. Wainwright, £6. The Rev. John Rogers gave £5, and Francis Wainwright £3. The two Whipples, John and Matthew gave two pounds each.

John 3, son of John 2, was born 1652. freeman, May 24, 1682, and died Sept. 11, 1739, (see epitaph 6.) He married Nov. 23, 1681, Elizabeth, daughter of the Rev. John Rogers, President of Harvard College, who survived her husband and died March 13, 1754, aged 91 years. He sustained several important offices. Was Town Clerk from March 29, 1687 ; Colonel of a regiment, Justice of the Court of Common Pleas, and Judge of Probate twenty years ; and of the Gov'rs Council twenty-five years from 1698.

Nathaniel 4, born December 9, 1693, graduated at Harvard College, 1712, ordained minister at Cambridge, October 9, 1717, and died Feb. 9, 1784, aged 91 years. Their daughters were, Elizabeth, wife of Rev Jabez Fitch ; Margaret, wife of President Holyoke ; Priscilla, the first wife of the Rev. Robert Ward of Wenham. They had a son William, born Oct. 15, 1686, and John born August 18, 1705, who probably died young. In his will dated February 8, 1734, he bequeathes to his wife Elizabeth "the improvement during her life of his house and land lying near the meeting house, adjoining to Mr. Edward Eveleth." Also "the Mansion house and all the buildings and land, adjoining which is my orchard." This house is yet standing. It was probably built about 1680, and descended, at the decease of his mother to Daniel, who dying in 1762, intestate, it was inherited by his daughters, Elizabeth, wife of the Rev. John Walley, first minister of the South Parish in Ipswich, and Mary, single woman, by whom it was sold, in 1768, to Daniel Noyes, Esquire, of whose heirs it was purchased in 18– by the late William Dodge.§ Col Appleton bequeathed to his son Nath'l "the old house and barn that was formerly my father Appleton's ; the land to extend northward from the said house twenty feet, and so to run from the highway over the hill to the Turtle pond, &c." This is the lot, next westward from the railroad station. To his two daughters, "the house and land near the Meeting house, known by the name of Lowds and Fosters lotts, bounded by the land of Mr. Edward Eveleth on the south ; the river on the east ; the highway on the northwest," after the decease of his wife. To Daniel the right to redeem by paying certain sums named. Daniel, residuary legatee with reversion of mansion house, &c., after his wife's decease.

Samuel 3, son of John 2, is designated in the probate records as Samuel, junior, and in the Town records as Samuel the third. He died August 16, 1693, and there were living at that time, his uncle Samuel 2, son of Samuel 1 ; and his uncle's son, Samuel 3, who was born in 1654. He left four sons, all minors :

Jose 4, born November 30, 1684, died March, 1707,

Samuel 4, born July 21, 1686,

Thomas 4 ;

John 4, married 1716, Mary Allen of Salisbury.

His widow Mary died June 9, 1712, aged 53 years.‡ (See epitaph 8) In 1701, July 5, as administratrix of the estate of her deceased husband, she sells to Michael Farley three acres of land, "bounded by land of Lt. Coll'n John Appleton, Esq'r at one end ; the other end by the mill course, &c., the one side by the said Michael's land ; the oth-

---

§ Mr. Hammatt resided in this house.—*Printer*.

‡ 1748, Sept. 17. Died Mrs. Priscilla Appleton, daughter of Mr. John Appleton : being the last of seven daughters dying with consumption within the space of three years.—*Ipswich Town Records*.

er by land said Mary is in possession of as it was her late husband's."
This indicates his residence as being near the mill, and in the neighborhood of his father's and grandfather's.

Jose 4, son of Samuel 3, was born November 30, 1684. His will
is dated December 30, 1706, and proved March 31, 1707. He appoints his "honoured Mother, Mrs. Mary Appleton," ex'x, and gives
to his brother John 4, a minor, his weaving shop, &c., provided he
"carries on the trade of weaver and clothier." Thomas 4 is mentioned in the will, but Samuel 4, is not.

Jesse 3, son of John 2, was born March 27, 1660. He became a
merchant in Boston, and died unmarried in 1721.

Samuel 2, son of Samuel 1, was born in England about 1626, and
came with his father to Ipswich in 1635. He married first Hannah,
daughter of William Payne, by whom he had a son, Samuel 3, who
was born in 1654. For his second wife he married Dec. 2, 1656, Mary
daughter of John Oliver of Newbury. She was born June 7, 1640,
and died Feb. 15, 1697. (See epitaph 5.) By her he had John 3,
born 1660. (See epitaph 7.) Isaac, born 1664. He lost a daughter Mary, June 5, and a son Oliver, June 14, 1676. He had a dau.
Mary born about Oct. 20, 1679, Joseph, born June 5, 1674, Oliver a
minor in 1696; Judith Walcott; Joanna Whipple; Hannah Downs,
who died before her father, and left one only child. He mentions in
his will, dated April 12, 1695, a cousin Thomas Jacob; probably a
son of Richard Jacob, who married his sister Martha. He was selectman, with title " Left." 1662 ; Major in the militia, and commanded a
regiment with great distinction in the war against King Philip in 1676.
He was elected Assistant from 1681 to 1686, six years, and was one
of the first council under the charter of William and Mary, 1692. He
bequeathes to his wife one half of the dwelling house, &c., during
her natural life. To Samuel his eldest son, the dwelling house, orchard, barn, &c. excepting what he has given to his wife. Mentions
his sons John 3, Isaac 3, and Oliver 3 to whom he gives the saw-mill,
&c., "if he live to the age of twenty-one years." He appoints his
wife executrix. He died May 15, 1696, (see epitaph 3,) and his widow died before the estate was settled, Feb. 15, 1697. The brothers
John 2 and Samuel 2 in the year 1653, purchased of Thomas Manning
a property thus described :—" Dwelling House situated in Ipswich
near the meeting-house, having the meeting house green towards the
north west, and the river towards the south east ; the land of John
Woodman towards the north east ; and the land of Mr. Symonds on
the south." The same year, May 20, they purchase of "John Woodam, a dwelling house, barn and houselot, containing by estimation

three acres with commonage belonging to the dwelling house as it now lyeth bounded and fenced to the ledge of rocks near the meeting house green, from the corner of the land from the meeting house green leading to the river, to the rock wall turning down to the house where John Woodam now dwelleth, and so from the corner of the land afforsaid to the houselot of Reonald Foster, and so over to the house lot of the Widdow Averill, and thence to the corner of the rock wall aforesaid near the meeting house green in the town of Ipswich." " In exchange for another house and house lot and thirty pounds in good pay ;" "viz. The dwelling house and house lot purchased of Thomas Manning adjoining to the house lot above mentioned, towards the north, & upon the river towards the south, and upon a houselot of Mr Samuel Symonds towards the west, and upon a houselot of the widdow Averill towards the east." This property was acquired when John the eldest brother was thirty one years of age, and two years after his marriage with Priscilla Glover. Samuel, the younger brother was twenty-seven years old, and was probably married the same year, their eldest son Samuel being born in 1654. It was probably the residence of both of the brothers in the early years of their marriage lives. In the later years of their lives their residences were on the Topsfield road, a little westward of where the railroad station now is. The lot above described became the sole property of John, who left it to his son John, from whom it descended to his son Daniel, whose widow and administratrix Elisabeth, in her account of administration, July 24, 1765, returns, " The old Homestead sold to Nathaniel Souther, £140, 00.§

Samuel 3, son Samuel 2, died Oct. 30, 1725, aged 71. (See epitaph and Coat of Arms, 5.) He married Elizabeth, daughter of William Whittingham, son of John of Ipswich. She survived her husband and married Rev. Edward Payson of Rowley.

In the latter part of the year 1673, and the early part of 1674, (the

---

§ " 101-2, Jan. 29. Liberty granted to Corn't Matthew Whipple, Mr. John and Joseph Whipple, and Mr. Isaac Ringe to build a shed for their horses of 40 feet in length and not exceeding 10 foot wide, about 20 foot from ye watch house southerly toward ye old meeting house, Ensign Wallis and his two sons to build a shed next, Serg't Lamson next, &c."
" 1702. April 9th. Consideration being had of ye prejudice of ye above grant, instead thereof have granted room for sd sheds against ye orchard fence where Mr. Samuel Appleton lives, beginning about two rodds from ye lane corner towards Mr. Appleton's Barn.—*Town Records.*

gloomy period of Philip's war,) there were great additions to the church.) In about four months, from December to April 12, nearly ninety were added, some in "full communion," and some by "taking the covenant," sixty-five of whom were males. On the three Sundays, Jan. 18, 25, and Feb. 1, twenty-four who are distinguished as of the "young generation," took the covenant. One of these was " Samuel Appliton, ye sonne of Major Appliton." He was then about nineteen years of age. He was justice of the court of sessions ; commander of a regiment in the expedition against Canada in 1690 ; representative of the town several years, and of the governor's council, 1713-14. His children were Samuel, a wealthy merchant of Boston, who died in London, September 15, 1728, of the small pox ; Whittingham, born December 29, 1706 ; Hannah Clark, Martha Wise, Elizabeth, a minor at the time of his decease in 1725. John 3 son of Samuel 2, died May 17, 1724. in the 64th year of his age. (See epitaph 7.) He is improperly distinguished as "senior," on his gravestone, his cousin John 3, son of John 2, being living, and his elder by eight years. He is so called in reference to his son John 4, who was born May 28, 1695. He married April 1, 1689, Rebeckah Ruck, daughter of John Ruck of Salem. She was living in December, 1697. He married August 31, 1700. the widow Elizabeth Dutch. March 24, 1749, died Elizabeth, widow of Mr. John Appleton. (See N. E. Hist. and Gen. Reg. vol. 8, 1843.) But whether the widow of John 3, or John 4 his son, or John 4 son of Samuel 3, it is not certain. Neither does it appear to which of them the following extract from the town records refers : " 1748, September 17. Died Mrs. Priscilla Appleton, daughter of Mr. John Appleton ; being the last of seven daughters, dying with consumption within the space of three years." Benjamin 4, son of John 3 and Elisabeth, was born November 14, 1702. He married Elizabeth, daughter of Capt. Thomas Wade, who survived him and married Mr. ——— Cogswell of Rowley. He died Feb. 12, 1731. (See epitaph 9.) He left daughters, Elisabeth, Mary and Sarah. His estate £373. Isaac 3 son of Samuel 2, died May 22, 1747, in the 83d year of his age. (See epitaph 13.) He married Priscilla, daughter of Thomas Baker, and grand-daughter of the Hon. Samuel Symonds of Ipswich. He left an only son Isaac 4, and six daughters : Priscilla Abbot, Mary Osgood, Elisabeth Fairfield, Martha White, and Rebecca who married January 19, 1728-9, William Dodge, then of Wenham, afterwards of Ipswich, and Joanna.‡ Isaac 4, son of Isaac

---

‡ Isaac Appleton subscribed 6s toward the bell 1699, and John jun'r, 12s.

3, was born May 30, 1704, and died December 18, 1794. (See epitaph 11.) His wife Elisabeth died April 29, 1785, aged 75 years. (See epitaph 12.) By his will, dated July 24, 1788, he appoints his son Samuel 5, his sole executor. His other children were Isaac 5 of New Ipswich, born 1731, died 1806, Francis 5, of New Ipswich, father of Jesse, President of Bowdoin College, Thomas 5, John 5, Daniel 5, William 5, deceased before his father, Joseph 5, graduated at Rhode Island College, 1772, ordained minister of North Brookfield, November 30, 1776, died July 24, 1795. Daughters, Elizabeth Bartlett and Mary Woodbury. Thomas, John, and Daniel settled in Maine. [Farmer.] Oliver 3 son of Samuel 2, was a minor in 1696. He died Jan. 9, 1759-60. He left a widow named Sarah (Perkins,) of Topsfield, married Nov. 16, 1701. His sons were Oliver 5, born 1702, died August 3, 1787, William 4, born 1703, died April 8, 1725, (see epitaph 10,) Joseph 4, born December 24, 1705, John 4, Samuel 4, (see epitaphs 14, 15,) Daniel 4, and Nathaniel 4. His daughters were Sarah Swain, Hannah Swain, and Mary Whipple. Sarah, widow of Oliver 4, died June 22, 1811, aged 90 years. Daniel 4, died April 7, 1807, aged 88 years. Nathaniel 4, died Feb. 15, 1798, aged 77 yrs. Samuel 4, died May 15, 1819, aged 81 years. Oliver 5, son of Nath'l 4, died December 11, 1797, aged 40. Samuel 5, son of Isaac 4, died May 15, 1819, aged 81 years. Mary, his wife, died Nov. 10, 1834, aged 88 years.‡

BAKER, John, possessed an house lot on High street in 1638. He appears to have been a man of property, his name standing against one of the 44 highest of 157 subscriptions to the compensation of Major Denison, the military leader, in 1648. He married Kathrin Perkins, May 13, 1667. He died in 1710. His widow Katherine took out letters of administration on his estate, April 14, of that year. His sons were Thomas 2, born Sept. 13, 1636, who settled in Topsfield, and married Priscilla, daughter of the Honorable Samuel Symonds, Nov. 26, 1672, and died March 18, 1718. John 2, and William 2, were probably his sons. He had a daughter Elizabeth who was married June 30, 1690, to Benjamin Dutch. In 1661, Sept. 20, he conveyed to his son Thomas 2, lands in Topsfield upon condition of the payment of ten pounds yearly to him and his wife during their lives.

---

‡ John 4, son of John 3, son of Samuel 2, born May 28, 1695.
John 4, son of Samuel 3, son of John 2, born about 1690.

John 2, junior, died in 1710, and left a widow named Hannah.* William 2, probably son of John 1, was a tythingman in 1695, and surveyor of highways for Scott's Lane, 1697-8 ; his wife, Sarah Fitts, married Dec. 30, 1686, died July 1, 1722, aged 60 years.  (See epitaph 17.)  He publishes an intention of marriage with the widow Ann Burrill, Feb. 3, 1722-3 ; his children were :

> William 3, born November 14, 1687,
> John 3, born March 18, 1696-7,
> Sarah, born Oct 22, 1692,
> Mary, born April 26, 1695,
> Damazen, born May 7, 1699.‡

Thomas 2, son of John 1, died March 18, 1718.   His children were

> Thomas 3, born Feb. 17, 1688,
> John 2, born January 6, 1691,
> Priscilla, born Dec. 8, 1674, married to Isaac Appleton,
> Rebecca, born Nov. 16, 1685,
> Elizabeth, married Feb. 16, 1716-17, Michael Farley.

He left also a grandson. Joseph Sargent, son of a daughter Martha, born Oct. 14, 1682, deceased.   His wife Priscilla was born  in  1648, married March 26, 1672, and died Jan. 2, 1733-4.  (See epitaph 18.) Gov. John Winthrop in a letter to his son John Winthrop, jun'r, dated Sept. 30, 1648, writes : " At Ipswich they are all in  health,  God be praised.  Your sister Symonds is delivered of a  daughter." This daughter was Priscilla Baker.   Thomas Baker§ bequeathed large pos-

---

* 1678, Sept. 24.   John Baker for his offence of being  drunk  and revelling, fined 20s and costs and fees.

1681, April 30.   Ordered by the Select men, that no  inhabitant of this town shall directly or indirectly give, or sell, or deliver  any  rum, wine, sider, brandy, strong beer, or any other strong drink,  to John Baker, less or more, under the penalty of ten shillings for one offence, he the said John Baker being so often abused with drink, and not able to govern himself.

‡ The will of William Baker 2, dated June 14, 1731, and  proved September 19, 1743, mentions a wife] Anna, and  sons William and John, daughters Sarah Waite,  Mary  Heard, Thomasen, Abbe,  and Margaret Stacey.

Coll. John 5, son of John 4, died June 9, 1785, aged 64  years.  Eunice, his widow, died January 10, 1821, aged 94 years.

§ Thomas Baker's will is dated Jan. 17, 1717, and proved April  7, 1718.   He mentions his wife, " Mrs. Baker," sons Thomas and John ; daughters Rebecca, Priscilla, and Elisabeth, to whom he  bequeathes an "hunrded pounds apiece at money price, or bills credit." A daugh-

sessions in Topsfield and Boxford to his eldest son, Thomas 3. To John 3, he gives all his "houses and lands and meadows at Argilla farm in Ipswich," with the commonages and all the stock of cattle that shall be there at his decease. The freemen of the town of Ipswich, in 1637, granted to Samuel Symonds a tract of land estimated to contain three hundred acres. The farm here made, from the circumstance of its abounding in clay, Mr. Symonds named "Argilla." The name has been extended to the district of the town in which the farm lies. Some years after the decease of Mr. Symonds, his heirs by a bond dated April 10, 1694, agree to divide the Argilla farm into two equal parts; after confirming the sale by the executor, William Symonds, their brother deceased, of thirty-five acres of upland, and eight acres of meadow to Bragg, and eight acres of upland sold to John Emerson, and four acres of upland sold to Thomas Baker toward paying legacies. One of the parts when so divided to be assigned to Harlackenden Symonds of Ipswich, John Emerson and his wife Ruth of Glocester, Thomas Baker and his wife Priscilla of Topsfield, Daniel Epes of Salem, and Symonds Epes of Ipswich. The other part to Joseph Jacob and his wife Susannah; Dorothy Symonds; Coll'n Wade as guardian of Mary and Elisabeth Symonds, children of William Symonds, deceased; all of Ipswich. The part of this estate which was inherited by Thomas Baker, and bequeathed to his second son John, has descended to John Baker the present owner. It is one of the very few properties which have been transmitted by inheritance from the original grantees to the present generation.

John 3, son of Thomas 2, was born January 6, 1690-1, and married for his first wife, Anna, daughter of Mr. John Perkins, who was born December 28, 1697, and died April 27, 1716. (See epitaph 20.)

---

ter Martha, deceased, left a child named Joseph Sargeant, to whom he bequeathes "thirty-nine pounds if he live to ye age of twenty-one years." "To son Thomas all my houses, and lands, and meadows, yt I have in ye town of Topsfield and Boxford, and commonage, &c., cattle, &c., and two thirds of all ye money that shall remain due to me." "My silver Tankard and silver spoon yt was my father's." "Also seven hundred acres of land and meadow, I bou't of Mr. Harlak'n Symonds." "Also two hundred and fifty acres I bought of Mr. Noyes of Salem, both parcels of land lying at Coxhall at the eastward, he paying two thirds of my debts, and take care of his mother in all particulars." "To son John all lands, and houses, and meadows at Argilla farm in Ipswich, with commonage, and the stock of cattle that shall be there at my decease." "Also an acre of salt marsh yt I bought of Bro'r Eppes." "Also eight hundred acres upland and meadow at Coxhall, he paying one third of all debts."

His second wife was Mary Perley of Boxford, with whom he was published on the 16th of November, 1717. She was born May 16, 1697, and died March 26, 1738, (see epitaph 21. He died August 1, 1734, (see epitaph 19.)

His sons were John 4, Samuel 4, and Thomas 4; and Mary the only daughter. His estate was appraised at about three thousand pounds. A portion of the property is designated thus: "One quarter part of westerly half of Argilla farm;" which was appraised five hundred pounds, "the prices in proportion to the value of our present paper currency, accounting 24 shillings thereof to be equal, and but equal to one ounce of silver coin." The estate seems not to have been settled until May 2, 1746, when it is thus assigned: "The farm called Baker's farm, contains about one hundred and seventy-nine acres." "First share one hundred and twenty six acres of Baker's farm, running by the farm that was Collonell Denison's on the north-easterly side, is assigned and settled on John 4, ye eldest son, he giving bond to pay to Mary, ye only daughter, the sum of £165, 16, in bills of the last Tenor." "Second share the rest of said Baker farm, containing about fifty-four acres is assigned and settled on Samuel, ye second son; he giving bond to pay to pay to Thomas £265 16. A Guardian appointed Feb. 2, 1742, to estate of John Baker, (son of John Baker, Esquire, late of Ipswich,) "a person non compos and distracted." His estate consisting of two fifths of houses and lands, formerly his father's is apportioned at £450.

BARTHOLMEW, William, (who wrote his own name Bartholmew,) took the freeman's oath at Boston, March 4, 1634. Had a houselot on High street, granted Feb. 19, 1637, adjoining Robert Lord. He subscribed 3s toward the bell, 1699.

In 1642, April 6, it was voted: "The Town doth trust Mr. Bartholomew to copy out the old waste book, and such other papers as the Recorder shall commit unto him, and he shall be paid for his paynes." The copy made in accordance with this vote, is the oldest record possessed by the town. It is in the handwriting of Mr. Bartholmew, and a very good specimen of the chirography of the age. He was town clerk, feoffee of the grammar school from is institution in 1650, to his removal to Boston about 1656, representative, or deputy as then called, to the General Court five years, from 1635 to 1650.

March 17, 1727, Thomas Baker a minor upwards of fourteen years of age, son of Thomas Baker, late of Ipswich, deceased, made choice of Benjamin Appleton for Guardian.

" 1639.  William Bartholemew was granted eighty acres of land, in consideration of charges in going to courts, lying near Mr. Hubbard's farm." In 1646 the "seven men," were Mr. John Whittingham, Mr. Samuel Appleton, William Bartholomew, Thomas Emerson, Daniel? Foster, Tho: Bishop, Will'm Adams. He was county treasurer, 1654. He sells in 1653 to William Evans, late of Glocester, several parcels of land in Ipswich, the deed of which his wife, named Ann, signs with a mark.  He is said by Mr. Felt to have died in Charlestown, Jan. 18, 1681.

BACHELLOR, or Bachelder, Henry, was a commoner in 1641 and in 1664,  He sells to Thomas Knowlton, March 26, 1645, a six acre lot lying on the hill on the north side of the river.  He died Feb. 3, 1678.  A warrant for the distribution of the estate of Henry Bachelder, late of Ipswich, deceased, is dated May 28, 1696.  His heirs were John, Elisabeth and Hannah Bachelder, children of Joseph, his brother, deceased ; John, Joseph and Hannah Bachelder, children of John, his brother, deceased ; to each of whom is ordered to be paid £11  13. The " Widdow Batchelder," died April 15, 1686.

BELCHER, Jeremy, came to New England in 1635, in the ship Susan and Ellen, being then twenty-two years of age.  He was a commoner in 1641 and 1664.  He died March 31, 1693, under which date Samuel Belcher, clerk, is appointed administrator on his estate. He had :

Judith, born August 19, 1658,
Mary, born July 12, 1660,
David. born 1662,
Richard Sept. 10, 1665.

The "widow Belcher," probably his relict, died in October, 1700. He possessed a farm on which Thomas Burnham, jun'r dwelt, 1664. In 1652, September 20, he conveys in trust to Robert Payne and Robert Lord of Ipswich, and Richard Brown of Newbury, certain lands, "there being an intent of marriage between myself and Mary Lockwood of Ipswich," &c.  March 14, 1655, he sells to John Appleton, a farm of one hundred acres situated between the farm of John Adams and the land of Thomas Safford.  1657, Oct. 10, he sells to John Appleton a house and eleven acres of land which he purchased of Thomas Rowlinson, late of Ipswich, bounded by the common north west, Daniel Warner south west, river south east, land of the said Mr. Appleton north east.  Also six acres of marsh in the hundreds near Rowley.  The name Serg't Belcher is in a "list of those that by law are allowed to have their votes in Town affairs," Dec. 2, 1679.

Richard 2, probably son of Jeremy 1, was a commoner in 1697. He was married March 20, 1689 to Mary Simson, grandaughter to Francis and Jane Gordan. They had children :

Jane, born March 26, 1690,

David, born December 19, 1691,

Richard, Oct. 22, 1693,

Thomas, May 29, 1696.

Samuel 2, probably son of Jeremy 1, on whose estate he was ad·ministrator, was born about 1640, and died March 10, 1714, (see epitaph 23.) His story is short and mournful. After receiving the honors of Harvard College in 1659, he preached the gospel at the Isles of Shoals and at Newbury many years, as is recorded in his epitaph. But our wary neighbors did not permit him to acquire what is technically called a residence ; and having outlived his popularity as a preacher, he was sent back to his native town to be maintained as a pauper. Thus says tradition. It may be hoped that a consciousness of having served his Master faithfully, sustained his spirit under the accumulated pressure of age, poverty and neglect. His wife, Mercy, survived him fourteen years, and died on the 14th of November, 1728. In the account of Nathaniel Lord, Town Treasurer, under the date, Feb 13, 1729, the town is charged with £3, 2, 10, paid "Doct'r Berry for Goode Belcher." Probably for medical attendance in her last sickness.

His destitution was not quite so great as might be inferred from the tradition. His effects at his decease were appraised at £58 10 8d, in the currency of that day, which is equivalent to about $175 of present money. Among his effects were nineteen ounces of old plate, valued at £7, 12, and books valued at £8, 10, relics of former prosperity. The rest of his property consisted of "living stock," probably a cow, valued at £5, wearing apparel, £4, 5, and various articles of household furniture, amounting in value to 33, 10, 8.

BEARCHAMP, Robert, was a commoner 1641 and 1648.

BENNET, Henry, a commoner 1664, and 1678 had right of commonage for Phillip Call, and a voter 1679. In 1654, April 1, Jonathan Wade and Susanna his wife, sell him a farm of two hundred acres, known by the name of "said Wade his farm, which was given him by the town of Ipswich." Bounded by land of Mr. Samuel Symonds on the north, Mr. Saltonstall, east, Mr. Rogers, west, a brook on the south. He married, May 20, 1685, Frances Burr. They had Mary, born March 3, 1685, died Jan. 12. 1707-8.

Mrs. Mary Bennett, wife of Henry Bennett, before widow of John Burr, and Phillip Call.

Henry and Margaret had Margaret born March 22, 1697; Frances, Sept. 8, 1694.

Jacob and Sarah had Ebenezer, born June 20, 1686, Jacob, Oct. 9, 1676, died March 5, 1685. Widow Sarah, inventory, £425 14 6. App'd by Daniel Epps and William Goodhue. Mary had a seat in the meeting house, 1702.

1700, Dec. 12. The inventory of the estate of Thomas Bennit, consisting of a house and land valued £120, with other property, making a total of £188 7, 8, appraised by Robert Kinsman, John Smith, and Nathaniel Wells, was exhibited by Elizabeth, his widow and administratrix. Stephen Bennett died "latter end of July," 1680.

BIGGS, John, came with John Winthrop the younger, and commenced the settlement of Ipswich, then called Agawam, March, 1633.

BISHOP, Thomas, a commoner, 1641, 1648, 1664, selectman, 1661, '62, '63, '65, '69. He contributes towards the cart bridge, in 1646. He sells a farm of one hundred and ten acres, lately bought of Mr. Woodmansy to Daniel Ringe for £180, bounded east by the mile brook; south by land of Matthew Whipple; north and west by Richard Jacob. 1670, May. Ordered that the constable take care about the repairing of the meeting house, and our Brother Bishop also be impowered about it.

He died Feb. 7, 1670. His will was dated Feb. 5, and proved March 28, of that year. He left a wife Margaret; sons Samuel 2, John 2, Thomas 2, Job 2, and Nathaniel 2.

Nathaniel son of Thomas, died May 10, 1673. He bequeathes a legacy to a "cousin Sarah Bishop." To his brother Paul of Kingston, a hogshead of tobacco to be sent over to him. He possessed a farm and a house in town and he bequeathes to his son Samuel‡ vessels and goods at sea, "after Mr. Dean is paid what belongs to him." His estate amounted to £5000.

---

‡ The deposition of Samuel Bishop, aged 40 years or thereabouts, and Jacob Perkins, 23 years or thereabouts, about the middle of march last past, (we three deponents were on board the sloop wr off Thomas Bishop was commander, being bound for the Barbadoes, ready in Ipswich harbor,) wr off Nathaniel Roper was on board, going as one of the men." " Brother John Roper should have my estate, and pay my debts and give to my cozen Nathaniel Dutch (John Dutch his son) ten pounds." Sworn to Sept. 29, 1685.

Samuel 3, son of Thomas 1, in a deposition Sept. 29, 1685, states himself to be forty years of age. He was commoner 1678. He had a house fronting on the meeting house green, and it seems possessed a disposition yet prevalent for encroaching on the public lands ; for we find under date of July 9, 1677, "at a meeting of the select men, ordered that a warrant be made to the constable to pull down the new end of Samuel Bishop his barn, that stands upon the common ground, on the Meeting house green, to pull it down from time to time as oft as he shall set it up, if he shall not remove it himself within two days notice from him, or else to chop it down."

His wife was Esther Cogswell, daughter of William Cogswell, married Aug. 10, 1675. They had :

Margaret, born May 17, 1676.

Samuel, born Feb. 1678.

Hester, born Aug. 21, 1681.

Thomas, born Sept. 21, 1683,

John, born Sept. 20, 1685.

He had taxes abated November 3, 1699.

After his decease his widow, Esther, married Thomas Burnham.§

Job 2, son of Thomas 1, had a wife named Johanna, who on the 31st of March, 1691, represented to the Court, "that the said Job went to sea, and has been gone three years," &c. Job and Johanna had :

Dinah, born June 19, 1657,

Sarah, born May 19, 1659,

Hannah, born Dec. 24, 1662.

Nathaniel, probably son or brother of Thomas 1, was of Boston 1652, when he sells "to John Wiate of Ipswich, the house in which

---

§1703-4, Jan. 17, Esther Burnham, "formerly widow of Mr. Samuel Bishop," represents that the property left by her late husband, was "litell a noufe to inable me to bring up five or six small children." "There being something of land belonging to my children, request your honor to grant administration to my eldest son, Samuel Bishop." 

John Burnham, sen'r will proved Jan. 24, 1703-4 ; dated Dec. 31, 1703. He mentions a wife Elizabeth, his eldest son John ; his second son Thomas ; his youngest child Mary ; "Joseph and Jacob if they be living." Jonathan, David and Abigail.

Jacob Burnham of Chebacco appointed administration of the estate of his brother Joseph, May 1, 1704.

Aaron Burnham married Nov. 4, 1701, Hester, daughter of Samuel Bishop).

the˙said Wiate now dwelleth, with the land, three rods more or less, having the land of Thomas Betham now in possession of Mr. Ralf Smith toward the north east; the meeting house green toward the south east, a lane toward the south west," &c.

BETYGOOD, Richard, a commoner 1641. " 1641, 12 day of 1st mo. Barnabas Horton of Ipswich, baker, sold unto Moses Pingry six acres of land within the common fence," "Richard *Bisgood* on the southeast."

BIRD, widow, had the right of commonage 1641.
Thomas Beard, freeman, May 31, 1671.

BIDLAKE, Christopher, and Sarah had a daughter born Aug 15, 1694, named Mary. Had a seat assigned to him in the meeting house, 1700, when his name is spelled Bedlock.

BOREMAN, Bourman, Boarman, Bordman: Thomas 1, had a houselot on High street, 1635, and a farm near Labor-in-vain, 1636. He was a commoner, 1641. His will dated Oct. 6, 1670, was proved June 19, 1673. In it he mentions his wife Margaret; sons David and Thomas; son Robert Kinsman, and a daughter Joanna unmarried. He provides for a brother Daniel, to be maintained out of the estate. His widow died 1679. Her will dated August 8, of that year, was proved on the 30th of the following March. She mentions daughters Kinsman, Loe, [Martha, who married Deacon Thomas Low of Chebacco,] and Fellows: sons Daniel and Thomas.

In a fragment of a letter dated " London, ye 5th of Sep'r, 1672," and signed " Lidia Bankes," which was probably addressed to Daniel Epes, there is a postscript as follows: " I desire my affectionate love to your wife and all your children, my service to your father Symonds, my cousin, and not forgetting ould Mr. Bourman, Mr. Rogers and their wives if alive."

At a Town meeting Feb. 1672. Ordered, that the select men together with Mr. Wade and Serg't Bowman, take speedy care to repair the meeting house.

Daniel 2, son of Thomas 1, married Hannah Huttchinson, April 12, 1662.

Thomas 2, son of Thomas 1, married Elisabeth Perkins, Jan. 1, 1667. They had:

Thomas, born August 8, 1669.
Jacob, born June 10, 1671,

John, born March 8, 1673,

Offin, born Dec. 1676,

Margaret, born April 4, 1681.

A daughter died Nov. 25, 1679. He was a voter in town affairs, 1679. We find the following vote on the town records: " 1696-7, March, voted, that Thomas Boreman, sen'r, make an acknowledgment for his affronting Lt. Thomas Hart, or pay a fine of five shillings." In 1714, Mr. Thomas Boreman is appointed on a committee, and in 1719 a seat is assigned to him in the meeting house. It appears from the inscriptions on their grave stones yet standing in the old burying place that he died Oct. 3, 1719, in the 76 year of his age; and his wife died Dec. 4, 1718, aged 68 years, 8 months, and 3 days. In these inscriptions the name is spelt Bordman.

Thomas 3, son of Thomas 2, with his wife Sarah, had a son John, born Feb. 13, 1697. They were appointed administrators on the estate of Abel Langley of Ipswich, "their only brother," December 24, 1711.

Offin, son of Thomas 2, married Sarah Heard, Feb. 28, 1698, and on the 16 of December following, had a son Offin.

Jacob 3, son of Thomas 2, subscribed 10s towards the bell, 1699. " 1706, December 26, Martha Boarman, wife of Jacob Boarman, widow of Jno. Rogers, son of Samuel Rogers," died June 11, 1740, aged 70. Jacob Boardman died Nov. 29, 1756, aged 86. Elizabeth their daughter died May 4, 1736, aged 22.

John 4, son of Thomas 3, married Abigail Choate, published Nov. 27, 1720, daughter of Thomas Choate 2, son of John 1.

Moses with his wife Ann, had a son Daniel, born Dec. 10, 1699.

BOSWORTH, Haniel, a commoner 1648, 1664 and a voter in town affairs 1679. 1676 agreed with Haniell Bosworth for his son Haniell shall keep the flock, &c. His will was proved Sept. 25, 1683. He directs his body to be buried in Ipswich burying place. He left a wife and two daughters, Abigail and Elisabeth. He had Mary born April 6, 1665, who died Aug. 9, 1666. He possessed a lot of land at Muddy River.

1675, Sept. 28, Benedict Pulcipher's wife, upon pr'stment for wearing silk hood and scarf, fined 10s, and costs, and fees. Arthur Abbott's wife, same, Haniell Bosworth his two daughters same, (remitted March, 1677,) Margaret Lambert, same. Thomas Knowlton's wife and Obadiah Bridge's wife, same.

1696-7, Feb. 23. Granted to Mother Bosworth, in order to relief her in her want, £1 0 0.

BOYNTON, Caleb and Mary, had a son
    Caleb, born  December 1685,
    Ann, born Jan. 30, 1678,
    Hepsibeth, Nov. 13, 1681,
    Mary, Jan. 21, 1692.


William, complained of for encroaching on the common, 1667.
William, sen'r, died Dec. 8, 1686.


BRADSTREET, Simon, possessed a planting lot in High street,
adjoining lands of the Rev. John Norton, and the Rev. Thomas Bracy
in 1638.   He was a commoner in 1641.   He purchased of William
Symonds, laborer, "a planting lot containing  seven acres, being on
the hill on the north side of the river," Dec. 28, 1647.   In 1658, Mch
10, with Ann his wife, being then of Andover, he sells  land in  Andover, to Richard Sutton of Roxbury, husbandman.   He  was  born in
Holling, Lincolnshire, England, March, 1603, was one  year at Emmanuel College, arrived at Salem, 1630, the place  where he  died 27
March, 1697, at the age of  94.   He was elected Assistant, March
1630, and was 48 years in office ; Secretary of the Colony 23 Aug.
1630 to 1643, Deputy Governor 1673-78 ; Governor  1679-86 ; and
again Governor after the imprisonment of Andros from  May 1689 to
1692.   His first wife, by whom he had eight children,  was Ann, dau.
of Gov. Thomas Dudley.   She was a woman of much  literary ability,
and died 16 Sept. 1672.


Humphrey 1, had a house lot 1635, commoner, 1641.   Had a house
lot granted to him in Mill street, having Mr. Cogswell on the  north
west, Dec. 9, 1645.   The grant is signed by Richard Saltonstall, Daniell Denison, Samuel Appleton,  Richard  Jacob,  Robert Lord,  and
John Payne, a committee appointed by the freemen for that purpose.
In 1646, Jan. 28, he sells to Thomas Knowlton his dwelling house and
lot, situate and being between the dwelling house of Andrew  Hodges
towards the south west, and the dwelling of Stephen Jordan  towards
the south east, having a  highway leading down  to the  river on  the
west side.   He sells to Richard Hutley, Nov. 20, 1645, ten acres lying
in the common fields on the north side of Ipswich  River.   His  farm
was, before his decease, annexed to the town of Rowley.   His will dated July 21, 1657, was proved Sept. 26, following.   He directs his
body to be buried in the  burying place in Rowley.   He left a wife
Bridget, who died in November, 1665, a son John 2, to whom he gave

the farm at Muddy river;‡ Moses 2, a minor, and five daughters; Hannah Rose, Martha Beale, Mary, Sarah and Rebecca; three grandchildren, Daniel and Hannah Rose, and Samuel Beale.

Moses 2, son of Humphrey 1, a commoner, 1663; voter in town affairs, 1679; married Elizabeth Harris, March 11, 1661; had

Moses, born Oct. 17, 1665,

Elizabeth, born March 22, 1667.

Capt. Moses Bradstreet died August 17, 1690, aged 47, and is buried in Rowley.

Bridget Bradstreet, widow of Humphrey died about 1665. Her will is dated Oct. 14 of that year. She mentions a son Moses, and daughters Martha, the eldest, Mary Kimball. Walter to whom she bequeaths " Mr. Cobbets Book," and Rebecka Longford. John died in 1699, and left a widow Hannah.

BRACY, Rev. Thomas, was probably an assistant with the Rev. Nathaniel Ward in 1635. He possessed an house lot and planting lot in High street adjoining the lots of the Rev. John Norton and Mr. Simon Bradstreet, April 16, 1638. He probably returned to England. He also possessed land "lying towards the neck," in 1635.

" 1635. There was granted to Mr. John Tuttle ten acres toward the Neck, having Mr. Bracy his land west, Mr. Tredwell east, Philip Fowler north, and a Creek south. Also a planting lot on heart break hill, having Mr. Dudley west, Michael Williamson, John Johnson, and the marshes east, and two little swamps north and south."

BIGGSBY, Joseph, subscribes to the compensation to Denison, 1648. He purchased land of Joseph Jewett, in Rowley, which he afterwards sold to Robert and Nicholas Wallis before 1661. He had

Mary, born Feb. 18, 1659,

Susannah, died Jan. 18, 1657,

Nathaniel, died July 11, 1658.

BETTS, Richard, subscribed to Major Denison's allowance, 1648.

---

‡1699, Sept. 21. Inventory of John Bradstreet, mariner, who dyed in the Island of Barbadoes on the 21st July, Ano Dom, 1699. Appraised as money, Housing and land, about fifty acres, £300. The eighth part of sloop Unity £20. A tankard; 3 spoons and a porringer, all plate, £12, 8. Beds and bedding, £51, 5. 18 pairs of sheets and as many pillow cases, £23, 16.

Had a house and land on High street, adjoining Edward Brown, which he sold to Cornelius Waldo, before 1654.

BRABROOK, Richard, purchases conditionally of William Whitred of Ipswich, Carpenter, one half of his farm, Oct. 15, 1653. In 1654, he has certain rights of commonage as the Widow Haffield's farmer. He removed to Wenham and died about July 7, 1680. In the will his name is spelled Brawbrook. Richard, probably his son was a town pauper, 1681.

BRAGG, Edmund, or Edward, is mentioned as servant to Mr. Symonds, Dec. 30, 1642; gives "a day's work carting voluntary, besides the rate toward the cart bridge," Nov. 19, 1646. He was a commoner, 1664, and a voter in town affairs, 1679. He had Deborough, born Dec. 22, 1658, a son Thomas died Sept. 24, 1675. He purchased an house lot, Feb. 28, 1643, of " William Knowlton, bricklayer, which he bought of John Andrews, who bought the same of Robert Hayes, to whom the freemen of the Town of Ipswich did grant the same," containing an acre, adjoining other lands of said Knowlton which he bought of William Lampson and William Storey, having a lane leading towards the house of Joseph Medcalf towards the east, and Ipswich river toward the west. He, together with Thomas Low, purchased of Thomas Firman, Oct. 6, 1647, twenty acres of land lying upon the Mile brook toward the south west. Elisabeth his wife, died May 28, 1691, and on the 28 of October of the same year, he married widow Sarah Redington.

1673, Nov. Edward Bragg bound to keep the town from any charge by his entertaining of Robert Starkweather and family.

1679. He is one of 24 chosen as Tythingmen:

" At a meeting of the select men the 15th December, 1679: In obedience of an order made by the Honored General Court, held at Boston, October 15, 1679—we ye select men of Ipswich, have chosen Tythingmen as followeth :

| | |
|---|---|
| Jeremiah Jewet, | Isaack ffoster, |
| Aaron Pengre, sen'r | Samuel Eyers, |
| Symond Stace, | Thomas Wade, |
| Thomas Lull, | Isaack ffellowes, |
| Mr. Chute, [James, b. 1649, | John Giddings, |
|    G. Reg. No. 23, p. 247.] | William Goodhue, |
| John Wainwright, | Joseph Everly, |
| Sergent Perkins, | Will Thomson, |
| Jaakob ffoster, | Richard Walker, [or Wattles] |
| Thomas Louewell, | Thomas Jaackob, |
| Edmund Heard, | John Adams, |
| Thomas Clark, winisimet, | Edward Bragg. |
| John Denison, | |

1700. In the new meeting house, January 16, 1700, a seat at the Table is assigned to Old Good'n Bragg.

The will of Edward Bragg, dated January 14, 1706, was proved August 23, 1708. He mentions his wife Sarah, and a daughter Mary Eveleth. He bequeaths to the children of his daughter Deborah Searls, his " Land and building in ye town of Rowley." He adds, " I give and bequeath to ye Church of Christ in Ipswich, which I am a member of, three pounds in money, to be layd out by my overseers in a peice of silver plate, for ye use of sd church for ever." Among the communion service plate belonging to the First Church is a silver cup, bearing the inscription :

$$\left. \begin{array}{l} \text{A}_*\text{D's} \\ \text{E}_*\text{B's} \end{array} \right\} \text{Gift to the Church of Ipswich.}$$

The initials in this inscription probably stand for the names of Andrew Diamond and Edward Bragg.

Timothy 2, probably son of Edward 1, married Feb. 24, 1685, Lidia Gott. They had children :

  Timothy, born June 5, 1690,
  Edward, born July 10, 1692,
  Thomas, born Sept 1, 1696,
  Ebenezer, born Nov. 13, 1699.

He was a surveyor of highways, 1695-6, and had the right of turning horses on the common, 1697. He subscribed 10s toward the bell 1699. The inventory of the estate of Timothy Bragg, Feb. 3, 1706-7, House and an acre and an half land, £28, 10 ; total, £96, 18, 8. Lydia, relict.

BIRDLEY, or Burley, Giles 1, was an inhabitant 1648, and a commoner, 1664. June 13, 1668, Goodwife Birdley had granted trees for 100 rayles, and 100 posts. His will was proved Sept. 29, 1668. In it he mentions sons :

  Andrew,
  James, born Feb. 10, 1650,
  John, born July 13, 1662.

Andrew 2, son of Giles, born Sept. 5, 1657, died Feb. 1, 1718, aged 60 years and 5 months. (See epitaph 29.) He had the title of Cornet. His wife's name was Mary Conant, married March 14, 1681 ; had a daughter, Rebeckah, born March 29, 1683 ; he left one son, Andrew, born June 14, 1694, and three daughters, Rebeckah, wife of Robert Kinsman, married June 28, 1705 ; Mary, wife of Samuel Adams, and Sarah, wife of Richard Kimball, born Oct. 6, 1698.

1687, March 20, I Andrew Burley  request to grant me ye liberty of making a kill of bricks a Jefferies Neck, I cutting there no wood down that is growing to burn them but what I shall prepare otherwise,  taking such drift wood as may be found by the water side, because it will be near to my land by Jefferies Neck Caseway,  where  I  purpose  to build an house for to dwell there.   Voted and granted.

In his signature in 1698, the name is  spelled  " Burdly."   Andrew Bardley, another variation of the name Burley, is one of the  subscribers for a "bigger bell," in 1699.

Andrew 3, son of Andrew 2, (see epitaph 30,) was married to Lidia Pingry. in 1717.   Their publishment is dated  Nov. 9,  of  that  year. After her death in  1736,  (see  epitaph  31,)  he married, January 9, 1736, a second wife, whose name was Hannah Burnam, who survived him, and died Sept 15, 1759.   He died December 15, 1753.

James 2, son of Giles 1, married Rebeckah Stace, daughter of Thomas and Susanna Stace, grand  daughter of the Rev. William Worcester of Salisbury, May 25, 1685.   She  was  buried Oct. 21, 1686.   In 1695 he had a wife named Elisabeth.   They had :

Joseph, born April 6, 1695,

Thomas, born April 5, 1697.

John 2, son of Giles 1, died Feb. 21, 1688.

The committee appointed January 16, 1700, to assign the seats  in the meeting house then recently built, appoint a seat for Mr.  Andrew Burley.   In 1702, they appoint seats to John Burley, Rebecca Burley and Mary Burley.   In 1719 seats are appointed to Andrew Birdley, Widdow Birdley, probably Mary, widow of Andrew 2, and Mrs. Birdley, probably Lydia, wife of Andrew 3.


BRIDGES, Edmund, was a subscriber to Denison's  compensation, 1648, and a commoner 1664, and a voter in town affairs, 1679.   His wife Elizabeth died Dec. 31,  1664.   He married  Mary Littlehale, April 6, 1665, had Mary, born April 14, 1667.   He is appointed one of the executors of the will of Thomas Scott, March 8, 1653.   He sold jointly with Anthony Potter, April 4, 1660, to Elder John Whipple, a six acre lot, which was sometime Henry  Kingsbury's.

1675, Nov. 25.   John Littlehale being slain in the  warr, ad'r  gr'd to Edmund Bridges and Mary his wife,  (late wife to  Richard Littlehale and mother to sd John.)

He died January 13, 1684, and his  widow Mary, Oct. 21, 1691. He was a blacksmith, and left property, £235, 6.

The will of Edmund Bridges is dated Jan. 6, 1694, and was proved

March 31, 1685. He mentions his wife Mary, and sons John and Josiah; daughters Faith, Bethiah, and Mary. He appoints Capt. Daniell Epps and Lieutenant John Appleton overseers: witnesses, Daniell Epps and Edmund Heard.

1695, March 17, debts due from Edmund Bridges estate: To Isaac Littlehale on account of partnership £14, 10. To John Littlehale's estate as Edmund Bridges was administer'r, £10, 17, 8.

John, married Sarah How, Dec. 5, 1666.

Obediah, married Mary Smith, Oct. 25, 1671. He died Oct. 22, 1677. He had Obediah, born July 2, 1671; Samuel, born Feb. 1, 1675. In 1669 he had granted to him the privilege of fire wood, feed for one cow, so long as he follow the trade of fisherman.

1672, Feb. Granted to John Brown the like privilege of the common as other tradesmen as John Knowlton and Obadiah Bridges.

1677, Nov. Obadiah Bridges dying intestate, administration granted to Elisabeth his widow.

Josiah, married Elisabeth Norton, Nov. 13, 1676. She died June 24, 1677; married Ruth Greenleaf, Sept. 19, 1677.

BRYER, Richard, possessed the right of turning horses on the common, 1697. His wife was named Mary. They had
    Samuel, born March 20, 1679,
    Robert, born March 8, 1680,
    Margaret, born April 7, 1682,
    John, born December 31, 1685,
    Martha, born Feb. 19, 1689.
He had a seat in the meeting house, 1700.

BRIDGHAM, Doctor, died May 2, 1721, in the 76 year of his age. (See epitaph 25.) Grad. at H. C. 1669. He was son of Henry and Elizabeth Bridgham of Boston. Henry Bridgham took the freeman's oath in Boston, May 10, 1643. (Savage.) To the notice of the death of Doct. Bridgham in the town Records of Ipswich, is added the following remark: "For many years past he proved himself a very skillfull and eminent Physician, his administrations being commonly attended with great success." He was a feoffee of the grammar school from 1714 to the time of his decease. A silver cup belonging to the First Church has this inscription: "The Gift of Doct'r John Bridgham to the Church of Christ in Ipswich, 1721." He had a seat assigned to him in the meeting house, 1700.

April 16, 1695. Granted to Doct. John Bridgham about half an acre of land near Goodman Bridges near the widow Clark's, provided he improve it for a Garden and to build on for his settlement here in this Town.

BROWN, Edward, possessed an houselot March 17, 1642, on the east end of High street, of one acre, adjoining the houselots of William Bartholomew and Mr. Bradstreet. He is a subscriber to Denison's allowance in 1648. He possessed land in 1654. He died Feb. 9, 1659.

27 day of July, 1638, Memorand that: Richard Lumpkin hath sold unto John Tuttle one house and a house lot with certain other lands, ————one house lot lying near the great cove of the town river having a house lot now in the possession of William Avery on the southwest, Robert Kinsman's houselot on the north west, the town river on the south east, a houselot now in possession of Samuel Hall on the east, also upon the said lot one dwelling house formerly built by Richard Brown now of Newbury, and by him sold unto Mr. Richard Saltonstall by whom it was sold unto the said Richard Lumpkin.

John, was a commoner, 1641, and a contributor to Denison, 1648, was entitled to share in Plum Island, &c., 1664, and with the title or distinction of *farmer*, has the right of having horses on the common, 1697. He had land in 1649, adjoining land which William Fellows sold to John Pierpont. He had a houselot on town hill, 1657. He purchased, Dec, 5, 1663, of John Woodam and Mary his wife, a house and land in High street, on the south side, between Phillip Fowler and Phillip Call lately deceased. He died Sept. 13, 1677.

1677, November. John Brown of Ipswich, dying intestate, admin. granted to his eldest son, John Brown; two daughters, £50 pounds each; brother Nathaniel, his mother, £16.

John, probably son of the preceding, has the distinction of junior, in 1664, when he was entitled to shares in Plum Island, &c. He died April 9, 1727, aged 88 years, (see epitaph 36;) his wife, Hannah, died Nov. 17, 1727, aged 76 years, (see epitaph 37.) He had:

 Elisabeth, born May 15, 1664,
 John, Sept. 29, 1666,
 Jonathan, born Nov. 4, 1668,
 Sarah, born Dec. 2, 1670,
 John, born July 1678.

1681, Jan. The select men having called John Brown before them, and having had comp. that the sd John doth neglect his occasions, and spend much time and expense in ordinaries, doe now forewarn him, the sd John Brown, that he doe not frequent any of ye ordinaries upon penalty of Law. John Knowlton same.

1672, Feb.   Granted to John Brown the like privilege of the common as other tradesmen as John Knowlton and Obadiah Bridges.

1679, April.   Ordered that no person whatsoever shall sell or give unto John Brown the glazier, any strong drink or strong liquor, &c.

Thomas, was a commoner, 1641.

Joseph, was commoner, 1664.

Nathaniel, joined the church by taking the covenant, March 8, 1673: his wife was named Judith Perkins, married Dec. 16, 1673; he had a daughter by a former wife, born April 25, 1668.

Nathaniel and Elisabeth, had a son Thomas, born Nov. 18, 1699.

John and Hannah, had a daughter Mary, born July 3, 1685.

Joseph and Abigail, had a son Daniel, born January 15, 1684.

Joseph, sen'r, died Sept. 30, 1694, and left a widow, Annah Affalbie, married Feb. 28, 1671; he had:

> Joseph, born Feb. 18, 1673,
> John, born March 12, 1674,
> Hanah, born Feb. 24, 1675,
> Thomas, born Dec. 26, 1678.

Sept. 1694.   Inventory Joseph Brown: Farming lands, and £275, 5, as pay; debts due, in pay £20, 1; in money, £52, 3, 5.

Nathaniel, senior, Nathaniel, junior, William, John, senior, shoemaker, and John, junior, were commoners, 1707.

The committee for seating the meeting house, January 16, 1700, assign seats to Nathaniel, sen'r, John, sen'r and John, glazier.   Feb. 23, 1702-3, seats are assigned to William, Thomas, James and Sary.

Jonathan, married Liddia Kindrick, daughter of John Kindrick, April 6, 1694.

BREWER, Thomas 1, a commoner, 1641, probably removed to Hampton.

John 2, probably son of Thomas 1, was a commoner, 1664, and a voter in town affairs, 1679, when he has the addition of senior.   He joined the church by taking the covenant, Jan. 25, 1673.   He died June 23, 1684.   In his will dated nine days previously, he mentions his "father Brewer of Hampton; wife Mary; grand children, Edward Chapman, John Chapman; son John; he appoints his brother Thomas Lull and Simon Stace overseers.   His widow died Dec. 10, of the same year.

1684, Oct. 2.   Mary Brewer, widow of John Brewer deceased "'relinquishes to John Brewer and Simon Chapman husband of sd Brewers daughter," the estate bequeathed to her by her husband, in consideration of a bond to pay five pounds each, " that is ten pounds a year, and also they shall pay for her clothing;" to be paid quarterly in provision suitable for her support.

Corp'll Brewer was a surveyor of highways.

Feb. 1662.   The constable was ordered, 1661, "to pay John Brewer 20s for charges he is out about building the fort."   He was one of the selectmen 1673, com'r 1679.

" Clarke Brewer" was chosen " Tithingman," Dec. 20, 1677.

Serjeant John Brewer was chosen town clerk, Oct. 2, 1683.   Voted that sd John Brewer shall transcribe the Records which are in the two old Town Books : (the books being shattered to pieces,) into another book.

John 3, son of John 2, was married June 3, 1689 to Martha Perkins, daughter of Abraham.   He had lost a wife Susanna Warner, married January, 1674, who died Nov. 20, 1688.   1697, Oct. 4, Martha Brewer appointed adminis'r of estate of John Brewer, renders account, estate £92, 16, 5.

1701, Oct. 8.   " Martha Brewer alias Ingols," guardian of John Brewer, son of John Brewer : his part of his father's estate, £30,  18, 10.   She was also guardian of Mary, daughter of John Brewer.

1723, September 27, died Abigail, wife of John Brewer.

BULLY, Samuel, married Elizabeth Webber, Feb 22, 1693, and had a daughter Elizabeth born May 17,1696.

BUTTON, Mathias, commoner 1641, was, according to Mr. Felt, a Dutchman, and removed to Haverhill in 1646.   He sold land in Ipswich to Thomas Wells, June 14, 1644.   He subscribed to Major Denisons allowance 1648, Dec. 29.

BUTLER, William and Sarah had a daughter Sarah born July 23, 1680 ; and twin sons Thomas and Ralf, born Sept. 15, 1682, and a son Ralf, May 1684, William born June 1, 1676.

1710, Dec. 4.   Stephen Herrick of Beverly, attorney to Mary Herrick of Preston, Connec'tt, Ephraim Fellows and Anna his wife of Plainfield, Conn'tt, both daughters of Robert Cross of Ipswich ; in consideration of twenty-three pounds current money of N-England, acquit to William Buttler of Ipswich, all claims on their father's estate.

In a list of commoners, March 9, 1707-8, are the names of William sen'r, William junior, and Thomas Butler.

BURNHAM, John, was a soldier in the war against the Pequot Indians, for which he received a grant from the town of eight acres of land, 1639. He subscribed to the compensation of Major Denison in 1648. He sold to Anthony Potter, June 1, 1648, "a house lot late of Humphry Griffin, situate near the water mill. Also a house lot containing three acres lying next the house lot of serjeant Jacob."

John, secundus, married Elizabeth Wells, June 9, 1669; was appointed with others "to run the line between Glocester and us," 1665. Was a tythingman 1677 and 1695. He had:

John, born April 8, 1671,

Thomas, born Sept. 22 1673,

John, senior, came into full communion with the church, August 12, 1674. [See Note, page 29.]

Thomas 1, probably brother to John, was with him a soldier in an expedition to the Indians in 1643. Had privilege of commonage granted to him, Feb. 1667.

Granted liberty to set a saw mill upon Chebacco river, 1667, May.

Corp'll Thomas, surveyor of highways, 1662, selectman, 1663,serg't 1669.

He was a subscriber to the compensation to Major Denison, 1648.

On the 10th of March 1683, he enters into a "contract or agreement with respect of marriage intended betwixt Misheck Farley and Sarah Burnham," [born June 28, 1664,] with Michael Farley, sen'r, by which they agree "to give the young couple a house lot and to build for them a house."

Mesech Farley, miller, son of Michael Farley, sen'r, and Sarah Burnham, daughter of Lieut. Thomas Burnham, sen'r, were married August 6, 1684.

Lieut. Thomas,* died May 19, 1694, his wife Mary, March 27, 1715, aged 92, (see epitaph 28.)

The surviving children according to his will, dated Jan. 10, 1693-4, of which Nehemiah Jewett and Philemon Dane were ————,

were Thomas, born Jan 19, 1666, John, James, Mary, Johannah, Abigail, Ruth, Sarah, and Hester.

Thomas 2, son of Thomas 1, was a carpenter, and worked upon the meeting house in repairing it, 1668. Freeman, May 31, 1671.

---

*1685, Sept. Sarah Wait came into court, owned she had comited fornication with Joseph Burnham, son of Lt. Thomas Burnham, fined 40s and fees.

John Wait and Catherine Carroll his wife came into court and owned there comitting fornication together—fine 40s each.

He married Lydia Pengry, Feb 13, 1665.   They had :

    Moses, born Jan. 24, 1668,

    Lidia, born Dec. 6, 1674,

    Aaron, born Sept. 12, 1676,

    Eleazer, born Sept. 5, 1678,

    Abigail, born June 2, 1680.

James 2, son of Thomas 1, joined the church by taking the covenant Jan. 25, 1678.   He was overseer of the poor in 1698.   His wife was named Mary.   They had :

    Mary, born May 25, 1678,

    James. born Nov. 1, 1679,

    Thomas, born June 27, 1681,

    Sarah, born March 3, 1685,

    Joanna, born March 19. 1689,

    James, born Jan. 30, 1691,

    Joshua, born August 19, 1694.

They lost sons James, May 10, 1677, and Nov. 10, 1679.

March 23, 1692-3, the town granted to twenty-three of the inhabitants as many "lots laid out by ye River side between Samuel Ordway's shop and ye Town Bridge, beginning by ye Bridge and so by ye River side."

James Burnham had the 20th of these lots measuring 18 feet front. The lots varied from 18 to 28 feet ; the whole extending 498 feet.

He subscribed £2 toward the bell, 1699.   He died June 30. 1729, aged 78, (see epitaph 39.)   His wife died Nov. 1738, aged 76, (see epitaph.)

Thomas, married December 16, 1685, Esther Bishop, daughter of William Cogswell, widow of Samuel Bishop, [see note page 29.] They had children :

    Susanna, born Jan. 29, 1692-3,

    Thomas, born Feb. 12, 1694,

    Benjamin, born Dec. 21. 1696.

Thomas and Liddia had Mary, born Oct. 18, 1685, and March 14, 1688, died Liddia wife of Serj't Thomas.

May 27, 1728, died Susanna widow of Serj. Thomas.

Job and Abigail had a son Job, born Dec 9, 1698.

John of Chebacco, had a son Jonathan born Nov. 3, 1695.

Moses and Ann had a son David, born Dec. 10, 1699.

Josiah of Chebacco died Oct. 25, 1692, and Abigail his wife the 31st day of the same month.

Robert, died 1691, June 12.   Administration on his estate was granted Sept. 29, of that year to Frances, his widow.   He left two

sons, Samuel and Jeremiah.  By his will he gives to his  son  Samuel
two hundred acres of land at "Lamperell river."  He gives to his son
Jeremiah, besides lands, &c., "all my carpenters tools," "he to maintain his mother, my wife Frances Burnham, as  long  as  she  lives."
He possessed a house and land at " Oyster river."  The witnesses  to
his will were Thomas Burnham, sen'r, Francs Burnham,  James
Burnham, who makes his mark, and John Newmarch, jun'r.  The inventory of his estate amounting to £99 13, was made by Jacob Foster
and Nathaniel Knowlton, March 21, 1681-2,

Doct'r Joshua died March 7, 1762, æ 51 yr 5 mo.  Susanna his wife
died May 19, 1759, æ 29.


BOWLES, Christopher, was an inhabitant 1678, had certain  rights
of commonage, 1697 ; and had a seat assigned to him in the  meeting
house, 1700.

Joseph Bolles died May 17, 1711-12, aged 5  yr  3mo.  11  ds, (see
epitaph.)


BUCKLEY, William, 1648, he subscribes to  Major  Denison's  al-
lowance.  Herdsman, 1661.  He had :
William, born Dec. 8, 1657, died 1659.
William, died Aug. 16, 1660.
John, born May, 1660.
William, born Oct. 14, 1666.
Elisabeth, born May, 1669.


BLADGETT, Jonathan, had a seat appointed to him in the  meeting house, Jan. 16, 1700.


BRITTON, John, had a seat appointed to him in the meeting house
Jan. 16, 1700.


BUGG, Goodman, had a seat assigned to him in the meeting house
Jan. 16, 1700.


BARRY, John.  John Berrye married Hannah Hodgkins, Jan. 17,
1670.  Hannah his wife died May 29, 1676.

John Barry and Marry Chapman were married Jan. 24, 1676.

1679, Sept.  John Barrye and his wife for fornication  before  marriage, fined £3 and costs and fees.  He had  rights  of  commonage as
tenant of Samuel Bishop, 1678.

BEBBER, Capt. Isaac Van, lost a wife named Elizabeth, Aug. 21, 1737, and married widow Elizabeth Harris, Jan. 22, 1738.   (See epitaph 22.)

BRACKENBURY, William. was published with Abigail Heard, July 19, 1707, who died July 20, 1712, (epitaph 24.)  He married for a second wife, Mary Walcut of Salem, with whom he was published August 15, 1730.

BISGOOD, Richard.   1641, 12th day, 1st mo, Barnabas Horton of Ipswich, baker, sold unto Moses Pingry six acres of land within the common fence.   Richard Bisgood on the south east,

BUR, John, sen'r, died April 22, 1673.
   Jonathan, born June 28, 1665,
   Elisabeth, born Dec. 29, 1667,
   Jeremiah, born July 10, 1670.
   Abigall, born Dec. 11, 1672.

CALDWELL, John, purchased a house and land, August 21, 1654, of Cornelius Waldo, which he purchased of Richard Betts, bounded by land of Edward Brown south east; Robert Collins north west; street west; Thomas Lovell north east.   He was a commoner, 1664, and a voter in town affairs 1679, and with his wife Sarah, joined the church in full communion, April 12, 1664.

1673, Nov.   Granted to John Caldwell all the salt marsh gras that growes upon the island cald Bagwels island, to him and his heirs forever.

His will is dated June 20, 1692 ; on the 7th of July,  the inventory of his estate was presented ; Sept 28 his will was proved.  In it he mentions his wife Sarah, § (see Appleton Memorial, page 84,) who

---

§ She was the daughter of John and Sarah Dillingham, who came from Leicestershire, Eng., in 1630.  In 1634 they were in Ipswich, where Sarah was born.  In 1636, both John and Sarah Dillingham were dead.  The will of Sarah Dillingham, is :—" This is the last will and testament of mee Sarah Dillingham of Ipswich widowe : ffor my soule I comend it into the hands of God in the mediacon of Jesus Christ : ffor my temporall estate : I give to my onely child Sarah Dillingham my whole estate in lands and goods (except such pticuler legacyes as hereafter are named) : And if my child dye before it shall be marryed or attaine to the age of one and twenty yeares, then my

died Jan. 26, 1724, aged 87 years ; sons John, the eldest to whom he gives a double portion of his estate ; Dillingham, born March 6, 1666 ; William, who died Feb. 19, 1695 ; Nathaniel, born Oct. 18, 1669. His daughters were : Anna, born August 23, 1661 ; Sarah Ayres, born April 2, 1658, wife of Joseph Ayres, married June 9, 1684 ; Mary born Feb. 26. 1671, and Elizabeth, born Oct 15, 1675.

" Agreed with John Caldwell for his son William ٿo keep the flock on the north side of the River." 1677.

An inventory of the estate of John sen'r was rendered July 7, 1692, by Sarah his wife, and John jun'r.  Amount of value, £221, 16, 4.

John 2, son of John 1, freeman May 23, 1677, married Sarah Foster, daughter of Jacob Foster, May 5, 1689, who died July 11, 1722. Their children who survived their father were :

 Martha Ringe, born Aug. 28, 1690,

 John 3, born Aug. 19, 1692,

 Jacob 3, born Feb. 26, 1694-5, died 1744 ; was deacon ; left a
  widow Rebecca, dau. of Tho: Lull.

 Sarah Ayres, born July 16, 1697,

 William, born Jan. 17, 1708, married Lydia Lull.

He had a seat in the meeting house, 1700, and was a commoner, 1707.  He died Feb. 7, 1721-2.

---

will is that the same shalbe devyded equally betweene my mother Thomasine Caly, my brothers Abraham Caly and Jacob Caly, my sister Bull and my sister Base, the wyves of John Bull and John Base, and my sisters Rebecca Caly and Anne Caly, or such of them as shal be lyving at the tyme of the death of said child, all wch my mother, brethren, and sisters are now lyving in England : Also I give to Mr. Ward, Pastor of the Church at Ipswich, ffive pounds, and to Richard Saltonstall esqr ten pounds, and to Mrs. Saltonstall his wife, a silver bowle, To Mr Samuell Appleton ffyve pounds, and to his wife a silver porringer : and of this my will I make executors the said Mr Saltonstall and Mr Appleton, comitting the educacon and government of my said child and the estate I leave her vnto their faithfull ordering intreating them in the bonds of Christian Love to see this my will fulfilled, my due debts paid, my body decently buyried and my child religiously educated if God give it life and that they will order the estate as they would doe their owne.  In wytnes that this is my true will made in my prfect memory though my body be weake and sicke, I publish it after it had beene read vnto mee in the presence of those whose names are vnder wrytten, this xiiijth day of July, 1636.

SARAH DILLINGHAM.

Tho : Dudley, Robert Lord, Phillip ffowler, (his mark.)

—Caldwell Records, pages 9-14.

John Caldwell 3, son of John 2, was born August 19, 1692, married Nov. 5, 1715, Elisabeth Lull, and was killed by the Indians in Maine, July 10, 1724.    Their children were :

   John, born July 11, 1717, died 1801, aged 84,
   Thomas, born May 10, 1719, died May 31, 1725,
   Aaron, born April 18,1721, died 1765,
   Stephen, born June 1, 1723, died Jan 14, 1754, (see epit. 49)

William 3, son of John 2, born Jan. 17, 1708, married Lydia Lull, Dec. 1729, died Dec. 27, 1759 ; his wife was born Nov. 22, 1715, died Jan. 19, 1787.

Dillingham 2, son of John 1, was a commoner 1697, and with Mary his wife had :

   Mary, born November 3, 1695, died Oct. 13, 1698,
   Daniel, born August 30, 1698, died Oct. 23, 1698,

Mary, the mother, died on the 21st of the same month.

His second wife was Mary, by whom he had :

   Daniel, born Oct. 5, 1701, married Elisabeth Burley.
   Mary, born Sept. 28, 1703, married Jeremiah Lord,
   Sarah, born Aug. 1706, married Nath'l Hart.

He subscribed 3s toward the bell 1699.    In 1725 he has the title Serg't ; he died May 3, 1745, aged 79.    Mary his widow died 1748.

Nathaniel 2, son of John 1, was a commoner, 1707, and had a seat assigned to him in the meeting house, 1702.    His will was proved Jan. 3, 1738.    He married Abigail Wallingford, 1703, who survived him, and is mentioned in his will, a son John, and two daughters, Mary and Hannah.


CARTWRIGHT, Mistress, possessed a house in High street, before 1659.

Michael was "paid 32s for work done at the bridge, and for carriage for the gun," March 17, 1642.


CALEF, Joseph, son of *Robert of Roxbury, was a physician ; his name is in a list of such as had horses on the common in 1697 ; he then has the title of Mr. and his name is spelt *Calf*.    In the meeting house which was built in the year 1699, there was one tier of pews against the walls which were assigned to the principle inhabitants for the use

---

* Samuel Caleff, will, dated August 19, 1720, proved Sept. 26,— " To my Hon'd Mother, Mary Caleff."—"as an heir to ye estate of my Grand father Robert Caleff, late of Roxbury, in ye county of Suffolk, dec'd,"

of their wives and families, while the men were obliged to take their seats in the body of the house. The committee appointed for that purpose assigned to " Mr. Joseph Caleff ye 5th pew on ye so. east side of ye great door for his wife and family." Mr. Joseph Caleff himself, was appointed to sit in the fourth seat; his wife was named Mary; their children were :

Robert, born Dec. 12, 1693,

Joseph, born May 20, 1695,

Samuel and Ebenezer, born Jan. 25, 1696,

and according to Mr. Felt. two others, Peter and Mary.

He died Dec. 28, 1707, in the 36th year of his age, (see epitaph 38.) He subscribed 9s to the bell, 1699 ; the name is spelled *Calliffe.*

Robert died July 12, 1730, (epitaph 39.)

Samuel died Sept. 1, 1720, aged 24, (epitaph 40.)

Robert 2, son of Joseph 1. married Margaret, daughter of Deacon John Staniford, published Nov. 23, 1683, and had two children, who were both living 1730. Margaret was born Nov. 29, 1695, and died Oct. 7, 1727, (epitaph 39, A.)

‡John 3, son of Robert 2, was born in 1725; married Margaret, daughter of Rev. Nath'l Rogers, baptized Dec. 14, 1729, died March 27, 1751. He was a physician and surgeon, and was in 1755, and several years after, representative of the town in the General Court. In 1755, Oct. 25. the town instruct him to oppose "the distressing and ruinous measures taken by Parliament against Ameria," and "to do all he can to repeal the acts passed or may be passed." When in 1768, the Earl of Hillsborough required the House of Representatives to rescind a vote respecting a union of the colonies, the House, June 30, resolve not to rescind by a vote 92 to 17. Doctor Caleff voted in the minority, and incurred the displeasure of his constituents by so doing.

Oct. 3, 1774, having been waited on by a committee of Ipswich, so that his views of late acts of Parliament might be known, gives them leave to have it published in the Essex Gazette of Salem, that he regretted voting, June 30, 1768, in favor of the royalists, that his purpose is to maintain the charter rights against the late acts of Britain. But being convinced against his will, it appears he remained "of the

---

‡ His house stood upon the site of the residence of the late Col. John Heard. It was sold about 1802 to Capt. Samuel Caldwell, and removed some rods east of the South Meeting House, where it now stands.—*Printer.*

same opinion still," for he continued attached to the royalist party, and when the revolutionary war broke out left the country and settled in the British province of New Brunswick, where at the the town of St. Andrews, he died in 1812, aged 87 years. He had a son Robert who died at Norfolk, Va. in 1801, at the age of 41. (Sabines American Loyalist.

CALL, Philip. His will is dated May 6, 1662, and was proved Sept. 30, of that year. To his wife Mary, he bequeathes a house and land in Ipswich, and "land in Old England, to help bring up the children." He mentions a son Philip, born Jan. 17, 1659, and a daughter Mary. His houselot was in High street adjoining John Woodam.
Philip, a shoemaker, 1683.

CARR, George, 1635, is possessed of an houselot about half an acre butting upon the south upon the town river, on the east by a planting lot of his own, on the north by the planting lot of Daniel Clarke's, with liberty granted him to fence the said lot as low as the low water mark, provided he leave a way or gate for passage by the river side.
1636.   He was possessed of an island of about 20 acres on the east side of Labor-in-vain, which John Andrews afterwards possessed and conveyed to Mary Webster, widow, Nov. 30, 1646. He removed to Salisbury, 1640.

CASS, Samuel, has a seat assigned to him in the meeting house, January, 1700.

CRESSY, William, had a right of turning horses on the common, 1697, and had a seat in the meeting house, 1700.

CATCHAM, John, subscribed to Major Denison's compensation, 1648. In 1647 he possessed land adjoining a grant to William Payne.

CHAPMAN, Edward 1, was a commoner, 1664. He died April 18, 1678; his will is dated April 9, and was proved April 30, 1678. His wife Mary died June 18, 1653; he left a wife Dorothy, daughter of Richard Swan of Rowley, with whom there had been a "covenant and contract" before marriage. His sons were Samuel, his executor; Symon and Nathaniel; he left a daughter Mary, wife of John Barry.
Richard Swan of Rowley, in a will dated April 25, 1678, mentions daughters Jane Wilson, Frances Quilter, Dorothy Chapman and Mercy Warner. Shoreborn Wilson had an account open with Robert Lord, January 18, 1683.

" At a meeting among the select men of Ipswich, 21, 12, 1705-6, whereas Mr Thomas Hamond of this town is come to reside upon ye ffarm yt his late grand father, John Cross gave to his daughter, ye sd Hamonds mother, sd Hamond being ye only surviving heir yt we know of to P. land and other lands of his late father Hamond dyed siezed of which was granted to Mark Symonds in or before ye year 1684,—which when granted these was comon land lying between sd land and Rowley lines and in January, 1644, sayd comon land was granted to Edward Chapman—about 16 acres.

Simon 2, son of Edward 1, was a voter in town affairs, 1679 : freeman May 12, 1675, and had a seat in the meeting house 1700.   With Mary his wife had a son Samuel, born Oct. 29, 1680 ; Steven, born Oct. 30, 1685.   Mary wife of Simon died Feb. 23, 1724.

Samuel 2, son of Edward 1, joined the church by taking the covenant, being one of the "young generation," January 25, 1673 ; commoner, 1678.   With Ruth Ingalls, his wife, married May 20, 1678, they had :

> Samuel born Feb. 12, 1678,
> Joseph, born April 6, 1685,
> Mary, born Jan. 2, 1690,
> Edward, died Oct. 17, 1688.

Ruth, his wife, died June 22, 1700.

Nathaniel 2, son of Edward 1, had a wife named Mary Wilborn, m. Dec. 1674, by whom he had a daughter Hannah, born February 8, 1691-2, and other children who died young.   In June, 1696, he married Ruth Davis.

John, married Rebecca Smith, Sept. 30, 1675 ; had John born July 7, 1676 ; joined the church, being one of the "young generation," the same day with Samuel, Jan. 25, 1678.

Samuel had a seat in the meeting house 1700.   He married Phoebe Bolton, Nov. 20, 1701.

Samuel, Joseph, John, Mary, and Dorothy, had seats assigned to them. Feb. 23, 1702-3.

William, and Elizabeth Smith, married March 30, 1682 ; had

> William, May 30, 1682.
> Elizabeth, born Nov. 29, 1684,
> Ann, born Jan. 19, 1690,

Samuel and John were commoners, 1707.


CHASE, Aquilla, was born July 15, 1688 ; he married Mary Smith —their intention of marriage was published at Ipswich, May 31, 1742, he died March 17, 1713-14, aged 26, (epitaph 44.)   He was the 4th child of Thomas, who was born July 25, 1654; and married Rebecca Follansbee, November 22. 1677.  Thomas was the fourth child of Aquilla, who settled in Hampton, New Hampshire, in 1636, and married Ann Wheeler, daughter of John Wheeler, of Hampton. and died at Newbury, Aug. 29, 1670.  (Hist. and Gen. Reg. vol 1, p. 69.)

CHOATE, John, whose name is spelt *Chote*, subscribes to Denison's allowance, 1648, and was a voter in town affairs, 1679 : he died Dec. 4, 1695 ; his wife Ann, died Feb. 16, 1727, being more than 90 years of age.  She joined the church in "full communion," Dec. 1673. Their children were :

> John, born June, 1661, the eldest son,
> Thomas,
> Samuel,
> Benjamin, grad. H. C. 1603, minister at Kingston, N. H.
> Joseph, a minor of 17 yrs, at his father's death.
> Mary, born Aug. 16, 1666.

*John 2, son of John 1, born June 15, 1661, was a Deacon of the church at Chebacco.  He married July 7, 1684, Elisabeth Graves ; May 19, 1690, the widow Elisabeth Giddings ; July 20, 1723, the widow Sarah Perkins ; March 12, 1729, the widow Prudence Marshall. Sarah died Nov. 17, 1728 ; and Prudence, Dec. 9, 1732.  He died July 11, 1733, aged 73 years.  He had by his first wife :

> John, born May 28, 1685 ;

by his second wife :

> Robert, born April 27, 1691,
> Ebenezer, born Jan. 23, 1694,
> Samuel.

In 1718-19, Feb. 13, he conveys to his son Robert, "in consideration of ye natural love and affection," half of his 'housings and land,' in possession of his " Mother Choate which was deeded to him by his brother Thomas Choate."

Robert 3, son of John 2, born April 27, 1691, married January 7, 1715, Eunice Perkins, daughter of Jacob Perkins, who died Nov. 23, 1755.  Their children were :

> Ebenezer, born Nov. 3, 1619,

---

*"1696-7, March 15, John Chote enters cossion to ye Honoured Judg of probate of wills that whereas I having matters of waight to offer that my fathers Will may not be approbated while I have opportunity to alleadg against it as witness my hand.    JOHN CHOTE."

Elizabeth, born Sept. 29, 1726, married Michael Farley,
   Nehemiah, born Dec. 6, 1730,
and three others who died young.

He married for a second wife, Mary Knowlton, widow of Isaac Knowlton.  Previous to marriage, July 1, 1758, he purchased of her a dwelling house which was left to her by her former husband.  This house§ is yet standing, the next building south of the Town House. He bequeathed it to his daughter Elizabeth Farley, and it remained her property until her death, 1795.

He died Sept. 26, 1763 ; by his will dared June 1, 1761, he bequeaths to his wife Mary, all the property which he received with her, and the house and garden, &c., which he purchased of her, during her life ; to his son Ebenezer, who married Elizabeth Brown, March 28, 1750, homestead, &c. ; to his son Nehemiah, house and land at Wade's island ; to his daughter Elizabeth, wife of Michael Farley, £65 "lawful money," also the house and homestead where I now live in town, after wife's decease.  Also "a riding horse and household goods which I have not given to my wife."

Thomas 2 son of John 1, with Mary his wife had :
   Anne born May 22, 1691,
   Thomas, born June 9, 1693,
   Mary, born March 18, 1695,
   John, born July 25, 1697,
   Abigail, born Oct. 20, 1699,
   Francis, born Sept. 13, 1701,
   Rachel, born Nov. 8, 1703,
   Ebenezer, born March 10, 1706,
   Sarah, July 24, 1708.

---

§ " July 1, 1759, Mary Knowlton sells to Robert Choate in con'n of £50, a dwelling house and a small quantity of land about it, being the homestead late of my husband, Isaac Knowlton of Ipswich, deceased, bounded westerly by street or county road leading to the town Bridge, —northeasterly and northerly on land of Thomas Lord till it comes to land of Doct. Manning  south easterly on said Manning till it comes to land of Henry Wise, southerly on said Wise till it comes to bounds first mentioned."

This house, in which Gen. Michael Farley at one time resided, was sold to Aaron Wallis, who, in 1820, sold it to Amos Jones, blacksmith.  Amos Jones resided in it till his death, 1846.  His widow, Elisabeth (Smith) Jones, sold it, and in 1862 it was taken down.  It was probably built by Samuel Younglove in 1635.  A sketch of this house is in possession of the *Printer*.

Capt. Thomas Choate married Mary Calef, widow, Sept. 24, 1734.

John 3, son of Thomas 2, born July 25, 1697, died Dec. 17, 1765, (epitaph 41,) his wife, Miriam, married March 3, 1717 at Gloucester, died March 1, 1769, aged 74 years, (epitaph 42.) He was a representative at the General Court fifteen years, between 1731 and 1760; he was colonel of a regiment and judge of probate many years. They had several children, all of whom died before their parents.

Thomas 3, son of Thomas 2, and Elisabeth his wife had:

 Josiah, born Sept. 16, 1715,

 Jeremiah, July 16, 1725, m. Eunice Giddings, Jan. 24, 1751.

 Stephen, born Nov. 1727,

 Mary, born June 20, 1731,

 Abigail, born July 18, 1734.

Francis 3, son of Thomas 2, with Hannah (Perkins,) his wife, married April 13, 1727, had:

 Francis, born Feb. 27, 1727-8,

 William, born Sept. 5, 1730,

 Abraham, born March 24, 1731,

 Isaac, Jan. 3, 1733-4.

Samuel 2, son of John 1, married Mary Williams of Roxbury, Nov 23, 1688, and had:

 Mary, born Dec. 31, 1690,

 Samuel, born Jan. 10, 1691.

Samuel 3, son of Samuel 2, with his wife Mary, had:

 Mary, baptized Sept 3, 1721,

 Ann, bap July 9, 1727.

Samuel married the widow Damaras Groton of Chebacco, March 4, 1728.

Daniel was published with Mary Adams Dec. 13, 1727, and Daniel son of Daniel and Mary, was born Jan. 19, 1728.

1747, June 28, died Daniel Choate, (*felo de se.*)

Ebenezer 3, son of John 2, in his will dated Dec. 15, 1718, bequeaths thus: "To my dear and well beloved Mrs. Mary Cogswell, daughter of Capt. Jonathan Cogswell of Ipswich, deceased, £30,—£15 of which to purchase mourning." He mentions brothers Robert and Benjamin; sisters Jane Wicom, Dorothy Brown, mother Elen'r, brother-in-law Parker Dodge, who had a son Parker. Mary Cogsweil makes her X mark to a receipt.

Benjamin 2, son of John 1, Feb. 9, 1702-3, in consideration of being brought up at College renounces all claim to his father John's estate.

Samuel 2, son of John 1, died about 1713; his estate was divided March 30, 1713, thus: To his widow Mary, one third, £33, 0, 4; to

Samuel two shares, £14, 13, 5; to Sarah, Mary, Stephen, William, Elizabeth, Margaret, John, £7, 6, 9, each.

1715, Sept. 16, Samuel Story married the widow Mary Choate.

John Burnham married Sarah Choate, daughter of John 1, April 13, 1693.

Joseph Choate, Nov. 28, 1706, sells to his "brother John Choate and Nathaniel Goodhue," certain lands, &c.

"Benjamin Choat of Kingston in ye provence of Newhampshire, clerk," conveys "House and about four acres of land in which my mother Anne Choate lives," "to Thomas Choat."

"1727, February 2, Thomas Choate in consideration of love and good will and respect I have toward my loving cousin Robert Choate of Chebacco,——gives commonage that belonged to my father Mr. John Choate, sen'r, of Ipswich."

Feb. 13, 1718-19, John Choate conveys to his son Robert, &c.

1734, Dec. 9, David Preston and wife Elisabeth, of Windham, Connecticut, received of Robert Choate £20 legacy from John Choate, father of Robert, to his grand daughter Elisabeth Preston, only child of his daughter Ann Martin deceased.

May 16, 1747, Robert Choate and Samuel Choate in possession of land formerly belonging to our grandfather, Mr. John Choate, sen'r.

CHALLIS, Philip, was possessed of a house lot, 1637, in the south side of the river, having on the east a highway leading to the river, on the south west a houselot granted to Robert Hayes. He removed to Salisbury, 1640, where he was commoner, 1650.

CHUTE, Lionel, school master. His will is dated 4th 7th mo. 1644, and proved November 7, 1645. He left a wife Rose, and a son James.

James, is appointed administrator of his father, James, estate, August 16, 1691, consisting of one half homestead, 6 acres marsh, 6 acres pasture land, cash, and 6 silver spoons £3, total £70.

James and Mary Wood, married Nov. 10, 1673, had
   Mary, born Feb. 16, 1674,
   Elisabeth, June 22, 1676,
   Ann, born Oct. 19, 1679,
   Lionel, born April 15, 1680.
   James, born June 15, 1686,
   Thomas, born Jan. 30, 1690.
Lionel was a commoner, 1641, and James 1648.

Mr. Chute was selectman 1661, commoner 1664, and 1678.

CHEEVER, Ezekiel, the first master of the grammar school from 1650 to 1660, when he removed to Boston.   He had born in Ipswich,

    Nathaniel, born June 23, 1657,

    Thomas, born Aug. 23, 1658,

    Nathaniel, died July 12, 1657.

He owned a piece of land on which he built a barn and planted an orchard, which on his removal was purchased by the Feoffees and added to the grammar school property.   It was probably that part of the lot on which some old apple trees are yet standing.   The noncupative will of the Rev. Nathaniel Rogers, taken July 3, 1655, appears to be in his handwriting, and is a very neat specimen of the chirography of the age.   The following is from Farmer's Register : " The celebrated Schoolmaster of whom an early poet says,—

> " Tis Corbet's pains and Chever's we must own,
> That thou New England art not Scythia grown,"

was born in London 25 Jan. 1615, came to N. E. 1637, and settled at New Haven, removed to Ipswich Dec. 1650, to Charlestown Nov. 1660, to Boston, 6 Jan. 1670, where he died 21 August, 1708, æ 93."

Mr. Samuel joined the church in full communion, Jan. 25, 1673.

COBBETT, Thomas, was born at Newbury, England; was a student at Oxford ; arrived in New England, June 26, 1637, settled first at Lynn, and afterward, in 1656, at Ipswich, of which place he continued to be the minister, until his death, Nov. 5, 1685.   In his will proved Nov. 23, 1685, he describes himself as being "nigh 73 years of age."   He mentions his "wife Elizabeth, with whom at our marriag I had a considerable portion."   " My dwelling house in Ipswich, confirmed lately to be my own by Mr. William Norton, impowered thereto by his Brother, Mr. John Norton his will."

This house is yet standing, a little eastward from the Methodist meeting house. ‡

August 11, 1696. " John Cobbett of Ipswich, Gentleman, sells to Francis Wainwright in consideration of seventy pounds, a house lot and tract of land containing three acres, more or less, bounded by land of John Baker, north-north-east ; by said Baker, east ; and south east by highway ; on the south-south west by said Wainwright ; and by Mr. Robert Payne, west and north west ; with ye house upon said

---

‡ Mr. Hammatt refers to the First methodist meeting house, since removed.

land." Signed John Cobbitt and Elizabeth his wife. Mr. Cobbett mentions in his will his son Belcher, and sons Samuel, freeman Mch 11, 1673 4, John and Thomas.

1661, Feb. 18, granted to Mr. Thomas Cobbitt twelve acres of land either at Mr. Paines paster or by the river beyond Goodman Harough his house wch he shall think meat.

Mr. John and Elizabeth had a son Thomas born Feb. 10, 1685.

Mrs. Elisabeth. widow of the Rev. Thomas, died August 5, 1686, at night.

1674, Mch 31. Mr. Jo: Rogers, Mr. Sam'l Cobbett, Robert Kinsman, Tho: Clearke, Daniell Hovey, Abra: Fitt, Joseph Goodhue, Joseph Whipple, Phile: Dane, James Day, being admitted to the freed of this Colony took the freeman's eath.

1673, Feb. 22, Mr. Samuel joined the church in full communion.

From Rev. Thomas Cobbet's Will:—" As to that sorry dust heap in itself, I mean my body, I leave that to the care of my within named executors to be decently buried close by deceased children here in the burying place at Ipswich, then to return again to its dust out of which it was originally taken, being through grace firmly parswaded from infallible of God's holy Word, and having thence a living hope that our Lord Jesus Christ at the last day will by his almighty power, and by virtue of his own blessed resurrection, assuredly raise it up again, and re-unite it to my soul again, so that both shall live as in the most desired blissfull communion and fellowship and fruition of the most pretious face, favour. and presence of the blessed father, son and holy ghost, so in the sweet company and fellowship of all the glorious angels and glorified saints forever and ever, Amen.

" First, as it hath been much and often in my heart, so now I actually will and bequeath to my dear wife Elizabeth Cobbet, with whom at our marriage I had a considerable portion—so much of my estate for her life time as in an ordinary way by God's blessing thereupon may put her in a capacity of comfortable maintaining herself and a maid servant to keep her without depending upon any of her children, and to be enabled rather to lend them help if need require, and to give to her grand children what she may see meet, or to other pious, charitable uses.

" The particulars, &c.,

" My dwelling house at Ipswich, &c.,

" The money and plate that I have left; also household stuff, and goods whatsoever.

" All my study books which are yet not so many as other ministers which live where they contribut money are enabled to get, five only excepted, given to Samuel Thomas and John Cobbet—also, all the corn and malt which hath been paid in for my use, either at Capt. Appletons or Capt. Whipples malt house," &c.

" Also what debts are due to us as from John Dutch forty shillings, from my sonne Belcher for what he oweth us for stockings and shoes for Samuel and for the one half of his diet since his mother died, being willing to bear the other half of his diet for that while, as I told him, besides what we wholly bear for four or five years formerly, and it being now about a year and a half since my daughter died, &c.

" Also all my other lands in Ipswich, that is the four acre pasture and the eleven acre corn lot, at the west end of Ipswich.

" Malt at old Goodman Lowe's malt house.

" Farm 500 acres near Haverhill, which our honoured general court gave me.

" One half of a dwelling house at Lynn."

Sons Samuel, Thomas, John.   Samuel double portion.

" Ten pounds to Samuel Belcher to be paid him when at the age of twenty-one."

" Ten pounds to Elizabeth Belcher to be paid when married."

" Samuel and Thomas already married," "widow of their deceased brother," [Elisha,] "grandchild Samuel Belcher and his sister Elizabeth Belcher."   No date to will.

November 6, 1685, agreed with respect to the Reverend Mr. Cobbitts funeral, That Deaken Goodhue provide one barrill of Wine and half a hundred weight of sugar, and that he send it to Mr Cobbitts house next second day of the week in the morning, for which he is to have in pay not money four shillings by the gallon and six pence a pound for the sugar.

That Mr. Rust provide if he can against the funeral, Gloves suitable for men and women, to the value of five or six pounds not money pay, and some spice and ginger for the syder.   That a man be sent to Lyn to acquaint friends with the solemn providence here.

That some persons be appointed to look to the burning of the wine and heating of the syder, against the time appointed for the funeral next Monday at one of the clock, and such as will be careful in the distribution.

Total expense £17, 19, 0.

[To Mr. Hammatt's account of Mr. Cobbett, we add an extract from Judge Sewall's Journal, and also a letter from Mr. Cobbett to Increase Mather.]

Judge Sewall says:—*Sabbathday, Nov. 8, 1685.* Going to Mr. Willard's, I understand Mr. Thomas Cobbet died last Thorsday Even,

*Rev. Thomas Cobbett's House, East street.*
*Drawn by A. W. Dowe, 1880.*

to be buried to-morrow, Nov'r 9th; was abroad at some of his Neighbors the Monday before.   Mr. Chauncey died on Tuesday last.   So
two Ministers dead this last week.

*Monday, Nov'r 9.*   Mr. Cobbet buried about four in the afternoon.
Flight of snow.

*Thorsday, Nov'r 12.*   Mr. Moody preaches from Isa. 57: 1.   Mr.
Cobbet's Funeral Sermon: said also of Mr. Chauncey that he was a
Man of Singular Worth.   Said but two of the First Generation left.

Extract from a letter of Mr. Cobbett (to Increase Mather,) concerning his son's captivity: printed in Hist. and Gen. Reg.   A very
interesting account is likewise given by Mr. Hubbard.   Mr. Cobbett
writes:

" As to what you querie whether there were not answers of prayer
respecting my captive son: [Thomas.] surely, sir, I may truly say,
his wonderful preservations in all that nine weeks' time, after he was
taken, and deliverance at the last, they may well be put upon account,
as answers of prayer; for he was constantly pleaded for by Mr.
Moody, in his congregation for that end from his first being taken, (of
which they first heard) till his redemption: so was he in like sort constantly pleaded for by Mr. Shepperd in his congregation at Charlestown, and by my desire signified that way, by Mr. Philips, Mr. Hale,
Mr. Higginson, Mr. Whitting, Mr. Buckley, in their congregations,
and I doubt not by yourself, Mr. Thatcher and Mr. Allen in the three
Boston Churches, besides the prayers going constantly that way for
him in the families and closets of godly ones who heard of his captivity and hazard.   He was constantly as there was cause, remembered
in our congregation for that end, and which I may not forget to mention.

When Mr. Moody by a Post sent hither, sent me the first news of
his taking by the Indians, and their further rage in their parts, calling
out for earnest prayers, now if ever I presently caused one of our
Deacons to call to our house that very day as many godly persons and
their wives as were near us, to spend some time in prayer together
about the same.   About thirty met, several of them prayed, and the
Lord was with them in it: and with me also, who began and ended
that service.

And having begged some amends at first of our wasted son Elisha
at home, as a pledge of desired mercies to our captived son abroad as
granted, my heart, as I must acknowledge to the Lord's praise, was
sweetly quieted in the close of that service, and I was even persuaded

that the Lord had heard our prayers in that respect, and could not but express as much to some of our godly friends. So was one of our sisters, (as since she informed my wife,) as confidently persuaded thereupon that she should ere long see Thomas returned—and that in comfortable plight—as if he were already come.

Verily as to my son Elisha bodily amending somewhat, God so ordered it that that very night he slept better than he had done a great while before, and thence forward he strangely began to get more clear of his dire cough, to voyd phlegm more freely; to fetch his breath better, to have a better stomach, and to gather strength; insomuch that he who could not walk up and down the room without staggering, could walk up that high hill (which you know of,) behind Mr Norton's now our house. So that Mr. Rogers concluded the worst was past as to his consumption. Only after this, unhappily he catched a sore cold, being alone in the chamber above an hour without fire, writing (unknown to us,) and by that means fell into an ague and fever for many weeks constantly once a day; and was brought rather low every way than ever; and after the ague left him and he began to get up again; and made us afraid of him, and although since also his ague hath left him, he is in a very wasting way again. O dear sir, with your prayer sustain, in our renewed griefs for him.

One passage more about my son Thomas I must tell you of. That after so many means used for his ransom at first and crossed, Mr. Moody had that passage in his letter writing thereof, that he would fain conclude that means failing God meant to do it only himself. Wherein indeed he spake to what was in my heart and mouth often to plead with the Lord, and who else but God alone sent him so seasonably to the place, where and when the opportunity was but then ordered by God, in the articles signed the 9th of December, 1676 for the captives to wit, under Madowandoe's the Penobscot Sachems power, and he sent to Penobscot under his tyranical master for powder (never imagining any such articles to be there made by his Sachem,) the 10th (which was the Lord's Day, the wonted special praying day for him,) and he arrived at the Sachem's wigwam the 11th Dec. that is on Monday, and his coming being heard of, and most desired by Capt More, and the Sachem was sent unto, to send him to them, or bring him himself aboard with him, enjoining that he should return with him, if he would not for to release him—and the Tuesday being foul weather, the Wednesday, that is the 13th, the Sachem came with him aboard, and when urged upon the articles to deliver him, and he conceiving that his master must consent and be satisfied first; and then any ransom he would demand to satisfy his master or him being offered

—he would that also fearing to be killed by Thomas his master if he yielded him up without he were there to consent: for he was he said a desperate man if crossed; and had crammed two or three in that way—and he feared the like for him in this matter, and when after a parting cup of wine and dram of liquors given to the Sachem and his company. he walked awhile to and again on the deck—and on a sudden made a stand, and said to Capt. Moore, " Well Capt. since it is so, take this man; I freely give him up to you, carry him home to his friend: "who but God alone when means failed gave that turn to the Sachems heart, (according to that Proverb 21 : 1,) which was what had been pleaded and expected before, and I count that providence in the arrival of our vessels the 7 of December; the concluding the articles making such way for his freedom the 9th Dec: his coming the 11th: to be when he might have the benefit of that opportunity; and the bringing the Sachem's heart so freely off the 13th to set him at liberty, following our general fast so very speedily (for that was the 7 Dec. 1676, on which day I am sure his case was strongly also pleaded for,) I verily conclude his redemption may therefore be put among the special answers of New England prayers.

COGSWELL, John, was an inhabitant of Ipswich, 1635, and had a house near the meeting house green, with a lot of eight acres at the " N. W. end of" Bridge street, granted 1638. He was a man of wealth, and had large grants of land principally in Chebacco, of which parish he became a resident. His family and descendants continued to reside in that parish many years. There does not appear to have been any of the name in the first parish when the meeting house was built in 1669, no pews or seats assigned to any such at the seating of the meeting house, Jan. 16, 1700. He died Nov. 29, 1669, aged according to Mr. Felt, about 58. This must be a mistake; his son William being fifty years old at the time of his father's decease. It may have been occasioned by a misprint for 78, the more probable age. He left a wife named Elizabeth, who died June 2, 1676. His children were William, John, *Edward, Mary Armitage of Boston, Hannah, wife of Cornelius Waldo, Abigail, wife of Thomas Clark. and Sarah wife Simon Tuttle.

John 2, jun'r, died about Sept. 27, 1653, and left a will of which— and the inventory of his estate,—only illegible fragments remain. He

---

* 1670, March 29, Thomas Bragg and Edward Coggswell for fighting in the meeting house on the Lord's day, in time of exercise, fined 10s a piece and costs and fees.

was probably son of John 1.

William 2, son of John 1, died Dec. 1700, aged 71.   He was a subscriber to Denison's compensation, 1648, commoner, 1664, surveyor
of highways, 1663, tithingman. 1677, a voter in town affairs, 1679.

A town meeting of the inhabitants of Ipswich. held on  the  17th of
December, 1700, "by  reason  of  several  persons being absent, and
gone to Mr. Cogswell's funeral, is adjourned·to next lecture day."

His children living at the time of his decease were :

> Elisabeth, widow of Col. Thomas Wade,
> Hester, wife of Thomas Burnham ;
> Susannah, wife of Benjamin White, m. Jan 21, 1681,
> Sarah, wife of William Noyes,
> William, born Dec. 4, 1659,
> Jonathan, born April 26, 1661,
> John,
> Adam, born Jan. 10, 1666.

He had besides :

> Anna, born June 5, 1657,
> A child  born May 12, 1665,
> Edmund, died May 14, 1680,
> Sarah, born Feb. 3, 1668.

William 3, son of William 2, died April 14, 1708.   He married Oct.
9, 1685, Martha Emerson, daughter  of  the  Rev.  John Emerson of
Gloucester.   His children were :

> Edward, the eldest son,
> William,
> Emerson,
> Martha, Dorothy, born Aug. 31, 1692, Lucy, Eunice.

Mr. Matthew Whipple was  appointed May 15, 1709, guardian  to
Dorothy and Emerson, who were minors.   Eunice was also a minor at
the time of her father's decease.

One charge on the estate was, " To dividing  the  Island  with  Mr.
Choate," May 16, 1717.   Administration is granted to " Matthew
Whipple, who married ye eldest daughter of William Cogswell."

Jonathan 3, son William 2. married May 24, 1686, Elizabeth Wainwright.   His will is dated July 9, and was  proved  August  7, 1717.
He has the title of Captain ; he gives  to  his  wife  Elizabeth, besides
other legacies : "my Negro man slave called Jack, and also my  Indian maid slave called Nell."

He left two sons : Jonathan, born May 1. 1687, his executor,  and
Francis, whom he directs "to be supported at College until he has the
degree of Bachelor of Arts."

Also six daughters of whom the names are mentioned :
Elisabeth Eveleth,
Ann Goodhue, born March 28, 1684,
Sarah, born August 21, 1696,
Lucy, the youngest.
John 3, son of William 2, with Margaret Gifford his wife, married
July 22, 1674, had :
Margaret, born Sept 6, 1675,
Elizabeth, born Aug. 1, 1678,
Gifford, born Aug. 4, 1679,
Sarah, born Sept. 16, 1681,
John born Sept. 6. 1683,
Mary, born Dec. 1685,
Susanna, born May 5, 1691
Samuel, born Feb. 23, 1693.
His will dated Sept 6, 1713, and proved July 20, 1724, mentions
his wife Margaret ; sons Gifford, Samuel, John ; daughters unmarried
Sarah, Mary, Bethiah, and Susanna.
John, jun'r, had :
Hannah, born March 27, 1693,
William, born Sept. 24. 1694,
Susanna, born March 10, 1696.
Adam 3, son of William 2, had :
William, born Dec. 15, 1687,
Abigail, born March 21, 1688-9,
Adam, born April 17, 1691,
Jeremiah, born Feb. 22, 1693.
Willlam 4, son of Adam 3.   The inventory of his estate exhibited
October 26, 1727, contains ``46 acres of land, homestead, which he
had by deed of gift from his father, Capt. Adam Cogswell."
William 4, probably son of William 3, married Elizabeth Appleton,
widow of Benjamin Appleton, March 13, 1734.
Francis 4, son of Jonathan 3, left a widow Elizabeth, and four sons
—Francis the eldest, John, Jonathan, William, the two last named,
minors ; and a daughter named Elizabeth.   By his will dated Feb. 25,
1755, and proved March 29, 1756, he bequeaths to his son Francis
his dwelling house and his "best schooner named Deborah," his
"flake room and stages at Jeffries Neck."
Francis 5, son of Francis 4, died Oct. 28, 1774, (epitaph 50, 51.)
By his will dated June 6, 1772, and proved November 25, 1774, he
bequeaths to his "well beloved Elizabeth, a suit of suitable mourning." The rest of his property, after legacies to his daughters, he gives

one half to his son Francis : and the other half to his son Joseph.

His daughters were Hannah Lane, Lydia Potter, Unice, wife of John Farley, married Sept. 1761, and Abigail wife of Abraham Dodge. Mr. Francis Cogswell was married to Elizabeth Rogers, March 15, 1728. A grave stone of which the bottom part only remains, stood close to that of Mr. Francis Cogswell, and appears to have been made of the same kind of stone, and of the same age. The foot stone is entire, and contains this inscription :

### Mrs. HANNH CAGSWELL,

In the meeting honse which was built in 1749, Francis Cogswell, Esquire, purchased the pew No. 24 ; and his son Francis Cogswell, jun'r, the pew No. 23. These were wall pews on each side of the north easterly door. Emerson purchased No. 51.

John Cogswell's will was proved Oct 5, 1719. He left a wife, a son John, and daughters Sarah, Margaret and Martha.

Mr. Jonathan, Mr. William, sen'r, Mr. William and Adam had horses on the common, 1697.

Adam, Jefferd, William, Lieut. John, and Mr. Cogswell's family, had rights of Commonage, 1707.

Francis Cogswell married Eunice Low, Oct. 22, 1756.

Emerson married Mary Pecker, Dec. 30, 1736.

COLES, Robert, was one of the twelve who came with John Winthrop the younger, and commenced the settlement of Ipswich, March, 1633. At a meeting of the freemen holden in November, 1634, there was "given and granted unto Mr. Robert Coles two hundred acres of land more or less, lying upon neck of land the Town standeth bounded by, a creek on the north side, and a creek on the west side, and the Town river on the south side, unto him or assigns forever." He possessed a house lot at the easterly end of High street near the cove.

In 1685, August 15, Robert and Mary had a daughter born, named Mary.

1671, Gilbert Cole had liberty of "trees for a house."

CLARKE, Thomas, sen'r, Tanner, had Mary born Feb. 18, 1669, a commoner, 1641, had a house lot, 1638, "in the stoney street, leading to the river," south of Stephen Jordain ; commoner, 1664. [See List of Tythingmen, page 34.]

Thomas, sen'r and Thomas, tanner, Serj't Clarke, Corp'l Thomas, Thomas, miller, were voters in town affairs, 1679.

Thomas, and Thomas, taylor, who had Elizabeth born Feb. 20, 1668, had horses on the common, 1697.

Thomas and wife came into full communion with the church Feb. 22, 1673.

Thomas and wife had:

    John, born Nov. 13, 1666,
    George, born Dec. 30, 1672,
    Nathaniel, born Nov. 5, 1674,
    Samuel, born April 30, 1676.

Serg't Thomas had a seat in the meeting house, 1700. He with Robert Peirce had liberty to build a wharf, 1661.

Mr. William Clerk was one of the twelve who came with Winthrop and commenced the settlement of Ipswich, 1632-3. Gov. John Winthrop in a letter to his son John the younger, then in Connecticut, Dec. 12. 1634, writes, " Mr Ward continues at your house this winter, and Mr. Clerk, (to give him content,) in his own." He was a subscriber to Major Denison, 1648.

" 1634. Given and granted unto Mr. William Clerke sixty acres of land lying eastward of Labour-in-vain, southward by the Town River, separated from all other lands by a small creek encompassing the same, unto him, his heirs or assigns forever."—*T. R.*

Serg't Thomas, Thomas, sen'r. and Thomas, tanner, were commoners, 1664.

Josiah, had horses on the common, 1697.

1691, May 14, Thomas Clark, sen'r inv.£128, 19. Josiah Clark, Executor.

1681: 82: March 14. Thomas Clark, seenor: sume time: sargent: give unto my son Freeman, &c. *will.*

Daniel, possessed a planting lot near the river, adjoining George Carr, 1635. Subscribed to Denison, 1648.

Thomas, will, June 24, 1688, son Josiah, ex'r, daughter Abigail wife of son Thomas deceased; daughter Sarah Hiskell and her children; Sarah, Abigail and Mercy; grand daughter Mercy Clark; son Josiah's children. Property: House, barn, orchard, &c., value, £128, 10. Inv. May 19, 1691.

1710, May 22, Nath'l Bayley and Sarah his wife of Rowley: Mercy Clark and Hannah Clark of Ipswich, receive their portions of their father Josiah Clark's estate.

Thomas, sen'r, "sometime Sargent," will, date June 24, 1668, proved May 14, 1691; son Freeman, wife Sarah: friends and neighbors, Mr. Francis Chute and Stephen Cross, overseers.

Freeman, will dated Dec. 26, 1692. Administration granted July

12, 1697, mentions a brother Thomas, and Josiah son of his brother Josiah. Philip Fowler, executor. Inventory, 80 rods of land, value £7, other effects, £14, 3.

Josiah and Mary had: Sarah, born Jan. 3, 1673, Hannah, Jan. 1, 1679, George, Sept. 19, 1686.

Josiah and Elisabeth had Nathaniel, born Feb. 24, 1694, and Elizabeth, Dec. 26, 1698.

Elizabeth, wife of Nathaniel, died Sept 3, 1720.

Samuel died Sept. 22, 1721. (Epitaph 46.)

Mary, widow of John, tailor, died Feb. 1723. He married 'ye widow Lord, March 15, 1701."

Thomas, died June 26, 1727, aged 56.

Abigail, "an antient widow," aged 87, died April 2, 1728.

Matthew, subscribed to Major Denison, 1648.

John, jun'r, commoner, 1707, in right of his wife. Serj't Thomas, Samuel.

1637, Sept. 23, "bounds of Mr. Clarke his farm," "recorded for Mr. John Clarke now of Ipswich late of Newbury." March 8, 1647.

1648, Nov. 20, John Ward sells to Simon Tompson, "house and ground that was sold me by Mr. John Clarke, eight or nine acres."

Thomas, possessed a lot on the north side of the river, 1657.

Daniel, possessed land butting on 150 acres which Samuel Symonds and Martha his wife sold to Isaac Cummins, April 1, 1652.

COWLEY, John, was a commoner, 1641. John Cooly possessed a houselot "in the street called west end," April 1639. " Granted to Thomas Smith a house lot one acre to the street called west end, a house lot granted to John Cooly south east, common near the common fence gate north west. 9th 2 mo. 1639."

CLINTON, Jacob, died Oct. 17, 1720 ; his widow Nov. 3.

Larence, married Rachell Hatsel, Dec. 1665 ; he was refused permission to be an inhabitant, June 5, 1673.

" 1677, March, Lawrence Clenton committed to Quartermaster Perkins to serve out his time.

November, Rachell, wife of Lawrence Clinton, desiring to be divorced, the court declared this court could not grant it.

1678, Sept. 24, Lawrence Clinton ordered to pay to Rachell his wife one peck of corn a weake."

CONWAY, Robert, and Mary had a son Matthew, born Oct. 22, 1687.

COBORNE, or Colborne, Robert, subscribes to Denison, 1648, commoner, 1664 ; died, Robert sen'r, May 2, 1685.

Edward, Mr. Saltonstall's farmer, had shares in Hog Island, &c., 1664 ; he was a voter in town affairs, 1679, was with others employed to run a line "between Wenham and us," 1665.   He had :
    Ezra, born March 16, 1658,
    Joseph, born June 16, 1661,
    Lydia, born August 20, 1666,
Joseph, was appointed guardian of Ebenezer Goodhue, son of Joseph, deceased, and Mary ; a minor of 12 years of age, Dec. 6, 1697.
Daniel son of Thomas, born Jan. 1, 1679.


COLLINS, Robert, had rights of commonage 1664, had
    Hester, born April 18, 1658,
    Robert, Feb. 15, 1659 died Jan. 19, 1662.
    Nathaniel, born June 18, 1662,
    Elizabeth, born Jan. 19, 1664.
James, married Hannah Dutch, Dec. 22, 1674.


CRELY, or Cressie, Michael or Mighill had rights of commonage 1664.   Married Mary Quilter, April 6, 1660 ; had Mighill, born April 1, 1661, died April, 1670.


COLMAN, James and Sarah, had
    Mary, born June 1, 1673,
    Samuel, died Nov. 18, 1677.
    James and Sarah, twins, born Nov. 7, 1681,
    Rebecca, born March 1, 1684,


COWES, Giles and Agnis, had
    Mary, born August 30, 1670,
    Berry, born Feb. 27, 1672,
    Thomas, born Oct. 15, 1673,
    A son, born Nov. 27, 1675,
    Hannah, born Oct. 16, 1677,
    Agnis, born April 6, 1680,
    William, born Aug. 12, 1683,
    Elizabeth, born March 26, 1691,
    Giles, born Jan. 28, 1692.
Agnis, "an ancient widow," died Sept. 15, 1731.   She was a commoner, 1707.
Giles had liberty to fall trees, 1670.

Appointed administrator of Thomas Berry, May 11, 1693.

He died August 14, 1696.   Est. £198, 17, 5d.

The estate of Giles Cowes was distributed August 15,  1698,  thus:
To Agnis, the widow, one third, viz: £37, 10s real, £26, 16, 2d personal; to William eldest son, £21, 8, 7d real, £15, 8, 4, 12 personal;
to Mary £10, 4, 3 1-2, real, 7, 13s, 2 1-2d personal, and  a  like  sum
to Hannah, Oliver, Agnis, Elisabeth and Giles.

COVINGTON,  John had a house  lot  adjoining  William  Fuller's
lot, 1635.

CURRIMARCH, ——— had rights of commonage, 1664.

CHESSON. Roger, had four acres marsh at Chebacco granted 1644.

CUTTING, John, had a seat in meeting house, 1700.

CROMPTON, Francis, and Elisabeth, had Francis b May 31, 1694.

CROSSE,  Robert, commoner, 1641, subscriber to  Denison,  1648,
entitled to rights of commonage, 1664, voter in town affairs, 1679.

His wife died Oct. 29, 1677.

Robert married Martha Treadwell, 1664.

     Ralf, born Feb. 15, 1658,

     Robert, born Jan. 21, 1665,

     Timothy, born Nov. 29, 1667,

     Martha, born March 15, 1670,

     Abiel, born April 5, 1676,

     Stephen, born April 27, 1678.

Robert, seat in meeting house, 1600.

1710, Dec. 4, Stephen Herrick of Beverly, allowing to  Mary  Herrick of Preston, Connec'tt, Ephraim Fellows and  Anna  his  wife  of
Plainfield, Connec'tt, both daughters of Robert Cross late of  Ipswich:
in consideration of  twenty-three pounds current money of N-England,
acquit to William Butler of Ipswich all claims on their father's estate.

Steven, had "liberty of firewood and one cow," 1664.   In 1686 he
had a wife named Elizabeth, and a son Nathaniel who died in infancy.

1704-5, January 22, Benja Dutch,  saddler,  appointed  guard'n  of
John Cross, son of Stephen Cross, a minor about seventeen years old,
George Hart and Thomas Norton sureties.

John, possessed a farm near Rowley, which he Dec. 1, 1650, bound
to pay ten shillings yearly towards a free school.   His will dated Nov.

5, 1650, and proved March 23, 1651, after providing for his wife Anne, gives to his daughter Susanna his farm, &c., and one hundred pounds, after his wife's decease. " But in case my daughter doth depart this life without issue leaving behind her, then my will is to give the said hundred pounds to the town of Ipswich to remain towards the maintainance of a Free School forever. The which is to be ordered and disposed of by the officers of the church of Ipswich for the said work." " Wife and loving friend William Inglish," executors.

[His daughter left a son—Thomas Hammond—who inherited the property. See page 49, first paragraph.]

George, had a son, Thomas, born March 10, 1689.

Ralf, had a seat in the meeting house, 1702.

Mary Cross, widow, appointed administrator of the estate of Ralph Cross, August 17, 1711. Jacob Foster, jun'r, Abraham Foster and Joseph Foster, sureties. Clear estate £39, 11, 3.

CUMMINGS, Isaac, was a commoner, 1641.

1652, April 1. Samuel Symonds and Martha his wife, sell to Isaac Cummings in consideration of £30 paid to my sons Harlakinden, John and William, &c. one hundred and fifty acres butting on land of Daniel Clark, &c.

CURTISS, Henry, had seat in the meeting house, 1700.

CRANE, Robert, had a house lot adjoining land of Mr. John Norton.

DANE, or Dean, John, senior, John, junior, and Francis, were commoners, 1641. John, senior, was probably Father of the other two. He probably died or removed soon afterwards.

John 2, without any addition to his name, subscribes toward the compensation to Major Denison, 1648. He was according to Farmer, born about 1618; his name with the addition of "senior," is in "list of those that by law are allowed to have their votes in Town affairs," 1679; tithingman, 1677; freeman, 1682; selectman, 1664-69. In the record of his death, which occurred Sept. 29, 1684, he is called John Dane, chirugeon. The inventory of his estate amounted to 469l. 11, 5.

Francis, probably son of John, according to Farmer, was "the second minister of Andover, came over it is said with Rev. Nathaniel Rogers in 1636. He was ordained about 1648; and died 17 Feb.

1696-7, in his 82nd year.§   He subscribed towards  the compensation
of Major Denison, 1648.   In a list of inhabitants that have shares  in
Plum Island, 1664, the name of John Dane,  without addition occurs
twice, once among those who are entitled to  a  share  and  a  half, or
four and a half acres, and again among those who are  entitled to  one
share, or three acres.   The people were  divided  for  the  purpose of
this distribution into three classes.   The first  class consisted of those
who "paid more than sixteen shilling in a single country rate, together with the magistrates, elders, Messrs John Rogers and Thomas Andrews."   These were entitled to a double share,  or  six  acres.   The
second class was of such as paid more  than  six  shillings  and  eight
pence, and not more than  sixteen  shillings.   These  had  one  share
and a half.   The third class were of those whose rates did  not exceed
six shillings and eight pence,  who  had  one  share, or three acres.
There were  twenty-seven of the first class ; sixty-nine of the second ;
and one hundred and thirty-four of the third.   It is probable that one
of these Johns was John 2, senior, and the other, John  3, junior,  his
son.

The will of *John 2, chirugeon, was proved Sept. 30, 1684.  He left
a wife and two sons, John 3 and Philemon 3 ; also  daughters, Elizabeth and Sarah ; a grand daughter, †Mary Chandler, and a grandson,
Daniel Hovey.

He gives to his son  John  his  farm,  he "bought of Mr. Richard
Hubbard."

John 3 son of John 2 married Abigail Warner, Dec.  27,  1671, and
had :

---

§ John Dean the elder had granted to him  a  houselot of one  acre
lying on the street called the west end, butting at the  south  west on
the same, the houselot of Richard Massey east, houselot of Thomas
Brewer west.

1676, March 28, John Dane, senior, releast from training, free.

*1684.   Will of " John Dane, Chirugion," labelled, " Doct.  Dean
Will."   Date, May 31, proved Sept. 30, 1684.   " To my beloved
wife during the tearnie of her life, I give that new house I  built upon
land I bought of Dan'l Hovey, sen'r, to be kept in repair  by  my  son
John."   " My will is that my son John and philemon have my  books
and manuscripts, and that philemon divide them and that John chuse."
Witnesses, John Brewer, Nehemiah Jewett.

† William Chandler of Andover  and  Mary  Dane  of  Ipswich were
married Aug. 24, 1658, by Mr. Simonds.—Andover Records.

John,

Daniel,

Nathaniel, born June 27, 1691,

Abigail, born Dec. 15, 1673,

Elizabeth, born March 6, 1678,

Susannah, born March 6, 1685,

Rebecca.

John 4, son of John 3, died in 1737. Appraisers of his estate were appointed June 3 of that year. His children were:

John, born Nov. 29, 2681, the eldest son;

Benjamin, deceased in 1756,

William,

Sarah Wheeler,

Elizabeth Knowlton,

Elizabeth Dodge.

Daniel 4, son of John 3, died in 1730. Mary, probably his widow, was appointed guardian to

John, aged 12 years,

Mary aged 10,

Lydia, aged 6,

Nathan, aged 4.

At the same time, John Dane was appointed guardian to Daniel, aged 15 years, children of Daniel Dane, late of Ipswich.

Nathaniel 4, son of John 3, born June 27, 1691, died in 1760. His will dated May 6, and proved June 23 of that year, mentions his present wife Esther, who was the mother of his younger children. His elder children were: Nathaniel, Israel and three daughters. The younger children were Edward, Nehemiah, Elizabeth, Mary, Anna, Abigail and Esther.

Philemon Deane 3, son of John 2, was a physician. He was admitted a freeman March 11, 1673-4. He joined the church in full communion Feb. 8, 1673 4. He married first, Mary Thompson, Oct. 7, 1685; second Ruth Convers, Dec. 25, 1690. By the last wife he had

Philemon, born September 16, 1693, died March 12, 1694-5.

Philemon and Edward, twins, July 17, 1695,

Ruth, (whose name is spelt on the record, Dean,) Aug 24, '98

He subscribed 6s toward the bell. He died Oct. 18, 1716, aged 70. (Epitaph 60.)

Doct. Philemon Dean and Mr. John Dean have seats in the new meeting house, 1700, and Lydia and Abigail have seats assigned to them in 1702. The widow Dean is a commoner, 1707. Mrs. Ruth Dean was living in 1728; widow Anstis Dean, 1751, kept shop 1753.

Philemon 4, son of 3 Philemon was born July 17, 1695, married Anstis Manning, pub. March 24, 1716, and removed to Newbury. He married Aug. 20, 1742, Hannah York of Ipswich.

Edward 4, son of Philemon 3, and twin brother of Philemon 4, died before his father, and left a widow. He married Lydia Emery, pub. 28, 2, 1716.

DARBYE, Roger, commoner, 1678.

DAVENPORT, Addington, of Boston, married Elisabeth Wainwright, Nov. 10, 1698, and had at Ipswich, born Aug. 18, 1699, a son to whom they gave the name of Addington.

DAVIS, John, commoner, 1641, subscribes to Denison, 1648. He sells to Daniel Rindge, Feb. 8, 1748, a six acre lot on Heartbreak Hill, bounded on the west by William Knowlton.

1642, April 15. Agreement with Jo : Davis respecting the herd on south side of the river. Davis makes his mark.

James Davis had a seat in the meeting house, 1702 ; he married Abigail, daughter of Joseph and Rebeckah Metcalf, who died Jan. 13, 1720, in the 33 year of her age, (epitaph 59.)

In the old burying ground may be seen three stones of rough granite, with inscriptions very rudely cut upon them, and all evidently by the same hand. One of them is intended to commemorate Deacon Jacob Foster, who died in 1710 ; another for Mrs. Elisabeth Hunt, 1706 ; and on the other may with difficulty be made out

### I A C O

### D A V I S

which was undoubtedly intended as a memento of Jacob Davis, son of Jacob and Mary Davis, who died June 9, 1703.

Hopkins Davis was commoner, 1678. The widow Davis, alias Quilter, died August 10, 1700.

DAY, Robert, commoner, 1641 ; subscriber to Denison, 1648, had a share and a half in Hog Island, &c., 1664, a voter in town affairs, 1679, selectman, 1663, '69, tithingman, 1677 ; his will is dated Aug. 11, and proved Sept. 25, 1683. In it he alludes to an engagement with his son John 2, upon his marriage with Sarah Pengry ; he gives him a dwelling house, &c. And he gives his son Thomas who married Ann Woodward, Oct. 20, 1672, a farm   The daughters mentioned are Hannah Lord and Sarah Fiske, wife of David Fiske, married June 17, 1674. Son James executor and residuary legatee. Witnessed by John Denison, senior, John Brewer, senior, and Rob't Lord. Estate £478, 10, 9.

John 2, son of Robert 1, died about 1690; his will is dated March 25, 1690; he left a widow Sarah, probably the Sarah Pengry mentioned, whom he married April 20, 1664; his sons were John, born Feb. 17, 1665, the eldest, and Moses, a minor. The daughters were Mehitable, born Jan. 26, 1669, Lydia, born March 18, 1676, Hannah, born Jan. 16, 1678. Inventory of his estate, October 11, 1692, house, barn and homestead in §Scott's Lane, £100. Total estate, £607, 12, 3. 1695, May 23, John Day, administrator to the estate of Sarah Day, executor to ye will of John Day, father to said John: Richard and Mehitable daughter of sd John dec'd: Moses Day, £220, 7, 6. Yet due to ye children, under age, £202.

John 3, son of John 2, married Jan. 27, 1691, Sarah Wells. They had Sarah born Jan 9, 1692, Liddia, Oct. 27, 1694, John. Sept. 27, 1696. Sarah, wife of John, died January 14, 1702-5; he died Feb. 28, 1722, aged 57 years and 10 days.

Thomas 2, son Robert 1, with his wife Anna, had a daughter Mary, who died August 27, 1685, and another to whom they gave the same name, born April 30, 1686. They had Ann, born Sept. 24, 1673, Sarah, born Jan. 4, 1674, Robert, March 14, 1679; he was freeman, May 7. 1673, commoner, 1707, and died March 19, 1717-18, aged 75.

James 2 son of Rob't 1, with Susanna, had Robert b. Jan 14, 1684.

DAVISON, George, purchased a farm of Thomas French, tailor, April 1, 1647.

Daniel and Sarah had Sarah born March 29, 1786, Daniel, born March 23, 1690. His will is dated Dec. 5, 1693; he left a wife and sons William, John, Thomas, Peter, and daughters Bridget, Dorcas, Margarate, born Sept. 24, 1658, Sarah, March 30, 1660. A child died July 1666. Property, house, barn, &c.

William, son of Daniel with Mary his wife, had Mary born Sept. 23. 1693, Margaret, June 22; 1695, Lydia, Jan. 21, 1697, Anne July 15, 1703. Daniel had a seat sssigned to him in the meeting house, 1700.

---

§ In a plan of the central part of Ipswich, drawn in 1717, and preserved among the Court Records at Salem, the road now leading from Damon's Block, opposite the depot, to the west end of Mineral St. (the extent of the plan in that direction,) is designated as "The great lane, called Scots lane that leades towards the mill to the street broad vp meeting house hill."—*Printer.*

DENISON, Daniel, son of William of Roxbury, who was born about 1612 ; admitted a freeman at Boston, April 1, 1634, when he has the title of Mr.   Under the marginal date, 1635, on the town records, he has a grant of "an house lot near the mill, containing about two acres, which he hath paled in and built an house upon."   This house and lot he sold to Humphrey Griffin.   Sept. 3, 1634, it is ordered by General Court that Mr. Daniel Denison and 8 others, "or the maior part of them, shall have power to sett out the bounds of all townes not yet sett out."   March 9, 1636-7, he receives his commission as "Captaine."   In 1648, Oct. 12, there is granted to him "two hundred acres of land lying upon the line between this town and Salem, on Jeffries Creek, beyond Mr. Hubbard's farm, not prejudicing former grant, nor the cow common, "for his better encouragment to settle among us."

1641, Jan. 19, Daniel Denison conveys to Humphrey Griffin a Dwelling house, &c., near the mill.

1648, 1st 4mo, John Burnham conveys to Anthony Potter a house lot late of Humphrey Griffin, situate near the water mill.

1661, January 19, Anthony Potter, and Elizabeth his wife, convey to John Safford a dwelling house and land three acres—north side of the river, near the mill, bounded with highway round.

1680, Feb. 7, granted to Major Gen'l Denison, twelve foot of land at the west end of his barn to the pound.

1639, Feb. 11.   Granted to Daniel Denison a house lot next Mr. Fawn's to come to ye seat of ye hill next ye swamp.

1636.   Granted to Humphrey Wyth in the year 1636, &c.,—also for a farm one hundred acres on the south side of the creek called the labor-in-vain, having land of George Carr west, Thomas Baroman north, Mr. Wards farm east, Mr. Denison's farm south.

1667, Sept. 24.   The judges of the Court were Mr. Symon Bradstreet, Mr. Samuell Symonds, Major General Denison, Major William Hathorne.

He was admitted a commoner by vote of the town, Feb. 28, 1644.

Under the date Dec. 29, 1648, is recorded " A list of those that did subscribe their names to allow *M*ajor Denison the sum of £24, 7, yearly, so long as he shall be their leader, to encourage him, in his millitary helpfulness."   The list contains 155 names, to eight of which is the title *Mr.* viz., Mr. Saltonstall, Mr. Symonds, Mr. Hubbard, Mr. Rogers, Mr. Norton, Mr. William Payne, *M*r. Robert Payne, and *M*r. Tuttle.   The highest subscription is *M*r. Robert Payne's—ten shilliags.   Ten others give five shillings or more, viz., *M*r. William Payne, William Bartholomew, Edward Waldern, John

Appleton, Samuel Appleton, John Andrews, jr., Job Bishop, John Perkins, jun., George Giddings, John Chote. The others give various sums from one shilling to four. It may be inferred from the eagerness manifested to obtain his military services that he had been in the army in early life, before he came to this country. He attained to great distinction in the colony, was a member of the House of Representatives many years, and Speaker in 1649 and 1659.

1636-41. " As also in order to the publick Safety of the Colony, it was about this time divided into three several regiments, that were to be managed by Colonels with their Lieutenants, which yet hath since been altered, and the military matters committed to a Major in every particular County, and to a Major General for the oversight of the whole."—*Hubbard.* Mr. Denison was appointed by the General Court, Major General of the Colony eleven years, between 1652 and 1680. In 1658 he has granted to him "one quarter of Block Island for his great pains in revising, correcting, and transcribing the colony laws." He wrote a book called " Irenicon : or Salve for New England's Sore," printed in 1684, after his decease.

He married Patience, daughter of Governr Thomas Dudley, who survived him. He died Sept. 20, 1682. In his will dated July 18, 1673, he mentions his wife Patience, and a daughter Elisabeth Rogers the wife of the Rev. John Rogers, President of Harvard College, (epitaph 127.) The grand children mentioned are Daniel Rogers, (epitaph 128,) and Elisabeth Rogers, afterward the wife of Coll. John Appleton, (epitaph 6,) John, Daniel and Martha Denison, the children of his deceased son John. His will is signed and sealed thus :

*Manu propria scripsi*

DANIEL DENISON.

John 2, son of General Denison 1, married Martha, daughter of the Hon. Samuel Symonds. He was selectman in 1662, 65. He died January 9, 1670-1, and left sons : John and Daniel, and a daughter Martha, who married Matthew Whipple, and died Sept 12, 1728, aged 60 years.

His wife survived him and married Richard Martyn of Portsmouth.

John 3, son of John 2, was graduated at Harvard College, 1684 ; he was elected pastor of the Ipswich church, April 5, 1686, but was not ordained ; he died Sept. 14, 1689, in the 24th year of his age.

He married Elisabeth, daughter of the Hon'ble Nath'l Saltonstall of Haverhill, who survived him and married the Rev. Rowland Cotton, of Sandwich, and died in Boston, July 9, 1726, aged 58 years.

John 4, son of John 3, was born in 1689. He was graduated at H. C. 1710, and according to Mr. Felt, studied divinity and preached a year or two; but his health failing, he became a lawyer; he was Col. of the militia, and Sheriff of the county, (epitaph 54.) He married Mary, daughter of John Leverett, President of Harvard College. She and one son, John, and one daughter, survived him. He died Nov. 25, 1724, aged 35. The publishment of Major John Denison and Mary Leverett is dated March 21, 1719.

John 5, son of John 4, was born in 1724, graduated at H. C. 1742,* died Aug. 25, 1747, in the 25th year of his age. (epitaph 55.)

[The Denison Coat of Arms, copied by Arthur W. Dow, from the gravestone of Mr. John Denison, who died, 1747. They are also upon the table stone over his father's grave.]

The male descendants of General Denison were singularly short lived. His only son died before him at about 35 years of age. His grandson, the Rev. John Denison died in his 24th year. His great grandson, Col. John, at 35; and his great-great grandson, John, the last of this line, in the 25th year of his age. Thus in 65 years from the decease of General Denison, 1682-1747, four generations of his descendants had passed over the stage of life.

Daniel 3, son of John 2, married Dec. 8, 1657, Margaret Low; and June 28, 1685, Sarah Dodge, and had Sarah born March 29, 1686, and Daniel, March 23. 1690.†

---

* The silver plate, from which he ate while at Harvard, is still preserved in the family of Mr. Joseph Farley.

† Sept. 1880, Rev. S. D. Denison, D. D., Honorary Secretary of the Committee on Foreign Missions of the Protestant Episcopal Chh, died at White Plains, N. Y., in the 70th year of his age. He was a native of Boston, and was a descendant of Major General Daniel Denison, the Commander-in-Chief of Massachusetts Colony at the outbreak of King Philip's war.—*Boston Journal.*

There was a John Denison 1, (see his name in List of Tithingmen, page 34,) who died 1683. He was a weaver by trade, and does not appear to have been related to the General. He left a widow Priscilla, who died Feb. 15, 1692, and a son, John 2. He also left daughters, Ruth, Sarah Perkins, Priscilla Persons, wife of Thomas Person, married Oct. 9, 1666 ; and a grand child, Sary Pritchett, who are mentioned as such in his will. A daughter Mary had died July 11, 1658. The following extract from his will tends to show the condition and station in society which he occupied : " To my son-in-law, John prichett, I do forgive all that he oweth me upon my books, excepting 18 shillings, and four pounds, which I lent him—upon this condition following : that he pay or cause to be paid to his son John and daughter Elisabeth forty shillings a piece in good New England money at their day of marriage." " Likewise I give to my son John Denison my houses and land, sheep, horse, hoggs, with the great Braise kettle, biggest iron pot, the table in the new room, the great chest in the parlour, & all my debts and whatever else is my estate which I have not already given out. John Denison 1, was a subscriber to Major Denison, 1648, commoner, 1664, voter in town affairs, 1679. He had six acres of marsh next Goodman How, granted Feb. 7, 1647.

John 2, son of John 1, had a wife named Ruth, who died Feb 2, 1694, and a second wife named Elisabeth, who survived him, and died Sept. 15, 1725. He was one of the "young generation," who joined the church by taking the covenant, Jan 25, 1673-4. By his wife Ruth, he had :

> Ruth, born June 7, 1686,
> John, died July 30, 1688
> John, born April 28, 1692, (epitaph 56,)
> Priscilla, Jan 14, 1694, died Jan 30, 1694.

John 3, son John 2, married Rebecca Wallis, Aug. 12, 1727, who died May 5, 1761.

DENNIS, Thomas, died May 23, 1706, aged about 68 years, (epitaph 53,) he married Grace Searle, Oct. 26, 1668 ; she died Oct. 24, 1686, aged 50 years,* (epitaph.) They had :

---

A pillow case spun and woven and sewed by Grace Searle Dennis, and embroidered with her initials, is in possession of the Printer, 1880. It has been preserved by the several generations, as follows : 1. Grace Searle Dennis : 2. Elisabeth Dennis Hovey ; 3. Elisabeth Hovey Caldwell, who was the great-great-grandmother of the Printer.

Thomas, born Novenber 30, 1669,

John, born September 22, 1673,

Elisabeth, married Ebenezer Hovey.

John had horses on the Common, 1697.

John and Elisabeth had seats in the meeting house, 1702.

Thomas, sen'r, had a seat assigned to him in 1700.

Elisabeth appointed adm'x of estate of Thomas, jr., Jan. 1, 1702-3.


DEAR, Edmund.   March 3, 1660, married Elisabeth Griffin who died Dec. 1677, had

Elisabeth, born August 28, 1662,

Edward, Feb. 27, 1664,

Thomas, Feb. 14, 1666.

He was commoner, 1678.   His will is dated August 12, 1696, and (proved October 14,) "being very sick and weak of body ;   son Edward Dear a double share, and each of the rest of my children shall have share alike; the six sheep aforesaid, I give to my grand children, the children of my son Edward Dear, to each alike : loving friends. Mr. Francis Wainwright, and Tho : Louell, sen'r. overseers. Thomas Louell, sen'r and John Frost, witnesses, Mary Edwards present.   (Signed) Edmond Dear.

1700, Nov. 20, Edward Dear appo. adm'r of estate of his brother Thomas Dear, Daniel Rindge, surety.

1703, July 12.   Hannah Deer, wido : Elisabeth Dowe, and Abigail Deer, petition for administration on the estate of "our Honoured father Deer, who died in the year 1693, and made a will and appointed ower brother Edward Deer, executor, who is dead, pray administration be granted to our sister Liddia Deer."

1712, Jan. 5, division of the estate of Edmond Dear,—real £94, personal, £66.   Edward Dear executor being deceased, and Elisabeth Dow also deceased without issue, Lydia Potter alias Deer, adm'r, *di bonis non*.   To Edward Deer or his representative, two shares, £62 18 2 ; Elisabeth, share divided between her sisters, Lydia Potter and Abigail Deer.

1700.   Edward Deer has a seat assigned to him in the new meeting house.   He had liberty to "fell three oaks for his trade," 1669.— He had a daughter Mary, born January 7, 1669.


DIX, Ralf, was a soldier to the Indians, 1643.   Dec. 4, 1643, "it is agreed that each soldier for their service to the Indians shall be allowed 12*d* a day, (allowing for the Lord's day in respect to the extremity of the weather,) and the officers double."   The pay amounted to three shillings for each soldier. He purchased in October, 1647, of William White, a farm of 200 acres, for £60. In 1651, Oct. 4, he purchased of George Palmer and Elisabeth his wife, a house and lot containing two acres and a half; also a six acre lot on the north side of the river of Ipswich, "within the common fence." In 1661, Mch 20, with Hester his wife, he sells to Ezekiel Woodward, in consideration of £60, a house and lot containing two acres and a half, bounded on the northeast and southeast by the Mill river, and on the south west by land of Samuel Younglove, and on the northwest by the highway. He was a subscriber to Major Denison, 1648. He had

John, born March 12, 1658,

Samuel, August 25, 1661.

Col. B. Church writes Sept. 30, 1690, "about the 19th one Dicks of Chebacco was killed near Casco."

1637. The Widow Dix had six acres of land granted.

DIAMOND Andrew, was administrator on the estate of the late Andrew Sargeant, May 10, 1697. He seems to have been a merchant and of considerable property. He was on a committee appointed to assign stations at the neck for fishermen. He subscribed liberally toward the bell and pulpit cushion in 1700; and had appointed to him (with the title of Mr.) a seat among the most considerable of the inhabitants in the new meeting house.

There were seats assigned at that time to 198 adult male inhabitants. To 27 of them is given the title of *Mr.* Various military titles from Coll'n to Corp'l are given to the same number; and two have the addition of Doct'r.

"Diamond Stage," a well known wharf and landing place, near the mouth of the river, received its name from this gentleman. His widow, Elisabeth, who was an Elliot of Boston, married Theophilus Cotton of Boston.

1708, June 14. Theophilus Cotton and Elisabeth his wife, app'd adm. of the estate of Andrew Diamond, late husband of Elisabeth. She signs the bond with a mark.

DIKE, Nathaniel, had a seat assigned him in the meeting house, 1700, and was a commoner, 1707.

Anthony was a commoner, 1707.

DILLINGHAM, Mr. John, was admitted a freeman at Boston, October 19, 1630. He had a grant in Nov. 1634, of six acres of land lying on the west end of the town on the south side of the great

swamp." And the same year it was "given and granted unto Mr.
Jo: Dillingham sixty acres of Meadow ground more or less lying on
the Rocky Meadow, and laid out by Mr. William Clarke and John
Shatswell, the appointed Committee for yt.   Also 30 acres upland
ground adjoining unto the same to him, his heirs or assigns."   He
came in the fleet with Winthrop; was from  Leicestershire ; was first
at Boston ; and died at Ipswich between November 1634 and March
1635.   His widow Sarah survived him, and died  in  1636.   [See her
will, pages 44-45.]   His daughter Sarah became the  wife of John
Caldwell.   [See Appleton Memorial, page 84.]

DODGE, Samuel, with Mary his wife, had :
   Samuel, born Jan. 22, 1668,
   Joseph, born Feb. 1670,
   Hannaniah, born June 9, 1673,
   Anna, born Dec. 20, 1674,
   Antipas, born Sept 7, 1677,
   Mary, born May 6, 1680,
   Amy, born August 27, 1682,
   Deborah, born April 16, 1685,
   Samuel, December 11, 1692.
He had a seat in the meeting house, 1700.   His wife survived him
and was a commoner, 1707.   His will is dated  June 26, and was
proved December 24, 1705.   He bequeathes one half of his  property
to his wife.   He left five sons : Joseph, Antipas, Jabesh, Parker,
and Samuel, the youngest born Dec. 11, 1692.   His  daughters were
Anna, wife of Jno. Edwards, Mary wife of Rice Knowlton,  Deborah.
   Richard, jr., had Martha, born May 29, 1696 ; Nath'l, born Oct. 8,
1698 ; Lucy, May 3, 1700.
   Joseph, probably son of Samuel, with his wife Martha, had
      Nehemiah, born June 1, 1696, died Dec. 25, 1697,
      Hannaniah, born May 22, 1698.
   Antipas, son of Samuel, died and left a widow Joanna Dodge, who
was appointed administratrix on his estate, May 5, 1707.
   William, then of Wenham, married January 19, 1728-9, Rebecca,
daughter of Mr. Isaac Appleton.   He settled in Ipswich, where he
became a prosperous merchant.   He died April 11, 1777, in the 77th
year of his age.   She died Oct. 15, 1794, in the 95th year of her age.
William, 3d., their son, was published with Susanna Smith, May 16,
1778.   She was the daughter of Capt. John and Mrs Hannah Treadwell Smith.
   Lt. William Dodge of Wenham, published with Mrs. Abigail Giddinge of the Hamlet, Oct. 28, 1737.

William Dodge and Mary Balch of Beverly, married June 16, 1736. There was a John Dodge in 1669.

DORMAN, Thomas, was admitted a freeman at Boston, March 4, 1634-5. He had granted to him four acres of meadow, 1634 ; he was a commoner, 1641. He had sold a house to John Morse previous to 1646 ; he purchased of Samuel Symonds, May 1, 1651, a farm of one hundred acres, adjoining the farm of Francis Peabody in Topsfield, where he died in 1670.

Thomas Dorman, senior, will dated April 24, proved May 3, 1670. About 70 years old. Sons Thomas, Ephraim, Daniell Bradly. Land in Rowley. To Thomas, land I bought of Mr. Firmans. Land on the south side of the river, one half to Thomas and one half to Ephraim ; my shop I give to my son Thomas children. Four days work and a half that John Worner oweth me for : and three days and a half that Thomas day oweth me for. Half a days work Robert Stiles oweth me for, and I do owe him for four days plowing : one bushell of indian corne I owe to William White of ipsige : I owe to Robert Kobarnd half a bushell of indian corne : too bushells wheat Thomas Ross doth ow me. John Morall doth ow me ten shillings. Twenty shillings William Smith oweth me. Mirall dounill oweth me. Three pounds that Martha Stanly oweth me. Witness Francis Peabody, John How.

*DOW, Thomas, had the right of turning horses on the common in

---

* Richard Kimball 1, was married twice ; Margaret his second wife survived him, but died March 1, 1675, the same year he died or the year after. She was the widow Dow of Hampton, N. H., probably widow of Henry Dow, whose will is dated 1659, 4th 8mo. Henry his son died in 1676, having had 12 children, two of whose names were Richard and John. His second wife named Elisabeth, who was before her marriage to him a widow Rayner, had no children. Benjamin Kimball 2, fifth son of Richard, styled Cornet, was in Bradford where he died June 11, 1696. He left a widow whose name was Marcy, and nine children, viz., Richard, David, born 1671, Jonathan, born 1673, Robert, born 1675, Hannah, Elisabeth, Samuel, born 1680, Ebenezer, born 1684, and Abigail.

Margaret the second wife of Richard Kimball, was widow of Henry Dow, sen'r, who died April 21, 1659, and left three children, viz., Mary, born 1640, Thomas, born 1652 and Jeremiah, born Sept. 6, 1657. Richard Kimball and the widow Margaret Dow were married Oct. 23, 1661.—*Lynn News*, Feb. 9, 1849.

1697.   With his wife Susanna they had
        John, born April 24, 1685, died 1688
        Ebenezer, born May 26, 1692,
        Thomas, born Nov. 29, 1694,
        Jeremiah, Dec. 12, 1699.

Susanna, wife of Thomas, died August 29, 1724.   He died July 12 1728, aged 76.

Thomas Dow made a noncupative will in the presence of John Eaton and Theoph : Shatswell, May 29, 1654, which was proved Oct. 2, 1656, at a court held at Salisbury.   He appoints his wife Pheby executrix, mentions sons John the eldest, Thomas, Stephen, dau. Mary and Martha.

Thomas his son made a will dated June 16, proved Nov. 14, 1676, by which it appears that he had a wife and son, and that he had expectation of another child.   He mentions his "unkill Benjamin Kimball," his brother Steven, and his sisters Mary and Martha.   Administration was granted to Henry Kimball of Haverhill.

1684, April.   Thomas Dow of Ipswich asks to be freed from training by reason of lameness he received at the fort fight at Narraganset. His wife Sarah died Feb. 14, 1680.

Jeremiah was a commoner, 1707, died June 6, 1723.   Epitaph 58.

Mary Dow, a maiden, aged 91, died Oct. 16, 1731.

Mary, wife of John Dow, died Sept. 1724.

Exercise, wife of Daniel Dow, died 1724-5.

Thomas and Jeremiah had seats in the meeting house, 1700.


DOUGLAS, William, was admitted a freeman at Boston, May 6, 1646, was a commoner, 1641.


DUNTON, or Downton, William with Mary his wife had
        William, born April 3, 1695,
        Mary, April 7, 1696,
        Elisabeth, June 4, 1698.

The name Mr. Dunton is on the list of such as had horses on the common, 1697.

Mary Dunton had a seat appointed her in the meeting house, 1702.


DUDLEY, Thomas, was born at Northampton, England, 1576 ; came to New England, 1630 ; resided in Ipswich from soon after its first settlement until about 1639, when he removed to Roxbury.   He was Assistant six years ; Dep. Gov. 13 years ; and Gov. 4 years.   He died July 37, 1653.   His wife Dorothy, died Sept. 27, 1643, and he

married again next year.    His widow married the Rev. John Allen
of Dedham.   His children were Samuel ; Ann, wife of Gov. Simon
Bradstreet ; Patience, wife of Gen. Daniel Denison ; Mercy, born
Sept. 27, 1621, who married the Rev. John Woodbridge ; a daughter
who married Major Benjamin Keaine of Boston ; Deborah, born Feb.
27, 1645 ; Joseph, born 1647 ; Paul, 1650.

Granted to Thomas Dudley, Esq , in October, 1635, about nine
acres of land between Goodman Cross on the West, and a lot intended
to Mr. Bradstreet on the east, upon which Mr. Dudley hath built an
house. ——— All which the said Thomas Dudley Esq., hath sold to
Mr. Hubbard.—*T.* R.

Samuel Dudley possessed a farm at Chebacco, having the farm of
Jonathan Wade on the south west, and the Sagamore hill on the north.

1635.   There was granted to Mr. John Tuttle ten acres towards the
Neck, having Mr. Bracy his land west, Mr. Treadwell east, Philip
Fowler north, and creek south.   Also a planting lot on heart break
hill, having Mr Dudley west, Michael Williamson, John Johnson and
the marshes east, and two little swamps north and south.

Samuel 2, son of Thomas 1, was born in England about 1606   He
was one of the very earliest settlers, and in 1638 possessed a house in
what was then called Brook street, but has since acquired the undig-
nified appellation of Hog Lane.   This street is in a gorge of the
Town Hill, and was the Path which led to the settlements of Rowley
and Newbury.   The spot where Mr. Dudley's house probably was
placed, must have been one of the most desirable situations for a gentleman's residence which could be found in this region.   It had a
copious spring of pure water, which gave name to the street.   It was
sheltered on the north and east by the hill, and opened towards the
south and south west on an uncommonly beautiful landscape.   Mr.
Samuel Dudley had a planting lot on Heartbreak hill, bounded on the
west by a lot of Thomas Wells, 1635.   He removed first to Salisbury,
1643, and afterwards to Exeter, of which place he became the minister and died there in 1683, aged 77 years.   He married Mary Winthrop, daughter of Gov. John Winthrop.   She died at Salisbury,
April 12, 1643.   He had many children.

DUTCH, Robert 1, was a subscriber to Major Denison, 1648.   Had
rights of commonage, 1664.   His will is dated April 22, 1691.   He
had :

>    Caleb, born May 1, 1659,
>    Benjamin, born December 4, 1665.

He signed with a mark R, 1661.   He left sons Robert, Benjamin,
Samuel, and a grandchild named Hannah.

John Dutch, died Nov. 5, 1685. The inventory of his estate consisting of house, barn and land to the value of £100, is dated March 11, 1685-6. His widow died about 1692. They lost a son Samuel, Feb. 14, 1671. John Roper, her brother was appointed administrator on her estate, March 29, 1692. Her children were then:

Elisabeth Ringe, aged 19, born Feb. 11, 1673, m. Isaac Ringe.
Susanna, aged about 16, born July 13, 1675.
John, aged 15, born June 17, 1677,
Benjamin, aged 12,
Nathaniel, aged 10, born Feb. 18, 1681,
Hannah, aged 7.

The deposition of Samuel Bishop aged 40 or thereabouts, and Jacob Perkins, 23 years or thereabouts, — about the middle of March last, (we three deponents were on board the sloop wr off Thomas Bishop was commander, being bound for the Barbadoes ready in Ipswich harbor.) wr off Nathaniel Roper was on board going as one of the men, — my brother John Roper should have my estate, and pay my debts, and give to my cousin Nathaniel Dutch, (John Dutch his son,) ten pounds, — sworn to Sept 29, 1685.

In Memory of
Mr
Benjamin Dutch,
who departed
this life Nov.
13th, 1760,
aged 80
years.

In Memory of Mrs. Sarah Dutch, wife of Mr. Benj'n Dutch, who departed this life, July 31st, 1748, aged 68 years.

Stephen son of Benjamin Dutch, died Oct 27, 1721. Age nearly obliterated; probably 6 years

John and Samuel Dutch had liberty for fire wood and one cow each, in 1664.

Robert Dutch 2, son of Robert 1, by his wife Hannah Lovell, m. Dec. 26, 1677, had

Ebenezer, born January 29, 1679,
Benjamin, born August 9, 1680,
Robert, born January 12, 1692.

Benjamin 2, son of Robert 1, married June 30, 1690, Elisabeth, daughter of John and Ketherine Baker. Had Elisabeth, born Sept. 20, 1692, died Oct. 22, same year. Elisabeth, born Sept 14, 1693. He was a commoner, 1707 With Sarah and Hannah, have seats up-pointed to them in the Meeting house, 1700.

Samuel 2, son Robert 1, with his wife Abigail Giddings, m. Feb. 12, 1673; they had,

Samuel, born November 3, 1674
Abigail, born November 8, 1678
Mary, born May 18, 1680
Jane, born August 14 1685

He has appointed to him with the title of Mr. a seat in the meeting house, 1700.

1712, Jan. 20 Samuel Dutch, estate, divided: widow, Samuel, John, George, Abigail, Mary, Dorothy, Martha, Jane. £8, 18. 2 1-2 each.

Abigail, his widow. died Nov. 14, 1713, aged 64. (Epitaph 61.)

1711, April 16, Abigail Dutch, widow of Samuel Dutch, renounces adm. of the estate of her husband, and Samuel, eldest son of the deceased is appointed. Inventory, house and homestead, £120, plate, £5, 8, 6. Total, £222, 1, 6.

There is a will of Benjamin Dutch, dated March 25, 1692, in which mention is made of a wife Elisabeth, and a child whose name or sex is not given.


DURGY. John, had a son John, born Nov. 23, 1689, and Andrew born Sept. 20, 1692, a seat in meeting house, 1700. See *Dirkey.*


DUMMER, Richard, second son of John Dummer, of Bishop-stoke, England, was born about 1591, came to New England, May 26, 1632, and admitted freeman November 6, of the same year. He was elected an Assistant in 1635 and 1636, being then of Roxbury, from whence he soon removed to Newbury, which he represented in 1640, '45, 47. He died 1679, Dec. 14, aged 88 He was an inhabitant of Ipswich in 1659, and had a son William, born May 28 of that year.

John Andrews and Sarah his wife, Nov. 14, 1659, convey to Mr. Richard Dummer of Ipswich, a house and four acres of land in the hill street, (commonly called by the name of the White house.) Richard Wattles north west, street north east; Philip Call south east; Henry Pindar south east; Widow Quilter south east; Mr. Ayres north west, said Richard Wattles north east in part; land of Mr. William Norton northeast in part.

In 1663, April 18, Richard Wattles, brick layer, conveys to Henry Russell of Marblehead, "my dwelling house and land about one acre, in the hill street having Mr. Richard Dummer on the south east, street north east, Mr. Dummer south west.

[We conjecture from these boundaries that "the Hill street," was a part of Meeting House Hill, extending from the Agawam House to the residence of **Mr. Manasseh Brown** ; and included also a Lane or street now extinct, which commenced at the rear of the Agawam House and continued to the rear of Mr. I. Brown's and Mr. I. K. Jewett's and from thence northerly to the homestead of the late Mr. John Stocker, where it opened into what was then called the Great Lane or Scott's Lane. The Quilter's lived near the Manning High School House, and the Pindar's lived at the rear of the house of the late Mary Baker—the most historic house in town. Mineral street is called Baker's Lane in early Records.—*Printer, 1881* ]

May 23, 1677. This may signify to whom it may concern yt
Mr. Richard Dummer &
Mr. Henry Shorte
are members in full comunion wth t'e churche of Newbury as affirms
JNO : RICHARDSON. Minister.

DWIGHT, William, and Martha his wife, had a daughter Martha born August 1668

DYAR, John, had a seat in the meeting house, 1700.

DIRKEY, William, married Martha Cross, daughter of Robert Cross, Dec 20, 1664 ; had son John. The name is probably spelt Durgy and Durgre.
John Durgy, had a son
John, born November 23, 1689
Andrew, born Sept 20, 1692.
He purchased of the Town, Dec 1, 1693. about one quarter of an acre of land, part of which he had before yt time sett his barn on, being of the comon land, near his house in Chebacco.
William Durgey, sen'r, had a seat appointed on one of ye short seats in the meeting house, 1700.
Thomas Dirgey married Elisabeth Lord, March 5, 1700.

DOWNING, John, had
John, born Nov. 31, 1675
Margaret, February 7, 1678.

## EMERSON.

*High Street Burying Yard. Copied by Arthur W. Dowe, 1880.*

Here Lyes ye Body of Mr Nathan'l
Emerson who Died Decemr ye
29 1712, aged 83.

EMERSON, Thomas 1, was a commoner in 1641 ; and one of the seven men in 1646.   He had granted to him 1638, sixty-four acres of land adjoining Goodman Mussey.   In 1648, he convers to his son John a farm of 120 acres, on conditions.   In the deed the name is written Emberson.   In 1650, June 13, he sells' to Joseph Jewett, a farm granted to him by the town of Ipswich, containing four score acres, scituate beyond the north river on the south side of Prospect Hill, having the land of Richard Kimball and John Pickard towards the south east and the land of John Cross towards the north east, a highway of two rods broad lying between the land of Rowley and said farm.

October 6, 1652.   Joseph Emerson and Elisabeth his wife, sell to his father, Thomas Emerson, meadow and upland at Labor-in-vain.

He sold to Daniel Ringe, by a deed dated Feb. 14 1648, and acknowledged Feb. 25, 1655, a dwelling house* and six acres of land lying next the dwelling house of John Dane towards the south.   He died May 1, 1666.   His will is dated May 31, 1653, and the inventory of his estate is recorded Nov. 3, 1666, in which record he is styled "Goodman Emerson, sen'r."  ● He left a wife Elisabeth, and sons Joseph, John, James and Nathaniel ; and a daughter Elisabeth, wife of John Fuller.   He bequeathes to his wife, "the yearly rent of the farm with the six head of cattle, also the house, &c. during the time that she doth continue my widdow."   To his "sonne Joseph the some of eighty pounds of current pay of Newengland."   To his "sonne James, the sume of forty pounds to be paid unto him if he shall come over into this country, or send by a certain surtifficate of his being living within two years after the decease of me & my wife   In case

---

* This venerable mansion still stands.   It is situated on Turkey Shore.   It was owned in 1648 by Thomas Emerson, and sold by him to Daniel Ringe.   Daniel Ringe died in 1661.   It was next owned by Uzael Wardwell, who sold it to William Howard, and it is still called the Howard House by aged people.   William Howard left it to his sons, William, Samuel and John.   Samuel Howard bought it, and at his death, in 1766, he left it to his son Stephen Howard.   Stephen removed to Connecticut and sold it to Samuel Ringe, a son of Isaac Ringe and grandson of Daniel Ringe above mentioned.   A little later it was owned by Capt. Ebenézer Caldwell, whose first wife was Lucy, daughter of Samuel Ringe. above mentioned, and Mary (Appleton) his wife   Capt Caldwell's second wife was Mercy, daughter of the famous sheriff William Dodge.   Capt Caldwell died in 1821.   Since then the house has been in possession of Aaron Wallis, and others. — A picture of this house, by Arthur W. Dowe, 1880, will be found in these pages in connection with the Ringe Family.—Printer, 1881.

my sonne dye before then, my will is that my sonne Joseph his sonne Joseph shall have ten pounds, and my daughter Fuller her four sonnes twenty pounds, and my son Nathaniel ten pounds."

To Nathaniel, "my house wherein I now dwell, with all my upland and meadow, and the marsh yt bought of my sonne Joseph wh was sometime Mr. Woodmansys." To his daughter, Elisabeth Fuller, "the best feather bed and boulstar, with a pair of blanketts and the best coverlet and the bedstead, to enjoy for her use until her daughter Susana atayne the age of twenty years or the day of her marriage, if should happen sooner, then she to enjoy them also." He gives her also, "the great carved chest and the carved box with a little trunck with all is in it, and a small carved chest with what is in it."

In a codicil dated Jan. 4, 1660, he mentions having given unto his son John, "his portion full in ye consideration of yt agreement between us about my farm," &c. He bequeathes legacies to his daughter Fuller's two daughters, Susanna and Elisabeth, to be paid to them at "ye age of twenty years or at ye day of marriage." [See Fuller, John.]

He appoints his "loving wife, Elisabeth Emerson, sole executrix, and doe desire my much honored and faithful friends, Mr. Samuel Symonds and Major Gen'l Daniel Denison, to be overseers to see yt this my will be fulfilled. The will was proved May, 1666.

John 2, son of Thomas, was graduated at Harvard College in 1656, at which time he must have been not less than forty years old. [John Emerson, aged 20, passenger in the ship Elisabeth Ann, for New England, 1635.] He was a subscriber to Major Denison's compensation in 1648; and received a deed for a farm of his father, the same year. He married in 1662. Ruth, daughter of Hon. Samuel Symonds, and settled as minister at Gloucester, October 6, 1663, where he continued until his decease, Dec. 2, 1700. He left his property which was large to the sole disposal of his wife; with nominal legacies to his son John and his daughters Ruth Newman, Martha Cogswell, (wife of William Cogswell, married October 9, 1685,) Mary Phillips, Dorothy Emerson. To his son he gave 40s in money, and to his daughters 20s, and adds, "which I do give them besides what I have given them already." His will is dated Feb. 3, 1697-8, and was proved Dec. 23, 1700. Besides large possessions in Gloucester, he had in Ipswich a farm "lying by the farm of Mr. Denison on the south east, having Mr Emerson, tenant." Another farm "having the Town river Lying upon the north west of the farm, having 20 acres of meadow land lying by the crick called the Labour-in-vain crick, having Capt. Ringe and Mr. Howard tenents." And another farm "in Argilla in Ipswich, John Ross and James Burly being tenants." The last mentioned farm he inherited from his father-in-law, Symonds.

John 3, son of John 2, according to Farmer, graduated at Harvard College 1689, was probably the preacher at Manchester, named in the Magnalia, and was afterwards ordained at New Castle and installed the first minister of the 2d church in Portsmouth, 28 March, 1715, died 21 June, 1732 aged 62.  He was sworn a freeman, March, 1684. He appears from the following extract from the town records to have possessed the farm which had been his father's at Labor-in-vain, in 1703.  " May 6, 1703.  Voted to allow Mr. John Emerson three pounds toward a highway to his farm,"  And "Thomas Emerson declared in town meeting yt he would freely lay down an high way thro his land from Nathaniel and Thomas Wells land to Mr. John Emerson's land."  He was a resident of Ipswich in 1713, when with his wife Mary, he lost an infant son, named John.  " Here Lyes interred ye Body of John, son to John & Mary Emerson, a minister of ye Gospel at Portsmouth, aged about 2 months, who expired June ye 7th, 1714."  The anachronism in the epitaph 'may be explained by supposing the grave stone to have been erected some years after the decease of the child, when the father had become the minister of Portsmouth    The wife of John 3, was Mary Batters of Salem ; they had six daughters.

Joseph 2, son of Thomas 1, and probably the eldest, was a subscriber to Major Denison's compensation in 1648.  October 6, 1652, he with Elisabeth his wife sells to his father, meadow and upland at Labour-in-vain ;  the farm probably afterward possessed by John 2.

He married (1) Elisabeth Woodmansy, daughter of Robert Woodmansy, and had :  Joseph, (who probably died in Boston leaving one daughter, Mary ;) and James.

He married (2) Elisabeth Bulkley, and had :  Peter, Ebenezer, Jane, Edward, (ancestor of Ralph Waldo Emerson,) Daniel.

Nathaniel 2, son of Thomas 1, died Dec. 29, 1712, aged 83.  [See page 85, inscription and Arms.]

Sarah, wife of Nathaniel, died August 3, 1670.

Lydia, wife of Nathaniel, died August 17, 1716, aged 76.  In a petition to the Court of Probate, August 6, 1694, Mrs. Lydia Emerson represents herself as the relict of Nathaniel Wells, late of Ipswich. Epitaph 63.

Martha Emerson 2, daughter of Thomas 1, married William Cogswell, and had :  Edward, William, Emerson, Martha, Dorothy.

Nathaniel 3, son of Nathaniel 2, died Sept. 16, 1738, aged 81 yrs and one month.  He was, accordingly, born in August, 1657.  He married Martha Woodward, Feb. 1, 1685.  They had

Nathaniel, born Dec. 26, 1686, married Elisabeth Whipple.

Stephen, married (1) Mary, (2) Widow Lydia Norman.

Joseph, born June 26, 1690, married Abigail Perkins.

Mary, born January 19, 1691.

Broster, born June 28, 1695, married Thankful Howland.

Mary, born Dec. 18, 1697, m Lieut. Jacob Tilton, 1723.

Hannah, born December 5, 1698, married Mr. Michael Farley

Annah, born Sept. 4, 1700, married Benjamin Studley.

By the following extract from the Court Records of Essex County, it may be feared he was not so strict in his early deportment as the manners of the age required : " March, 1673. Nathaniel Emerson for being in company with Peter Cross and others at Jonas Gregory's and drinking thyr of stolen wine, was admonished and to pay costs and fees." At this time he was not more than 16 years old, and it may be hoped that he benefitted by the legal admonition, and afterward kept better company than Peter Cross and Jonas Gregory, who do not appear ever to have been citizens of Ipswich.*

Thomas 8, son of Nathaniel 2, possessed a farm near Labour-in-vain adjoining his cousin John Emerson's. He married Nov 20, 1685, Phillipa Perkins. She died April 26, 1738, aged 67 yrs 5 months.— They had :

Sarah, born July 6, 1691, married William Hunt, 1710.

Elisabeth, born July 16, 4693.

Thomas, born March 1696.7.

Thomas, June 4, 1699,

Mary, born April 20, 1704, married Stephen Story, 1721.

Mehitable, married Solomon Burnham, October 17, 1729.

Elisabeth, married Francis Goodhue, Jan. 5, 1733.

Phillipa, married John Hurlbert, 1759.

James 3 son of Joseph 2 and Sarah his wife, had, ("taken from his book after his decease,")

James, born March 13, 1692,

John, born June 9, 1694,

Joseph, born Dec. 18, 1696.

Nathaniel 4, son of Nathaniel 3, married Elisabeth Whipple, pub. Nov. 19, 1715. They had :

---

Jonas Gregory is mentioned in 1687, but it does not appear that he possessed any property,

1677, March. Jonas Gregory, the whipper, for abusing the court, sentenced to be whipped.

1678, March. Jonas Gregory allowed 29s a year for his employ as whipper on year past out of which his fine is sett off.

Elisabeth, born  2   10   1716,

Sarah, born 9   1   1718, married John Brown, Dec. 8, 1736.

Mary, born June 12, 1720, m. John Andrews, Mch 13, 1741.

Martha, born Aug. 19, 1722, m. Nath'l Adams, 1746.

Nathaniel,

Priscilla, married William Adams.

Hannah, married Nath'l Howe of Topsfield.

Isaac, born 1728 died 1730.

Broster 4, son of Nathaniel 3, published with Thankful Howland, March 24, 1727.  He was drowned at Plumb Island Oct. 15, 1728, and Widow Thankful Emerson married Ebenezer Smith, July 2, 1729.

Joseph 4, son of Nath'l 3, married Abigail Perkins, 1722, and had :

Joseph,

Abraham, born Nov. 13, 1726

Broster, born April 12, 1830

Abigail, born August 29, 1731.

Stephen 4, son Nath'l 3, had wife Mary, who died Oct 22, 1732, aged 30.  They had :

Stephen, born Dec. 1, 1728, died 1732.

Mary, born May 3, 1730.

He married (2) Widow Lydia Norman of Boston, and had :

Anstice, who m. Wm. Badger of Newbury, 1751

Stephen went to Buxton, Me  1735 ; to Newmarket, 1758.

Thomas 4, son of Thomas 3, and Sarah, had ;

Sarah born Oct. 31, 1724, m. Sam'l Cummins of Uxbridge.

Mary, b  June 20, 1727, m. Samuel Baker, jr., 1748.

Lucy, b. May 15, 1729, m. Johathan Cole of Beverly, 1747,

Elisabeth, June 27, 1733, m. James Emerson of Uxbridge,

John, b. July 30, 1734, m. Dorothy Foster, 1755

Ruth, b. March 12, 1737.

Nathaniel 5, son of Nathaniel 4, married Deborah Burnham, 1773 ; his daughters Deborah m  Abner Poland, and Mary, David Lull

1746, Joseph Emerson 5, probably son of Joseph 4, m. Mehitable Wheeler, of Gloucester ; his second wife was Mary.  He had Mehitable, Joseph, Benjamin

The following has reference probably to daughters of Nath'l 2 :—

Phillis Emerson died Aug. 1693, Deborah Emerson appointed adm'x.

Martha Cogswell, was daughter of John 2, and gr-dau. of Thomas. Wrongly stated on page 88.  We have added to Mr. Hammatt's sketch, gleanings from Town Records and from Prof. Emerson's MSS, (Amherst College.)

ELINGTHORP, or Elethorp, Nathaniel had a share and a half in commonage, 1664.

 Thomas, born March 15, 1662
 Abigail, December 9, 1665.
 Margaret, July 24, 1672.
 Nathaniel, July 10, 1675.

EASTON, Mr. Nicholas, took the freeman's oath at the same time with Mr. John Spencer at Boston, September 3, 1634. The same year they entered into a stipulation with the freemen of Ipswich to erect a mill at the place where the cotton factory now stands. In addition to the mill site there was granted to each of them "20 acres of land lying near the river on the south side thereof." They soon gave up the contract respecting the mill and probably also the grants of land, and removed to Newbury. Easton was representative to the General Court from Ipswich in 1635. He became involved in the Hutchinson controversy about "covenant of works," and "covenant of grace," and having signed a petition to the Court, or remonstrance against their proceedings in the case of Mr. Wheelwright which was adjudged to be "scandalous and seditious," he with the other petitioners or remonstrants was ordered to be disarmed. The following extract from the order of Court is from Savage's Winthrop, Vol. 1, p. 247 : " Whereas the opinions and revelations of Mr. Wheelwright and Mrs. Hutchinson have seduced and led into dangerous errours many of the people heare in Newe England insomuch as there is just cause of suspition that they as others in Germany in former times, may upon some revelation make some suddain irruption upon those that differ from them in judgment : for prevention whereof, it is ordered that all those whose names are under written, shall (upon warning given or left at their dwelling houses,) before the 30th day of November, deliver in at Mr. Cane's house at Boston, all such guns, pistols, swords, powder, shot and match, as they shall bee owners of, or have in their custody, upon paine of tenn pound for every default to bee made thereof, which arms are to be kept by Mr. Cane till this Court shall take further order thereon. Also it is ordered upon the penalty of X£ that no man who is to render his arms by this order, shall buy or borrow any guns, swords, pistols, powder, shot or match, until this Court shall take further order therein."

To the foregoing order is attached the names of fifty-eight of the inhabitants of Boston, five of Salem, Mr. Dummer, Mr. Easton and Mr. Spencer of Newbury, Mr. Foster and Samuel Sherman of Ipswich, "which are to deliver their arms to Mr. Bartholomew ;" five of Roxbury, and two of Charlestown.

Gov. Winthrop in speaking of Mr. Easton calls him "one Nicholas Easton, a tanner, a man very bold. though ignorant; that gifts and graces were that anti-Christ mentioned in Thessalonians. and that every one of the elect had the Holy Ghost and also the Devil indwelling."

Nicholas Easton is distinguished with only four others, out of a list of 54 freemen admitted at a General Court, 3 September. 1634, by the title of respect. The Rev. Messrs Parker and Noyes were admitted at the same time, and I conclude that he accompanied them.

In March after, Easton was deputy from Ipswich. and he probably followed his spiritual guide, to Newbury.

He was Governor at Rhode Island four years. and the station was filled five years by one whom I presume to be his son,—John Easton. He died in 1675, aged 83 —*Farmer.*

[A more complete history of Nicholas Easton and John Spencer, by Charles A. Sayward, Esq., is printed in the Ipswich Chronicle, October 30, 1880.]

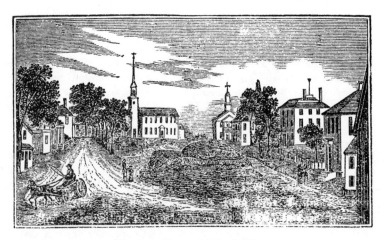

*Meeting House Hill. 1839.*

EPES, Captain Daniel, 1, is said by Farmer to have been the son of Daniel Epes of Kent, England, and to have come with his mother, who married Dep. Gov. Symonds. He was a subscriber to Major Denison's allowance in 1648. He married Elisabeth, daughter of the Hon. Samuel Symonds, May 20, 1644, and had, according to Farmer, eleven children, whose names and dates of birth are given from 1647 to 1659. This list does not contain the name of his son Symonds, who was born about 1662, and survived him. One other of his children, Daniel, born March 24, 1649, only survived him.

[Savage gives his children; Samuel, born 24 Feb. 1647, H. C. 1669, died 1685 at London; Daniel, born 24 March, 1649, H. C. '69; Nathaniel 1650; John, 1651; Joseph, 1653; Martha, 1654; Mary, 1656; Lionel, 1657; infant, 1658; Richard, 1659; Symonds, 1662.]

His wife Elisabeth died May 7, 1685:

> Here lies ye Body
> of Mrs. Elizabeth Epes,
> (wife of Capt. Daniel Epes, Esq'r,)
> who died May ye 7th, 1685,
> Aged abou 61 years.

After her death, he married Lucy, daughter of Rev. John Wood-bridge, and widow of Rev. Simon Bradstreet. He died, 1692:

> Here Lyes Buried
> ye Body of Capt.
> Daniel Epes, Esquire,
> who died January
> ye 8h, 1692, aged
> about 70 years.

His property consisting principally of the Castle Hill Neck estate, which he purchased, December 1, 1664, of his father-in-law Symonds, was appraised at £1411, 5s., and was divided January 1, 1693, into four shares, which were assigned to the heirs as follows:

To Daniel the eldest son, two shares; the Homestead called Castle Hill, 130 acres, bounded southerly by the cut creek, westerly by Sagamore Hill creek and Ipswich town river, northerly by the sea, south easterly by a stone wall in part, and ditch and creek.

To Major Symonds Epes, the "whole island," in another record called the "hole island," containing about 100 acres, near Castle Hill, and bounded northerly by the cut creek; south easterly by little Chebacco river; south westerly by Ring's marsh; north westerly by a branch of Sagamore Hill creek.

To Robert Greenough and Daniel Greenough, grand-children of said Daniel Epes, Esquire, £100 a piece.

To Lucy Epes, relict, £100.

Samuel, 2, eldest son of Daniel 1, born Feb 24, 1647, graduated at H. C. 1669 ; came into full communion with the church April 12, 1674 and died before his father, who was appointed adm'r of his estate, September, 1685.

Daniel 2, son of Daniel 1, was born March 24, 1649 ; graduated at Harvard College, 1669 ; freeman, May 27, 1874 ; was a member of the "executive counsell," and died in November, 1722. He resided at Salem, where he was a school-master, 1682. He came into full communion with the church at Ipswich, April 12, 1674. He married April 17, 1672, Martha, daughter of William Bordman, of Cambridge, and had two sons and seven daughters.

Daniel 3, son of Daniel 2, born Oct 28, 1679. Farmer says he married Hannah Higginson of Boston, in May, 1704, but it appears by the Ipswich Records that he was published, April 27, 1705, with Hannah Hicks of Boston. They had according to Farmer, seven sons and two daughters.

Symonds 2, son of Daniel 1, was born about 1662, and died Aug. 30, 1741, aged 79. He married Mary Whipple, March 26, 1715, who was probably his second wife. She survived him and became the third wife of President Holyoke, and died at Cambridge, March, 1790, in her 92d year. He left a son Samuel, [see Quincy's Hist. Harv. Univ. v. ii, p. 142,] and a daughter Elisabeth who married Edward Eveleth. He had the military title of Major and was a justice of the Court of Sessions, and a member of the Governor's Council ten years, 1724-34. The year of his daughter's marriage with Mr Eveleth, m. Dec. 5, 1715, he sells to him for the consideration of £300, "a dwelling house and land near ye meeting house, containing by estimation eight acres, bounded northwesterly by meeting house green, and Sadler Rogers his land ; north-easterly by Coll'l John Appleton ; easterly and southerly by Town River ; north-westerly and south-westerly by Wardwell's land." A part of this lot contained the town residence of his grandfather, the Hon. Samuel Symonds. [The Seminary of Rev. J. P. and Mrs. E. C. Cowles stands upon the site of Mr. Symonds' town house ; and the Public Library upon the site of a residence of an Appleton, who afterward erected a house on the Topsfield road.]

EVELETH, Joseph, with his wife Mary, had
      Isaac, born October 11, 1676
      Edward, born July 25, 1679

Moses, born Feb. 13, 1681

Mary, born Nov. 13, 1683, m. Stephen Perkins, July, 1706. See tythingmen, p. 34.

Hannah, born October 1, 1685

Isaac, died July 4, 1685, and left a widow Abigail. His estate, consisting of an house, land, &c. amounted to £115, 7s.

Edward, married January, 1704, Elisabeth, daughter of Abraham Perkins.

Here Lyeth Buried
ye Body of Mrs. Eliz
abeth Eueleth
(wife to Mr. Ed
ward Eueleth)
who died Mar
ch y 11, 1712-13.
aged 33 years.

She left a son Joseph and a daughter Elisabeth. He married for his second wife, Elisabeth, daughter of Major Symonds Epes, who died August 24, 1733. And a third wife, Mary Wise, August 10, 1737.

EVANS, Philip, died Aug. 20, 1693, and left a widow, Deborah, The inventory of his estate amounted to £40, 12s. Returned by Tho: Lovell and Sam'll Wallis.

EDWARDS, John, was a tenant of Mr. Humphrey Vincent in 1664, and was entitled to a share in certain common lands. He married Mary Sams, November 24, 1658. They had

John, born January 22, 1659, died 1694

Mary, born October 15, 1661

Elisabeth and Lucy born February 28, 1666

Elisabeth died 1666

William, born March 13, 1668

William, born March 27, 1669

Samuel, born June 1, 1671

His second wife was named Margaret; they had,

Francis, born December 29, 1678

Hannah, born July 7, 1681

Frances, born September 30, 1682

He had the right of turning horses on the common in 1687.

Thomas Edwards, was possessed of the right of turning horses on the common.

"Old Good'n Edwards," had a seat assigned to him "behind ye pulpit," 1700.

1703, December 6, Joseph Edwards and Hannah his wife, who signs with a mark, daughter of Joseph Goodhue, to "her brother Thomas Knowlton, her guardian."

The will of John Edwards, dated April 1, 1706, proved Jan. 6, 1706-7   He left a wife, and sons, Samuel the eldest; and John; dau. Mary Wait, Lucy Kimball, Elisabeth Burch, and Hannah Wardwell. He makes Francis Whipple residuary legatee, and his son-in-law, Caleb Kimball, executor.

There was a Rice Edwards mentioned 1699.

John Edwards, Drum-Major, died April 26, 1723, aged 64th year.—*Inscription*.

EASTY, Joseph, had a seat appointed to him in the Meeting House, 1700.

FARLEY, Michael, 1. came from England with his two sons, Michael and Mesheck, and settled in Ipswich about the year 1675.

It appears from the Registry of Deeds of Essex Co. under the date, April 27, 1682, that there was a covenant respecting a mill, between Richard Saltonstall, Esquire, on the one part, and Michael Farley and Michael Farley, jun'r, on the other part, dated June 24, 1675. This covenant expired March 26, 1682, when another was entered into between same parties, including Mesheck, the younger son of Michael.

1683, March 10, Michael, sen'r, and Lieut Thomas Burnham, enter into a contract "with respect of a marriage intended betwixt Mesheck Farley and Sarah Burnham, in which, upon compleating said marriage said Farley engages upon his paternal love and care of his said son, and for his further settlement, to give said Mesheck a small parcel of land, granted unto the said Michael by the Town of Ipswich, together with half such a sum as said Burnham should be at in ye building parties a dwelling house upon said land." The deed of the land was executed March 8, 1698 9, by the said Michael, with the consent of his "now wife." This land remained the property of the family about 150 years.

1679, September, Mr. Mighill ffarley, licensed to sell liquors by the gallon and quart.

1684, License renewed.

1680, Sept. 28, he sued John Caldwell for a debt, £3, 8s. 3d.

1679.   Mr. Farley's two sons worked on highways.

1683, Feb. 11, Michael Farley and Meshack Farley petition the town to grant them "eight or ten rods of ground for to build a small dwelling uppon where we may be near to attend ye towne service," "near the end of John Safford's orchard." "If you see not good to bestow it freely on your servant for his son : I will pay ten shillings per rod within a twelve month." "This petition was voted in the affirmative and granted freely."

Michael 1, died June 15, 1700. His wife died Dec. 12, 1736, aged 78 years. She was probably a second wife, and could not have been the mother of his children.

Michael 2, son of Michael 1, was born as early as 1654, and married Nov. 1708, Mary Woodbury of Beverly, who died in 1712 :

Here lyeth buried ye body of
Mrs Mary Farley,
(wife of Mr. Michael Farley,)
who dyed ye 21st of October,
1712, aged 38 years.

As you are
So ware we
As we are
You shall be

It does not appear that he had any children. He married April 15, 1724, Hannah Emerson, by whom he had three children,—Jane, Hannah, Nathaniel. It seems from the following extract from the Town Records that he was not exempt from the usual troubles that affect old men who marry young wives :

" Memo : Mr. James Burnham and Mr. Michael Farley appeared before me, the subscriber, Town Clerk of Ipswich, ye 8th day of April, 1727, and said Mr. Farley declared that he allowed no body but his wife to sit in the pew granted to him and the sd Burnham, & as for his wifes Bros and sisters he had never given them leave to sit in the said pew, nor never should, nor any of their relations, but forbid them all, and desired an entry might be made hereof. John Wainwright, Town Clerk."

He subscribed £1, 10s, toward the bell, 1699. He died in 1736. An inventory of his estate dated January 28, 1736-7, exhibits a total of nearly £3500. His children were placed under the guardianship of Increase How. His widow married Abel Huse, jr. of Newbury, with whom she was published April 22, 1738.

Nathaniel 3, son of Michael 2, was published Nov. 7, 1754, with Elisabeth, daughter of Jonathan Cogswell. Esq., then deceased ; she died in 1763, and he married Mary Wise, published Nov. 17, 1764.

Mesheck 2, son of Michael 1, was born about 1662. He married August 6, 1684. Sarah Burnham, daughter of Lieut. Thomas Burnham. They had :

Mesheck, born June 1, 1685
Michael, born August 2, 1686
Jane, died March 6, 1692

He died in 1696, and left his sons under the guardianship of his brother Michael. The inventory of his estate is dated Dec. 23, 1696. It was taken by Matthew Perkins and Edward Dear, and amounted to £164, 8, 2. The house and homestead were appraised at £60, money, £15, 4s ; among the "personal chattles" were Child-bed linen, £2, 10 ; Pewter, 4, 6s. Brass and Iron, 8, 4s. It was rendered January 18, 1696-7, and signed, Sarah Farlo. His estate was distributed thus : To Sarah, (widow,) £49, 9, 9 1-2. To Mesheck the eldest son, 35, 15, 3. To Michael, 17, 7, 7.

*M*esheck 3, son or *M*esheck 2, died March 6, 1715, without issue.

Michael 3, son of *M*esheck 2, married February 2, 1716-17, Elisabeth, daughter of Capt. Thomas and Priscilla Baker of Topsfield. She died Feb. 26, 1745   He died *M*ay, 1757, and left sons Michael and John, and a daughter Jane, wife of Samuel Heard, married Mch 1747. His will, in which he styles himself "cordwayner." is dated April 10, 1751, and was proved June 4, 1757. The following are extracts :— " Being aged, &c., I give to my son John Farley, my dwelling house I now live in with thirty rods of land, bounded southerly by John Safford's land,* westerly by ye highway, &c., also one half my outlands (excepting my four neck rights) with one half of all my household goods, and leather, and shoes, and tools, and cattle, except what I shall hereafter give to my daughter Jane Heard, to be equally divided between my two sons Michael and John ; but if my son should die without having a child, then I give all that is given to him to my son Michael Farley and his heirs forever. I give to my daughter Jane Heard, &c. I give to my son Michael Farley and his heirs forever, my four neck rights at Jeffries Neck, and the other half of all my outlands what I have given to my son John Farley, and the other

---

* 1641. Daniel Denison conveys to Humphrey Griffin a dwelling house near the mill.

1648, 1, 4mo. John Burnham conveys to Anthony Potter a house lot late of Humphrey Griffin situate near the water mill.

1661, Jan. 19. Anthony Potter and Elisabeth his wife, convey to John Safford, dwelling house and land three acres, north side of the river, near the mill, bounded with high way round.

The houselot thus described is now known as the site of the ancient house, till lately the residence of Mrs. Hannah Dennis Lord. On this land Major-Gen. Daniel Denison built his earliest Ipswich house.— *Note 1881.*

half of all my leather, &c., to be equally divided, &c., I have already given to my son Michael Farley, a deed of the old house, and Michael Farley sole executor.

Michael 4, son of Michael 3, was baptized April 24, 1720. He was published December 21, 1745 with Elisabeth, daughter of Robert Choate, born Sept. 29, 1726; the inscription upon her gravestone is:

In memory of<br>
Mrs. Elisabeth Farley,<br>
Consort of the late<br>
Gen'l Farley<br>
who died<br>
July 6th, 1795,<br>
Æt 69.

My children and friends when these you<br>
see remember me.

Michael and Elisabeth (Choate) Farley had:

 John, baptized October 5, 1746
 Ebenezer, baptized November 27, 1748
 A daughter, baptized January 14, 1750, d. e.
 Michael, baptized December 3, 1752
 Jabez, baptized October 13, 1754
 Eunice, baptized October 26, 1756
 Robert, baptized February 4, 1759, d. e.
 Robert,* baptized April 27, 1760
 Susanna, baptized January 17, 1762, d. e.
 Susanna, baptized February, 1764
 Thomas, baptized February 21, 1766
 Sarah, baptized July 6, 1768

General Farley died June 20, 1789. The stone erected to his memory is inscribed:

Erected to the memory of the<br>
Hon'bl Michael Farley, Esq'r, Major<br>
General of the Melitia and Sheriff<br>
of the County of Essex; who died<br>
June 20th, 1789, Æt 70.

With a mind open, honest and generous<br>
with a heart alive to humanity and<br>
compassion, he served for many<br>
years in various stations, private, publick

---

* When Robert was about 16, he went to war; his mother helped him to equip, and as he left the house, charged him to behave like a man. See Felt's Ipswich, pages 184. 187-8.

> and honourable, his neighbours,
> and his Country, with such integrity, zeal
> and diligence, as merited an extensive
> approbation and rendered his death
> justly regretted.

> Here mixed with earth his ashes must remain
> Till death shall die and mortals rise again.

Gen. Farley held for many years the principle offices of the town : was feoffee of the Grammar School, representative to the Provincial Congress and General Court from 1766 to 1779, High Sheriff of the County, Major-General of the Militia, and one of the Executive Council which exercised the functions of government during the revolutionary interregnum, 1775-80. Felt in his History of Ipswich, gives a brief but interesting sketch of the Gen'l and his wife, p. 184.

John Farley, son of Michael 3, married Sept. 1761, Eunice. dau. of Francis Cogswell.

FAWN, John. Had a houselot granted in 1634 in High street, on the north side, between Mr John Baker and Mr. Thomas Bracy, which lot he sold to Thomas Firman. He possessed also a farming lot of 25 acres at Chebacco, which his assignees sold to John Webster In 1650, Oct. 10, with the title Gent. he quit-claims to John Whipple an houselot in Ipswich. He also possessed an houselot adjoining Mr. Appleton, six acres near the mill, near where the rail-road station now is, adjoining General Denison's lot. He removed to Haverhill. His wife, according to Farmer, was named Elisabeth and one of his daughters married Robert Clement.

FANCY, Thomas, died about 1700. He possessed an house and land ; his wife, Elisabeth, administered on his estate, April 22, 1700. [See Thomas Fossy.]

FELLOWS, William, 1, was a commoner, 1641, and 1664. His will is dated Nov. 29, 1676, and was proved Nov. 27, 1677. He left sons, Ephraim, Samuel, Joseph, Isaac ; daughters Mary, Elisabeth, Abigail and Sarah.

Ephraim 2, son of William 1, was a voter in town affairs 1679. Commoner, 1678. His wife, Mary, died Feb. 23. 1671. With his second wife, Ann, he had

> Elisabeth, born September 14, 1685
> Anna, born February 26, 1693

He had a seat appointed to him in the meeting house, 1700.

Joseph 2, son of William 1, had a wife named Ruth, married Aug. 19, 1676. He was entitled to certain rights of commonage in 1664, and was a voter in town affairs, 1679, freeman, May 26, 1682. He died in 1693. The inventory of his estate, amounting to £791, 15, was rendered by Ruth, his widow, Nov. 7 of that year. His children living in 1697, were:

> Mary, born May 3, 1676
> Joseph, born 1578, married Sarah Kimball Nov. 18, 1701
> Ruth, born 1681
> Sarah, May 17, 1685
> Abigail, born 1688
> William, born 1690.

His estate in 1697, amounted to real—$451, personal £235, 15. It was distributed one third part to the widow, on real £150, 6, 8, personal 85, 11, 8. To Joseph the eldest son real £85, 18; personal 48, 8, to each of the other children, real, 42, 19, personal 24, 8. The widow Ruth charges April 15, 1697, to keeping three children 3 1-2 years to this time £15. She died April 14, 1729, and is mentioned on the record as an "ancient widow."

Isaac 2, son of William 1, was a voter in town affairs, 1679 and possessed rights of commonage, 1697 and 1707, and with the title of Corp'l has a seat appointed him in the meeting house, 1700. See list of Tythingmen, p. 34. He married Joanna Bourne Jan. 29, 1672. They had

> Isaac, born Novhmber 27, 1673
> Samuel, born February 8, 1676
> Ephraim, born September, 1679
> Jonathan, born September 28, 1682
> Joanna, born November 19, 1689

He died April 6, 1721, aged "84 years and upwards."

Jonathan, was a commoner 1707, and together with Ruth and Sarah had seats assigned to them in the meeting house, 1702. With his wife Rachel he had a son named Varney, born March 25, 1694.

Samuel 2, son of William 1, settled in Salisbury, where he was commoner, 1650.

FARROW, George, was entitled to one and a half shares in Plum Island, &c., in 1664, which shows that his taxable property was greater than that of the average of the inhabitants. He possessed land before 1636, which in that year had become the property of John Webster. He is styled Mr.

1661. Feb. 18, granted to Mr. Thomas Cobbitt twelve acres of land either at Mr. Paine's paster or by the river beyond Goodman ffarough his house wch he shall think meat.

FIRMIN, Mr. Giles, took the freeman's oath in Boston, March 4, 1633-4. He was, according to Farmer, son of Giles who came from Sudbury, England, in 1630, and settled in Boston, where he was chosen Deacon in 1633, and died in September, 1634. He was born in Suffolk, England, educated at Cambridge. It appears from the following extract from a work by him, published many years after his return to England, entitled "The Real Christian, or a Treatise of Effectual Calling," that he did not come to America until after his father's decease. Speaking of his father with reference to some "christian duty," the performance of which was a subject of controversy, he says: "When he was dead, his minister who wrote to us the news of his death, said this of him, *He lived much desired, he died much mourned for*   Yet this, my godly father, would scarcely be esteemed for a serious christian by some for not performing that duty according to the question, though I suppose a year or two before his death he did take it up, but then I was far distant from him." p. 315 He settled in Ipswich, where he practiced physic. Jan 4, 1638, 100 acres were granted him near Mr. Hubbards farm. He was a commoner in 1641, and continued to reside in Ipswich until about 1654, when he returned to England and became a minister when more than fifty years old. After his return to England he sold his house and six acres of land in Ipswich to Mr. William Goodhue. [See Goodhue] In a sermon before the House of Lords and Commons and the Assembly of Divines at Westminster, he said: "I have lived in a country seven years, and all that time I never heard one profane oath, and all that time never did see a man drunk in that land." He died at Ridgewell, England, in April, 1697. His wife was daughter of Rev. Nath'l Ward.—*Farmer.*

Firmin, Thomas, took the freeman's oath at Boston, May 22, 1639, was commoner with the title of *Mr.* 1641. He was a merchant and seems to have possessed large property. He purchased of John Proctor, May 1 1647, a dwelling house with about two acres of land, being the lot situated next southerly to where the stone bridge now is. [It is now the residence of Capt. Samuel N. Baker.] He sold at the same time to Proctor a farm. He purchased of Richard Haffield in 1639, a house and lot being in the "cross street leading to the meeting house, bounded by the highway leading to the mill on the south." Oct. 5, 1647, he sells to Thomas Low and Edward Brage twenty acres lying upon the Mile Brook towards the south west; and Nov. 29, to Thomas Howlett and William Goodhue 22 acres of marsh, part of farm called Thornhill; he died about 1648, and the inventory of his estate was rendered by Sarah Firmin, his widow, April 10, of that year. The house "that was Goodman Proctor's" is appraised at £18, 10s.

*Seal of Robert Fitts.  1665*

FITT, Robert, said by Farmer who spells the name Fitts, to have been of Salisbury in 1640; was a commoner of Salisbury, 1640-52; was among those "voted to be townsmen and commoners" of Salisbury, 3d 12 mo. 1650, and is assessed 11s 3d in Mr. Worcester's rate for £30 the 25th Dec. 1650.  Also in a rate made 18th 5 mo. 1652, for his half year due 24 : 4mo 9s. 7d.  His name, spelled Fitch, is in a list of the inhabitants of Ipswich, who have shares in Plum Island in 1664.  He died May 9, 1665.  His will in which the name is spelt Fitt, was proved June 26, 1665.  It has a seal attached to it, the device of which is represented by the above figure.  He left a widow named Grace who died April 25, 1684, and a son Abraham.

Abraham 2, son of Robert 1, married Sarah Thompson, dau. of Simon Thompson, and came from Salisbury to dwell in Ipswich at the request of his father-in-law, who conveys to him an house and land which he bought of Humphrey Griffin containing three acres, having the Rocky Hill towards the west, John Fuller south, the highway east and north east : together with other lands.  He joined the church in full communion February 22, 1673, freeman March 11, 1673-4, and died March 27, 1692.  The inventory of his estate exhibited a total of £366, consisting of a house, orchard, and 50 acres of upland and meadow; he also possessed land in Salisbury.

To his first wife, Sarah Thompson, he was married May 16, 1655; they had :

Sarah, born February 21, 1657, died June 14, 1660.

Robert, born March 31, 1660, died Jan. 15, 1661

Sarah, born March 15, 1661

With his second wife he had Robert, born May 2, 1670; Richard, born Feb. 26, 1672; Isaac, born July 3, 1675.

Abraham 3, son of Abraham 2, joined the church by taking the covenant Feb. 1, 1673-4. He married (1) Rebecca Burley, (2) Margaret, and had

> Robert, born July 19, 1690
> Margaret, born January 25, 1691

His wife Margaret died February 28 following, and he married Jan 9, 1693, Mary Ross, and had

> Mary, born January 8, 1694
> Mercy, born March 3, 1695
> Sarah, born March 15, 1697
> Samuel, born August 16, 1699

He became a freeman March 31, 1674, and died 1714.

> Here Lyeth ye Body
> of Mr Abraham
> Fits who died
> August ye 18,
> 1714, aged
> 59 years.

Richard 3, son of Abraham 2, married March 18, 1694, Sarah Thorne, and had

> Isaac, born December 19, 1695, died August 10, 1696
> Sarah, born July 11, 1697

Isaac, wife Bethia died August 22, 1722.

From Town Records: Richard Fitts and Rebeccah Fitts, widdow, relict of Abraham Fitts of Ipswich, deseased, enter into an agreement dated this twenty & fifth day * * * Anno Dom: 1693. yt whereas sd Abraham in his last will & testament bequeated & left to sd Rebeccah & Richard Lands in Ipswich & Salisbury to be to their use & improvement during ye natural Life of sd Rebeccah: the Land and Marsh Grounde in Salisbury being sd Richards after sd Rebbeccah's decease: it is considered yt sd Rebecah shall have the whole Lands & Meadows given them in Ipswich to be to her use, benefit and improvement during her natural life and shall Quit claime to the sd Richard of all Lands & meadows given him by deed of Gift by his father in Salisbury.

FISK, Joseph, with his wife Susanna, lost a son named Joseph, December 5, 1698. He had a soat in the meeting house assigned to him in 1702; and his name with the title *Mr.* is on a list of commoners in 1707.

1681, October, Mr. John Fiske, undertakes to use means for the recovery of John Bridge; in case he cure him, to have 25s. at prsent, & the rest when he is cured, &c.

David Fiske and Sarah Day married June 17, 1674.

FAIRFIELD, Walter, with Sarah his wife, had
    Samuel, born February 22, 1695
    Benjamin, born February 1, 1697 died February 9.
    Sarah, born October 7, 1699
He possessed a farm in 1673, was complained of for felling trees in 1667, was a commoner in 1707.

John Fairfield, probably father of Walter, died about 1662. The inventory of his estate dated November 30, 1672, amounts to £241, 5, 6. He had "land in ye great meadow and upland undivided with his brother, valued £52; his house and land were appraised £200; his children John and Elisabeth were of Muddy River near Boston, 1692.

FOSTER, Reginald, according to an article in the New England Gen Register, vol. 1, p. 352, was descended from an ancient and respectable family settled in the west of England. He came from England in 1638; and with his family was on board a vessel embargoed by King Charles 1: he settled at Ipswich with five sons and two daughters: Abraham, Reginald, William, Isaac, Jacob, Mary and Sarah; his daughter Sarah married William Story, ancestor of Judge Story. Mary, married (1) a Wood, and (2) Francis Peabody. He resided near the bridge, and is one of 24 of the inhabitants who in 1646, "promise carting voluntary toward the cart Bridge, besides the rate, a day work a piece." He was a commoner in 1641. In 1648, he and his son Abraham are subscribers to an allowance for Major Denison. 1661, he was a surveyor of highways; his name with the names of his sons, Abraham, Reginald, Isaac and Jacob, are in a list of the inhabitants that have shares in Plum Island, &c., Feb. 14, '64. The same names are on a list of those that by law are allowed to have their votes in Town affairs, Dec. 2, 1679. October, 1664, Judith, his wife, died. He lived, says the writer above quoted, to an extreme old age; but the time of his death does not occur on our records.

Abraham 2, son of Reginald 1, was born at Exeter, England, about 1620, and died in Ipswich, January 15, 1710, aged 90. He joined the church in full communion, April 12, 1674; his children were:
    Ephraim, born Oct 9, 1651, m. Hannah Eames, lived Andover
    Abraham, born October 14, 1659
    James, born June 12, 1662
    Benjamin, 1670
    Ebenezer, July 15, 1672
    Mehitable, October 12, 1675
    Caleb, Nov. 9, 1677, pub. Mary Sherrin, April 26, 1702.

He had a seat assigned to him "behind ye pulpit," in the meeting house then recently built, 1700.

Reginald 2, son of Reg. 1, married Sarah Martin, Sept. 1665; his will is dated July 11, 1704, was proved Jan 19, 1707-8. In it are mentioned his wife Elisabeth, and three sons and three daughters :

        Isaac.

        John, born July 15, 1664

        Nathaniel, born September 19 1678

        Elisabeth,

        Judith, born January 20, 1659

They had lost children :

        Mary, born June 18, 1662

        Rebecca, born Feb. 25, 1666, died July 1, 1684

        Ruth, born December 19, 1671, died 1671

        Hannah, born October, 1675

        Naomi. born May 6, 1679

Isaac 2, son of Reginald 1, married (1) Mary Jackson, May 5, 1658, she died November 27, 1677 ; (2) Hannah Downing, Nov. 25, 1678; (3) Martha Hale, March 16, 1679 ; he died Feb. 8, 1691, being then according to his will about 62 years of age ; he was freeman, May, 31, 1671. He had :

        Jonathan, born January 9, 1658, d. e.

        Mehitable, born September 1, 1660, d. e.

        Benjamin, born August 3, 1661.

        Jacob, born February 9, 1662

        Eliezer, born April, 1665

        Elizabeth, born April 20, 1667

        Daniel, born Nov. 14, 1670

        Martha, born August 1, 1672

        Ruth, born February 20, 1673

        Prudence, born May 23, 1675

        Hannah, October 24, 1676

Jacob. Daniel and Eliezer, and twin daughters whose names are not mentioned were living at his death.

Jacob 3, son of Isaac 2, is designated as Jacob tertius on the Records ; he married March 5, 1696, Mary Caldwell, daughter of John and Sarah (Dillingham) Caldwell, and they had

        Jacob, born May 9, 1697

        William, born May 11, 1699

        Mary, born March 9, 1700-1, m. Jacob Louden, 1721

        Abigail, born September 27, 1703, m. Wm. Holland, 1724

        Israel, born March 3, 1706-7

The inscription  on  the gravestone  of Mary (Caldwell)  Foster: —

> Here lies  Buried  Mary
> ye wife of  Jacob  Foster
> who  Dyed  April  ye 2
> 1709 aged 37

Jacob 2, son Reginald 1, was born about  1635 ;  he  married  (1)
Martha Kinsman, daughter of Robert  Kinsman,  January 12,  1658.
They had :

> Judith,  born October 29,  1659,  d.  e.
> Jacob, born  May  15,  1662,  d.  e.
> Mary,  d.  e.
> Sarah, born  August 3,  1665,  married  John  Caldwell

He married  (2)  Abigail  Lord,  Feb.  26,  1666, who  survived him.
They had

> Abraham, born  December  4,  1667
> Jacob,  born  March  25,  1670
> Amos,  born  August 15,  1672
> Abigail,  born  July  3,  1674
> Nathaniel,  born  October  7,  1676
> Samuel,  born  September  10,  1678
> Joseph,  born  September  14,  1680
> James,  born  November  12,  1682
> Mary,  born  December  20,  1684

He died  July  9,  1710, in the 75th year of his age.   His widow, Abigail, died June 4,  1729.

> Here Lies  Dec'n
> Jacob  Foster
> who died  July
> ye 9th  1710
> In  ye 75  yr  of
> His  Age.

He was a Deacon of the church, and  his  name—Jaakob  ffoster,—is
is among the Selectmen, 1679.   He gave by his will to his sons Abraham and Jacob, ''land at Muddy river that was  my  father  Foster's
adjoining to land that was my father Lord's.''

Abraham 3, son Jacob 2, with Mary his wife had  Abraham,  born
June 11,  1696.   Dec. 17, 1697, Abraham Foster, a  soldier wounded
in the public service is to receive £8 out of the public treasury.  ''Here
Lies Mr. Abraham Foster,  Died December ye 25, 1720, aged 53 yrs.''

Daniel 3,  son  Isaac  2,  with  Mary his wife, had Ketherine, born
August 21, 1696 ;  Mary, d. e. Mary, born Jan. 23, 1698.

Thomas and Elisabeth had Liddia, born January 6. 1691, Hannah,
born February 25, 1694.

March 10, 1700, Daniel Foster, adm. of est. of Benj. Foster, ex-hibits his account : estate according to inventory, £6, 7, 2. Debts and charges paid, £2, 4. Signed by Jacob Foster, Elisabeth Foster, Robert Grant in right of Mary Foster, Daniel Foster, Prudence Fos-ter alias Borman.

FOSSY, ffaccy, ffacie, Thomas, married Rayner, Feb. 4, 1685. He died March 27, 1700. He kept the herd 1673.

March 7, 1692. Thomas Fossey petitions the town that they would be pleased to grant him liberty to set up a little house by the prison during the time of his life and his widows during her widowhood, and then leave it to the town. Granted about 4 rods ; he was keeper of the Prison, 1696.

1700, April 12. Inventory of Thomas Fossy, late deceased, ex-hibited by his widow, Elisabeth, total estate, £85, 11, 3. House and land £40 ; appraised by William Baker and Edward Dear. Children, Elisabeth, aged 13, Lydia, Hannah aged 6. Elisabeth the widow, guardian.

FRINK, John. His will is dated December 16, 1674 and was proved Sept. 29, 1675. He left a wife Mary, and two sons John and George. Will proved by Deacon Goodhue and Mary Wilson. He had granted to him liberty for firewood as a seaman, November, 1673.

FOWLER. Philip, was among the earliest inhabitants of Ipswich. He took the freeman's oath in Boston, Sept. 3, 1684. He had a house lot granted to him in 1635, in the cross street called meeting house lane ;* being about one acre of ground, having John Gage his house lot on the south east, and Thomas Scott's houselot on the north west. Christopher Oogood‡ in his will dated April 9, 1650, appointed his "father Phillip Fowler," of the overseers of his will.

Mary his wife, died August 30, 1659. He lost a son Philip, June 15, 1676, born Nov. 27, 1675. He married widow Mary Norton.

---

* This cross street or lane, ran from the rear of the Agawam House to house of the late Mr. John Stocker. It is distinctly traced on plan made in 1717, which is among the Court Records at Salem.

‡ On an old Powder Horn in possession of Mr Clark Osgood of Cape Elisabeth, Me. is an inscription, " Christopher Osgood, of Or-rell, England, come to America, Feb. ye 14, 1634."

Matthew A. Stickney, Esq., has prepared history and genealogy of Philip Fowler's descendants.—*1881*

In 1663, his residence was High street, the south side adjoining the house lots of John Woodam and Philip Call. He joined the church by taking the covenant, March 8, 1673 and died June 24, 1697.

1635. There was granted to Mr John Tuttle ten acres towards the Neck, having Mr Bracy his land west; Mr Tredwell east; Philip Fowler north, and a creek south.

1679, Sept. Phillip ffowler dying intestate adm'r granted to Peter ffowler his grandchild.

1664, Feb 14. His name is in a list of those that have shares in Plum Island, Castle Neck, and Hog Island.

Thomas Fowler married Hannah Jorden Apr 23, 1660, and had Hannah born June 7, 1661.

Joseph 2 son of Philip 1, conveyed lands, &c. to his "father-in-law, Richard Kimball, wheelwright," Jan. 12, 1650.

Philip 2 son Philip 1, born Oct. 8, 1648, married Elisabeth Herrick Jan 20, 1672; was a commoner in 1709; being entitled to the right of commonage in consequence of possessing a dwelling house. He was a voter in town affairs, December, 1679. With six others he purchased the old meeting house, March 2, 1703-4, and engaged to "give £20 money for the for the said house, and to remove it from the ground whereon it stands within the space of nine months (which money shall be improved toward building the new Galleries in the new meeting house.")

His wife Elisabeth survived him and died May 6, 1727; he had horses on the common in 1697, and was a commoner in 1707. In the allotment of pews in the new meeting house, there is assigned "To Mr. Phillip Fowler ye 3d pew on ye nor side ye pulpit for ye children and John Treadwell's wife who is confined thereunto—otherwise one of ye heads of ye families." To Mr Philip Fowler himself is assigned a place on one of the seats, No. 3, in the body of the house. He had a son John born Jan 12, 1684, and a daughter Martha April 6, 1689.

> Here Lyes Jntarred
> what was mortall
> of Mr Philip Fowler
> who died Nouember
> ye 16th 1715 aged 67
> wanting 39 days

FILBRICK, Robert, had eight acres of land granted to him for his services as a soldier against the Pequot Indians, 1639.

1643, Dec 4. It is agreed that each soldier for their services to the Indians shall be allowed 12d a day (allowing for the Lord's day in

respect of the extremity of the weather,) and the officers double.——
Robert Philbrick received 3s.  He subscribed to Gen. Denison's com-
pensation in 1648.  1658, April 13, John Philbrick, inventory by
William Fivefield and Moses Cox.

FRANKLIN, William, had the grant of a houselot in 1634.

1634.  Given and granted unto John Newman, William Sargent
and William Franklin about 12 acres of land more or less to every
one of them a like portion or share of the same lying on the south side
of John Perkins the elder his land, &c.

Franklin soon after removed to Newbury and thence to Boston and
Roxbury. At Roxbury he was admitted to the church ; he was hanged
in 1644 for the murder of an apprentice boy.  Gov. Winthrop says :

" The case was this : he had taken to apprentice one Nathaniel
Sewell, one of those children sent over the last year for the country ;
the boy had the scurvy and was withal very noisome and otherwise
ill-disposed.  His master used him with continual rigor and unmerci-
ful correction, and exposed him many times to much cold and wet in
the winter season, and used divers acts of rigor to him : as hanging
him in the chimney, &c. ; and the boy being very poor and weak, he
tied him upon an horse and so brought him (sometimes sitting and
sometimes hanging down,) to Boston, being five miles off, to the
magistrates, and by the way the boy calling for water, would give him
none, though he came close by it, so as the boy was near dead when
he came to Boston ; and he died within a few hours.  This man had
been admitted into the church of Roxbury about a month before, and
upon this he was cast out ; but the church in compassion to his soul,
after his condemnation, procured license for him to come to Roxbury,
intending to receive him again before he died, if they might find him
truly penitent.  But though presently after his condemnation he judged
himself and justified God and the Court, yet then he quarrelled with
the witnesses and justified himself, and so continued even to his execution, professing assurance of salvation, and that God would never
lay the boy his death to his charge, but the guilt of his blood would lie
upon the country.  Only a little before he was turned off the ladder,
he seemed to apprehend some hardness of heart that he could not see
himself guilty of that which others did."

FRENCH, Thomas. a tailor, took the freeman's oath at Boston,
Nov 6, 1632 ; was a member of the church at that place, from which
he was dismissed to Ipswich January 27, 1639 ; he was possessed of
an house lot in Ipswich lying in Mill street between Thomas Scott and
Robert Mussey ; he was commoner, 1641 ; and subscribed to Gen.

Denison's compensation, 1648.  His will is dated August 3 and proved Sept 28, 1680; he left a wife Mary; and sons Thomas, John, Samuel, Ephraim and daughter Mary Smith; his son Thomas adm on his estate Sept. 1680; he had land in the "flat called Pequitt Lots." He had the title Sergeant, 1655.  In 1664 his name is on a list of those who have shares in Plum Island, and he is then called Ensign; with the same title his name is on a list of those that by law are allowed to have their votes in town affairs, 1679.  He died August 8, 1680.  He sold a farm to George Davision, 1647.

Thomas 2 married Mary Adams, Feb 29, 1659, and had
  Thomas born November 30, 1661, died December 14
  Mary born March 9 1662
  Thomas born May 21, 1666
  Abigail born June 27, 1668
  Hannah born Jan 30, 1670
  William born Nov 30, 1673
  Hester born June 2, 1676

1678.  Thomas French and John Safford are appointed to mend the highway from the meeting house down the Mill street and Topsfield and Andover road.

John 2 son Thomas 1, was a Denison subscriber 1648, and was entitled to a share in Plum Island, 1664.  He had
  Thomas born May 25, 1657
  Mary February 27, 1659
  Samuel February 26, 1661
  Hannah March 8, 1664

Edward was of Ipswich 1637; he was an inhabitant Salisbury, 1640. commoner 1620, and died 1675.  In his will dated April 13, 1675, he speaks of his great age; he bequeaths legacies to grand children: Joseph, Symond, Edward, sons of Joseph French; John eldest son of John French; Samuel eldest son of Samuel French; and a "son of my son John now newly born."

Susan. widow of Joseph French, died August, 1656; probably the widow French, who was commoner, 1641.


FULLER, William, aged 73, in 1681, was of Ipswich in 1635; but his name does not appear on a list of commoners, 1641; he removed before that time to Hampton; he possessed an houselot near the river, abbutting on the lot which Mr Samuel Symonds purchased of Mr Henry Sewall in 1637.  In 1635 he had "an house lot wh. he bought of John Hassell," also he had a houselot granted him by the town, joining to half an acre he bought of William Simmons.

John Fuller was one of Gen. Denison's subscribers in 1648, surveyor 1663, commoner 1664; he married Elisabeth daughter of Tho: Emerson; he possessed land near *Rocky Hill; he died June 4, 1666, leaving and children:— William, John, James, Thomas, Nathaniel, Joseph, and daughters, Susanna, Elizabeth. Mary.

The following are extracts from his will, proved Sept 25, 1666, by Mr Willm Hubbard, jr., and Symon Tompson:

" I give to my son John twenty pounds.

To son William five shillings when he is of age; to him and his brother John I bequeath no more because their uncle hath undertaken to give sufficient portions.

To my daughters Susanna and Elisabeth I give ten shillings apiece at the day of their marriage, or when they are 20 yrs of age; to whom also I give no more because their grandfather hath lately given them portions. [See Thomas Emerson.]

I make my wife and my son James executors; but in case my wife shall marry, my will is that James shall have the disposing of my whole estate; until his other brother come of age.

Son James shall pay his mother seven pounds a year during the time of her natural life, or else suffer her to enjoy her thirds.

My estate to be divided into seven equal parts, and as much as one seventh part amounts to shall be paid by my said executors to each of my children not already mentioned, viz. Thomas, Nathaniel, Joseph, Sarah, and yt wch is to be born, after they come to age, and my son James to enjoy the remainder to himself.

I desire the Honbl Mr Symonds and Major Denison would be ye overseers of this my last will.

Thomas 2 son of John 1, died about Sept 24, 1689, when his brothers John, James, Joseph and Nathaniel appeared as his heirs.

James 2 son James 1 married Mary Ring, Oct 20, 1672, had
    James born December 2, 1673
    Mary born May 30, 1675
    John born February 20 1676
    Elisabeth born February 25, 1678
    Daniel born February 24, 1680
    Nathaniel born February 18, 1682

He died June 21, 1725; Mary, his widow, died October 16, 1732, aged 85 years.

---

* The house built by Theodore Andrews, Esq., and now (1881) owned by Mr. Burnham, is on the site of John Fuller's house at Rocky Hill.

James 3 son James 2 was commoner, 1707.

Joseph 2 son John 1, married Mary Hayward Oct 1685, had

   Joseph born August 13 1690

   Thomas born April 6 1692

   William born March 7 1693

   John born May 16 1698

He was commoner 1707. In the new meeting house, 1700, he had a seat assigned him. He had the title of Serj't; he died August 22, 1731, aged 73 years; he had granted to him the third lot of 28 feet between Samuel Ordway's shop and the town bridge, March 1692-3; he subscribed 10s toward the bell, 1699.

Nathaniel had a seat in the meeting house, 1700; Daniel, ditto.

GILBERT Humphrey, was a commoner, 1648. He purchased of John Woodham, Feb. 5, 1650 "The house and land the said John Woodam bought of John West, 28 June, 1649." His will is dated February 14, and was proved March 30, 1657-8. In it his name is spelt Gilbard. He left a wife named Elizabeth, a son John, and four daughters.

Dea. John Gilbert was of the Hamlet; was Commoner Feb 15, 1678, married Elizabeth Killam Sept. 27, 1677, and had John and others  He died March 7, 1722.

1670, May.  Mr Thomas Gilbert being presented upon suspicion of being overtaken with drink. The Court finds not the presentment: yet saw cause of counsell & admonish him & order him to pay the witnesses returned by the jury & fees of court.

A more thorough account of Humphrey Gilbert has been given by Henry F. Waters, Esq., which we insert:

## HUMPHREY GILBERT.

BY HENRY F. WATERS, ESQ., SALEM, MASS.

Humphrey Gilbert, born about 1616, according to his deposition on file in the office of the Clerk of the Courts of Middlesex Co., in East Cambridge, seems to have had two wives. By the first (whose name is not known,) he had four daughters; by the second, Elizabeth ——, one son. He is said to have died 13 Feb. 1657, which may have been a mistake of one day; for his will purports to be made the 14th of 12th mo (Feb'y.) 1657, probably while he lay at the point of death. His widow, Elizabeth, was married 24 Sept. 1658, to William Reiner, who died 26 Oct. 1672. She next became the wife of Henry Kimball, who died before the 16th 4th mo. 1676, which was the date of the taking of his inventory. Among the items in this inventory was "a house & 12 acres of land wch was the widows before she marryed with him, 40 00 00." Among the debts were, "to ye remainder of legacies to Humphry Gilbert's children 00 06 11," "to 2 oxen & 2 cowes mentioned in Hum: Gilbert's will prized at 02 05 00," "to ye price of about 2 acres or land belonging to Hum: Gilbert's farm, which Wm: Rainer recd of Tho: fisk & gave bond yt ye hiere should give a deed of it when he come of age, being 05 00 00." Her last husband was Daniel Kilham, sen'r, with whom she sells to John Lambson, 19 June 1684, the commonage that was of Humphrey Gilbert's house formerly.

Mr. Gilbert's will was not recorded but remains on file in the Probate Registry of Essex County. It is as follows:

The 14 of thi 12 mo'th, 1657.

The last will & Testement of Humfrey Gilbard haueing his perfect memery dwelling in the boundes of Ipswich after my debtes being payde:

I giue unto my son John all the middow-Vpland wch is my farme one hundred Ackers more or less & that this farme be let out or Improued acording to my wifes discretion for the bringing of my Child vpp till he com to age or be able to Improue it himselfe | and it is my will that twentie pounds be payde oute of the Incom of my farme to my foure daughters when they are seaventene years of age & in case god take any of them a way by death be fore the age specied that her proportian shall be aqually divided to the rest of the sisters or if a second or a third still it to com to she that doe remaine moreouer it is my will that tow oxen and tow Cows that I haue now In possession be let oute with the farme I doe also give Vuto my daughter Abbigall one heffer of foure yeares olde | I doe giue Vnto my loueing and deare wiffe Elisebeth Gilbard twelve ackers of Vpland with my dwelling Howse | I doe likewise giue Vnto my wiffe my fetherbed wth the furniture thereunto belonging.

It is my will In case my son shold die in his nonage that what I haue given to my son should be equially deuided a mongst my daughters.

*Witnesses:* Charles Gott        *The mark* **H** *of Humfre Gilbard.*
　　　　　　Thomas Hobes
　　　　　　Richard Hutton

Administration Granted to Elizabeth Gilbard late wife to Humphrey Gilbert to order the estate acording to the will aboue writtan.
　　Recd in Court held at Ipswich the 30th of March 1658
　　　　　　　　　　p me Robert Lord cleric.

The 100 ackers spoken of in the will he bought 25 (3) 1650, of Edmund Frost, Edmund Angier, Nathaniel Sparhawk and John  Cooper, feofees of the estate of Nathaniel Sparhawk, late of Cambridge, dec'd, described as in some part of Ipswich bounds towards Wennam.

The children that Humphrey Gilbert is known to haue had were :

Martha, m Richard Coomer, 23 8 1663

Hannah, m Peter Harvey, January 1670

Mary, m Richard Palmer, 24 9 1672

Abigail, m Moses Elberne (or Aborern)abt 1679

John, born about 1656-7, m 27 Sept. 1677, Elizabeth, dau of
Daniel and Mary (Safford) Kilham

John Gilbert, only son of Humphrey Gilbert, lived in Ipswich Hamlet, near the Wenham line.  He was a member of the church at Wenham until the formation of the church at the Hamlet, of which he was chosen one of the first deacons, 9 Nov. 1714 ; he died 17 March, 1722-3, aged 67 years,—says gravestone.  By wife Elizabeth he had a number of children, of whom the births of only two have been found recorded, and the careless records of baptism kept by the  Rev'd Joseph Gerrish of Wenham throw very little light on the matter :

John, born 14 July, 1678, m Martha Dodge of Beverly, pub.
23 Dec. 1799, removed to Kettle Cove ; ancestor of the
Gloucester Gilberts.

Daniel, born about 1680, (gravestone,) m Elizabeth Porter of
Wenham, pub. 2 Dec. 1710, lived in Marblehad.

Mary, baptized before 1682

Mary, born 10 January 1682

Elizabeth, bap. between 1682 and 1685, m John Davis 23
Dec. 1711

Mary, bap between 1685, '88, m  John Hull, pub Nov. 1706.

Martha, bap 1688 or 1689

Joseph and Benjamin, twins, said to have been born 1 Feb. 1691,
Joseph removed to Littleton, m (1) Mary Cogswell, 1718,
(2) Elizabeth Whipple, 1739 ; Benjamin m Esther, dau of
John and Mary (Fiske) Perkins of Wenham,  Aug. 1716,
he died in North Brookfield, 24 June 1760.

Lydia, bap 1702

Noah, bap 21 Nov 1703, m Sarah Allen 12 Feb. 1727-8 :  no further records

Sarah, m Nathaniel Gott about 1708

GILMAN Edward. with his sons Edward and John  were early inhabitants of Ipswich.   Edward the son granted to his father a piece of land July 28, 1648, which land Edward sen'r sold to his "brother Richard Smith," October 2, 1651.   He also sold land to his son John, December 10, 1650.

Belknap statss: Elisabeth dau of Richard Smith of Ipswich, m Edw Gilman, jr.   In Sept. 1648, he sold to his father his place in Ipswich, which had been given to him by his father-in-law, Richard Smith, and settled in Exeter.   He was active, enterprising and judicious, and immediately became a leading and popular man.   About 1652 he went home to England for mill gearing, and never returned; he was lost at sea.

GIDDINGS, George, was a commoner 1641; one of Major Denison's subscribers 1648: one of the 20 sworn free-holders who paid the highest rates out of 240, in 1664; selectman 1661, '75; he died June 1, 1676; his widow Jane died March 2, 1680.  The inventory of his estate, June 19, 1676, exhibited a total value of £1021 12s. of which 152 acres of land with six acres of marsh at Plum Island were app. at £772.   Sept 26, 1676, an agreement between the sons of George Giddings, deceased, viz. Thomas the eldest, John, James and Samuel respecting a division of their father's estate was entered into.

John, commonage granted Feb 1667; tythingman 1679; inventory amounting to £269 15 10, rendered Feb 20, 1690; estate distributed March 29, 1692.   Sarah Herrick relict. Children—George 28, Eliz'th Haskell, Jane Harradine, Sarah 20, John 17, Job 15, Solomon 13, Joshua 12, Thomas 9, born May 19, 1683, Mary 6.

Thomas, married Mary Goodhue Feb 23, 1668: was a voter in town affairs 1679, commoner 1678; his estate divided among his children, Thomas, William and Mary, May 16, 1694.

Job,—Sarah Giddings appointed adm'x of her husband Job Giddings, April 5, 1709.

Thomas,—Elizabeth Choate, adm'x of her husband Thomas Giddings, April 24, 1710.   Thomas was freeman May 12, 1675; his widow married John Choate.   The heirs of Thomas were William Giddings, Thomas Manning, gunsmith, in right of his wife Mary, Jane, Dorothy by her guardian Thomas Manning.

Samuel and Hannah Martin m October 4, 1671; had Samuel born November 1674. Lawrence born March 30, 1685.

George, had a dau Elizabeth born July 29, 1699.

James and James jr. had horses on common 1697.  James had a son George May 1683.

William and George were commoners, 1707.

Joseph the inventory of his estate appraised by John Andrews and

William Goodhue, jr., amounting to £206 6 12; rendered Dec 10, 1690; he had Joseph, born June 9, 1672.

1667, March 26, Stephen Crose, William Andres and Joseph Giddings for their great misdemeanors in pulling up bridges, &c. fined.

GAINES, John, had a share in Plum Island, &c. 1644; he died about 1688, and left a wife, one son, and four unmarried daughters.

His will dated Sept 14, and proved the 24th, 1688, bequeaths to his four daughters "sixteen pounds that is to say to each of them four pounds to be paid to them by the sum of 20s a year." He bequeaths his house and land to his wife with reversion to his son John; he appoints his wife ex'x and John Harris, sen'r overseer. The witnesses were John Harris, Wm Baker, Thomas Lord, jr.; his property was appraised at £136 6s. of which was house and land about it £70. " In ye shoemakers shop, lasts," &c., 17s. He m Mary Treadwell in 1659 and had

 John
 Mary born June 11, 1660
 Martha born November 17, 1661
 Sarah born November 23, 1665
 Abigail born December 29, 1677
 Elizabeth born March 19, 1669
 Abyell born May 6, 1672

GOULD, Henry, had the right of turning his horses on the common in 1697; his wife was Sarah, and they had,

 Sarah born November, 1678
 Isaac born November 1, 1679
 Joanna born November 19, 1681
 Henry born March 4, 1688
John Gould married Sarah Baker, Oct 14, 1660, had John Dec 1 61

GOODENOUGH, David, died in 1698. The inventory of his estate rendered Feb 6, 1698-9, amounted to £9 6 6, by Francis Crompton, adm. He had a son Robert born Feb 27, 1682. 1700, Nov 24, Philip Fowler and Michael Farley appraised the estate of David Goodenough all that Mr Crumpton put in our hands.

GAGE, John, was one of the 12 who came with John Winthrop the younger and began the settlement of Agawam in March 1633. In 1652, " The town having appointed John Gage, Daniel Bradley, and Humphrey Gilbert to run the line with Wenham men between the town of Wenham and Ipswich." &c. The return is signed " Austin

Kilham, mark **K**, Edward Kemp, William Fisk, John Gages mark **I**, Humphrey Gilberts mark **G**."

1636, February, " Mr. Winthrop, Mr. Bradstreet, Mr. Denison, Goodman Perkins, Goodman Scott, John Gage, and Mr. Wade, are chosen to order Town business for three months following." "Order-ed to lay out Mr Dudley, Mr Bradstreet, and Mr Saltingstalls farme, before the 14 of May, 1637." John Gage was a commoner, 1641; and one of the Denison subscribers, 1648, and had a share and a half in Plum Island, 1664, was freeman 1635, and one of the seven men, 1636; he had an houselot in the "cross st called meeting house lane," 1635; his wife Amy, died June 1658, and he m Sarah Keyes, Nov-ember 7, 1658.

GEDNEY, Bartholomay, son of John of Salem was baptized June 14, 1640, admitted freeman 1669, elected assistant 1680-83: one of Sir Edmond Andros' council 1687; one of the first council under Wil-liam and Mary, 1692; died March 1, 1698, æt 58.—*Farmer.* He was Judge of Probate for the County of Essex from the institution of that court until his decease; his wife Anne died Oct 15, 1697, aged 56 years, and was buried in Ipswich. [Her first husband was Mr. William Stewart of Ipswich, who "dyed August ye 3, 1693."]

[Sewall writes; "Oct. 17, 1697. Col. Gedney had his wife to Ips-wich, as he went to Newbury Court, and she falls sick and dyes there in about three weeks time. Died on Friday night last. Heard not of it till this day."]

> Here Lyeth Byried
> ye Body of Mr'is
> Anne Gedney ye
> wife of Co'll Bartholo-
> mew Gedney aged
> 56 years departed
> this Life October
> 15          1697

Col. Gedney left a large property in Salem, from some items of which it appears that he was engaged in commerce, in distilling and in the manufactory of tobacco; he was appointed to a town office in Ipswich, Feb 23, 1696.

GLAZIER, Zacerias, m Hannah Emerson April 24, 1685, and had Joseph born October 15, 1691.

GRANGER, Lancelot, a Denison sub. 1648, moved to Newbury.

GARDNER, Edmund, had granted to him with the title of *Mr.* "a house lot where his house now standeth," Feb 1636. He possessed

land in 1640.  1642, 21st 7th month.  It is agreed between the Town
and Mr Edmund Gardiner for the making and constant keeping of the
meeting house tight as followeth, viz.  Mr Gardiner doth undertake
and covenant that he will within one month set the meeting house
water tight, and that he will constantly keep and preserve the same in
the like condition so long as he shall live and abide in Ipswich.

GOODHUE, William, took the freeman's oath, Dec 7, 1636 ; he
had a houselot in Ipswich, 1635, and afterward much other land by
grant and purchase.  1639.  Granted to William Goodhue six acres of
planting ground on the south side of the town river, butting on the
same river north west, and upon meadow grounds of John Perkins, jr.
south east, having a planting lot of Mathias Buttons on the east and
a planting lot of John Perkins on the west.  Also six acres of land
lying on the town river about half a mile above the mill having a parcel of ground of Thomas Birds on the east, and a planting lot of
Henry Archer's on the north, and ten acres of land granted to Nath'l
Bishop on the south.  Also a parcel of land about two miles up the
town river, encompassed on the south east and south west by the river
and running from the east from a dry pit to the west, &c.  26 acres
more or less.  Also he is possessed of a house being about three
roods of ground lying in the street called the east end bounded by the
said street on the south east, having a houselot of John Winthrop on
the southwest and a houslot formerly granted to Robert Cole and now
in possession of Isaac Cummings on the north-east.  This houselot he
bought of Joseph Medcalf who bought it of Robert Cole.  Entered on
Town Book 9th day of second mo. 1639.  1644, Feb 27, granted to
William Goodhue eight acres of marsh and four of upland.

1646, April 5, he purchased of John Newman an house in " Brook
street alias Hog Lane," between the dwelling house of Francis Jordan and Joseph Morse.  In the deed which was acknowledged April
19, 1649, he is styled William Goodhue, weaver.

In 1649, he possessed an houselot at the east end of High st. near
the river, adjoining an houselot of Mr John Winthrop ; and also an
house with six acres of land which his father-in-law Watson purchased
for him of Doct. Giles Firman in London, after Doct. Firman had removed from this country.  Mr. Goodhue seems to have possessed considerable property and to have attained to rank and influence ; he was
a commoner in 1641 ; one of Major Denison's subscribers in 1648 ; of
the 27 who paid the highest taxes in 1664 ; select man 1664 ; and had
the right of voting in town affairs in 1679.  He was deacon of the
church from 1658 ; and representative to General Court eight years,

between 1666 and 1683 ; he was one of those who was fined and imprisoned for resisting the arbitrary proceedings of Sir Edmund Andros in 1687 ; his first wife was Margery Watson who died Sept. 30, 1668, by whom he had, Joseph, William, Mary. He m for second wife Mary Webb, Sept 7, 1669, she was a widow and the dau of Henry Osborne.

1697, July 29, William Goodhue and Mary his wife who sign with marks, release to Henry Osborn claim to estate of Mary Marchant, John Osborne and Henry Osborn the same. Wm Goodhue was tythingman 1697 ; he died about 1700 aged 85 years.

Joseph 2 son of William 1, was freeman March 11, 1673-4 ; representative 1672-3 ; he came into full communion with the church February 22, 1673-4, was selectman 1697 ; he died Sept 2, 1697 ; he m July 13, 1661, Sarah dau of Elder John Whipple, who died July 23, 1681, and left ten children. About ten days before her decease she wrote a *Farewell*, directed to her "husband and children with other near relatives and friends." This was printed at Cambridge, 1681. He married a second wife, wid. Rebecca Todd, Oct. 15, 1684 ; and July 4, 1692, a third, the widow Clark, who probably survived him. Mary Goodhue was appointed guardian of Samuel son of Deacon Joseph her husband, being under 2 years of age, December 6, 1697.

1699-00, Feb. 5. Thomas Knowlton appointed guardian to Hannah Goodhue daughter of Mr Joseph Goodhue, yeoman, &c. "being a minor 14 years of age & upwards." 1700-1, Mch 10, John Kimball appointed guardian of Joseph Goodhue son of Joseph, 14 years of age and upwards. "An accompt of Sundry Goods Deacon Joseph Goodhue late of Ipswich took into his hands of estate of Josiah Clark Deceased upon his marraige to Mercy Clark the relict of sd Josiah." Mr Joseph Goodhue had the 12th lot of 18 feet between the bridge and Samuel Ordway's shop, March 23, 1692-3.

The children who survived him according to Mr Felt were, William, Mary Norton, Margery Knowlton, Sarah Kimball, Susanna Kimball, Joseph, and Anna Todd his step-daughter. Anna Todd afterward married Edmund Heard. He also had Ebenezer, Benjamin, Samuel.

William Goodhue 2 son of William 1, was a Captain and also a Deacon of the Church at Chebacco, a freeman Oct 12, 1682, selectman 1696, '98, representative nine years between 1691 and 1711 ; he married Nov 14, 1666, Hannah Dane, by whom he had

> William born Nov 13, 1667
>
> Hannah, born July 4, 1673, m 1 Lieut. John Cogswell, 2 Thomas Perley.
>
> Nathaniel, born October 24, 1672

Joseph, born March 5, 1676

Francis, born October 4, 1678, 1699 became the minister of Jamaica, Long Island, and died at Rehoboth, when on his way to Ipswich, September 16, 1707.

Elisabeth, December 19, 1680

Margery, August 12, 1683, m Giddings

John born August 2 died Sept 19, 1685

In his will dated Oct 3, 1712 he mentions his wife Hannah and sons Nath'l Joseph, and John.

William Goodhue 3, son of Joseph 2, and Mary his wife had

Mary born August 3, 1690, died April 10 1694

John born August 28, 1693

Sarah born May 24, 1695

Elizabeth born February 7, 1696

Hannah born March 27 1699

He died 1722, and Mary his wife died 1729 :

Here Lies ye Body of Mr William Goodhue who died July the 10, 1722, aged about 56 years.

Here Lies ye Body of Mrs Mary Goodhue ye wife of Mr William Goodhue who died Septemr ye 4, 1729 in 63 year of age.

Joseph 3, with Abigail his wife had

Francis born June 2, 1710

Joseph born August 14, 1712

William born May 8, 1715

Abigail born August 7, 1717

David and Jonathan born February 14, 1722

1688, Dec 6, died Bethiah wife of Deakn Goodhue.

1689, Dec 3, married Deacon Goodhue and the widow Remember Fisk. 1701-2, Feb 16, died Mrs Remember Goodhue. Remember Goodhue's will dated Feb 14, 1701-2, proved March 31, 1702 ; dau. Elizabeth ffisk being in needful circumstances she bequeaths to her all her property ; friend Daniel Rogers and son Joseph Ayres to have inspection. Witnesses, Daniel Rogers, John Sparke and Joseph Ayres.

1721, August 18, died Capt Nathaniel Goodhue at Chebacco.

William Goodhue who m a Lord, son William who m an Adams died in January, 1808, aged 80. Moses son of William born Oct 10, 1766 ; Aaron November 1761.

GROVE, John had liberty for firewood and one cow on the common in 1664 ; he died Jan 19, 1727, aged "upwards of 90." He m Hannah Lord Dec 15 1669, and had

John born Dec 8, 1670, died 1671
Samuel born Decemher 3, 1671
John born December 16, 1673
Hannah born January 3, 1679
Nathaniel born September 18, 1682
Thomas born February 20, 1684
William born November 22, 1690

Samuel and Ruth had
Mary born May 17, 1695
Samuel born August 31, 1696
Ruth born February 14, 1698

John and Samuel had horses on the common in 1697, and the name is then written GROW.

GRIFFIN, Humphrey. 1639. The Town doth refuse to receive Humphry Griffin as an inhabitant to provide for him as inhabitants formerly received, the Town being full.

Mr Griffin however soon became a commoner by purchase. Jan 19 1641, he purchased of Daniel Denison the dwelling house and land near the mill which was granted to Denison in 1635 ; also meadow at Labor-in-vain, and a planting lot at Heartbreak hill. He seems to have removed to Rowley ; he died about September 19, 1662, leav-in a widow Elizabeth. His wife Joan died July 17, 1657.

Samuel and Lydia had a dau Elizabeth who died Oct 2, 1684.

1641, Jan. 19. Daniel Denison conveys to Humphrey Griffin a dwelling house near the mill. 1648, 1st 4th, John Burnam conveys to Anthony Potter a house lot late of Humphrey Griffin, scituate near the water mill. 1661, Jan 19, Anthony Potter and Elizabeth his wife convey to John Safford, dwelling and land three acres. north side of the river near the mill, bounded with highway round.

GREEN, Henry, was a commoner, 1641, and possessed a dwelling house and land which he mortgaged May 12, 1642 to Daniel Denison.

Thomas Green, Denison subscriber, 1648.

GUTTERSON, William, was a subscriber to Major Denison, 1648, and had a share in Plum Island in 1664 ; he died June 26, 1666 ; he had William born September 20, 1658, died 1669
Mary born August 8, 1660
John born March 24, 1661
Sarah born July 3, 1665

GREGORY, James, witness to Thomas Lee's will.

Jonas Gregory, (see Emerson,) m Hannah Dow 1670, she died Feb 22, 1671, m Elizabeth Hely, May, 1672. 1677, March, Jonas Gregory, the whipper, for abusing the Court sentenced to be whipped. 1678. March, Jonas Gregory allowed 20s a year for his employ as whipper on year past out of which his fine is set off.

GRANT, Robert, married Mary Foster, Feb 27, 1686. 1708, The will of Roger Grant dated September 8 and proved the 27, 1708, mentions sons Roger, John and Robert; and daughter Allis Escott, and grand-daughter Joanna Henderson.

GOSS, Richard. Here Lies ye Body of Mr. Richard Goss, who died January ye 24, 1714-5, aged 52 years.

> For this departed soul
> And all the rest
> That Christ hath purchased
> They shall be blest.

GAMAGE John, had a son John born Jan 6, 1676, Nath'l born Feb 10, 1678, Mary born July 15, 1681.

GRAVES, Samuel, born 1624, had a share in Plum Island 1694, with his wife Joanna he had:

> Samuel born August 5, 1658, died Nov 22, 1679
> John born August 1, 1660
> Elizabeth born June 29, 1667
> Hannah born Dec 19, 1663

He had a seat assigned to him among the most elderly men behind ye pulpit, 1700. He is mentioned in 1678 as hatter.

Samuel probably his son has a place assigned to him in meeting house, 1700, on seat No 8.

Martha is appointed July 21, 1699, adm'x on the estate of John Graves her husband, which consisted of an house and land. Sept. 4, she was appointed guardian of Martha and Sarah, dau. of John Graves corwainer.

In 1674, Francis Graves, a boy, came to New England and a few months before had been preceded by his brother John. Both were consigned to Mr. Symonds; and became his charge; they were nephews of Mr Samuel Hall, mentioned in Felt's history, and came to Ipswich by his sanction and advice.

HARRIS. Elizabeth, widow, became the wife of Deacon Stitson of

Charlestown and died Feb 16, 1669-70, aged 93 years; was the mother of John, Thomas, William. Daniel Harris and Mrs Annie Maverick relict widow of Elias Maverick, so mentioned by Dea Stitson in his will made April 12, 1688, as the children of his first wife.

William son of Elisabeth is known to have had a houselot assigned him and to have lived a short time in Rowley, where John, Thomas and Daniel Harris also had houselots assigned to them at or about the same time.

Thomas one of twenty soldiers sent against the indians under Serj. Howlet in 1648; he was a Denison subscriber in 1648; with Martha his wife he sells lands in Rowley to Thomas and Richard Holmes and Richard Baley in 1652, tithingman 1677. In 1674 he is witness to the will of John Perkins; his will is dated July, 1687; witnessed by Daniel Epps, sen'r and James Chute, sen'r, and was proved Sept 14; he bequeaths to his wife Martha, whom he appoints exec'x, "house, barn, orchard, garden," &c. during her natural life. To his son John he gives the new house which he built in Ipswich; he gives legacies also to sons William and Ebenezer: the inventory of his estate amounted to £576 11 3. Martha Harris represents in a petition to the Court January 1695, that she is widow and executrix of Thomas Harris who left three sons, John, William, Ebenezer and also two other children, viz. Elizabeth wife of John Gallop and Margaret wife of John Staniford, not mentioned in her husband's will,

Thomas Harris and Martha Lake were married Nov. 15, 1647, [see Antiquarian Papers, September, 1881; and May, 1882,] She was dau. of Mrs. Margaret Lake, who died about Sept. 1672, and bequeathed property to her and to another dau. Hannah Gallop. The will of Margaret Lake of Ipswich, widow, will be found under head of Lake, Margaret.

There appears to have been another Thomas Harris in Ipswich, cotemporary with the above, whose wife was also named Martha; his widow had in 1683, become the wife of Samuel Burnham; his children were Thomas, John, Elinor, Aquilla and Mary.

A Thomas Harris had a share in Plum Island in 1664.

Anthony, son of Elizabeth, was a member of the artillery company in 1644, and was one of Major Denison's subscribers, 1648; he was of Chelsea in 1664, and there made his will April 23, 1651, wherein he named his wife Elizabeth, and his brothers Daniel, Thomas and Elias Maverick. He died Dec. 30, 1651.

William 3 son of Thomas 2, was born Dec 12, 1664; his wife was Sarah, daughter of Thomas Newman.

John and Ester had Margaret born May 22, 1685.

John and Mary had John born Nov 19, 1690; Joanna born Jan 18, 1691; Mary July 19, 1694; Thomas Oct 10, 1696; Sarah 1698.

John, quartus, and Margaret had Daniel born April 24, 1696.

Ebenezer son of Thomas and Martha (Lake,) married Rebecca Clarke Sept 15, 1690, and had Thomas born March 22, 1692-3: Ebenezer July 11, 1694.

Nathaniel and Mary had Nathaniel born Feb 7, 1697.

John joined the church March 1, 1676; commoner 1675.

John, jr. John, quartus, mash'll, and Thomas and William had horses on the common, 1697.

Sergt John and John 3d, fishermen, so designated in 1699, were commoners in 1707.

John Harris and Widow Susannah Wardwell m Nov 19, 1700.

John Harris, mars. subscribed to the bell 1699.

William Harris died Dec 31, 1751, aged 93.

Here Lyeth ye Body of Mr John Harris under Sheriff who died Sept ye 15, 1714 & in ye 64 Year of his age.

[To Mr. Hammatt's gleanings we add a Paper by a young man, prepared in 1882, concerning Serjt Harris, who was perhaps son of John Harris of Rowley, cousin of Rev. Nath'l Rogers; if so he was born October 8, 1649, married Elisabeth Wells October 27, 1677; she was buried December 29, 1679. In 1685 he is the husband of Grace and a resident of Ipswich. Can any one give light on this?]

## SERJEANT JOHN HARRIS, OF IPSWICH,

### And some of his Descendants.

#### BY WILLIAM SAMUEL HARRIS, WINDHAM, N. H.

Serjeant John Harris died in Ipswich, November 21 1732, Ætatis 82; he was born therefore about 1650. He married January 8, 1685, Grace, daughter of William and Grace Searle of Ipswich. She died June 10, 1742. Serjt John and Grace had the following children born in Ipswich:

William born November 26, 1690
Rebecca born January 11, 1692
Samuel born April 9, 1695
Martha born December 2 1698
Daniel born November 22, 1700
Richard baptized November 25, 1705

Richard Harris and Martha Foster were published May 10, 1735; she was the daughter of Jacob and Martha Foster, and was born in Ipswich the 16th of the 10th month, 1710, and died in Harvard Sept 8, 1756. He married (2) Mrs Phebe Atherton, nee Wright, widow of John Atherton. Richard Harris removed from Ipswich to Harvard in 1743 and died there Dec 20, 1776, aged 71 years and 26 days. Richard and Martha had ten children.

Jacob, the fourth child, was baptized in Ipswich Feb 15, 1741.

Rebekah, the seventh was born in Harvard March 25, baptised 27, 1748.

*Dea. Jacob Harris, 1741–1826.*

Jacob, whose portrait is given above, lived in Harvard from the age of two years until early manhood, when he settled in Ashburnham. He joined the Congregational church in Ashburnham, 1769; was Deacon from 1788 till death. In 1826 he went to Windham, N. H., and died there Sept. 26, of that year; is buried in W. He married (1) October 26, 1769, Elisabeth, daughter of Rev Jonathan Winchester, first minister of Ashburnham. He married (2) August 21, 1783, Mrs. Anna M. Warren, *nee* Merriam; married (3) 1792, Mrs Ruth Pratt, *nee* Pool, widow of Edward Pratt. Dea. Jacob had seven children, one of whom was Rev. Samuel Harris, Pastor of the Prespyterian church in Windham, N. H. from 1805 to 1826; another was Jacob, jr., a ruling elder in the same church many years. The above portrait was copied [by A. W. Dowe] from a hand sketch drawn in 1826, shortly before his death at the age of 85.

Rebekah Harris, sister of Deacon Jacob, married Grover Scollay Nov 4, 1779; lived in Ashburnham; she died in Rindge, N. H. Mch 21, 1819. Grover and Rebekah joined the Cong'l church in Ashburnham, 1796. They had five children of whom the oldest was Samuel, born January 21, 1781.

Samuel Scollay, (see profile,) was graduated at H. C. 1808; taught in a private family and studied medicine a few years in Virginia, and graduated in medicine at the University at Pennsylvania, 1816. Practiced in Smithfield, Jefferson Co. Va. (now West Va.) where he

*Samuel Scollay, M. D.*

died Jan 11, 1857.   He was one of the most distinguished physicians in Jefferson Co.   He married (1) Jan 21, 1822, Harriot Lowndes; he m (2) Jan 21, 1842. Sally Page Nelson, granddaughter of General Thomas Nelson, a signer of the Declaration of Independence.   She still lives in Smithfield.   Dr. Scollay had eight children   The profile was made [by Mr. Dowe,] from the original made in 1822.

HAFFIELD Richard, had an houselot granted to him in 1635, beyond Mr Hubbard's having the highway to Chebacco on the south, and an houselot of Robert Andrews on the east; he sold an house and lot entered on record in 1639, to Thomas Firman being in the cross st to the meeting house, bounded by the highway leading to the mill on the south.   He probably died before 1641, in which year the widow Haffield is recorded as commoner.

1641. Jo: Lee accused for stealing of a Bible of the widow Haffield is found guilty; he shall restore 15s to the widow and pay Xs fine for lying.

1665, Aug. 30, voted at a meeting of the seven men to the widow Haffield four rods of ground by the corner of William Averill's fence near the mill dam for 12 pence, to build a little house upon, allowing no privilege of a houselot to it.

1662, June 11, Martha Haffield will: daughters Mary Cobbit, Sarah ———? Marthe Coye, Ruth White, Rachel Haffield; house and land now in hand of Richard Brabrooke. Richard Hubbard ex., witnesses, Samuel Younglove, David Warner, sen'r. Proved Mch 31, 1668. Inventory £349 16 6. Farm £300. A small house and 4 rods of land £6 10s. Among the articles mentioned—one silver bowle two silver spoons, one silver-tipped jugge. Inventory by John Whipple, sen'r, Rich: Hubbard.

HADLEY, George, was an inhabithnt in 1689, and was a voter in town affairs 1679; married Deborah Skelling October 28, 1668. He died Sept 30, 1686.

John Hadley married Susan Piffis Sept 3, 1682.

HARDYE, Thomas, was one of the twelve who came with John Winthrop, jr. and commenced the settlement of Agawam, March 1632 3. Perry in his Historical Sermon at Bradford speaks of John and William Hardy, brothers, who came to New England in the family of Gov Winthrop as laborers to whom the Gov. gave land in Ipswich. In 1636 he had a house lot near the river adjoining Robert Adams and Thomas Howlet. He was one of Major Denison's subscribers, 1648.

Robert Lord in his account book without date, but probably about 1680, charges William Hardy for proving and recording his father's will and inventory, 9d.

HASSELL, John, took the freeman's oath at Boston, March 9, 1636-7. He had a houselot in 1635, near the river, adjoining Wm White which he sold to William Fuller. He was one of Major Denison's subscribers in 1648, and had a share in Plum Island, &c. in 1664 Margaret his wife died Feb 5, 1660.

HAYES, Robert, was an inhabitant in 1638; he had a houselot granted to him which he sold to Thomas Bishop, who sold it to John Andrews, who sold it to William Knowlton, who on the last day of February 1643 sold it to Edward Bragg.

HAYWARD, (see Howard,) William and Tabitha had Samuel b October 3, 1685; commoner 1698. In 1695 his son William m Martha Hodgkins.

April 15, 1686, died "old Thomas Hayward." By an account with Robert Lord in 1678 he appears to have been a hatter; in this acc't he is charged for "recording a marriage and birth," "for recording three births."

Nehemiah Hayward, will dated Mch 22, 1664-5; mentions wife Anna, and children not named. He desires his loving brethren Nath'l Hayward and John Dickey and father Nicholas Hayward to have oversight of the children  Proved Sept 26, 1665.

HANCHET, John, had granted to him six acres of planting ground, 1638, Nov 19, towards the reedy marsh, having a planting lot of Mark Symons southeast, a planting lot of Edward Treadwell northwest.

HALL, Samuel. He had a house lot near the present south meeting house, described as follows,—" 27 day July, 1638, memorand that: Richard Lumpkin hath sold unto John Tuttle one house and a houselot with certain other lands. One houselot lying near the great cove of the town river having a houselot now in the possession of Wm Avery on the south west, Robert Kinsman's houselot on the northwest the town river on the south east, a houselot now in possession of Samuel Hall on the east; also upon the said lot one dwelling house formerly built by Richard Brown now of Newbury and by him sold unto Mr Richard Saltonstall by whom it was sold unto the said Rich : Lumpkin.

1636. Samuel Hall is ps'ed of eight akers of planting ground by act of ye towne as in ye ould booke anno 1636, lying near ye highway going to ye Labour in Vayne meadowes, Butting to ye east upon ye planting ground of ffrancis Pebody.

Granted since unto Samuel Hall as in the old book 20th February 1686 and laid out the 20th of Februasy, 1637, as followeth, 14 acres of upland lying north east of Stephen Jordan and butting on the North west upon the land of Alexander Knight six acres of meadow lying south east of Stephen Jordaine and on the north west upon the land of Wilson

The first or original list of ye townsmen of Salisbury in ye book of Records contains the names of Mr. William Worcester, Mr Henry Byly, Mr Sam : Hall and Mr John Hall.  This was in 1640.

Mr Byly probably died soon after ; for his widow Rebecca married

Mr John Hall, who, dying, his widow married August 22, 1650, the Rev William Worcester, after whose death she married the Hon. Samuel Symonds.

Samuel Hall who was probably brother to John remained in Salisbury until after 1652 and was the person mentioned in the following extract from Felt's History of Ipswich :

" 1682    Mr. Samuel Hall sometime a resident in Massachusetts had died in Langford near Malden, co. Essex, Eng.  He bequeathed £100 to those who lost by the great fire in Boston and by Indian wars in this colony.  Mr John Hall of Assington near London, was his executor, who sent an order to his mother, Mrs Rebecca Symonds of Ipswich, to dispose of the bequest.

[1882.  We recently read and by kindly permission copied extracts from Letters in the archives of the American Antiquarian Soc. Worcester, written by Mr. John Hall, Assington, Eng. to his mother, Madame Rebekah Symonds of Ipswich ; one of these letters gives the following statements concerning the Hall Legacies :]

" May 23, 1681.   Yt [business] of Mr Sam : Hall and his wife Lie heavie on mee, they hauing given a peise of Land to sel to pay Legacies and it being remote from London about 33 miles as is said in an aguish country Essex, cannot get any one to bid near the value of the Legacies charged vpon it, wch I have offered to Rebate more yn a quarter part of what they at first purchased it for, yet it hath been refused.   And though I have a 12 months time to pay the Legacies, many of the Legaties being poore and others Importunate am forced to disburse moneys to pay ym to allay passionate claments, they fearing the consequences of my mortality.  I therefore doe request and order (if not otherwise disposed of) that the cattle in my Brother Epps hand be sould for money as much as they will yeild ; To enable mee to pay somewhat of the New English Legacies, viz. the 50lb to Boston poore pple yt were made soe by the great fire their ; and the 50 Lb to such poore as suffered of the Massachusetts colony by the Indian warr in the distribution wherof I purpose to entrust my worthy friend Mr Stoughton, the matter being by Samuel Hall will left to my discretion vnlesse you know particular freinds to commend to mee soe qualified as may Receive it whome in my Instructions to Mr Stoughton, I resolve shall be preferred, and I thinke Moses Woster as you did Intimate was a sufferer, and shall be one.

Your servt ffrancis Graves hath a Legacie of five pounds ; but John Graves [his brother] it seems in returning nothing of what he received lost his uncle and Ants favour quite.  [Mr S. Hall paid the passage money of John and Francis Graves, two lads sent over as servants of Mr Symonds. Francis refunded his passage money according to agreement, but John neglected to. The legacy was the same amount as the passage money had been.]

He writes again, March 30, 1682. "Moses Worcester was one; and if any of old Barnards of Salisbury New Towne children be poore by reason of their father's massacre, I leave their relief to your consideration. I would also have ffrancis Graves to have his five pound Legacie that his uncle Hall gave him."

Mr Hammatt gives the names of the following persons who received legacies :

Martha Graves, eight pounds ;

Moses Worcester of Newichiwanack, ten pounds, son of the Rev. William Worcester.

Francis Graves, five pounds ;

Martha Coy, three pounds ; fled to Boston, widow of John Coy of Brookfield, slain ;

Susannah Ayres, 33 shillings, widow of Thomas Ayres, slain.

HART, Thomas, was a commoner, 1641 ; one of the Denison subscribers, 1648 ; had a share and a half in Plum Island, 1664 ; selectman 1663 ; surveyor, 1661. He died March 8, 1673-4 aged 67. His gravestone bears the earliest date but one yet found in the old High street Burying place. His wife Alice died June 8, 1692. In his will dated February 12, 1673, he bequeaths to his two sons Thomas and Samuel a Tan Yard and other property. He mentions a grandchild Thomas Hart and two daughters Sarah Norton and Mary. He appoints his wife ex'x.

Thomas 2, Leftenant, son of Thomas 1, was born about 1640 and died Dec 31, 1717 ; he married Mary Norton Oct 12, 1664. They had

Mary, born August 25, 1665

Thomas, born November 15. 1667

George, born January 11, 1669

Lydia, born March 10, 1671

Samuel, born August 16, 1674

Nathaniel, born April 3, 1677

John, born December 20, 1678

Joseph, born November 18, 1680

See epitaphs 82, 83, 84.

Jan 18, 1696-7. At a meeting &c. voted that Thomas Boarman sen'r, make an acknowledgment for his affronting Lt Thos : Hart or pay a fine of five shillings.

In November, 1698, he was appointed with ten other of the most considerable men to fix a plan for building and paying for a new meeting house.

Samuel 2 son of Thomas 1, commoner, 1678; town treasurer; subscribed to the bell 1699; died Aug 31, 1725 in the 80th year of his age   His widow, Sarah Norton, (m Feb 2, 1678) died May 2, 1727, aged 81 years.

George 3, son Thomas 2, married Elisabeth Wells, May 5, 1698, and had

> Thomas, born March 25, 1699
> Nathaniel, called a currier.
> John, designated as joyner.

Elisabeth, his wife, died July 13, 1722, and he m (2) Martha —— see epitaph 84; he was commoners attorney, 1720; is designated in legal papers, cooper.

1728. George Hart son of Capt Samuel Hart of Portsmouth, died August 19, 1728, aged 19.

William, son of Lieft. Nathaniel Hart died Feb 15, 1732, aged 20 years 6 months.

Abigail, wife of Nathaniel ye third, died Aug 17, 1736, aged 31, "with fower of her children, viz. Henry, Abigail, Lydia, William."

HEIFER, Samuel, was one of Major Denison's subscribers, 1648. He sold a piece of land of about two acres to Robert Payne who gave the same to the Grammar School about 1650; it is part of the lot the school house now stands on.

HODGES, Andrew, who was a commoner 1641; Denison sub 1648, share in Plum Is. 1664; with Lydia his wife he sold land Nathl Piper Mch 18. 1662; m Lydia Brown Nov 27, 1659; he lost a wife Ann, Nov 15, 1658.   Mr Hodges house had right of commonage Feb. 15, 1678; he died Dec 1665.

HORTON Barnabas, 1641, 12 d 1st mo. Barnabas Horton, baker, sold unto Moses Pingry six acres of land within the common fence, Richard Bisgood on south east.

HILL, Henry, 1691, packer and guager.

HOLDRED, William, possessed a houselot and other land on so. side of the river adjoining Daniel Hovev, April 9, 1639.   Removed to Salisbury, 1640.

HOW James, was a commoner 1641, one of Denison subscribers 1648, with the designation of James, sen'r, he had share and half in Plum Island 1664, tithingman 1677. In 1679 he was a voter in town affairs; died May 17, 1702, aged 104 years; he gave testimony relating to the line between Ipswich and Rowley a short time before he died. His wife, Elisabeth, dau of John Dane, died Jan 21, 1693.

Abraham How and Sarah Peabody m March 26, 1678, had
     Love born January 15, 1678
     Increase, born April 12, 1680
     Abraham born June 27. 1686
     Israel born January 24, 1682
     Mark, born May 28, 1695
He died Jan 21, 1717. A seat in the meeting house was assigned to Corp'l Abraham How in 1700.

Mark How with wife Hepsebeth lost eight children, of throat distemper in the course of 23 days—Nov 5-28, 1736,—four sons and four daughters.

Increase How m (1) Mary, who died Aug 31, 1721; he m (2) Susanna Kinsman, May 10, 1723. Widow Susanna How m Capt John Smith, supposed to have been the richest man of his day in Ipswich.
  Increase How was a prominent Inn Keeper; his Tavern stood where Mr Cushing's residence is. He was bitterly opposed to the erection of the first meeting house of the south parish on the Green, as it obstructed the view of his windows.

James, jun'r, m Elisabeth Jackson May 5, 1658, was entitled to a share in Plum Is. 1664, voter in town affairs 1679; he died Feb 15, 1701; he had
     Elisabeth, born June 1, 1661
     Mercy, born February 25, 1664
     James died 1666
     John, born April 17, 1671
     Abigail, born December 3, 1673.

John and Hannah How had
     Martha, born June 13, 1691
     Sarah, born February 8, 1692
     James born March 29, 1694
He died May 22, 1697. Inv. real est £61, personal £16, 19; rendered July 1, 1697.

## HODGKINS.

**COLONEL JOSEPH HODGKINS.**
*Died September 25, 1829, aged eighty-six years.*

HODGKINS, [with genealogical additions to Hammatt.] William Hodgkins, first in Reading afterward in Ipswich   In 1691 he was 69 years old, and was therefore born about 1622.   His widow was Grace, dau. of Osman Dutch of Gloucester, and sister of Robert Dutch, Ipswich, of Brookfield notoriety.   [See Ipswich Antiquarian Papers, December, 1881.]

Children of William Hodgkins :

William, joined the church January 25, 1673
Samuel, born November 2, 1658, lived in Gloucester
Mary, born April 6, 1661
Edward, had wife Martha and dau Mary born June 26, 1685
Hezekiah
Thomas, born 1668 d 1719, m Abigail Hovey
Christopher, m Tabitha Howard ; he was drowned 1724
John, joined the church Jan 25, 1673 ; died Jan 20, 1690
Martha, m William Howard, 1695
Abigail died unmarried November 13, 1720
Hannah, m John Berrye Jan 17, 1670
He had a share in Plum Island, &c. 1654 ; he died Dec 26, 1693.

Samuel 2, born Nov 2, 1658, lived at Gloucester, and had 15 children, viz :

Samuel born October 24, 1684
Hannah, May 18, 1686
John, June 6 1688
Philip, January 25, 1690
William, March 2, 1691
A daughter, May 5, 1694
Jedediah, March 8, 1696
Patience, August 21, 1697
Abigail, June 11, 1699
Mercy, July 28, 1700
David, April 14, 1702
Martha, January 4, 1704
Anna, April 5, 1705
Jonathan, July 1, 1706
Experience, January 31, 1708

The descendants of Samuel 2 are still to be found in Gloucester ; see Babson's History and Notes.

*House in which Col. Joseph Hodgkins died.*

Christopher 2, lived in Ipswich; he married Tabitha Howard, dau of William Howard, January 22, 1689.

Tabitha Howard Hodgkins died September 15, 1735

Christopher Hodgkins was drowned in comieng over Squam March 4, 1724: William Fuzz all so out of a canoe: Thomas Cook, over Squam bar.

The children of Christopher 2 and Tabitha:

Christopher, born December 8, 1690, died Dec 15, 1753
Martha, born October 4, 1693. m Wm Pattison Oct 25 1718
Tabitha, born Nov 29, 1695
Mary, born October 1, 1697, m Neh'h Wood Dec 25, 1725
Hezekiah born July 28, 1701
William born Aug 12, 1703

Grace, born July 20, 1702.

John 2, son of William 1, wife Elizabeth. He died in 1705, leaving a family of young children.

William Hodgkins joined the church "by taking the covenant," January 25, 1673; and John Hodgkins, February 1,—both being of "ye young generation."

Hezekiah 2, son of William 1, was evidently a living boy: 1692, March. Hezekiah Hodgkins being brought before ye Court for bringing a pack of cards into ye watch house, fined £5. The sd Hodgkins complained against himself, and half the fine remitted.

To Mr. Hammatt's notes of this strong and most sensible Ipswich family, we add the following

## HODGKINS GENEALOGY.

Augustine Caldwell. 1884.
—o—

William Hodgkins, the ancestor of the Ipswich Family of Hodgkins, was born in the year 1622: came to Ipswich about 1640; and made the town his home until his death, December 26, 1693, in the 72d year of his age. It is evident that he was sometimes in Gloucester; but his home was in Ipswich. The names of his family can be gleaned from our Town Records.

In 1666, he built 100 feet of posts and rayles.

In 1668, he built a house.

In ffeb. 1676, he was one of nine to see that the Town orders were observed.

In 1684, his son-in-law, Robert Cotes, the husband of his daughter Mary, came from Lynn to reside for a time (1684-9,) in Ipswich. According to the then requirement, William Hodgkins was obliged to furnish a signed and sealed document that the said young man and his family should not be burdensome to the town. It was one of the quaint early customs to require all travellers to furnish sponsors. The paper presented to the Selectmen by Goodman Hodgkins is still upon file :

" 1684. Know all men by these presents ; that I William Hodgkins, Senior, of Ipswich, do bind my selfe, heirs, executors, and administrators in the ps'nall sum of fifty pounds currant pay ; unto the selectmen of Ipswich, or

their successors ; that where as my Son in Law, Rob't
Cotes is Lately come to dwell here in Ipswich, he nor his
familie shall be come to any charge of the Towne during
his or their residence in Ipswich, as witnesse my hand this
twentieth day of January, 1684.    William Hodgkins, s'r.

In 1687, William Hodgkins, Sen'r, Jacob Perkins and
Matthew Perkins, built twenty feet of wharf in the Cove.

In 1691, we glean from a Court record, something concerning his age and his residence in Ipswich.   He called
himself sixty-nine years of age, and testified to the use of
Little Neck Beach for fifty years, more or less.   This was
two years before the record of his death,—Dec. 26, 1693.

The wife of William Hodgkins was Grace Dutch of
Gloucester.   Her father was Osman Dutch, who filled out
a century.   It is on record at Gloucester that he died December, 1684, aged one hundred years !   His wife,—Grace
Dutch,—died October 10, 1694.

There were, at least, four Dutch children, viz., Hezekiah ; Robert, whose name is in history in connection with
the fatal Bloody Brook battle, where he was left among the
slain,—but lived, nevertheless, and came back as one from
the dead ; Esther, who married Samuel Elwell ; and
Grace, who married William Hodgkins and came to
Ipswich to live.

The Ipswich Hodgkinses have been remarkable for
longevity ; and it may be that this propensity to live, came
into the blood through Grace (Dutch) Hodgkins, the
earliest mother of the Ipswich family, and a daughter of a
centenarian.  A great-grandaughter of Grace (Dutch)
Hodgkins, Mrs. Abigail (Hodgkins) Burley, died November, 1825, aged ninety-nine years and four months ;  it was
estimated that she left two hundred and twenty-nine
descendants.

Robert Dutch, the brother of Grace (Dutch) Hodgkins,
lived in Ipswich.   It is thought his home was on the site
of the residence of the late Hon. and Col. Charles Kimball.
This estate remained in the Dutch family and name for
generations.   When Col. Kimball purchased, the ancient
house was removed to Elm street, and was owned and occupied by William Tozer and Samuel Caldwell, s'r.—
Caldwell had recently come from Essex to Ipswich.

William Hubbard, the historian, tells the story of the escape of Robert Dutch from the heap of the slain :

"As Capt. Mosely came upon the Indians in the Morning, he found them stripping the Slain, amongst whom was one Robert Dutch, of Ipswich, having been sorely wounded by a bullet that rased to his Skull, and then mauled by the Indian Hatchets, was left for dead by the Salvages, and stript by them of all but his skin ; yet when Capt. Mosely came near, he almost miraculously, as one raised from the Dead, came towards the English, to their no small Amazement, by whom being received and clothed, he was carried off to the next Garrison, and is living and in perfect Health at this Day.

"May he be to the Friends and Relatives of the Rest of the Slain, an Emblem of their more perfect Resurrection at the Last Day, to receive their Crowns among the Rest of the Martyrs that have laid down and ventured their Lives as a Testimony to the Truth of their religion, as well as Love to their Country."

Another account printed the same year in London is somewhat magnified :

"The next day they came up againe, the Indians were gone ; they had stript the Dead men of all their clothes, Arms and Horses ; amongst which dead was one who had Life in him, and was found by a Friend Indian ; he took him up and said : Umb, umb poo poo Ingismon, mee save yoo Life ! me take yoo to Capt. Mosee. He carries him 15 Miles the Day after to Captain Mosely, and now this Man is well again and in good Health."

William and Grace (Dutch) Hodgkins had twelve children, and all but one lived to maturity. We give their names as we have discovered them :

i. William, wife Elizabeth. Dead in 1706.
ii. Samuel, born Nov. 2, 1658, died at two years.
iii. Samuel, lived at Gloucester. I think Babson's History gives the register of this large family.
iv. Mary, born April 6, 1661. She married Robert Cotes of Lynn, who was a soldier in 1676, under Capt. Turner, and all but one of her children were born at

Lynn.  She had Robert, Mary, William, Obadiah, Hannah, Joseph ; born between 1683 and 1696 ; and of these, Mary was born at Ipswich, Aug. 25, 1685.

v. Edward, wife Martha, daughter Mary born June 26, 1685.  He did not live in Ipswich.

vi. Hezekiah, of whom it has already been stated that he was arrested and fined for playing cards.  Imagine a Puritan boy of 1692, with a pack of cards !

vii. Thomas, born 1668, died 1719, m Abigail Hovey.

viii. Christopher, married Tabitha Howard.  From them have descended the Hodgkins' of Linebrook.  Several families settled in New Hampshire.

ix. John, wife Elizabeth.  Joined the church, Feb'y 1, 1673.  He died Jan. 20, 1690, leaving little children.

x. Martha, m William Howard, 1695.

xi. Abigail, died Nov. 13, 1720.

xii. Hannah, married John Berrye, Jan. 17, 1670.

William 2, (William 1.) Wife Elizabeth.  Joined the church January 25, 1673; in 1684, was employed to tar and caulk the Town Bridge.  He had three children :

i. William, who was 21 years old in 1713

ii. Elizabeth, who married Richard Wilcomb, 1710.

iii. Hannah, who had £8 from her father's estate, in 1707.

In 1706, William and Elisabeth were dead ; and the children were spoken of as minors.

William 3, son of William 2, married and had two sons : Christopher 4. and William 4.

William 4, was fourteen years old in 1743, and his guardian was Philemon Dane, as his father was dead.  In 1752, Christopher 4, was guardian; and Anstice Dane, widow, paid him for a hat and jacket.  From this date the descendants of William 2, disappear from the records.

Serg't Thomas Hodgkins 2, (William 1,) was born in 1668.  He married Abigail Hovey, December 12, 1689.  Abigail was daughter of Daniel and Abigail [Andrews] Hovey.  Her grandfather Hovey built the old house and wharf at the end of Turkey Shore, which still exist. (1884.)  Her grandmother, Esther (Treadwell) Hovey, lived ninety years,—dying January 4, 1730.

Serg't Thomas Hodgkins died November 16, 1719, aged 51.  His funeral expenses were £14.  Widow Abigail

(Hovey) Hodgkins died November 28, 1754.

Children of Serg't Thomas 2 and Abigail [Hovey] were:

   i. Daniel, born Oct. 14, 1690, died June 1, 1773, aged 84.

  ii. Thomas, born 1692, died Dec. 30, 1778, aged 86.

 iii. Ezekiel, died Sept. 13, 1777.

 iv. Hannah, married John Lakeman, 1735.

   v. John, bap. Aug. 16, 1713, died 1797, aged 84 years. He was known in his manhood as "Carpenter John"

Daniel 3, (Serg't Thomas 2, William 1,) m (1) Abigail Hunt, 1714; (2) Margaret Harris, 1737, who survived him and administered on his estate. He died June 1, 1773, aged 84 years. The children were:

   i, Abigail, bap. Oct. 9, 1715, m William Stone, 1741.

  ii. Daniel, bap. April 10, 1716, m Abigail Heard, 1739.

 iii. Benjamin, bap. Dec. 6, 1718, died Jan. 4, 1748.

 iv. Sarah, bap. July 2, 1721, died early.

   v. George, bap. May 19, 1723, died Oct. 1, 1726.

 vi. Ezekiel, bap. Nov. 14, 1725, married Rebecca.

 vii. Sarah, bap. Oct. 19, 1726, died early.

viii. Sarah, bap. May 19, 1728.

 ix. George, bap. Oct. 25, 1730.

  x. Elizabeth, bap. Dec. 10, 1732, died Jan. 11.

Thomas 3, (Serg't Thomas 2, William 1,) married Sarah Ayres, Dec. 1721; she died June 13, 1728. He married widow Hannah [Warner] Stanwood, Jan. 20, 1729. Children:

   i. Sarah, bap. Nov. 18, 1722, m Francis Webber, 1744.

  ii. Thomas, bap. June 21, 1724, m Anna Goss, 1749, and had Anna, 1750, and Thomas, 1751, who was known as "Capt. Thomas." Went eastward.

 iii. Abigail, bap. July 3, 1726, married Thomas Ross and Andrew Burley. She was ninety-nine years old at her death, and because of these many years the children of the town went to her home to look upon her coffined face.

 iv. Mary, died July 3, 1728.

   v. John, born Dec. 26, 1731, m Patience Webber, died September 5, 1815, aged 84.

 vi. Daniel, bap. Aug. 22, 1736, married Mary Spillar.

 vii. Hannah, died at the home of her niece "at the eastward."

viii. Joseph, [Col. Joseph of Revolutionary memory,]
      born 1743, died Sept. 25, 1829, aged 86 years.

Ezekiel 3, (Serg't Thomas 2, William 1,) married Margaret Lakeman, Jan 20, 1731; she died March 1, 1744; he
married widow Deborah [Heard] Hovey, 1745; he died
Sept. 13, 1777.  His children :
  i. Ezekiel, born Nov. 19, died Nov. 26, 1732.
  ii. Margaret, baptized Nov. 11, 1733.
  iii. Sarah, bap. Aug. 3, 1735; died 1804.
  iv. Abigail, bap. Sept. 1737.
  v. Ebenezer, bap. Feb. 1744.
  vi. Ezekiel, *non compos*, guardian, John Baker.
  vii. Deborah, bap. December, 1747.
  viii. Judith, bap. February, 1749.

John Hodgkins, 3, (Serg't Thomas 2, William 1,) was
bap. Aug. 16, 1713, he married Elizabeth Hovey, October
1738.  He was called "Carpenter John" to distinguish
him from another John, then a citizen of the town.  In
legal papers he was designated as "shipwright."  He lived
and had a shipyard at the river-end of Summer street.  His
house still stands.  He was the great-grandfather of Mrs.
Rev. John P. Cowles, Mrs. Rev. Francis V. Tenney, Mrs.
Hon. James G. Blaine, Gail Hamilton, and others of
familiar name.  The children were :
  i. Elizabeth, baptized June, 1741.
  ii. Elizabeth, bap. October, 1743, married Perkins.
  iii. John, baptized October 27, 1745.
  iv. Frances, baptized July, 1748.
  v. Abram, baptized April, 1751.
  vi. Mary, baptized March 29, 1752.
  viii. John, baptized September, 1753.
  ix. Salome, baptized February 16, 1756.
  x. Eunice, baptized May 7, 1758.
  xi. Eunice, born 1758, married Capt Isaac Stanwood,
      Feb. 28, 1778, died Feb. 3, 1840, aged 82 years.
      Capt. Isaac Stanwood died Oct. 15, 1821, aged 66.

Daniel Hodgkins 4, (Daniel 3, Serg't Thomas 2, William 1,) was bap. April 10, 1716, m. Abigail Heard, dau.
of Edmund and Deborah [Osgood] Heard, published Oct.
27, 1739.  He was lost at sea in 1763, and Daniel Heard

was appointed guardian of the minor children.  There is a
curious story told traditionally among his descendants:—
"Abigail [Heard] Hodgkins, his wife, was much im-
pressed by a dream.  It seemed as if she were upon a most
desolate island, vainly endeavoring to dry what was at
that time worn as socks and nippers.  She wandered about
completely covered with the sense of desolation.  Such
was the depth of depression, that she went to her neighbors the next day, thinking that some expression would
dispel the shadow ; but it proved indeed a *foreboding*,—her
husband perished in the seas."  After several years of
widowhood she married David Pulcifer.  She died in 1786.
One of her grandchildren [Abigail Caldwell] went to see
her when she was dying ; she laid her hand on the child's
head in benediction, but her tongue was palsied.  The day
of her death there was a snow storm so severe that the
doors and windows were covered.  And at her burial the
bier was carried over the roof of a one-story house that had
been completely transfigured into a hill of snow.

The children of Daniel and Abigail [Heard] Hodgkins :
i. Abigail, baptized October 12, 1740; m. John Caldwell ;
  m. (2) Samuel Henderson.  Died Dec. 17, 1833.
ii. Deborah, baptized March 13, 1742, died early.
iii. Daniel, baptized Nov. 18, 1744, married Elizabeth
  Perkins in 1776, and went to New Hampshire.
iv. Deborah, bap. Feb. 22, 1746, m Jona Lakeman, 1772.

John 4, (Thomas 3, Serg't Thomas 2, William 1,) born
Dec. 26, 1731 ; married Patience Webber who was born in
1736.  Their children were :
i. John, born Sept. 13, 1756, married Abigail Lord, 1779,
  went to Bath, Me.  His son went to Woolwich ; his
  daughter married William Mack Rogers.
ii. Thomas, born May 19, 1760 ; married Priscilla Kinsman, Nov. 10, 1793 ; went to Portland.
iii. William, born August 15, 1762 ; m. Mary Staniford,
  March 1, 1792.
iv. Patience, born June 13, 1764, married Isaac Lummus.
v. Benjamin, born September 6, 1766.
vi. Joseph, born Aug. 7, 1768, m Abigail Swasey, 1793.
vii. David, born January 29, 1771, married Polly Wilson of
  Marblehead, Sept. 15, 1797.
viii. Betsy, born May 16, 1773, m John Jewett Sept 27, 1792

David Hodgkins 4, (Thomas 3, Serg't Thomas 2, William 1,) married Mary Spiller, Nov. 28, 1757. He died July 30, 1769. His widow, Mary, married Moses Smith, 1778. The children of David and Mary:

   i. Mary, bap. Nov. 25, 1758, m Daniel Boardman, 1778.
  ii. David, baptized July 27, 1760, died April 14, 1824, married Carter.
 iii. Thomas baptized May 30, 1762.
 iv. Abigail, bap. Feb. 22, 1767, went "to the eastward."
  v. Lucy, married James Merrifield, March 19, 1806.
 vi. a daughter married Knowlton.

Col. Joseph Hodgkins, 4, (Thomas 3, Serg't Thomas 2, William 1,) a most respected citizen of Ipswich, an officer of the Revolution, and an honor to his name. His mother was Hannah (Warner-Stanwood) Hodgkins. He was born in 1743, and died Sept. 25, 1829, aged 86 years. He was three times married:

  1. Joanna Webber, of Methuen, 1764; she died January 20, 1772.
  2. Sarah Perkins, daughter of Dea. Jeremiah Perkins, married Dec. 3, 1772; she died March 13, 1803, aged 53.
  3. Mrs. Lydia (Crocker) Treadwell, widow of Elisha Treadwell, and daughter of Dea. John Crocker. She died Dec. 8, 1833, aged 78 years.

The children of Col. Joseph Hodgkins were many, and all died before him:

    i. Joanna, born Aug 11, 1765, m Wm. Fuller Andrews.
   ii. Joseph, born June 14, 1767.
  iii. Mary, born July 10, 1768.
   iv. Hannah, born 1770, died 1771.
    v. Hannah, born Dec. 21, 1771, died 1772.
   vi. Sarah, died April 5, 1795, aged 22 years.
  vii. Martha, married Francis Pulsifer, June 12, 1806; her daughter Martha married Asa Wade, Nov. 20, 1832.
 viii. Hannah, married Nathaniel Wade, 1803, died at 40 years. She was the mother of Francis Wade.
   ix. Polly, died May 29, 1794, aged 12 years.
    x. Elizabeth, died March 2, 1806, aged 18 years.
  Two others died in infancy.

Capt. Thomas Hodgkins 5, (Thomas 4, Thomas 3, Serg't Thomas 2, William 1,) married Katherine Fuller, 1774; she died June 24, 1788, and he married Martha Choate, Nov. 21, 1790.   It is said that he went to Maine. The children born in Ipswich were :
  i. Thomas, baptized March 21, 1779.
 ii. Katherine, baptized August, 1784.
iii. Joanna. baptized April, 1786.

William Hodgkins 5, (John 4, Thomas 3, Serg't Thomas 2, William 1,) married Mary Staniford, March 1, 1792. He was born August 15, 1762.   His widow Mary, married Dr. Nathan Jacquis, and had one daughter, Caroline. The children of William Hodgkins were:
  i. William, born September 1, 1793.
 ii. Mary, born January 9, 1795.
 iv. James born March 31, 1797.

Joseph Hodgkins 5, (John 4, Thomas 3, Serg't Thom. 2 William 1,) married Abigail Swasey, Nov. 7, 1796.   She was the daughter of Maj'r Joseph Swasey, grandaughter of Henry Wise, and great-grandaughter of the Rev'd John Wise of Chebacco.   Joseph Hodgkins died July 3, 1825, aged 56 years.   His children were :
  Patience, Elizabeth, Sarah Bartol, Joseph Swasey,
  Abigail, married John Graves,
  Susan, married Tirrel of Salem,
  Charlotte Swasey, lived with her Uncle and Aunt,
    Rev. and Mrs. Hubbard.

David Hodgkins 5, (John 4, Thomas 3, Serg't Thomas 2 William 1,) born January 21, 1771, married Polly Wilson of Marblehead, Sept. 15, 1797.   Their children :
   i. David, born December 27, 1798
  ii. John, born May 28, 1800.
  iv. Joseph Wilson, July 15, 1801.
   v. Mary Wilson, August 9, 1803.
  vi. George. February 28, 1805.
 vii. Azor, September 28, 1806.
viii. Sarah Jane Wilson, November 9, 1808.
  ix. Eliza Waitt, born April 10, 1811.

We now take up another son of William Hodgkins 1 :

John 2, (William 1,) died January 20, 1690, in the midst
of his years.    His widow, Elisabeth, married Symonds
Wood.    The following request was filed at Court by Elizabeth Hodgkins :

" 1705, June 11.    Account of Elizabeth Hodgkins, Administratrix of the estate of Her Husband, John Hodgkins, who departed this Life January 20, 1690. pray
Alowens for bringen op my Children, they being Left
yong—the oldest not above eight years old, one being born
after the deth of my husband."

The children of John and Elizabeth were, John, Nathaniel ; and a daughter born Feb. 1, 1690, who married
Timothy Keysan of Haverhill in 1711.

John Hodgkins 3, (John 2, William 1,)  m Patience
Sands, 1714, she died Nov. 13, 1720 ; he  m.  Martha How-
ard, Dec. 24, 1720. She died Nov. 8, 1798, aged 97 years.
The children were :

   i. Elizabeth, born Aug. 19, 1716, m Samuel Waite, 1752.
  ii. Patience, born August 3, 1718, died early.
 iii. Thomas, born August 2, 1719, m Katherine Bryant,
       and had Lucy, 1740, and Joseph, 1742.
  iv. Patience, bap. October 23, 1720.
   v. William, bap. December 3, 1721.
  vi. John, bap. April 11, 1725.
 vii. Samuel, bap. April 9, 1727.
     Two named Mary, died early.
   x. Moses, bap. Sept. 28, 1733, m Elizabeth Quarles.
  xi. Martha, bap. January 1, 1737, married Jona : Wells.
 xii. John, baptized November 11, 1739.
     Mary and Sarah died early.
  This large family disappears from the Town Records.

Nathaniel Hodgkins 3, (John 2, William 1,) born Jan.
29, 1684, married Joanna Giddings, 1706.    He died Aug.
22, 1740.    Children :

   i. Nathaniel, born May 5, 1710, lost at sea, April 7, 1737.
  ii. Susanna, born April 6, 1712, died early.
 iii. Joseph, born September 26, 1714.
  iv. Benjamin and Stephen, twins, Feb. 20, 1716.
   v. Elizabeth, born September 21, 1718.
  vi. Joanna, born July 23, 1721.
 vii. Susanna, born August 1726.

Moses Hodgkins 4, (John 3, John 2, William 1,) bap. Sept. 23, 1733. He was a soldier and at Crown Point in 1750, and "at the eastward" in 1754. He married Elizabeth Quarles, Nov. 27, 1754. She died Oct. 30, 1797, aged 71 years. I find the following memorandum without date : " Moses Hodgkins, Master of sloop Elizabeth, wrecked back of Cape Ann, two miles from Pigeon Cove. Two passengers were washed into the sea and drowned."

Children of Moses and Elizabeth :

i Elisabeth, born 1755.

ii. Lucy, baptized November 27, 1757.

iii. Moses, bap. October 11, 1761, married Hannah Lord, November 27, 1787.

Nathaniel Hodgkins 4, (Nathaniel 3, John 2, Wm. 1,) born May 5, 1710, lost, with six others, at Canso, April 7, 1737. His estate was administered by Andrew Burley. He married Martha Smith, Feb. 26, 1733; his children :

i. Mary, born Oct 13, 1734, married Henry Spiller, 1754

ii. Joseph, baptized Oct. 10, 1735.

Benjamin Hodgkins 4, (Nath'l 3, John 2, William 1,) bap. Feb. 20, 1716, married Elizabeth Bennett, 1740. He was a soldier, 1760, and having returned from Albany, was seized of the small pox, and died, December of that year. Gen. Michael Farley became the guardian of his minor children. Elizabeth Bennett, his wife, was the daughter of Joseph Bennett. Their children were :

i. Mary, bap. Jan. 8, 1741, died 1791.

ii. Elizabeth, bap. December 8, 1743.

iii. Lydia, bap. Feb. 22, 1746, married Benjamin Pindar.

iv. Margaret, baptized July 19, 1746.

v. Benjamin, baptized November 17, 1751.

vi. vii. Joseph and Margaret, twins. 1757.

Stephen Hodgkins 4, (Nathaniel 3, John 2, William 1,) twin brother of Benjamin 4, baptized Feb. 20, 1716. Wife Elizabeth, 1739. He was a soldier at Lake George ; and in July, 1758, he, being small of stature, pursued a tall Frenchman, threw him down, forced a knife from his hand, and with a string which he had in his pocket he tied him fast and strong. Stephen was dead in 1760, and widow Elizabeth administered. The children were :

   i. Stephen, bap. Sept.1743. In 1760 Thomas Harris was his guardian.

  ii. Nathaniel, bap. June 25, 1745, drowned 1796, at the West Indies.

 iii. Capt. Thomas, bap. Feb. 15, 1746, m. Abigail Ross.

 iv. Elizabeth, bap. April, 1751, m. Samuel Stone, 1785.

  v. Joanna, born 1775, married Frazier.

vi. vii. Sarah and Abigail.

    Capt. Thomas Hodgkins 5, (Stephen 4, Nathaniel 3, John 2, William 1,) was bap. Feb. 25, 1746, died June 4, 1797, aged 51 years.   He married Abigail Ross, 1770, she died Oct. 22, 1737, aged 87 years.   Children :

   i. Thomas, married at Newburyport.

  ii. Capt. John, born Jan. 21, 1774, m Anna Lummus.

 iii. Stephen. iv. Joseph, born 1778.

  v. Daniel, died at sea. His dau. Mary m. Richard Potter.

vi. William, born 1782, m. Jane McMurphy, had three daughters, Sarah, died at 21 years ; Abby died at 15; Mary Jane, died 1890.

vii. Sarah, born 1784, married 1, Baker, 2, Dea. Chase of Portland, died at the age of 90, burial at Ipswich.

viii. Joanna, born 1786, married John Fellows, [son of John and Martha Shatswell Fellows,] lived at Roxbury.

 ix. Abigail, married Dr. John Scollay Osborne.

  x. Susan, married 1, Capt. Nathaniel Dennis, 1800, m 2. Capt. William Low of Salem.

    Capt. John Hodgkins 6, (Capt. Thomas 5, Stephen 4, Nathaniel 3, John 2, William 1,) was born Jan. 21, 1774, married Anna Lummus, Nov. 22, 1798, she was born May 25, 1777, and died April 21, 1866.   He died April 22, 1855. Their children :

   i. Anna, born Jan. 7, 1800, m. Robert Stone June 7, 1818 died Feb. 1820, aged 20 years.

  ii. Abigail, born Sept. 6, 1801, m Asa Lord, Nov. 3, 1825

 iv. Susan Dennis, born Nov. 8, 1803, m. Charles Smith Feb. 27, 1823, died June 18, 1861.

  v. Martha, born Oct. 30, 1805, m. Foster Russell, January 29, 1829.

vi. Thomas, born August 7, 1807, m. Julia A. Johnson, Nov. 2, 1830, died June 17, 1853.

vii. Mary, born Feb. 21, 1810, m. George Willett, Dec. 9, 1830, died August 17, 1866.

viii. Daniel Lummus, born Feb. 1, 1813, m. 1, Mary Willett, Sept. 6, 1835. She died March 2, 1869, aged 56 years. He m. 2, Sarah G. Fellows.

ix. Lucy L. born Oct. 30, 1815, died Oct. 23, 1819.

x. John, born Oct. 26, 1817, m. Caroline Hazeltine, Jan. 27, 1846.

Another line of the descendants of William 1 :

Christopher Hodgkins 2, married Tabitha Howard, January 22, 1689. She died Sept. 15, 1735. Children :

i. Christopher, born December 8, 1690.

ii. Martha, born Oct. 4, 1693, married William Pattison.

iii. Tabitha, born Nov. 29, 1695, m. Richard Abbott.

iv. Mary, born Oct. 1, 1697, m. Nehemiah Wood.

v. Hezekiah, born July 2, 1699, m Sarah Harris 1726.

vi. Grace, born July 28, 1701, died at the Hamlet, 1737.

vii. William born August 13, 1703.

Hezekiah Hodgkins 3, (Christopher 2, William 1) married Sarah Harris, July 31, 1726. Children :

i. Sarah, baptized February, 1726.

ii. Hezekiah, bap. Aug. 8, 1728, m. Lucy Chapman.

iii. Henry, baptized October 18, 1730.

iv. Samuel, baptized October 13, 1732, m Lydia Galloway

v. Stephen, died 1760, unmarried.

vi. William, bap. December 5, 1736.

vii. Tryphena, baptized November 9, 1749.

William Hodgkins 3, (Christopher 2, William 1,) married Elizabeth Clark, 1724 ; and widow Elizabeth [Clark] Hodgkins married Ezekiel Hunt, 1744. Children :

i. William, baptized Jan. 30, 1725, m Abigail Urann.

ii. Elizabeth, born Feb. 1727, m John Harris, 1752.

iii. Christopher, born June, 1730, m Dorcas Wallis, 1758, and had son Christopher who m Martha Giddings, 1780, and settled in Gloucester.

iv. Francis, born 1732 ; v. Sarah, born 1734 ;

vi. Samuel, born 1736.

William Hodgkins 4, (William 3, Christopher 2, Wm. 1)
bap. Jan 30, 1725, m. Abigail Urann, 1748.  She died May
5, 1790, aged 71 years.  Children :
  William, bap. February 3, 1750.
  Daniel, bap. February 20, 1757.

Hezekiah Hodgkins 4, (Hezekiah 3, Christopher 2,
William 1,) born February, 1726, married Lucy Chapman,
1752, she died July 8, 1801, aged 71 years.  They lived at
Linebrook.  Hezekiah was a Revolutionary Soldier; he
and his eldest son were slain in battle.  His daughter Sa-
rah, (afterwards Mrs. Emmons,) was six years old at the
date of his death; and she was "brought up" by Moses
Treadwell.  The children were :
  Lucy, born 1753; died in infancy.
  Amos, removed to Troy, New Hampshire.
  Pelatiah, joined his brother at Troy, N. H.
  Betsey, was for many years the respected servant in the
    family of the Rev. Dr. Joseph Dana.
  Eunice, married Capt. Ebenezer Hovey, Nov. 10, 1793.
  Sarah, married Daniel Emmons, March 26, 1799.  He
    died Sept. 15, 1861.
  Effie, died in childhood.

We subjoin a few Hodgkins names whose appropriate
places in the family lines, we are not able to tell.  Perhaps
they are children of Hezekiah Hodgkins 2 and Hannah
his wife; for Hezekiah was a resident of Ipswich in 1692,
and his wife, Hannah, died in Ipswich in 1727.  These
supposed children of Hezekiah 2 and Hannah, are :

  John 3, m Abigail Pierce, Aug. 28, 1705.  He was dead
    in 1730, when his widow Abigail m. Ephraim Fitts.
    No children recorded, but it may that the following
    were of their blood :

  Jedediah, married about 1727.
  John, married Patience Smith, 1729.
  Mary, married Samuel Pulcifer. 1735.
  Anne, married Samuel Holland, 1739.

Another name, which may have been an unrecorded son
of Hezekiah 2, and Hannah his wife, is :

Solomon Hodgkins 3, m. Mary Chase, 1715. She was a descendant of Aquilla Chase, the schoolmaster, and one of her children bore his baptismal name:

Mary, born 9 mo. 4, 1717.
Abigail, baptized August 21, 1720.
Mehitable, baptized Feb. 25, 1721, died 1723.
Solomon, baptized April 12, 1724.
Mehitable, born July 17, 1726.
Aquilla, born 1729, died 1730.

A third supposed son of Hezekiah 2, and Hannah his wife was,—

Hezekiah 3, married Martha Harris, 1716. Children:

Martha, baptized 7 mo, 15, 1717.
Hezekiah, bap. 7 mo. 21, 1718.
Thomas, bap. Dec. 4, 1720.
Sarah, bap. May 12, 1723.
John, bap. March 20, 1725, died 1773 ; deaf and dumb.
Jacob, bap. July 14, 1728, died early.
Lucy, bap. Sept. 27, 1730.     Jacob, bap. Nov. 5, 1732.
Anna, bap. Sept. 30, 1734.
Stephen, bap. July 11, 1736, a soldier, died 1760.
Martha, bap. Oct. 1739, died 1786.
Elisabeth, baptized July 12, 1741.
[This family disappears from the Town Records.]

The children of Jedediah 4, (John 3, Hezekiah 2?)
Sarah and Deborah, twins, born May 5, 1728 ; Jedediah, born July 5, 1730; Mary, born Feb. 4, 1732.

There was "weaver" John Hodgkins, whose name is familiar yet in tradition. He lived on East street, below Cross street. He may have been a son of "Weaver" John Hodgkins of Rowley.

HOW. James 1, was a commoner, 1641; one of Major Denison's subscribers, 1648. With the designation of James, sen'r, he had a share in Plum Island, &c., 1664; Tithingman, 1677; voter in town affairs, 1679. He died May 17, 1702, aged one hundred and four years. He gave testimony relating to the line between Ipswich and Rowley a short time before he died. His wife, Elizabeth, daughter of John Dane, died January 21, 1693.

James How 2, son of James 1, married Elizabeth Jackson, May 5, 1655. He was entitled to a share in Plumb Island, &c., 1664, and was a voter in town affairs, 1679. He died Feb. 15, 1701. Children:
James, died July, 1660.
Elizabeth, born June 1, 1661.
Mercy, born February 25, 1664.
John, born April 17, 1671.
Abigail, born December 3, 1673.

Abraham How and Sarah Peabody, m. March 26, 1678. He died January 21, 1717. Children:
Abraham, born June 27, 1686.
Israel, born January 24, 1692.
Mark, born May 28, 1695, wife Hephsibah.
Increase, born April 12, 1680.
Love, born January 15, 1678.
Corp'l Abraham How had a seat in the meeting house assigned him in 1700.

John How and Hannah his wife, had:
Martha, born June 13, 1691.
Sarah, born February 8, 1692.
James, born March 27, 1694.
He died May 22, 1697; the inventory of estate,—real, £61, personal, £16, 19; rendered July 2, 1697.

Mary, wife of Increase How, died August 31, 1721.
Increase How m. 2, Susannah Kinsman, May 10, 1723.

Mark and Hepsebeth How buried eight children—four sons and four daughters,—in twenty-three days, November 5-28, 1736. Throat distemper.

HOWLETT, Thomas, had granted to him in 1635 a "houselot in the town adjoining Thomas Hardy's, in the cross way leading to the mill."

In 1637, he purchased of John Perkins, the Elder, forty acres of land, for seven pounds ten shillings.

His name with the title of *Ensign* is among "such as promise carting voluntary toward the cart bridge, beside the rate, a day work a peice," Feb. 4, 1646.

In 1643, Sergeant Howlett, and ten soldiers, are empowered in some service to the [assistance of the neighboring Indians] for which they were voted twelve pence a day for each soldier, and the officers double. They were absent three days ; and Sergeant Howlett's compensation was six shillings.

He was a commoner in 1641 ; and had a share and an half in Plum Island, &c., in 1668.

He was deputy to the General Court, 1635.

He died in 1678, aged seventy-nine years.

Thomas Howlett, his will, dated December 21, 1667, and proved March 31, 1668. He left a son and two daughters; house and land valued at £220, being one hundred acres ; other property, making a total of £340.

His wife, Alice, died June 26, 1666. He left a widow, Rebekah. At his death his children were :

Samuel ;

Sarah Cummings ;

Mary Perley;

Nathaniel Howlett, his son, died April 28, 1658.

Thomas Howlett 2, son of Thomas 1, died December 22, 1667. He left a wife, Mary. His will is dated in December, 1667. " In case my wife be with child and have a son, I do give and bequeath to him half as much more as to any one of my daughters." The names of his children are not given. He mentions his "father Peabody." He possessed a house and farm of one hundred acres, valued at £220 ; five cows, £20, and other property.

William Howlett, was a voter in town affairs, 1679 ; and had a seat assigned to him in the meeting house in 1700.

John Howlett, was a commoner in 1707, Deacon in 1723.

HEARD, Luke. "The first or Original list of ye townsman of Salisbury in ye booke of Records," printed in the Gen. Reg. vol. iii, p. 55, without date, but probably 1640, contains the name of Luke Heard. He probably soon after that date removed to Ipswich.

Luke Heard took the freeman's oath at Boston, Sept'r 6, 1639, and died in Ipswich in 1647. His will is dated 1647, 28th, 7 mo., and witnessed by John Wyatt and Simon Tompson, both inhabitants of Ipswich. In the record of the will he is said to have lately deceased. He leaves the disposition of his property to his wife, Sarah; and directs that his two sons, John and Edmund, shall be "brought up to reading and writing;" and at the age of twenty-one years, they shall receive,—John, the eldest, ten pounds; and Edmund, the youngest, five pounds. He also directs that his books be equally divided between these two sons.

John Heard 2, son of Luke 1, settled in Andover where he died in 1696. His brother Edmund was appointed administrator on his estate, October 12, 1696. being "his only brother and heir" to a property of £20, 3, 9.

Edmund Heard 2, son of Luke 1, was one of "ten of the young generation who took the covenant," Jan. 18, 1673-4. He was appointed a surveyor of highways in 1696; a sealer of leather in 1699; and was for many years one of the selectmen. He had a seat assigned to him in the meeting house in 1700. He subscribed 8s toward the bell, 1699. In 1679. "we ye select men of Ipswich, have chosen [Edmund Heard] Tythingman." He had half a share in Plum Island, &c., in 1664; and in 1697 had horses on the common.

He died in 1713; the inventory of his estate amounting to £141 real, and £70, 7, 10 personal; rendered Dec. 28, 1713. His estate was divided July 18, of that year. He left a widow, Elizabeth, daughter of Daniel Warner; she died 1724, in the 77th year of her age. They were married Sept. 26, 1678. Three sons and three daughters, viz.,

Edmund, the eldest, born February 22, 1681.
Nathaniel, born September 1, 1685.
Daniel.
Elizabeth, born May 7, 1674.

Sarah, born May 6, 1676.
Abigail.

Edmund Heard 3, son of Edmund 2, Luke 1, was published with Annah Todd, November 2, 1706.

> Here Lyes Ye
> Body of Annah
> Heard Deceased
> June ye 13
> 1709
> Aged 26 Years

November 7, 1713, he is published with Deborah Osgood of Andover, who died August 29, 1723.

> Here Lyes Ye
> Body of Deborah
> Heard wife to
> Edmund Heard Aged
> 37 years Dec'd
> Aug ye 29th
> 1723

He is published Sept. 5, 1724, with Rebekah Knowlton, a widow, who dying Sept. 21, 1728, he, on the 11th day of January following, was published with Martha Kimball. She died Oct. 19, 1730, and on the 11th December, 1731, he is published with his fifth and last wife, Elizabeth [Lull] Caldwell, widow of John Caldwell who had been "slaine by ye Indians" on the coast of Maine.

In 1706, Edmund and Nathaniel Heard with ten others, have granted to them "to raise ye fourth Seat in ye front southwest gallery of the meeting house."

On the town records, under the date, March 9, 1726-7, is recorded, "Robert Potter prays for a grant of a small piece of land on the front of Edmund Heard's land on the north easterly side of Heard's brook."

Edmund 4, son of Edmund 3, with his wife Priscilla, had
 Edmund, baptized Sept. 4, 1743;
 Mark, baptized June 19, 1748.
In the meeting house which was built in 1749, Edmund

Heard, Jun'r, became the purchaser of the pew on the westerly corner of the gallery, No. 25.

Nathaniel Heard 3, son of Edmund 2, was born Sept. 1, 1685. His mother's name was Elizabeth. In 1706, he has a seat assigned to him in the meeting house. In 1709, Dec. 10, he publishes an intention of marriage with Agnes Hunt. In 1724, he is appointed by the town a sealer of leather.

In his will, dated January 9, and proved February 2, 1730-1, he mentions his children:

John,    William,    Elizabeth,    Sarah,    Hannah.

He remarks that Agnes, his wife, is weakly and his children are young.

> Nathaniel
> Heard    the
> son   of   Nathaniel
> and    Agnes
> Heard    Died
> Ianuary    ye    27
> 1718-19,   Aged    7
> Years   &   11   Days

Daniel 3, son of Edmund 2, married Mary Baker, dau. of William Baker. She was born April 26, 1695. Their publishment is dated November 5, 1715. He with seven others, January 26, 1710, were granted liberty to build a gallery over ye stairs on ye southeast corner of ye meeting house. In 1722, he was a surveyor of highways.

> William
> Heard    Son
> of   Daniel   &
> Mary    Heard
> Died    April
> ye   9   1720
> Aged   6   We
> eks   &   2   Days

Here Lies William Heard Son of Mr Daniel &
Mrs. Mary Heard who Died Oct ye 12 1726
aged about 5 years

At the sale of pews, Nov. 6, 1749, in the meeting house
which was built that year, the pew No. 32 was purchased
by Daniel Heard, Jun'r, probably son of Daniel 3, and continued the property of his family until the house was
taken down in 1846.   He was Deacon 1752.   Children :
    Nathaniel, baptized March 31, 1734.
    Daniel, born May 16, 1742.
    John, baptized May 1, 1744.
    Samuel, baptized April 5, 1747.

> Here  Lies  Samuel
> Heard   of  Salisbury
> Died   September
> ye 14 th 1720
> Aged  20  Years
> & 6 months.

HOLMES, Robert.  In March, 1677, Hester Holmes,
relict and administrator of Robert Holmes ; inventory less
than £20, clear estate ; two children.  The Court order
the estate to be left to her for the bringing up of the
children.

James Holmes 2, and Mary his wife, had :
    James, born June 27, 1694.

Robert Holmes 2, and Sarah Wastcut, married  January
4, 1701.   Their son—
Francis, born March 14, 1706.   He became a physician.

Dr. Francis Holmes 3, published with Mary Gibson,
March 29, 1732.

> Here is interred
> the Body of
> Dr.  Francis  Holms
> Who  Departed
> This  Life  May
> 12th 1758
> in  the  53  Year
> of his Age.

1747.   Robert Holmes, tailor.   Warner's Acc't Book.

HOVEY, Daniel. was an inhabitant of Ipswich, 1637 ; one of Major Denison's subscribers, 1648 ; had a share in Plum Island, &c., 1664 ; was a voter in town affairs 1679.

Sarah Stone, wife of Deacon Stone of Watertown, sells to Daniel Hovey of Ipswich, June 20, 1660, twenty acres in Topsfield, being the land that Towns-men of Ipswich did grant to Richard Lumpkin at that place called pye-brook.

1666, Aug. Granted liberty to Daniell Hovey to fell trees for his son James to work at his trade—and to fell timber to build a house for John ; and for a shop for James.

He died April 24, 1692.

March 12, 1693-4, Daniel Hovey 3, was named executor, together with his uncle Thomas Hovey, on the will of Daniel Hovey, sen'r. The said Daniel 3, made it appear he was twenty-one years old.

In his will, dated March 21, 1691-2, Daniel, sen'r, describes himself as "aged 73 and going into 74." His sons were :—Daniel, John, Thomas, James, Joseph, Nathaniel. The grandson, Daniel, son of James. The daughters,— Priscilla Ayres, wife of John Ayres ; Abigail Hodgkins, wife of Thomas Hodgkins.

Among his property is "upland called Hovey's Island."

Oct. 5, 1700. Thomas Hovey, executor, exhibits an account of his father, Daniel Hovey's estate, amounting to £606 10. Debts paid, £227, 12 7.

We give below a more thorough study of the Hovey Family of Ipswich :

## HOVEY RECORDS.

Augustine Caldwell.—1884.

The will of Daniel Hovey, sen'r, March 21, 1691-2 :

I Daniel Hovey, sen'r of Ipswich, considering the changes of man Doe Desyre by the helpe of the Lord to setle my concernes as may be for the glory of God and the good of my family.

my soul I desyre to resigne and commit into the hand of my Loving father in Jesus Christ, who is the Lord my righteousness. My body to be decently buried in earth in hope of a glorious and blessed resurrection by Christ. Amen.

Item.  The estate which God of his grace hath given me, I have disposed of as followeth :

To my oldest sons Daniel and John Hovey and my daughter Ayres : I have given them their portions of that estate I had, to our mutual content.  The one at Ipswich the other at Topsfield, now in their possession, Abigail paid by my son John to my son Ayres.

Item.  to my son Thomas and James his son Daniel, I give all that my Yland called Hovey's Yland, which with the thatch banks and Low marsh belonging to me on the other side of the creek, which I allowed Quarter Master Perkins to improve, holding my possession till I had occasion for the same.  Also all that houses and Land in Ipswich that I shall not dispose of before death.

Item.  I give to my sons Joseph and Nathaniel Hovey, one hundred rods of ground a piece ; Joseph bounded next to Mr. Emerson's land from the highway to the land of Daniel Ringe.  Nathaniel, one hundred rod of my land next to my son Daniel, with the Dwelling house, barn, part of the orchard to butt on Daniel Ringe ; half planting lot, about three acres, with a way to it over the bridge I made to go to it ; three acres at Plum Island also ; which lands I leave in the hands of my executor and overseers that is left after my death, to be disposed of as follows :

The children of Joseph Hovey to have an equal proportion of what is left after my death as to their father Legase.

The children of son Nathaniel to have an equal proportion amongst them ; only Nathaniel Hovey, the son of Nathaniel Hovey to have a double proportion, if he lives to the age of one and twenty.  If not, then to be divided amongst the other children of that family.

Item.  My moveables to my son Nathaniel ; those sheep he hath of mine to his children ; my cart and plow, irons, chains, great tramel, great brass kettle. Iron Kettle, little Iron pot.

My pewter porringer, and drinking cup, and my wife's wearing apparel to Nathaniel's children.

The others to Joseph his brothers's children : all my wearing cloaths, my great brass pot, and pewter quart pot.

And my great Bible and books as follows : Come to Christ and Welcome ; Cotton on the Covenant ; Mather's Seven Sermons to Nathaniel children.

To Daniel grand child those sheep with which ——— and books also, : Christian Warfare, Calvin on Job, Ten Divines, The Golden Scepter, with what other books undisposed of by me of mine, and such tools for his trade as are suitable of mine.

To Abigail Hodgkins, wife of Thomas Hodgkins, the brass pan and pewter salt seller.

My part of the mare and colt to grand child Daniel and Ivory.

Item.   My interest of Brookfield and Swampfield I give to my son Joseph and Nathaniel children.

Item.   I make son Thomas Executor, and would have his nephew [Daniel] in case he lives to age, if capable, to join in the same with him—and he pay out of his part to his brother James and sister Priscilla and John Ayres ten pounds a piece within three years after his possession, and in case of his death, I put James Hovey in his room, and let them four equally divide his part.

My bed, bolster and pillow with my green rug, a pair blankets with the bedstead, to Daniel grandchild.

I would have my son John at Topsfield to take his possession with his books.

I would appoint my loving sons Daniel Hovey and John Hovey to be over seers of this my last will, and see to discharge my funeral charges, which I allow four pounds estate, and to take an inventory of my estate, and discharge all my debts, and make probate of my will, and see his nephews have their equal proportion, Joseph and Nathaniel children who have lately deceased, for which I allow my overseers three pounds a piece for their care and trouble

This is my will as witness my hand and seale :

Daniel Hovey, sen'r, aged 73,
and going into my 74 this 21 of March, 1691-2.

Wit :   philemon Dane,   Thomas Hodgkins.

Proved October 3, 1692.

Daniel and Abigail (Andrews) Hovey had eight children who lived to maturiy :

i. Daniel, born 1642, married Esther, daughter of Thomas Treadwell.

ii. John, lived in Topsfield and was twice married. His first wife was Dorcas Ivory ; and this rather unusual surname has been a baptismal name to the present generation.

iii. Thomas, born in 1648, married Sarah Cook, and lived in Hadley ; he had one son, Daniel, born 1694, who died at 22 years : and eleven daughters.

iv. James, was killed in the Indian War, August 2, 1675. His son, Daniel 3, was "brought up" in the family of Daniel 1 and Abigail (Andrews) Hovey.

v. Joseph, married Hannah Pratt in 1676, and died at Milton in 1690. He had six children, none of them resided in Ipswich :—Joseph, 1677 ; Ebenezer, 1680 ; Hannah, 1682; John, 1684 ; Caleb, 1687 ; Thomas.

vi. Nathaniel, born March 20, 1657, married Sarah Fuller, Nov. 1679. He had two children born in Ipswich: Sarah, Sept. 19, 1680 ; Elizabeth, March 2, 1682, m. Joseph Ford, 1704.

vii. Priscilla, married John Ayres.

viii. Abigail.

Only one of these eight children has transmitted the Hovey name to the present generation in Ipswich,— Daniel 2, the eldest born.

Daniel 2, (Daniel 1,) was born in 1642. He married Esther Treadwell, who lived to be ninety years old :— " Esther Hovey, widow of Daniel Hovey and daughter of Thomas Treadwell, died January 4, 1730, aged ninety." Her husband died thirty-five years earlier, May 29, 1695. They were married Octo. 8, 1665, and had eight children :

i. Daniel, born June 24, 1666.

ii. Nathaniel 3.

iii. Abigail, married Thomas Hodgkins, 1689.

iv. Thomas 3.

v. John, born August 13, 1675 ; died August 17, 1720, aged forty-five. He married Mehitable Safford.

vi. Mary, born June 27, 1678.

vii. Ebenezer 3.

viii. Mercy; "the youngest child."

John Hovey 2, (Daniel 1,) married 1, Dorcas Ivory of Topsfield, Aug. 13, 1665 ; 2. Mercy Goodhue, 1712. He died, 1718. He established the Topsfield family of Hovey. Children :

i. John, born December, 1666.

ii. Dorcas, born January 16, 1668.

iii. A child born and died, 1671.

iv. Elizabeth, born January 18 1672.

v. Susanna, 1674.

vi. Luke, May 3, 1676.

vii. Ivory, 1678, married Ann Pingry, 1707.

viii. Abigail, born April 28, 1680.

Three at least of the grandchildren of John and Dorcas (Ivory) Hovey, came to Ipswich for wives :

John Hovey of Topsfield married Mary Lakeman of Ipswich, 1725 ;

John Hovey of Topsfleld married Mary Abbott of Ipswich, 1737 ;

Aaron Hovey of Topsfield married Sarah Ray of Ipswich, 1740.

Nathaniel Hovey 3, (Daniel 2, Daniel 1,) born October 9, 1667 ; died 1696. Wife Mary. He had :

Nathaniel 4, who settled in Ipswich.

Thomas Hovey 3, (Daniel 2, Daniel 1,) born May 28, 1673; wife Martha. He had :

Thomas 4, who married Sarah Rust.

Ebenezer Hovey 3, (Daniel 2, Daniel 1,) born January 11, 1680, deid 1729, aged forty-nine years. Wife, Elisabeth Dennis. He had:

Thomas 4, who married Rebekah Lakeman, and has had many descendants in Ipswich.

Thomas Hovey 4, (Thomas 3, Daniel 2, Daniel 1,) married Sarah Rust, December 17, 1729. He had Lydia, who married Benjamin Pindar, 1764 ; and Thomas, born 1736, who may have been the father of "Rebeka, dau. of Thomas," born 1778.

Nathaniel Hovey 4, (Nathaniel 3, Daniel 2, Daniel 1,) married Hannah ffossee, 10, 8, 1719. He died, 1775. His children :

Nathaniel and John and Daniel died early ;

Esther, bap. Feb. 23, 1728, m. Moses Treadwell, 1752.

John, bap. Oct. 24, 1731 ; married Rebekah Leatherland 1754 ; she m. 2, William Pulcifer of Douglas, 1761.

Joseph, bap. Feb. 10, 1733, m. 1, Elisabeth Caldwell, 1757 ; 2, Mary Burnham, 1762. He had : Hannah ; Joseph who m. Sally Burnham (and had Joseph B. who m. Margaret Stacey, 1806 ;) Nathaniel ; Sarah ;

Hannah, born 1739, m. 1, Eben'r Smith, 2, Wells ;

Elisabeth, born 1741, m. Daniel Martin.

Thomas Hovey 4, (Ebenezer 3, Daniel 2, Daniel 1,) was born May 9, 1710. He is styled yeoman, in legal papers. He died in 1772, and his brother John Hovey was adm'r. He married Rebekah Lakeman in 1738. She died Nov. 25, 1785. Their children :

John, born 1739, died at sea, 1763, aged 24 years. He married Elizabeth Huse ; his daughter Hannah was born shortly after his death ; she became the wife of Nathaniel Fuller. The widow, Elisabeth (Huse) Hovey, m. Nath'l Perkins in 1776. In the appraisal of the estate of John Hovey, 1763, his wardrobe is : "A crimson jacket, a scarlet jacket, a blue double-breadth jacket, a beaver hat and wig, silver shoe buckles, a blue coat, a black coat, a great coat, and the sea-clothing."

Ebenezer, baptized Sept 30, 1744, m. 1, Sally Holmes, 2, Eunice Hodgkins.

Francis, born Feb. 24, 1747, m. 1, Hannah Lewis, 2, Lydia [Lewis] Gray.

Rebekah, married Samuel Dennis, 1762.

Elizabeth, m. 1, Thomas Newmarch, 1762 ; 2, Capt. Gideon Parker, May 30, 1782. He was a Revolutionary officer and a prominent citizen of Ipswich.

Sarah, married Philip Abbott, 1773.

Capt. Ebenezer Hovey 5, (Thomas 4, Ebenezer 3, Daniel 2, Daniel 1,) born Sept. 1744, died July 23, 1817, aged 72 years. He m. 1, Eunice Dutch, 1773 ; 2, Sally Holmes, 1783 ; she died Oct. 7, 1792, aged 32 years ; he m. 3, Eunice Hodgkins, Nov. 10, 1793, she died August

27, 1837, aged seventy-four years.   Several children died
in infancy ; others were :

John Holmes, born Nov. 12, 1790, died 1884.

Eunice, died Oct. 20, 1819, aged twenty-one years.

Stephen, born Dec. 16, 1795, died March 8, 1870, aged
seventy-five years ; m. Isette S. Hook, 1842.

Francis Hovey 5, (Thomas 4, Ebenezer 3, Daniel 2,
Daniel 1,) was born February 24, 1747, died February 4,
1829, aged 82 years.   He m. 1, Hannah Lewis, born in
Boston February 26, 1746, died April 26, 1802.   He married 2, Lydia (Lewis) Gray, born in Boston, Oct. 16, 1761 ;
died February 15, 1826.

His son, Francis 6, in a diary, 1792,  makes this mention
of his father, Francis 5 :

" When  my father was a boy he went to Wenham to
live with one Mr. Dodge, a farmer.   I have heard him tell
of being chased by two black  snakes in a day.   Then he
went  to  Boston  and  learned  the  trade  of bricklayer, of
one Mr. Huse.

" When he was twenty-one years old,—or free,—he married  Hannah Lewis.   After she died, he married her sister
Lydia.   My grandfather Lewis was an Englishman ; he
came to this country  when he  was  almost  fourteen  years
old.   He  lived  in  Boston  in  New  North Lane, close by
Clarke's shipyard.   He was a block-maker, and served his
time on Parson's wharf.   He died at 85 years old,  and was
a pious, good man."

The  same  writer  says again :  " In  February 1791,  my
father, Francis Hovey, broke his knee-pan.   He had  Doc-
tors Manning, Clark and Lord.   He kept the house  three
months, and was lame a year.   He walked with two crutch-
es. and a strap round  his boot and over his neck to  steady
his leg.   *   *   In 1792, my father undertook to build  the
County House and to build the Powder House."

The same pen wrote out the family record of Francis 5 :

i. Francis, born April 24, 1771.   Unmarried.

ii. Thomas Lewis, born Aug. 29, 1772, m. 1, Mary Perkins, Dec. 30, 1794. 2. Cynthia Markoe ; he lived at
Hallowell and had nineteen children.

iii. Hannah, born November 20, 1774, died early.

iv. Hannah, born Dec. 16, 1776, died Aug. 56, 1836, aged sixty years; unmarried.

v. Rebekah, born April 2, 1779, died Nov. 19, 1836.

vi. Polly, born June 30, 1781, ; m. William Stone; he was lost in a sloop of war, 1812; seven children.

vii. John, born Nov. 26, 1783, m. Elisabeth Fuller, Oct. 28, 10. He died Oct. 23, 1865. Nine children.

viii. Lydia, born Aug. 26, 1785, m. Francis Caldwell, 1811 Seven children.

ix. Joseph, born Sept. 28, 1790, married Mary Andrews, born Dec. 1813, and married Feb. 26, 1837.

x. Levi, born April 25, 1792, married Sally Chase, Nov. 20, 1817. She died Aug. 2, 1871, aged 77 years.

xi. George, born July 29, 1804, died at Battavia, Aug. 9, 1826, aged twenty-two years.

Levi Hovey 6, (Francis 5, Thomas 4, Ebenezer 3, Daniel 2, Daniel 1,) married Sally Chase, Nov. 20, 1817, and had: Eliza H. married William Kingsford, 1840; Lydia, d. May 9, 1840, aged 14 years; Sarah, m. Parsons; Joseph died 1851, aged twenty-four.

John Hovey 6, (Francis 5, Thomas 4, Ebenezer 3, Daniel 2, Daniel 1, born Nov. 26, 1785, died Oct. 23, 1865, married Elizabeth Fuller, October 38, 1810. Children:

John, married Mary Ann Carr.

Elizabeth, died Nov. 7, 1837, aged twenty-five years.

Abigail Mansfield, died early.

Thomas.

Francis.

Abby, married Charles Estes.

Nathaniel, married Lydia Boardman.

Hannah Lewis.

George Lewis.

HOWARD, (or Hayward,) William, had liberty "to fall trees," 1670.  Commoner, 1678.  He had:

William, born June 25, 1673.

Marcy, born October 8, 1675.

Martha, born March 31, 1678.

He died July 25, 1709.  His will is dated July 23, 1709. In it are mentioned his sons: William, John, Samuel, weavers;

Daughters : Mary Fuller, (born Dec. 1667) Tabitha Hodgkins ; Mercy Hovey ; Martha Howard ;

His sister, Hannah Howard ;

His wife, but her baptismal name not given.

> Here  Lys  ye  Body
> of   William   Houeard
> who   Died   July   ye
> 25th,   1709,   &   in   ye
> 74  year  of
> His   Age

William Howard 2, and Martha his wife, had:

William, born September 26, 1696.

Hezekiah, born October 1, 1698.

Hezekiah Howard 3, son of William 2, left a widow, Susanna Howard, who died August 6, 1725.

Hannah Howard, 'a very ancient maid,' died Feb. 1725.

The names of Howard and Hayward are confounded on our records.  Christopher Hodgkins is recorded to have married Tabitha Hayward, January 22, 1689.  She was undoubtedly the daughter of William Howard 1, and she was born January 21, 1669.  [See Hayward, p. 129.]

"Old Thomas Hayward" died April 15, 1686.

HUNT, William, and Sarah Newman, were married June 9, 1684.  Their children :

Sarah, born June 6, 1685.

Annice, born April 5, 1689.

Mary, born February 12, 1690.

Abigail, born December 30, 1692.

Elizabeth, born December 20, 1694.

Rebeccca, born April 21, 1697.

Sarah, wife of Serg't William Hunt, died August 18, 1723. He had horses on the common, 1697. And had a seat assigned to him in the Meeting-house, 1702.

Samuel Hunt, had a share in Plum Island, &c., in 1664 ; surveyor of highways, 1675 ; had horses on the common, 1697. He and Elisabeth his wife had :
Peter, born August 8, 1668.
Peter, born May 16, 1670.
Samuel, February, 4, 1678.
Elisabeth, wife of Samuel Hunt, died,—

Elis : Hunt
aged  72  ys
Deces'd  Feb
15   1706
A   tender   Mother
A   Prudent   wife
At   God's   Command
Resined   her   life.

1693, March 29. Francis Palmer of Rowley sheweth : Joseph Reding of Ipswich, deceased, gave his whole estate to Agnes, his wife, during her life, and after her decease to be equally divided amongst ye children of his daughter, ye wife of Samuel Hunt. The names of which wre Samuel, William, Joseph, Elizabeth and peeter Hunt.
Before our marriage, said Samuel, her father made great promises what he would give his daughter : as much as any man in Ipswich should (except five) give theirs for portion.
Some estate I have rec'd which the sd Samuel saith, now his daughter is dead, is part of sd Joseph Reding's legacy to his daughter who I married, but it was inconsiderable to what he promist with his daughter when he engaged my Father palmer give me half his lands in Rowley.

William Hunt had the seventh lot of 18 feet beyond the Town Bridge granted to him March, 1692-3.

HUTLEY, Richard, commoner, 1641. He was one of the soldiers sent to the assistance of the Indians, 1643. In 1645, Nov. 20, he purchased of Humphrey Bradstreet, ten acres of land lying on the common fields on the north side of Ipswich river.

HOBBS, Jonathan, had:
Rebecca, born March 30, 1677.
Jonathan, born December 23, 1678.
John, born April 25, 1680.
Mary, born February 7, 1681.
Caleb, May 10, 1683.

HUNKEN, John, had horses on the common, 1697. 1673, November. Joseph Leigh bound to protect the town from charge from entertaining of Sarah Hunkin. The constable to warn Joseph Lee not to entertain John Hunkin.

HOOKER, Matthew. Had son Matthew born Nov. 3, 1678. Quartermaster John Perkins "shall save the town harmless by his entirtaining Mathew Hooker, a Jersie man, to be inhabitant, by taking him for a tenant into a farm of his."

HUBBARD, William, came to Boston in 1630, and made application to be freeman to the General Court, October 19, of that year.
He settled at Ipswich, in 1635, and was one of the wealthiest and most respectable of the first inhabitants.
1643, 4th, 2d mo. Granted to Mr. William Hubbard the parcel of land, &c., containing about fifty-one acres; twenty-five whereof is in consideration of the highway that leadeth through his farm; and the other twenty-five acres are for work to be done towards making the great swamp sufficient.
Mr. William Hubbard gave an acre of land toward the founding of the GRAMMAR SCHOOL; and was a feoffee of that institution from its foundation in 1650, until his removal to Boston in 1662. The lot he gave was probably that part of the lot on which the school house [1854] stands.
He was deputy to the General Court six years, between 1838 and 1646. He was commissioned by the General Court to marry people in 1651. He died between June 8 and August 19, 1670, leaving sons
William,
Richard,
Nathaniel.

William Hubbard 2, son of William 1, was born in England about 1621, and came to America with his father in
1630.  He was of the first class that was graduated at
Harvard College, 1642.

He commenced his ministry as colleague with Mr. Cobbett, July, 1656; and continued to officiate until August 2,
1702,—on which day, as it appears by the church record:
'' The Rev'd Mr. Hubbard detained the Brethren of the
Church and signified and declared his inability (thro age)
to carry on the work of the ministry any longer among
them, and desired that they would take care and procure
help to carry on sd work.''

He expended his patrimony which was large, and left
his widow in indigence at his death, Sept. 14, 1704.

He mortgaged to John Richards of Boston, July 20,
1674, his Dwelling house in the Town of Ipswich; and
thirty acres of land being part of Hattfields farm; and
twelve acres of other land for £324 sterling.

At a Town Meeting held Oct. 26, 1704 it was voted That
ye twenty pounds due to ye sale of ye old Meeting house,
ye Treasurer shall pay ye said twenty pounds toward ye
defraying Mr. Hubbard's funeral.''

His first wife was Margaret Rogers, daughter of the
Rev'd Nathaniel Rogers.  She, dying, he married the
widow of Samuel Pearce (who had died in 1698.)  This
marriage, Mr. Felt says, was not agreeable to most of his
parish.  They would allow her to be a worthy woman, but
not of sufficient distinction to be their minister's wife.

At a Town Meeting held '' March ye 14, 1709-10, Voted
that twenty pounds money be added to the Town rates for
supplying Mrs. Hubbard in her distressed condition.''
She died in 1710-11.

> Here  Lyes  ye  Body
> of Mis' Mary Hub-
> bard (late wife of
> ye Reuerend Mr.
> William  Hubard)
> who  died  February
> ye  28,  1710-11  Aged
> 53  years

Rev. William Hubbard left two sons, John and Nathaniel; and one daughter Margaret, who married John Pynchon, and removed first to Boston and afterwards to Springfield. While they resided in Boston she joined the church of Ipswich by "taking the covenant," Jan. 18, 1673.

Mr. Hubbard wrote a work entitled "Present State of New-England," which was printed in London in 1678. This was afterwards recast and printed under the title of *Indian Wars*. The General Court appoint a committee May 19, 1680, to peruse his History of New England and report, so that they may judge "about having it printed."

In 1663, they vote him £50, a "half of this sum to be paid him now, if he procure a fayre coppie to be written, that it be fitted for the presse." This "fayre coppie" remained in manuscript until the Massachusetts Historical Society, aided by a donation from the General Court, had it printed in 1815.

John Hubbard 3, son of William 2, came into the church in full connection, Jan. 25, 1673. Freeman Oct. 11, 1676.

Richard Hubbard 2, William 1, was graduated at Harvard College in 1653. His father when he removed to Boston in 1662, gave him a valuable farm in the part of the town called the Hamlet,—now the town of Hamilton.

In 1664 he had a double share in Plum Island, &c., which indicates him as being one of twenty-seven of the richest out of 230 freeholders. He was selectman, 1665; feoffee of Grammar School, 1665; tithingman, 1677. He died May 3, 1681. He left a widow Sarah; sons Richard, Nathaniel, John, Simon; and a daughter Sarah, wife of John Cotton. A son William was born Nov. 29, 1666.

His farm consisted of 220 acres, with a dwelling house, out houses, orchard.

1691, April 22. Richard, son of Mr. Richard Hubbard, chose his uncle, the Rev'd William, guardian; John, chose Daniel Epps; Nathaniel chose Capt. Thomas Wade.

INGALLS, John, was one of Major Denison's subscribers, 1648. He was son of Edmund Ingalls who came from Lincolnshire, England, and settled at Lynn, 1629.

Samuel Ingalls was commoner, and had a share in Plum

Island, &c., 1664.  He purchased of William White, Jan. 16, 1659, "ye part of his farm which he sold unto John West and purchased it of him again."

He with his wife Ruth, (married Dec. 9, 1657,) came into full communion with the church, March 1, 1673.  Voter in Town affairs, 1679.  He was freeman, Oct. 12, 1681 ; selectman, 1683 ; representative to General Court, 1690. His children :

Ruth, born March 19, 1657.
Edmond, born July 23, 1662.
John, born August 26, 1664.
Joseph, December 30, 1666.
Mary, born March 13, 1668.
Anna, born March 8, 1671.
Elizabeth, born September 27, 1673.
Nathaniel, born February 9, 1675.

Lievt: Ingalls, Samuel and Joseph, had horses on the common, 1697.

Samuel and Joseph were probably the sons of Lieut. Samuel.

1714, August 30.  Died lately, Samuel Ingalls.  He left a wife, and children : Mary Butler, Anna Giddinge, Joseph, Nathaniel, and a daughter, the wife of Samuel Chapman.

IRELAND, Philip, and Grace his wife, had a son Solomon, born January 24, 1691 ; Grace, died May 13, 1692.  He was a wool-comber.

JACOB, Richard, took the freeman's oath in Boston, May, 1635.  He was commoner, 1641 ; was entitled to two shares in Plum Island, &c., in 1664, which indicates him as one of the 27 richest men in Ipswich.  He had a house-lot in Mill street, 1635.  He married Martha, daughter of Samuel Appleton.  She died Sept. 8, 1659.  At his decease in 1672, he left a wife whose baptismal name was Joanna.

He directs in his will, proved October 5, 1672, his eldest son Thomas, to pay a legacy to his mother-in-law, "my wife Joanna."  He appoints his son Richard his sole executor.

He left children :
Richard,
John,
Nathaniel, a minor,
Joseph, a minor,
Thomas,
Martha,
Judith,
Lydia Jacob, a grandaughter, and daughter of his son Samuel, deceased.

He had the title of Serg't ; and possessed, in 1660, a farm on the south side of the river, which was originally granted io Mr. Winthrop, near to the farms of Daniel Rindge and Matthew Whipple.

Richard Jacob 2, son of Richard 1, married Mary Whipple, January 15, 1673. She died January 27, 1675 ; and he died 1676. A daughter Mary was born January 20, 1675, and died in June. His will is dated June 8, and proved Sept. 26, 1676. He bequeathes property to his brothers,—Nathaniel, Thomas, Joseph, John ; and to his sisters Martha and Judith. He. appoints his two uncle Appletons, [John and Samuel, sons of Samuel,]overseers.

Joseph Jacob 2, son of Richard 1, married December 18, 1660, Susan Symonds, daughter of William and granddaughter of the Hon'ble Samuel Symonds ; and had a son Samuel born Dec. 1, 1691, and died aged thirteen days ; and Joseph, born March 12, 1692.

1697, December 6. Inventory of Estate of Joseph Jacob. Farm, £452, 10.

Debts due from estate, £288, 6, 9.

Among which are,—To sister Moody, £6. To sister Hasey, £4. To Bro. Willard, £7, 13. To Bro. Willard for boarding ye boy, £5. To Abra : ffits, for boarding ye child, £4.

Ensign Thomas Jacob 2, son of Richard 1, married Sarah Brown, December 21, 1671. He was Freeman, 1674, voter, 1679. Thomas Jaackob, Tythingman, 1679 ; subscribed to the Bell, 1699, and had a seat assigned "at the Table," in the Meeting-house, 1700.

Nathaniel Jacob 2, son of Richard 1, voter 1679; commoner, 1678. His will is dated Nov. 4, 1688. He bequeathes to his brother Thomas twenty pounds ; to brother Jno : Jacobs, thirty pounds ; sister Judith Hasey, twenty pounds. "I give to ye standing minister or ministers twenty shillings per year, during ye continuance of such a ministry as is now settled in Ipswich as to Doctrine & form." " I also give vnto my Lo : Coss'n, Lev't Jno : Appleton, five pounds." The rest was given to his brother Joseph.

JACKSON, John, possessed a houselot in 1635 ; was a commoner in 1641 ; a subscriber to Major Denison, 1648, —the year of his death. The inventory of his estate is dated Sept. 18, 1648. His widow Catherine married William White, and sold the John Jackson land and house to John West, before June 28, 1649.

INGLISH, William, possessed land near Reedy Marsh, 1638.

JEWETT, Jeremiah,—the eldest son of Joseph Jewett of Rowley,—was a commoner in 1664.
Of his father, [Joseph Jewett of Rowley,] we gather the following :

1660, February 15. Joseph Jewett of Rowley, his will: goods to be divided equally among my seven children, as well those two that I have by my last wife as the five I had before. Always provided that my eldest sonne, Jeremiah Jewett, must have a double portion of all the estate I have, both in New England & old England : provided that one hundred pounds I have already payed to my sonne Phillip Nelson, that shall be counted as part of what I doe now give him.
I doe give to my sonne Jeremiah Jewett, the farm I bought of Joseph Murry. I mean all such lands bought of him or any other that are on the northwest side of the river called Egypt River, with all the meadow I bought of Robert Lord, senior, & Nathaniel Stow, provided he accept of it at five hundred pounds.
As to my two youngest children and their portion, I leave to the disposing of my brother, Maximillian Jewett,

and who he shall appoint when he departeth this life. And
I make executor of this my last will and testament, my
Brother Maximillian Jewett, and my sonne Phillip Nelson,
my cosin John Carleton and my sonne Jeremiah Jewett.
Witnesses : Ezekiel Northend, Mark Prime.

1661, February 1. Ann Jewett, will : It being that I
have at my own disposal one hundred pounds * * I will
that this one hundred pounds shall be equally divided
among the four of my children, to witt : John Allen, Ann
Allen, Isaac Allen, Bossom Allen. And as for those several perticulers that are at my disposal in that covenant
between Mr. Joseph Jewett and me, &c., &c. Daughter
Priscilla. John Allen shall have a gould ring & the silver wine cup. Witness : John Harris.

Joseph Jewett 1, of Rowley, purchased a house and
lands in Ipswich, of Nathaniel Stone and Elisabeth his
wife, June 12, 1656 ; having the house and land of Henry
Archer towards the Northwest ; street Northeast ; John
Woodman Southeast ; Henry Pindar south west.

Jeremiah Jewett of Ipswich had property, the value of
which as indicated by his having a share and a half in
Plum Island, &c., was greater than the average of the
inhabitants. His name is not on the list of those by law
allowed to have their votes in Town affairs in 1679, but is,
with the title of Mr. among those who "have horses yt goo
upon ye common, 1697. He had children :

Jeremiah, born in Ipswich, Dec. 30, 1662.
Joseph, born April 17, 1665.
Thomas, born January 29, 1667.
Mary, born January 24, 1674.
Ephraim, born February 2, 1679.
Caleb, born March 22, 1681.

His last wife was Elizabeth Kimball, whom he married
January 4, 1687-8. He had a seat assigned him in the
Meeting-house in 1700, "at the table." He died May 20,
1714, aged seventy-seven years.

Nehemiah Jewett 2, son of Joseph 1, was a prominent
man. He was a voter in town affairs in 1679 ; tithingman,
1667 ; selectman, 1680.

In 1700, he was one of a committee "impowered to appoint seats and to allot the pews in ye New Meeting house." The pew allotted to himself was "ye 2d pew on ye so-west side of ye great door, for his wife & family," while he was appointed to sit "at ye Table." He subscribed 12 shillings to the Bell in 1699.

He was Representative to General Court sixteen years, between 1689 and 1709, and Speaker of the House 1693-4 and 1701.

He died about January 1719-20. His wife, Exercise Jewett, was living in 1685. His children were:

Mary, born August 9, 1673, died August 30, 1681.
Nehemiah, born August 8, 1675.
Joanna, born May 8, 1677
Nathan, born October 25, 1679, died Nov. 8.
Joseph.
Benjamin.
Nathaniel.

He had a son-in-law, Daniel Dow; and a grandson Nehemiah Skillion. His sons Nathaniel and Joseph were commoners in 1707.

Jeremiah Jewett, junior, and Elizabeth his wife had:
Moses, born October 13, 1695.
Aaron, born Feb. 10, 1693, died June 27, 1694.
Aaron, died January 23, 1698.
Aaron, born June 13, 1699.
Jeremiah was a commoner in 1707.

John Jewett and Elizabeth his wife, had
Sarah, born March 7, 1668.
Abigail, died August 3, 1672.
Samuel, born September 12, 1673.
Abigail, born Sept. 13, died Nov. 14, 1675.
David, born April 3, 1677.
Mary, born May 27, 1679.
Daniel, born November 12, 1681.

Nehemiah, Nehemiah 3d, and Ephraim Jewett had seats assigned them in the Meeting-house, 1702.
Isaac Jewett was a commoner, 1707.
George Jewett had George born Sept. 17, 1680.

JOHNSON, John, Schoolmaster; was of Ipswich in 1635. He possessed a planting lot of six acres on the Town Hill, which he sold to Mark Quilter; and Quilter bequeathed it to his son Mark, who sold it Nov. 30, 1657, to John Woodman. He also had in 1635, a planting lot on Heartbreak hill, near to Mr. John Tuttle, Mr. Dudley and others, toward the marshes.

JORDAN, Francis, commoner, 1641, one of Major Denison's subscribers, 1648 ; had a share in Plum Island, &c., 1664; surveyor of Highways, 1675.  Died April 24, 1678. His will is dated April 23, 1678.  He gives all his estate to his wife, Jane, to dispose of it to his children and grandchildren ; and "may give it to them who behave themselves best towards her;" with liberty "to sell what part she may have occasion for her comfortable maintenance."

The will of his widow, Jane Jordan, (who was commoner 1678,) is dated Dec. 20, 1689, and was proved Oct. 28, 1693. She appoints Richard Belcher, who was probably her son-in-law, executor.  She mentions a grandaughter, "Mary Simson, so called before marriage," and a daughter, Jane Ward.  She then directs her estate to be divided into six equal parts, and given to her grandaughters, Mary Belcher, Sarah George ; daughters, Hannah Fowler, Mary Kimball, Lydia White, each one sixth part ; and one sixth part to the children of Deborah, late wife of Benjamin Goodridge, viz., Benjamin, Joseph, Daniel, Josiah.  She mentions having paid Jno : Kimball more than any of the rest.  Inventory, £159, 18, 6.  Lieut. Symon Stace and John Harris, sen'r, overseers.

Stephen Jordan, was of Ipswich in 1637 ; and one of Major Denison's subscribers in 1648.  He removed to Newbury, where he died, February 8, 1670.  He possessed land adjoining that of Mr. Samuel Hall, 1637.

JONES, Nathaniel. [With additions.] Nath'l Jones
and Rachel Bradford married January 3, 1704. Children:
  i. Nathaniel, born October 18, 1705.
  ii. William, born October 31, 1707.
  iii. Hannah, born April 8, 1711.
  iv. John, born January 28, 1712.
  v. Benjamin, born in Beverly, December 4, 1716.
  vi. Bethia, born August 9, 1719.

Nathaniel Jones 2, (Nathaniel 1,) lived at the Hamlet,
and had: Hannah, born 1727; Sarah, 1729; a child, 1750.

William 2, (Nathaniel 1) born October 31, 1707; married Joanna Lord, October 13, 1728. He died November,
1782. He is styled "Feltmaker" and "Hatter." He
built in 1728, the Jones house, nearly opposite the Town
Hall, which has continued in the family till now. [1874.]
He was converted under the preaching the Rev'd George
Whitefield, in 1740; and the renowned evangelist was his
guest during a part of his Ipswich visitation. The guest
chamber was specially regarded afterwards by the household, as the "Whitefield room." William 2, bought a pew
in the new Meeting-house of the First Church, November
6, 1749, which was occupied by his descendants till 1846,
when the beautiful old house was taken down. He was a
man of wealth, but lost a large share in his old age. Prov.
11, 15.) He was remembered by his grandchildren as one
of scrupulous care in demeanor, language, and dress;
and thereby commanded respect from the younger and
older people. His wife, Joanna Lord, daughter of Thomas
and Elisabeth Lord, was baptized October 5, 1712. They
had fifteen children:
  i. William, born June 6, 1731; died July 4, 1731.
  ii. William, died June 17, 1732.
  iii. Joanna, born 1733, died 1736.
  iv. Mary, born Novem. 24, 1734, married Capt. James
      Thurston, Exeter, N. H.
  v. Joanna, born Feb. 5, 1736, married Capt. John Hol-
      land, published August 16, 1755.
  vi. A son born 1738, died June 24, 1742.
  vii. Abigail, born August 10, 1740, married Dr. Wallis
      Rust, published Nov. 17, 1664, died July 28, 1792.

Dr. Rust died Dec'r 1, 1792, aged fifty-one years. Children : Wallis ; William ; Joanna, married Jonathan Howard of Boston ; John.

viii. Sarah, born March 28, 1742, marched James Fuller. She died June, 1816.

ix. Thomas, born March 11, 1743.

x. Nathaniel, born December 22, 1745.

xi. Daniel, born August 30, 1747, married Ellzabeth May, published September 25, 1763.

xii. Samuel, born January 22, 1749, lived in Salem.

xiii. Joseph, twin, born August 13, 1751, lived at Washington, N. H.

xiv. Dr. Benjamin, twin, born August 15, 1751 ; settled at Lyndeboro, N. H.

xv. John, born May 1757, died November, 1787.

John Jones 2, (Nathaniel 1,) born January 28, 1712, m. Mary Whipple, August 20, 1734. He lived at the Hamlet. Children :

Mary, born August, 1735. Died early.

John, born ,1737.

Mary.

Benjamin 2, (Nathaniel 1,) was born in Beverly, Dec. 4, 1716. He became a physician in Beverly. He married three times : 1. Mary Woodbury, and had,

i. Benjamin, born October 5, 1736, married Mary Lodge 1763. He died January 4, 1776.

ii. Mary, born February 8, 1741-2, married Billy Porter of Wenham. She died October 15, 1763.

iii. Nathaniel, born February 8, 1743, died Sept. 1779.

iv. Lydia, born June, 1746 ; married Thomas Lancaster.

Dr. Jones married 2, Ginger Leach. She died Dec. 13, 1756, in her thirtieth year. Her children :

v. Hannah, b. June 17, 1750, m. Henry Herrick, jr. 1772

vi. William, born December, 1752, died January 1761.

vii. John, born 1755, died November, 1781.

Dr. Jones married 3, Sarah Endicott, December 3, 1757.

Thomas Jones 3, (William 2, Nathaniel 1,) born March 11, 1743, married Hannah Smith, [daughter of John and Hannah Martin Smith,] published September 18, 1773, died May 6, 1814. Hannah died October 25, 1822. They had eleven children:

i. Thomas, born October 14, 1774, married Eunice Harding, Feb. 22, 1797, lived at Tamworth, N. H.

ii. Amos, born March 2, 1776, married Elisabeth Smith, [daughter of Simon and Mary Shatswell Smith,] he died March 23, 1846. Two children, William, who m. Lydia Hamilton of Chatham, Mass, and had Charles Franklin, George Galen and Lydia, all died unmarried; Mary, daughter of Amos, married Samuel Caldweil. Six children.

iii. Abigail, born April 13, 1778, drowned in Ipswich River, February 26, 1787.

iv. John, born July, 1780, died early.

v. Hannah, born September 11, 1781, died March 23, 1846, a few hours before her brother Amos. She married John Smith, 1801. He died six weeks later. He was son of Simon and Mary Shatswell Smith. She married 2, Samuel Henderson, April, 1820. Children: John, William, Mary, Eunice, Elizabeth.

vi. John, born January 13, 1784. Died early.

vii. Elizabeth, born February 26, 1786, married David Pindar, Dec. 9, 1810, died at Malden, March 9, 1853. He was lost at sea, 1815, aged twenty-eight years. Two children, Abigail Jones, unm.; Elisabeth, m. Horatio Hall. of Malden.

viii. John Smith, born April 28, 1788, wife Mary, one son, Alfred Caldwell, died at twenty-one years, unm.

ix. William, born June 15, 1790, lived at Salem; m. Elisabeth Giles, of Marblehead, March 21, 1813; died May 8, 1860. Children: Samuel G. John S. Elizabeth, Caroline.

x. Abigail, born August 28, 1792. Died early.

xi. Eunice, born August 11, 1793, died July 3, 1825, aged 32 years. A life of singular religious devotion.

Nathaniel Jones 3, (William 2, Nathaniel 1,) born Dec. 22, 1745, married Susannah Harris, Dec. 5, 1768. Chil:

i. Nathaniel, baptized November 25, 1770.

ii. William, baptized August 2, 1772.

iii. Susannah, baptized December 22, 1776.

Dr. Benjamin Jones 3, (William 2, Nathaniel 1,) born August 13, 1751, died January 12, 1819. He married Elizabeth Cleaves of Ipswich ; she was born October 20, 1752, and died June 6, 1819. He was a physician in Lyndeboro, N. H. and especially skillful as a surgeon. Children,

   i. Benjamin, born May 18, 1774.
  ii. Elizabeth, born December 18, 1776.
 iii. Joanna, born January 27, 1779.
 iv. Mary Cleaves, born January 19, 1781.
  v. Huldah, born March 26, 1783.
 vi. Dr. Joseph of Wenham, born March 29, 1785.
vii. Nathaniel, born June 22, 1787.
viii. William, born July 14, 1789.
 ix. Sarah, born March 5, 1792.
  x. Nathan, born April 25, 1794.

Of this Ipswich family, two of the sons of Nathaniel 1, became men of estate : William of Ipswich and Dr. Benja. of Beverly.

Of later generations several have left worthy record :
    Dr. Benjamin Jones, of Lyndeboro, N. H.
    Dr. Joseph Jones, Wenham, Mass.
    Rev. William Thurston, Manchester, Mass.
    Rev. James Boutwell, Dunkirk, N. Y.
    Rev. William Thurston Boutwell, Missionary to the
       Ojibwa Indians, Wisconsin.
    Rev. James Thurston, West Newton, Mass.
    Benjamin Jones Boutwell, Worcester, Mass.
    John Smith Jones, Salem, Mass.

KIMBALL. In the ship *Elizabeth*, of Ipswich, England, William Andrews, master, which sailed April, 1634, there came passengers, viz.,

> Henry Kemball, aged 44 years.
> Susan, his wife, aged 35 years.
> Elizabeth, aged 4 ; Susan aged 1 and a half years,—their children.
> Richard Kemball, aged 39 years, uxor, Ursala.
> Their children :
> Henry, aged 15 years ; Richard, aged 13 years ;
> Mary, aged 9 years ; Martha, aged 5 years ;
> John, aged 3 years ; Thomas aged 1 year.

Richard Kimball took the freeman's oath in Boston, May 6, 1635. He had a houselot granted to him in Ipswich, February 23, 1637, adjoining goodman Simons, "att ye west end of ye town." He was a commoner, 1641 ; one of Major Denison's subscribers, 1648 ; had a share and a half in Plum Island, &c., 1664.

He had a farm in the northerly part of the town, near Prospect Hill, having the farm which Thomas Emerson sold to Joseph Jewett on the north west. He also possessed a lot on the town Hill.

Thomas Scott in his will, March 8, 1653, calls him his brother.

In 1650, Joseph Fowler sells him lands, in the deed of which he styles him,—Richard Kimball, wheelwright, his father-in-law.

He died June 22, 1675. His will was proved September 28. He mentions his wife, without giving her name ; and her children, Thomas, Jeremiah and Mary ; and there was "forty pound due to her according to compact of marriage."

His children, mentioned in his will, were :

Henry, the eldest son ; John, Thomas, Benjamin, Caleb, John Stevens, son-in-law, Elizabeth, Mary, Sarah.

He mentions his "cousin Haniel Bosworth."

The inventory of his property, June 17, 1676, amounted to £986, 5; of which his house with 132 acres of land valued at £370.

The name is written upon our records—Kemball, Kimball and Kimbole.

The Massachusetts Observer says:

Richard Kimball, 1.  He was married twice.  Margaret, his second wife, survived him.  She died March 1, 1675. She was the widow Dow, of Hampton, N. H., probably widow of Henry Dow, whose will is dated 1659, 4th, 8m.

The second wife of Richard Kimball, was the widow of Henry Dow, sen'r, who died April 21, 1659, and left three children, viz., Mary, born 1640; Thomas, born in 1652 ; Jeremiah, born September 6, 1657.

Richard Kimball and the widow Margaret Dow were married October 23, 1661.

Thomas Dow, in his will dated November 14, 1676, mentions his "unkill Benjamin Kimball."

Henry Kimball 2, son of Richard 1, died in 1676, leaving twelve children, two of whose name were Richard and John.  The second wife of Henry Kimball was the widow Elizabeth Rayner.  She had no children.

Benjamin Kimball 2, fifth son of Richard 1, styled Cornet, was in Bradford, where he died June 11, 1696.  He left a widow, Marcy Kimball ; and nine children, viz.,

Richard ;    David, born 1671 :    Jonathan, born 1673;
Robert, born 1675 ;    Hannah ;    Elizabeth ;
Samuel, born 1680 ;    Ebenezer, born 1684 ;
Abigail ;    Margaret.

1681, 5, 10.  Agreed with Richard Kimball of Bradford, for his keeping and providing for his grandfather, Thomas Smith, for the year ensuing, £13.—*Ipswich Records.*

Richard Kimball 2, (Richard 1,) was one of Major Denison's subscribers in 1648.

John Kimball 2, (Richard 1,) born 1631, married Mary, daughter of Francis Jordan, October 8, 1666.  He had a share and a half in Plum Island, &c., in 1664; was a voter in Town affairs, 1679.  He joined the church by taking the covenant, March 8, 1673.

He died May 6, 1698.  His will is dated March 19, 1697-8. In it he mentions sons :

Richard, born March 16. 1668.

John, born Nov. 3, 1657.  (A son John died Feb. 24.)

Moses, born September, 1672,
Benjamin, born July 23, 1670.
Joseph, born January 24, 1675.
Daughters:
Mary, born December 10, 1658.
Sarah, born January 24, 1661.
Rebeckah, born February, 1664.
Richard and Elizabeth, born September 22, 1665.
Abigail, born March 22, 1667.
Hannah,
Aaron, born January, 1674.
Benjamin and Joseph were executors aad residuary legatees.
He gave his sons six shillings and his daughters four shillings each.
Inventory, £131, 9, 11.   July 4, 1698.

Richard Kimball 3, son of John 2, married January 13, 1685, Lidia Wills, and had,—
Liddia, born October 18, 1690.
Richard, born August 17, 1691.
Aaron, born January 10, 1692, died at 37 years old.
Liddia, born September 14, 1694.
He had horses on the common, 1697.   He died 1716:

> Here : Lyes : Bvried
> ye : Body : of : Mr : Rich
> ard : Kimball : who
> Died : May : ye : 26 : 1716
> Aged 50 years
> As . you . are . so
> Were . we . Bvt
> As : we : Are : so
> yov : shall : be

The gravestone of Aaron 4, son of Richard 3, is inscribed:

Here Lyes ye Body of Mr. Aaron Kimball, Dec'd February ye 12, 1728-9, in ye 37th year of his Age.

[Aaron, son of Aaron and Elizabeth Kimball, died November, 1731, aged thirteen years.]

John Kimball 3, (John 2,) and Sarah his wife, had twin sons :

John and Joseph, born October 19, 1693. Joseph died
February 2, 1693.

Mary, born February 24, 1697.

Moses Kimball 3, (John 2,) with Susanna his wife, had

Moses, born January 26, 1696.

Ebenezer, born March 20, 1698, died of small pox,
December 3, 1721

He had a seat assigned to him in the Meeting house in 1700.

Benjamin Kimball 3, (John 2,) with Mary his wife, had:

John, born October 21, 1695.

Mary, born October 24, 1697.

He had a seat assigned to him in the Meeting house, 1700.

Here Lyes Buried
ye Body of Mr Ben
Jamin Kimball
who died
May ye 28 1716
aged 45 years
Here – Lyes – His
Dust – Until – ye
Resurection – of
ye Just.

Thomas Kimball 2, son of Richard 1, born 1633 ; had a share and a half in Plum Island, &c., 1664. He was one of the first settlers of Bradford, where he was killed by the Indians, May 3, 1676. And his wife and five children, —Joanna, Thomas, Joseph, Priscilla, John,—were taken prisoners and carried forty miles into the wilderness, but were returned on the 13th of June. He had a daughter Hannah, born in Ipswich, January 27, 1661.

Caleb Kimball 2, son of Richard 1, was commoner, and had a share in Plum Island, &c., 1664. He married Anna Hazelton, November 7, 1660. He had :

Caleb, born September 8, 1662.

Anah, born December 11, 1664.

Elezebeth, born September 8, 1666.

Abigail, born July, 1668.

Richard, died April 10, 1673.
Abraham, born June 29, 1675.
Benjamin, born March 27, 1678.
Sarah, born May 19, 1681.

Caleb Kimball 3, grandson of Richard 1, married Lucy, daughter of John Edwards, Nov. 23, 1685.  They had
John, born March 6, 1687.
Thomas, born September, 1691.
Lucia, born September 19, 1693.
Anna, November 24, 1695.
He subscribed three shillings to the Bell, 1699.

Hannah Kimball, widow of Serg't Caleb Kimball, died January 3, 1721.
Widow Anna Kimball, died April 9, r688.
Sarah, widow of Richard Kimball, died Dec. 22, 1725.
Benjamin and Robert Kimball, brothers, 1704.
Benjamin Kimball, blacksmith, will proved December 4, 1704.  He bequeathes all his effects to his brother Robert Kimball.
In the inventory of the estate of Robert Kimball, dated June 4, 1705, there is among other property, "twelve acres Land at Bradford, rec'd p ye Dec'd as part of portion— accounted £18."
Caleb Kinsman husbandman and Robert Kimball marinor, join  in a bond, dated October 1, 1702.  In the first year of Her Maj'tyes Reigne.
Robert Kimball married October 25, 1699, Alice Norton, sister of Deacon Thomas Norton, and died in England June 27, 1703.  His brother-in-law, Thomas Norton, was app'd adm'r of his estate, January 24, 1703-4.  His widow died in 1733.  Her will, in which the baptismal name is spelled *Allis*, is dated June 9, and was proved October 30, 1733.  The following is extracted from it :
" To ye ministers of ye Church of which I belong  unto, ten pounds, viz, to ye Revd Mr. John Rogers five  pounds, & to ye Revd Mr. Nathaniel Rogers five pounds.  Alsoe, I give unto ye Church, ten pounds more.

" I give unto my well beloved Kinsman, Thomas Norton, son to my brother, Thomas Norton, all my plate,
viz., a silver Tankard, Can, a pepper box & two silver
porringers."

A silver cup belonging to the communion service of the
First Church has the following inscription, which, from
the date [1730,] appears to have been a previous gift to the
bequest of her will :

### THE GIFT OF ALLIS KIMBALL
TO THE FIRST CHURCH IN IPSWICH IN PART
AND OF THE CHURCH STOCK, 1730

KNOWLTON, John, a commoner, 1641.  A subscriber
to Major Denison, 1648.  He purchased of Theophilus
Wilson, January 28, 1646, land which Wilson bought of
John Warner.  In the deed, Knowlton is styled, *shoemaker*.

His will is dated November 29, 1653, and was proved
March 20, 1654.  He leaves his house and land to his wife
Margery, "for her use and bringing up of the children."
His children were:  John, Abraham, Elizabeth.

He mentions brother William, brother Thomas, and
brother Wilson.

Thomas Knowlton 1, brother of John 1.  January 26,
1646, Humphrey Bradstreet conveys to Thomas Knowlton
a dwelling house and lott, situated between the dwelling
house of Andrew Hodges towards the southwest, and the
dwelling of Stephen Jordan towards the southeast; having
a high way leading down to the river on the west side.

He was one of Major Denison's subscribers in 1648.  His
will is dated 1653.  In it he mentions his sisters Elizabeth
Wilson and Margery Knowlton.  He gives to John Knowlton twenty pouuds ; "and the rest of his sisters children
ten pounds a piece : "Elizabeth Knowlton, Abraham
Knowlton, and Seaborn Wilson ; and to his brother Wilson's son Thomas, three pounds, and the rest for his mother's use during her life.

William Knowlton 1, brother of John 1, was commoner

in 1641. He styles himself *bricklayer*, in a deed of land, which he sells Feb. 28, 1643, to Edward Bragg. This is the description, "All my commonage with the appertainings belonging to the house lot which I bought of John Andrews, who bought the same of Thomas Bishop, who bought the same of Robert Hayes, to whom the freemen of the Town of Ipswich did grant the same for a houselot, and whereupon there hath been a house built, and upon occasion removed, the said land containing an acre; and it adjoineth to the other lands where I now dwell, which I bought of William Lampson and William Storey, having a lane leading towards the house of Joseph Medcalf towards the east, and Ipswich river towards the west.

John Knowlton 2, son of John 1, died October 2, 1684. He had :

Nathaniel, born June 59, 1658.

Elizabeth, born March 1, 1659.

Thomas, born May in, 1662.

Susan, born August 15, 1663.

The inventory of his effects was rendered October 8, 1684. He had a legacy from his brother Thomas, Feb. 14, 1653. He was commoner, and had share in Plum Island, &c., 1664. He had granted to him Feb. 22, 1669, privilege of firewood & feed for one cow, as long as he follows ye trade of fisherman.

In 1672, it is noted on the records, that he has ye tradesman's privilege of ye common.

In 1671, the selecimen doe now forewarn him not to neglect his occasions, & spend much time in ordinaries.

Deacon Thomas Knowlton 2, was probably son of William 1. He had a share and a half in Plum Island, &c., 1664. Was Tithingman, 1677. Voter in Town affairs, 1679. He with Susannah, his wife, sold to Sarah Stone of Watertown, county of Middlesex, Feb. 26, 1655, land lying in a flatt or field, called pequitt Lotts, having Sargeant French's on the west ; William prichett east, the town river south, the town common north.

In March, 1627-8, he possessed a houselot on the north

side of the river, adjoining Robert Pierse, near Ipswich river.

The wife of Thomas Knowlton wore a silk hood to meeting, and was fined ten shillings for the elegance.

His wife died November 20, 1688, and he died April 12, 1692.

John Knowlton 3, probably son of John 2, had liberty of firewood and one cow on the Common, 1664. With Sarah his wife, he had a daughter born Sept. 19, 1685.

Abraham Knowlton 2, son probably of John 1. Was one of ten members of the young generation who recognized the covenant, January 18, 1673.

At a Court held in May, 1664, Abraham Knowlton is fined for playing cards.

Deacon Nathaniel Knowlton, 1697. Had horses on the common. He married Deborah Grant, May 3, 1682 ; had
Samuel, born November 9, 1682.
John, born December, 1685.
Thomas, born November 8, 1692.
Abraham, born February 27, 1698.
Abraham, born March 27, 1699.
Elizabeth, born September 15, 1702.
David, born May 15, 1707.
Deborah, his wife, died April 25, 1743.   His epitaph is :

Here lies ye body of
Deacon Nathaniel
Knowlton who died
September ye 24
1726 in the 69
year of his age.

Thomas Knowlton and Margery, his wife, had:
Robert, born September 7, 1693.
Margery, born March 25, 1695.
Joseph, born March 9, 1697.
Deborah, December 31, 1698.

Thomas Knowlton and Marcy his wife, had a daughter Marcy, born August 7, 1694.

Joseph Knowlton married Mary Wilson, August 14, 1677, and had :

Joseph, born February 1, 1680.

A son, born April 1, 1686.

A daughter, died April 1, 1693.

February 17, 1684. Joseph Knowlton takes possession of the farm that was Mr. Batchelder's, dec'd, by purchase.

Samuel Knowlton and Elizabeth Witt, married April, 1669. Had :

Elizabeth, born May, 1669.

Sarah, born January 16, 1670.

The will of Samuel Knowlton, husbandman, is dated January 15, 1696-7, in which are mentioned wife Elisabeth, sons Samuel, the eldest, Jonathan, born March 16, 1678, Ebenezer; daughters Sarah and Elizabeth. Witness : Jonathan Dike, John Witt.

Mr. John Knowlton, sen'r, shoemaker, died April 11, 1720.

Sarah, wife of Abraham Knowlton, dec'd July 29, 1724.

1692-3, March 23, Thomas Knowlton, senior, lot 22 ; Thomas, Knowlton, junior, lot 21 ; John Knowlton, jun'r, lot 11, each of ten feet front, granted to them, lying between Samuel Ordways shop and ye Town Bridge.

Nathaniel Knowlton, subscribed twelve shillings towards the Bell, 1699.

1690. Robert Knowlton, being by God's providence in an exposition against a potent enemy where eminent danger may be, makes his will, dated April 30, 1690 ; which was proved March 31, 1691. In this will are mentioned brothers Thomas and Ezekiel, and sisters Deborah and Susannah. He was probably in the Canada expedition under Major Samuel Appleton.

John Knowlton married Rebekah Young, May 29, 1703.

Nathaniel Knowlton married Reform Jewett, June, 1717.

John Knowlton died September 11, 1720, and left a widow named Sarah ; and sons Abraham and Isaac. He was a shoemaker.

Nehemiah Knowlton married Rebecca Jewett, May 3, 1682.

Isaac Knowlton married Mary Dear, October 12, 1723.
He owned the house next south of the Town House, late
the residence of Amos Jones.  He left it to his widow,
Mary, who sold it July 1, 1755 to Robert Choate, who soon
afterwards married her for his second wife.

[It became the early married home of Major Robert
Farley.  Later it was purchased by Aaron Wallis.  He
sold it to Amos Jones, who died in 1846.  After his death,
his widow, Mrs. Elisabeth (Smith) Jones, sold this old
domicile of a hundred and fifty years, to Mr. Augustine
Heard, who demolished it.  A picture of it is in the Ipswich Antiquarian Papers.]

Additional.

## IPSWICH KNOWLTONS, LITCHFIELD, MAINE.

By O. B. Classon. Attorney at Law, Gardiner, Maine.

—o—

Thomas Knowlton, born in Ipswich, 1732, died in Litchfield Maine, March 12, 1796, aged 64 years.

Sally Knowlton, wife of Thomas, born in Ipswich, 1735,
died in Litchfield, March 12, 1811, aged nearly 76 years.

Their children :

Sally, born Jan. 10, 1768 ; married James Lord ;
died January 8, 1820;

Mary, born August 15, 1775 ; married Thomas
Lord ;. died March 16, 1855;

[I think another daughter married a Lane, and
lived at Monmouth, Maine.]

Jacob, married Abigail Hodgkins.

Jacob Knowlton, son of Thomas and Sally Knowlton,
came from Ipswich, and settled in Litchfield, on what is
now known as the Knowlton Place.  He married Abigail
Hodgkins, December, 1791.  She came from Ipswich, and
her sister, Salome Hodgkins, married John Dennis of
Litchfield.

Jacob Knowlton died July 14, 1814.  Abigail, his wife,
died November 17, 1850, aged 83 years.

Children of Jacob and Abigail (Hodgkins) Knowlton:
Mary, born July 3, 1799. Died September 30, 1819.
Abigail, born March 14, 1801. Married Moses True.
Thomas, born August 31, 1802. Married Cynthia
     Savage.
David, born March 18, 1804. Married Eliza Lom-
     bard, of Windham. Lived in Augusta.
Joseph, born August 18, 1806. Married Rachel
     Cole. Lives in California.
Jacob, born August 20, 1808. Married Mary
     Rogers of Phippsburg.
Caroline, born November 6, 1810.
Francis, born September 18, 1813. Married Caro-
     line Matilda Billings. Lived in Detroit. Died
     December 6, 1856.

KINGSBURY, Henry, was a commoner in 1641, and
one of Major Denison's subscribers in 1648. He came with
Gov. Winthrop, in 1630, and appears to have been one of
his family. In writing to his wife, " From aboard the
Arbella, riding at the Cowes, March 28, 1630," Gov. Winthrop says : " Henry Kingsbury hath a child or two in the
Talbot sick of the measles, but like to do well." After
their arrival, in writing to his son, John Winthrop, jun'r,
from Charlestown, July 23, 1630, he again mentions him.
   Henry Kingsbury seems not to have remained long in
Ipswich. He sold a farm of thirty acres to Thomas Safford, February 8, 1648. He possessed a six acre lot
which he sold to Edmund Bridges ; who sold the same to
Anthony Potter and Elder John Whipple, April 4, 1660.

KNIGHT, Mr. William, was a commoner, 1641, received a grant of two hundred acres of land in 1639 ; began to preach in Topsfield, July, 1641, and died, it is supposed, in 1655.

Alexander Knight, possessed land in 1636 ; was a commoner, 1641. His will is dated Feb. 10, 1663 ; proved,
March 29, 1664 ; witnesses ⊦ John Whipple, James Chute,
who wrote the will, and Robert Lord. In it are mentioned

a son Nathaniel, born October 16, 1657, wife Hannah, and three daughters,—Hannah, Sarah and Mary. He bequeathed his house and house lot and planting land to h's wife, during her life. The house with thirty-two acres of land were appraised, at £137, 18, 11, by Walter Roper and Francis Wainwright. He appointed his wife and William Inglish, of Boston, executors.

Robert Knight and Abigail had a son Joseph, born February 27, 1690.

KINSMAN, Robert, had a house lot of one acre, granted to him near where the South Meeting-house now stands in 1637. He was commoner, 1641 ; one of Major Denison's subscribers, 1648 ; a commoner entitled to a share in Plum Island, 1664. He died January 28, 1664. His will is dated January 25. He left a son and five daughters :

Robert.

Mary, wife of Ursual Wardwell.

Sarah, wife of Samuel Younglove.

Hannah.

Martha, wife of Jacob Foster.

Tabitha.

He also mentions Isaac and Sarah Ringe, children of his daughter Mary, minors ; and his cousin, Richard Nichols.

He purchased, June 7, 1642, of John North, a house and lot on the south side of the river.

Also, a planting lot upon the Neck, near Labor-in-vain, so called.

In 1638, Richard Lumpkin sold unto John Tuttle one houselot lying near the great cove of the town river, having Robert Kinsman's houselot on the north west. On this Lumpkin house lot, was a dwelling built by Richard Brown ; and sold by Brown to Mr. Richard Saltonstall; and by Mr. Saltonstall sold unto the said Richard Lumpkin.

Robert Kinsman 2, son of Robert 1, has the title of Quartermaster. He was appointed to that office in 1691, to a company of which Thomas Wade was Captain, and

Samuel Ingalls Lieutenant.  He had one and a half shares in Plum Island, &c. in 1664; was a voter in town affairs in 1679.  He came into full communion with the church, Feb. 22, 1673.  Freeman, March 31, 1673-4; selectman, 1675 ; tithingman, 1677.  Had horses on the common, 1697. Seat appointed to him at the table in the meeting house, 1700.  It is recorded :

"1674, March 31.  Mr. Jo: Rogers, Mr. Sam'l Cobbitt, Robert Kinsman, Tho : Clarke, Daniell Hovey, Abra : Fitts, Joseph Goodhue, Joseph Whipple, Phile : Dane, James Day, being admitted to the freed of the Colony, took the freeman's oath.

Quartermaster Robert Kinsman was fined and imprisoned for opposing the arbitrary measures of Sir Edmund Andros in 1687.  At a town meeting holden Dec. 28, 1704, it was voted to give Nathaniel Rust, jr., two acres of land by his house iu Chebacco, up ye hill,—which land is accepted in full satisfaction for ye loss and damage ye sd Kinsman sustained under Sr Edmund Androse Government.

Previous to this the town took measures to make reparation to some of those who had been imprisoned :

"24 Dec. 1689, voted yt mr. wise & ye Selectmen draw up ye Townes abuses with respect to ye Rates taken, and ye Calumnies cast upon ye Towne and psons have suffered by ye late Gour'mt in Sr. Edmd Andros his rule, psent them to ye Towne next lecture day after Lecture."

Quartermaster Kinsman sent in the following petition:

Ipswich, March 14, 1692-3.  Gent'n & ffriends: my Requst is that you would be pleased to consider me something for my loss that I met with at Boston about five or six years agoe.  As I am a townsman make your cause mine ; and I doubt nott you will stirr up your hearts to pittie & merice, so that you will be willing to contribute something to my loss that I have sustained thereby.  I have long been patient.  I pray let not that hinder me, but be pleased to doe for me as you have for others In ye Like Case, and so I Rest Your Faithfull Friend and Servant.

ROBERT KINSMAN.

The response to this petition is on record :

Voted and Granted : That whereas there was many sufferers with quarter master Rob't Kinsman, In ye like maner
if the money Raised by Selling Incroachments be over and
above what the town hath already promised, that it shall
be divided proportionably amongst those sufferers, that
have not been yett considered until their Loss be In Some
Measure made up as others have been.

The children of Quartermaster Robert Kinsman :

Robert.

Mary, born December 21, 1657.

Sarah, born February 19, 1659.

Thomas, born April 15, 1662.

Joanna, born April 25, 1665.

Eunice, born January 24, 1670.

Joseph, born December 20, 1673.

Pelatiah, born November 10, 1680.

Margaritt, born July 24, 1668.

Robert Kinsman married Mrs. Lydia More of Boston,
April 4, 1700.

Mr. Robert Kinsman had the sixteenth lot of eighteen
feet, laid out between Samuel Ordway's shop and ye Town
Bridge, beginning by ye Bridge, and so by ye River side :
March 23, 1692-3.

In 1699, he subscribed eighteen shillings towards the
bell.   His gravestone has the record of his decease :

Here lieth buried
ye Body of Quarter
Master        Robert
Kinsman      who
Died February ye
19, 1712, Aged
83 years.

Robert Kinsman 3, probably son of Robert 2, married
June 28, 1705, Rebecca daughter of Cornett Andrew Burley.   They had a daughter who died at fourteen years :

Here lies·
Rebekah Kinsman
ye Dafter of
Mr. Robert &
Rebekah Kins
man          died
December ye
17, 1719, in ye
14 year of her Age.

A son Robert was baptized May 3, 1713.

Robert with Rebecca his wife, in consideration of £60, acquit unto their brother Andrew Burley, all share in the estate of their father, Cornett Andrew Burley, February 8, 1718-19.

Thomas Kinsman 3, (Robert 2,) and Elisabeth had a son :—

Thomas, born April 3, 1693.

Mary, born October 14, 1695.

Thomas died soon after the births of his children. His widow, Elisabeth Kinsman, and Isaac Ringe published their intention of marriage.

1701, June 12, Elizabeth Kinsman, widow and administratrix of Thomas Kinsman, exhibits an account, in which she charges : " For schooling three children,  viz : Steven, Eliz'h, Thos.  Mary's maintenance five years ye 15 July. For Tho's Ditto three & halfe. For Eliz'h Ditto two year. For Steven 11 weeks Ditto & 3 years Clothing."

1701, June 30.   Elizabeth Rindge, wife of Isaac Rindge, alias Elizabeth Kinsman, guardian of Elizabeth, daughter of Thomas Kinsman, under fourteen years of age ; Mary, under fourteen years of age ; Steven, thirteen years of age: or thereabouts, &c.

Joseph Kinsman 3, (Robert 2,) and Susanna, had :

Joseph, born September 1, 1701.

Unice, baptized June 23, 1705.

He had the title, Lieutenant.

Epitaph of Susanna, his wife :

> Here lyes Buried
> the Body of Mrs.
> Susanna Kinsman
> Wife to Lieut.
> Joseph Kinsman
> who departed this
> Life Noubr 9th
> 1734, Æ tatis Suæ 60.

Stephen Kinsman married Lucy Kimball, daughter of Caleb Kimball. Epitaph :

> Lucey Kinsman
> who was Daugh
> er of Mr Caleb
> Kimball & wife
> of Stephen
> Kinsman Died
> February ye 22
> 1715 : 16 Aged
> 23 Years

KENDRICK, John, married Lydia Cheney, Nov. 12, 1657. He had a share in Plum Island, &c., 1664, and had a seat assigned to him in the Meeting-house, 1700. He had,

Hannah, born Sept. 18, died Dec. 20, 1661.
Sarah, born July 11, 1666.
Lydia, born and died December, 1669.
Katherine, born June 16, 1674.
John, born December 7, 1678.
George, born May 1, 1681.

Granted to John Kindricke to fell eight white oaks, June 17, 1661.

KILHAM, Austin, took the freeman's oath in Boston, June 2, 1641. His will, in which his name is written Killam, is dated June 2, and that of his wife, Allice, July 3, 1667. Their children were :

Daniel, who had a wife.
Lott.
Elizabeth Hutton.
Sarah Fisk.
Mary Killim, a grandaughter.
Thomas Fisk, son-in-law, was a witness.

Daniel Kilham 2, (Austin 1,) was a voter in town affairs, 1679. He was a member of the Artillery company. He was styled senior in 1679, and also in 1707, when his name, spelled Killum, is on the list of commoners.

Daniel Kilham 3, (Daniel 2,) had a seat assigned to him in the Meeting-house, 1700. He had the title of junior, 1673. Children :
Mary, born March 10, 1673.
William, born July 1680.
Hannah, born January 15, 1682.

KENNING, Jane, lately deceased, December 1, 1654. She possessed a dwelling house and half an acre of land, near the Meeting-house, having John Knowlton southeast: Goodman Peitchett northwest side: John Wyatt northeast end of it.

KENT, Cornelius, had the fifth lot of eighteen feet front, granted to him by the town, between Samuel Ordway's shop and ye Town Bridge, March 23, 1692-3. Mary Kent, his wife, died April 25, 1671.

Richard Kent had four acres of land near Chebacco river, granted to him 1634. John Harris, deputy sheriff, appointed administrator of the estate of Richard Kent, laborer, November 5, 1705.

KEERKE, Henry, hath liberty settle in the town, and make use of his trade of a currier, February 14, 1664.

LAIGHTON, John, is one of Major Denison's subscribers, 1648, when the name is spelt Layton. He was constable, 1663; was appointed to lay out Castle Neck,

1665. He had a share in Plum Island, &c., in behalf of Mary Jewett, in 1664 ; tithingman, 1677 ; commoner, 1678: voter in town affairs, 1679.

His will is dated March 14, 1693. In it is mentioned his wife, Pennell; cousin John Laighton of Rowley; Thomas Snell, formerly his servant, Mary Newmarsh, wife of Thomas Newmarsh ; and the children of his brother, Richard Laighton, deceased, viz., Ezekiel. Mary, Sarah, whom he makes his residuary legatees.

He was one of the soldiers to the Indians, 1643.

John Laighton 2, probably "cousin" of the above John, died about March 27, 1694, when his will was presented for proof by his son, John 3, executor. In this will the name is spelled Laighton. Robert Lord, under date of April, 1683, charges John Leighton for proving and recording his ffah: will & inventory, 5 shillings.

John Leighton 3, married, and speedily buried, Sarah Perkins :

> Here Lyes ye Body
> of Sarah Laigh:
> Ton Daughter
> of Mr Jacob Per :
> kins & wife
> to John
> Laighton
> Died March
> ye 1, 1716, Aged
> 19 Years 2
> months &
> 5 Days.

LANGTON, Roger, took the freeman's oath at Boston, March 4, 1634-5, when the name is spelt Lankton. He was commoner, 1641 ; subscriber to Major Denison's compensation, 1648. He possessed a house in Brook street, in 1655.

LAKEMAN, Richard, commoner, 1707.

William Lakeman, born 1651, died 1707, leaving wife, Margery Lakeman, and ten children.

Here lys ye Body
of William Lake
man who died
January ye 24
1707 aged
56 years

His children were : Annis Roberts ; Richard ; Elizabeth Downs; John; William; Jonas; Hercules; Lieut. Sylvanus, (married Mary Lull;) Solomon; Sarah.

The inventory of the estate of William Lakeman, February 24, 1706-7, gives a total of £454, 9, 3. Among the items were a house bought of Major Francis Wainwright, £45 ; Fishing Shallop, £60, 10 ; Housing and one acre & half belonging, £105.

The will of William Lakeman is dated Dec'r 11, 1706 and was proved August 24, 1707. He bequeathes to his wife, Margery Lakeman, the use of all his estate, during her widowhood. He gives to his eldest daughter, Annis Roberts, five pounds, "having given liberally unto her before." To his son Richard, "twenty shillings in consideration of what I have formerly given him." To his daughter, Elizabeth Downs, and her children, five pounds. To son John, twenty shillings, "having been at the charge of a trade for him." Son William, ten pounds, "he having no trade. Sons Jonas and Hercules, to each five pounds, "in consideration that I have given them trades ;" son Sylvanus, five pounds, when of age. Son Solomon, thirty pounds, "in case he will live with his mother, and abide under her jurisdiction, until he arrive at the age of twenty-one years ; but, if he will learn a trade, ten pounds." He bequeathes a legacy to his youngest daughter Sarah, "if she arrive at the age of eighteen years." And to each of his grandchildren "that are now born," ten shillings. His wife and Thomas Newman, sen'r, executors. Witnesses : Thomas Newmarch, Thomas New-march, jr., and J. Staniford.

Elizabeth Lakeman, wife of Archilaus, died May 29, 1723.

Elizabeth Lakeman, wife of William, died May 12, 1724.

[Additional.] Lieut. Sylvanus Lakeman 2, (William 1,) and Mary Lull were married October 23, 1714. She was the daughter of Thomas and Rebekah (Kimball) Lull, and was born October 22, 1690. Their children :

Mary, born September 2, 1716.

Rebekah, born December 28, 1718, died early.

Sylvanus, born July 23, 1720, married Mary Dow, 1745, died at sea, 1750.

Rebekah, born November 25, 1722.

John, born October 3, 1724.

Elizabeth, born June 4, 1727.

Abraham, born October 5, 1729.

Thomas, born May 19, 1734.

The *Caldwell Records* give an account of the spirit and valor of Sylvanus Lakeman :

John Caldwell of Ipswich, was killed by the Indians on the coast of Maine, July 10, 1724. He had married in 1715, Elisabeth Lull, the sister of Mary (Lull) Lakeman. He owned a shallop, and sailed "to the eastward." It required considerable daring to run along the shores of Maine. The Indians, instigated by the French, were alert for booty and slaughter. The year proved a sad one to many on land and sea. Again and again fishing shallops were seized ; and at last the Indians captured a schooner that had two swivel guns. This they manned and became a terror.

On the tenth of July, 1724, John Caldwell was in his shallop and with him his sister's husband, Daniel Rindge, junior, and others. Within sight of him was the shallop of Sylvanus Lakeman. They were near Penobscot. Suddenly the Indian privateer appeared, and opened its guns. The contest was short. John Caldwell and his men were slain. The Indians then pursued Sylvanus Lakeman, but the favoring winds carried him beyond their reach ; and he speedily returned to Ipswich.

The Indians sailed into Penobscot with the scalps of their slain. At Penobscot was a captive—Joseph Goodhue, of Ipswich,—taken the 22d day of June, and his skipper was then killed. The scalps of the slaughtered men were rubbed jeeringly in the face of Goodhue.

Sylvanus Lakeman stirred and enflamed all Ipswich by the intelligence ; and sixteen men at once declared their readiness to go with Lakeman to the east. Mr. John Wainwright applied to Lieut. Gov. Dummer, (Gov. Shute was in England,) in behalf of these Ipswich boys, and Sylvanus Lakeman was commissioned, and with the noble sixteen, sailed away to Maine.

Dr. Jackson of Kittery, was also commissioned, and sailed with twenty men. Niles gives the story :

" Doct'r Jackson from Kittery, and Sylvanus Lakeman from Ipswich, gave them chase, and fired on them with their small arms. The enemy had two great guns and four paferaros, which did damage to their shrouds, yet they pursued and drove them into Penobscot ; and there being a great body of Indians to cover them, our men thought unadvisable to follow any further."

LARCKUM, Mordicah, had Mordicah, born September 16, 1658.

LAMPSON, William, was a commoner, 1641 ; one of Major Denison's subscribers, 1648. He sold land to William Knowlton before 1643. He died February 1, 1658.

Joseph Lampson 2, son of William 1, born Octo. 1658.

John Lampson was a voter in town affairs, 1679. Freeman, May 27, 1644. With Martha Perkins, his wife, (married December 17, 1668,) he had

John, born November 21, 1669.
Phebe, born August 13, 1673.
William, born August 19, 1675.
Martha, born March 21, 1677.
Thomas, born January 3, 1682.

Samuel, born February 25, 1684.
With his second wife, Abigail,
Abigail, born December 14, 1695.
John, born November 4, 1698.
John Lampson and his wife came into full communion with the church, March 1, 1673.

1703-4, March 2. Liberty granted to Serjt John Lamson to set up a shed for his horses at ye east side of Major Epes bard ; provided it be common, &c. Subscribed 10s toward the bell, 1699.

LAMBERT, James, had horses on the common, 1697.

Sarah Lambert, Sept. 29, 1680. Son Benoni.

Jane Lambert, probably of Rowley, died in Ipswich about May 24, 1659, the date of her will, and left sons : John, the eldest ; Jonathan, Gershom, Thomas, Ann. She appoints Mr. Ezekiel Rogers and Mr. Joseph Jewett, overseers. Witnesses : Joseph Jewett and Thomas Seaver who wrote the will. Estate, £539, 16.

William Lambert, had
James and Mary, born March 11, 1658.
Sarah and Elisabeth, born April 4, 1661. Elizabeth died in May.
Elizabeth, born November 14, 1665, died April 8, 1667.
David born June 30, 1668, died Sept. 30.
Margery, born August 25, 1671.

LITTLEHALE. 1675, November 25. John Littlehale being slain in the warr, ad'r gr'd to Edmund Bridges and Mary his wife (late wife to Richard and mother to sd John.)

1676. Inventory of the estate amounting to £18 8 4 of John Littlehale, being slaine with Capt. Lathrop, rendered March 28, 1676.

1685, March 17. Debts due from Edmund Bridges estate : To Isaac Littlehale, on account of, partnership, 14 10. To John Littlehale's estate as Edmund Bridges was administrator, 10, 16, 8.

Isaac Littlehale, and Elisabeth his wife, had
    John, born July 15, 1691.
    Elizabeth, born June 5, 1694.
    Mary, born June 30, 1698.
He was surveyor of highways, 1696 ; had horses on the
common, 1697.

> Here  lies  Mr.  Jsaac
> Litelehal  Died
> Aprel  ye  4th  1718
> in  ye  58  year
> of  his  age

Richard Littlehale married Sarah Collins, Oct. 23, r676.
    Sarah, born January 27, 1678.
    Richard, born January 30, 2679.

LEE, John, commoner 1641 ; subscriber to Major Denison, 1648.  With the addition of "senior," his name is on
the list of those who have a share and a half in Plum Island, &c., 1664.

1667, March 26.  John Leigh upon his presentment for
working in his swamp on the Lord's Day, upon his Answer
it appeared by testimony that it was to stop the fire : was
discharged.

His will is dated June 12, and the inventory of his estate is rendered in July, 1671,  He left a wife named
Anne; and two sons, John and Joseph, who were executors.  The Rev. William Hubbard and the Rev. John
Rogers were the witnesses.  He appoints his friends, Major
Denison and Mr. William Hubbard, overseers.  He gives
the income of his property, which consisted principally of
farming lands, to his wife, with reversion to his two sons,
with the exception of a legacy of £20, to Mary Hungerford
(who appears to have been a domestic,) to be paid on her
marriage, provided she remains with his wife until that
event happens.

The will is in the handwriting of Mr. Hubbard, the historian.  The seal contains the device of a martlet, and a
motto which is illegible.

In the will the name is spelt Leigh.   In the inventory
which was rendered by his sons, it is Lee.

He possessed lands near Heartbreak Hill.

1641.   Jo : Lee accused for stealing of a Bible of the
widow Haffield, is found guilty.   He shall restore 15
shillings to the Widow, and pay X shillings fine for lying.

1648.   Granted that John Lee shall enjoy all the profits
of the highway and all the common ground lying at the
foot of Heart Break Hill, to him and his heirs forever : he
or they always maintaining the highway from Rocky  Hill
to William Lamson his lott.

John 2, eldest son of John 1, was a surgeon in the  navy.
In 1681, he lived with his mother and brother Joseph.

1677, March.   John Lee, for his offence knocking down
Daniel Hovey, is fined and bound to good behavior.

Joseph Lee 2, son of John 1, married Mary  Woodhouse,
or Woodis,—and had

Woodis, born Oct. 17, 1679, died Nov. 28.

Joseph, born October 16, 1680.

Mary, born July 14, 1682.

Ann, born May 17, 1684.

Henry, born May 16, 1686.

John, born September 10, 1688, died December 16.

Woodis, born December 18, 1689.

Hannah, born April 10, 1691.

November, 1673.   Joseph Leigh bound to protect the
town from charge from entertaining of Sarah Hunkin.

The constable to warn Joseph Lee not to  entertain John
Hunkin.

1681.   Ordered that Joseph Lee be sued for cumbering
the highway by the  gate  neare  Ensign  Burnham's near
Rocky Hill.

He was constable in 1691

Joseph Lee removed to Concord as early as 1696.   He is
mentioned April 9, 1696, as ''formerly of Ipswich.''

Joseph Lee and Mary Wigly married at Concord, November 13, 1697.   Mary, wife of Joseph Lee, died Nov.
25, 1708.

Joseph Lee and Mary ffox married January 28, 1712-13.

Woodis Lee and Elisabeth Wood married Aug. 4, 1715.

In the burying ground at Concord are gravestones erected to the memory of Doct. Joseph Lee who died October 5, 1736, aged 56 years.

Ruth Lee, his wife, died March, 1761, aged 70 years.

Doct. Joseph Lee, died April 10, 1797, aged 81 years.

Lucy, his wife, died April 10, 1806, aged 58 years.

John Lee, died Feb. 7, 1761, aged 43 years and 49 days.

Woodis Lee, died Sept. 6, 1796, aged 77 years.

Jonathan Lee, died July 7, 1766, aged 40 years.

At Ipswich, Mr. John Lee and Johannah his wife had Johannah, born January 9. 1697.

Thomas Lee 1, brother of John Lee 1, was commoner 1641 ; one of Major Denison's subscribers, 1648.

1642, March 16.   Agreed to pay six bushels of Indian corn to Mr. William Payne for Ambrose Leach ; and also to pay him 7£ more in corn or cattle, in full discharge of a six acre lot which the Town did purchase of Thomas Perry ; and the said Thomas Perry did assign the debt to Thomas Lee, and the said Tho : Lee to Ambrose Leach.

Thomas Lee, with Alice his wife, sell land to Symon Tompson, May 2, 1659.   He had previously sold commonage to John Lee.   His will is dated March 19, 1661.   He died March 23, at the age of eighty-two years.   The following is extracted from his will :

" My mind and will is, that Alice, my beloved wife, shall have the sole disposing of my farm and the rest of my estate, upon these considerations, that is to say : That my Grandson, Richard Lee, shall live and abide with her until he shall be two and twenty years of age.   Then my whole estate to be divided, and Richard shall have an equal share with my wife; only my wife shall have the use of my now dwelling house during the time of her life, unless she shall be willing that they both may live together.   But if my wife should marry, my mind is that she shall have five pounds every year out of my estate, during the time of her life.   And the above mentioned Richard, to have my estate at ye age of two and twenty.

"My mind also is, that if my wife shall continue a widow, and enjoy such a share of my estate as is aforesaid, that after her decease, my aforesaid grandchild shall inherit all that estate she shall leave,—twenty pounds being excepted, which I give and bequeath to my daughter Susanna, now in England, or her children, if any of them be here to demand the same, within the space of seven years from this present time.

My will is that Richard, my grandchild, shall not have liberty to Alien, sell or bargain my farme, or any part thereof, but that it be reserved entire to him and his heirs.

If my wife shall not think meet that Richard my Grandchild, should abide with her for the psent, shee shall have liberty to dispose of him to some good service till he shall come to bee at the age of two and twenty."

Signed by Thomas Lee, his mark [T] and his seal. Witnessed by Richard Brabrook and James Gregory.

At a meeting of the seven men the 13th of March, 1650: It was granted to Thomas Leigh that the land that is laid out to him by Thomas Bishop and Simon Tomson in exchange for another part of his Farm he shall enjoy to him and his heirs.

Richard Lee, grandson of Thomas, was commoner, 1678; had horses on the common, 1697; was surveyor of highways, 1679.

1674. June. The selectmen are informed that some fences are set up at or about Richard Leighs land wch encroach on ye common.

Richard Lee's children were:

Thomas, born February 20, 1671.
Susannah, born February 20, 1675
Jonathan, born June 19, 1677
Richard, born June 20, 1679
Mary, born January 20, 1681
Joseph, born January 23, 1683
Benjamin, born November 25, 1685
Eleanor, April 10, 1688

[See Genealogy of Thomas Lee and his Descendants.]

LEEDS, John.    Had  a  share  in  Plum  Island,  &c., 1664, as servant of John Kimball.  1669.  He kept the cow-herd with Haniel Bosworth.  1671.  Haniel Bosworth is allowed 30 shillings for goodwife Leeds enter't in his house for ye time past and until May day.

John Leeds had daughter Abigail born June 1, 1676.

He was a soldier, and probably died in the Canada war, in  1700;  for  we  find  that  Joseph  Hunt  was  appointed administrator  on  his  effects,  January 29, 1700-1.  He is entitled, "A soulder in ye Country's service."  His property consisted of £1, 4, 4d,—Wages received ; and £1, 4, 4, —wages  due.

LADD, Daniel.    Had a grant of six acres of land, 1637.

LOCKWOOD, Mary.    Was of Ipswich, Sept. 30, 1652, when there was a contract of marriage between her and Jeremiah Belcher.

LUFKIN, Thomas.    Was a commoner, 1707.  With his wife Sarah, he had :

> Sarah, born December 11, 1693
> Thomas, born September 30, 1695
> John, born November 28, 1697
> Jacob, December 9, 1698

LUMPKIN, Richard.    Was admitted  freeman, 1638, and was Representative the same year.  A commoner, 1641. He  had  land  granted  to  him  "at  that  place  called  pye-brook,"  which  is  in  the  part  of  the  town  since  called Topsfield,

27th day of July, 1638.  Memorand that :  Richard Lumkin hath sold unto John Tuttle, one house and a houselot with certain other lands,—one house lot lying near the great cove of the town river, having a house lot now in the possession of William Avery on the south west ; Robert Kinsman's house lot on the north west ; the town river on the south east ; a house lot now in possession of Samuel Hall on the east; also upon the said lot, a dwelling house formerly built by Richard Brown, now of Newbury, and by him sold unto Mr. Richard Saltonstall, by whom it was sold unto the said Richard Lumkin.

He was "lately deceased," March 26, 1645.

Sarah Lumpkin, probably widow of Richard, adminis-tered on the estate of Sarah Baker, "her Kinswoman," September 30, 1651.

LORD, Katherine, widow. Was a commoner, 1641.

Robert Lord 1, took the freeman's oath at Boston, March 3, 1635-6 ; was one of Denison's subscribers, 1648 ; had a share in Plum Island, &c., 1664 ; was a voter in Town affairs, 1679.

1645.  He was on a committee with Richard Saltonstall, Daniel Denison, Samuel Appleton, Richard Jacob, John Payne, empowered to grant houselots to the settlers.

1639.  He had a houselot on High street, next east from Mr. William Bartholomew ; which property yet remains a possession of his descendants.  [1847.]

He was Town Clerk, and Clerk of the Court, and Reg-ister of Deeds, for many years,—till his decease in 1683.

He was selectman, 1661, and many years after.

He was Representative in 1638.

He died August 12, 1683, in the eightieth year of his age.  His will is dated June 28, and was proved Septem-ber 25, 1683.  In the will he mentions his wife, Mary, "with whom by God's good providence we have lived comfortably together in a married condition almost fifty three years."  He bequeathes to her all his estate during her life.

His wife was Mary Waite, whom he married, 1630.

In an account book, under date of 1660, he mentions his "sister ffitt."

He gives legacies to his eldest son, Robert 2 ; to his daughter Sarah Wilson ; to his sons Nathaniel 2 ; Thomas 2, who removed to Charlestown; Samuel 2, who removed to Charlestown ; to the children of his daughter Chan-dler, deceased, viz: Mary, William, Joseph and Samuel ; to his daughters Susannah Osgood, Abigail Foster, Han-nah Grow (wife of John Grow,) and to his grandchild, Robert Lord 3.

His houselot on High street was granted to him February 19, 1637. It adjoined the homestead of Mr. Humphrey Vincent.

Robert Lord 2, son of Robert 1, married Hannah Day. He had a share in Plum Island, &c., 1664. He was a voter in Town affairs, 1679. He was one of twenty-four of "the young generation," who joined the church by taking the covenant, between January 18 and February 1, 1673. He was Marshal of the Court, as early as 1669 ; and is usually designated as Marshal Lord.

He died November 11, 1696 ; and left a widow Hannah, who possessed the rights of commonage, and had horses on the common, 1697.  His sons were :

Robert 3, born December 26, 1657
John
Thomas
Joseph, born January 8, 1674
James, born January 27, 1676
Nathaniel, born April 30, 1681
A son fourteen years old in 1699

Robert Lord 3, son of Robert 2, born December 26, 1657. In 1697 his name is on a list of such as have horses on the common, and at this date he has the title of Serjeant. He subscribed, 1700, toward "procuring a bigger bell for ye good of ye Town." He was one of the Selectmen, 1707.

He had a son, Samuel 4, who had a son Samuel 5, who married and removed to Dunbarton, N. H.

He married Abigail Ayers, June 7, 1683.  Children :

Hannah, born July 18, 1685
Susannah, born October 7, 1687
Robert, born March 6, died May 14, 1689
Samuel, born April 14, 1691
Abigail, born June 17, 1693
Ruth, born September 9, 1695
Ebenezer, b. August 25, 1697, d. July 2, 1698
Ebenezer, born May 16, 1699

Robert Lord, jun'r, had the fourteenth lot between Ordway's shop and ye Town Bridge,—eighteen feet front, granted to him March, 1692-3.

John Lord 3, son of Robert 2, married Elizabeth Clarke, December 9, 1695.  Their children :

    John, born Oct. 8, 1696, (left no children.)

    Elizabeth, born December 12, 1668

    Thomas, born July 19, 1703

    Robert, born 1712, lived at Boston.

Thomas Lord 3, son of Robert 2, married Mary Brown, May 24, 1686.  Their children :

    Thomas,    John,    Jonadab

    Mary, born March 21, 1691

    Robert, born April 2, 1694

He died September 26, 1694.

James Lord 3, (son of Robert 2) and wife Mary, had :

    James,

    Joseph,—left no children

    Nathaniel

He was commoner in 1708 ; and had a seat assigned him in the Meeting-house, 1702.  Mary Lord, his wife, died April 11, 1724.

Joseph Lord 3, son of Robert 2, removed to New Jersey.

Nathaniel Lord 3, son of Robert 2, lived at the Isles of Shoals.  Left no children.

Nathaniel Lord 4, son of James 3, born 1718 ; married Elizabeth Day, and had :

    Nathaniel 5, born 1747, who lived at New-

        market, N. H.

    Abraham 5, born 1751

    Isaac 5

Isaac Lord 5, son of Nathaniel 4, had

    Isaac, born 1777

    Joseph, born 1778

    Nathaniel, 1780

    Levi, 1784

Nathaniel Lord 2, son of Robert 1, was born about 1653.  He married Mary Bolles, December 31, 1685.  Mary was then a widow,—the daughter of Philip and Mary Call.  She was born about 1658.  They had :

    Nathaniel 3, born about 1687

    Philip, born March 5, 1691

Elizabeth, born November 4, 1683
Jeremiah, born Novemper 10, 1696
Samuel, born October 28, 1700
He was Town Treasurer ; he died December 18, 1733.
Nathaniel 3, son of Nathaniel 2, died in 1770 :

Here Lyes the Body
of Mr. Nathaniel Lord
who died August 10th, 1770,
aged 83 Years.

With Anna Kimball, his wife, he had :
Nathaniel 4, born 1721
Caleb, born 1726, (he had many children ; all died
in infancy)
Daniel, left no children
Aaron, born 1732
Joseph, left no children
Nathaniel Lord 4, son of Nathaniel 3, had Nathaniel 5,
born 1753; and Nathaniel 5, had
Daniel 6, born 1780
Nathaniel,    Ammi.
Philip Lord 3, son of Nathaniel 2, born March 5, 1691,
married Tryphena Staniford February 2, 1720. Children :
Philip, born Feb. 25, 1724, married Sarah, daughter
of Benj. Brown, born Dec. 1729.
Samuel, born 1726
Jeremiah, born 1728. Lived at the Isles of Shoals
John, born February 26, 1736
Ebenezer, born 1740
Jeremiah Lord 3, son of Nathaniel 2, born Nov. 10,
1696.  He had :
Jeremiah 4, who left two sons, Jeremiah and Bems-
ley, who removed "into the country."
Ebenezer 4, born 1738
Samuel Lord 3, son of Nathaniel 2, born October 28,
1700.  He had : Samuel, Moses, Jacob.
Nathaniel Lord 4, son of Nathaniel 3.  He had :
Nathaniel 5, born 1753
Joseph 5, born 1763

Joseph Lord 5, son of Nathaniel 4, Nathaniel 3, had Joseph 6,   George W. 6,  Warren 6.

Aaron Lord 4, son of Nathaniel 3, born 1732, had :
    Aaron, born 1757
    Daniel
    Stephen
    Nathaniel, born 1775

Philip Lord 4, son of Philip 3, had :
    Philip 5, born 1749
    William, born 1750
    Charles, born 1753
    David, born 1756
    Benjamin, born 1761
    John, born November 25, 1764

Samuel Lord 4, son of Philip 3, born 1726.   Children :
    Samuel, lived at Boston ; William ; Thomas, died young ; Daniel Bolles ; Josiah, died young.

John Lord 4, son of Philip 3, born 1736.   Had :
    John 5, lived at Portland, Maine
    William, lived at Portland
    Ebenezer, died young

Ebenezer Lord 4, son of Philip 3, born 1740.   Children :
    Ebenezer 5 ; Abraham, died early ; Jacob ; Josiah.

Moses 4, son of Samuel 3, had : Moses ;  Caleb, (left no children ; Jacob, lived at Salem.

From an old manuscript of Nathaniel Lord 2, son of Robert Lord 1 :

these cattel were Lost and killed that were of the stoke that father Left when he dyed :  before that I took them into my hands :

| | £ | s | d |
|---|---|---|---|
| one cowe killed for the family november : 83 | 3 | 10 | 0 |
| nine sheep killed by the woolves novembr 83 | 1 | 12 | 0 |
| 2 Calves dyed that winter | 1 | 04 | 0 |
| one hefer dyed of the giddy may : 84 | 1 | 10 | 0 |
| the colt dyed in the yard feb : 84 | 0 | 15 | 0 |
| one cowe dyed in the myer April :· 54 | 3 | 10 | 0 |
| one ox killed for the family no'r : 84 | 5 | 00 | 0 |
| one cow killed for the family no : 85 | 3 | 10 | 0 |
| | 22 | 6 | 0 |

Additional.
# IPSWICH LORDS, LITCHFIELD, MAINE.
———o———
Furnished by O. B. Classon, Attorney at Law, Gardiner, Maine.

James Lord 3, was born in Ipswich, Mass., in 1737, and
died in Litchfield, Maine, February 13, 1830. He served
in the French and Indian Wars three years, and in the
Revolutionary War four and one half years. He held the
commission of First Lieutenant, given to him soon after
the battle of Lexington. It was signed by John Hancock,
President of the Senate.

Lieut. Lord had command of his Company at the battle
of Bunker Hill. He was wounded in the right thigh at
the battle of Long Island, July 27, 1776; and was ever
after lame, from the effects of the wound. He was put on
the Pension Roll, March 30, 1818.

Lieut. Lord came to Litchfield with his family in 1788.
He lived on the farm afterwards owned by Hon. Samuel
Smith. He was prominent in town affairs, and was a member of the Board of Assessors of the plantation of Smithfield, during its existence.

The wife of Lieut. Lord was Elizabeth Brown, born in
Windham, Conn., March 1, 1742. She made the journey
from Windham to Ipswich, on horseback, to be married.
The wedding day was August 7, 1762. She died in Litchfield, July 21, 1831.

Lieut. Lord's grave is in the burying ground in the
Grant neighborhood. No stone marks this resting place of
the Old Soldier.

Children of James 3 and Elizabeth (Brown) Lord:
James, born Dec. 31, 1763, married Sally Knowlton
Thomas, born October 26, 1765, married Mary
    Knowlton, September 29, 1795
Elizabeth, born Oct. 2, 1767, married Thomas
    Lakeman, July 8, 1790, died in Hallowell,
    May 25, 1862.
Lucy, born 1769, married Thomas Pickard, in
    Ipswich; lived in Litchfield, died in Alna.

Ephraim, born August 4, 1771 ; married Sally
Dennis, October 16, 1796 ; died June 2, 1824.
Lived in Hallowell.

John, born August 1, 1773. Married (1) Hannah Johnson, March 11, 1809 ; (2) Dorcas
Springer. Died February, 1822.

Mary, born 1775 ; married Andrew Tibbetts
June 14, 1795

Annie, born Oct. 26, 1777. Married Tristram
Locke, May, 1794. Died in Gardiner, 1846.

Joseph, born June 8, 1783 ; married Sally Magoon
August 9, 1804

James Lord 4, son of Lieut. James Lord 3, came to
Litchfield with his father. He served in the Revolutionary Army with his father. He died February 16, 1847.

Children of James 4 and Sally (Knowlton) Lord :

Sally, born Jan. 22, 1796, married Charles
McCausland, Dec. 5, 1820

James, born Oct. 1, 1797, died Dec. 4, 1803

Thomas Knowlton, born June 13, 1799. Married
Amelia Woods, Jan. 16, 1825

Abigail S. born April 15, 1802, m. Daniel Gilman

Deborah Woodbury, b. Feb. 24, 1806, d. May 8, 1828

James, born May 12, 1808, died Nov. 12, 1809

Mary Elizabeth Knowlton, born Jan. 10, 1811.
Married Oliver H. Johnson, 1836. Died
July 1, 1848.

Thomas Lord 4, son Lieut. James Lord 3, married Mary
Knowlton, and lived in Litchfield. He died February 21,
1858. Mary, his wife, died March 16, 1855.

The children of Thomas and Mary :

Mary, born June 22, 1796. Married John True,
March 18, 1820. Died Dec. 5, 1821.

Abigail K. born Jan. 20, 1798. Married Jonathan
Folsom, Nov. 19, 1819. Died Dec. 23, 1878.

Phebe Steel, b. Jan. 21, 1800, d. Aug. 20, 1802.

Thomas, born Sept. 1, 1802. Married Eliza Mun-
roe, June 9, 1825. Died Sept. 28, 1877.

Elizabeth B. born Dec. 31, 1804. Married Edward
G. Smith, Nov. 27, 1834
Lucy Pickard, born May 25, 1807. Married Eli-
phalet Palmer, Nov. 26, 1838, died Sept. 3, 1897
James Henry Kendall, born Feb. 11, 1810. Mar-
ried Ann R. Rich, July 14, 1836, d. Aug. 31, 1870
Daniel Brown, born July 27, 1812. Married Sarah
A. Blackwell, Jan. 1, 1846. Died June 25, 1877,
in Gardiner.
William Stinson, born July 10, 1815. Went to
Nashville, Tenn.
Joseph Stacy, born Oct. 14, 1817. Married Eme-
line True, March 14, 1844, died Nov. 27, 1885

LOW, Thomas. Was one of Denison's subscribers,
1648; had a share and a half in Plum Island, &c. 1664.
He with Edward Bragg purchased of Thomas Firman 20
acres of Land lying upon the Mile Brook towards the South
west, Oct. 5, 1647. His will is dated April 30, 1677. He
left a wife named Susannah ; his children : John, Thomas,
Abigail, Sarah. He mentions in his Will the following
grandchildren : Thomas Low, Sarah Low, Margaret Davison, Sarah Safford.

John Low 2, son of Thomas 1, married (1) Sarah Thorn-
dike, December 10, 1961. His children :
John, born April 24, 1665
Elizabeth, born October 10, 1667
Margaret, born January 26, 1669
Dorcas, born November 3, 1673
Martha, born September, 1979
with wife Dorcas, he had :
Hannah, born July 13, 1685
He died about 1695, and left a widow, Anna. The in-
ventory of his estate, amounting to £165 19, personal
property, is dated Dec. 18, of that year. Anna, his wid-
ow, was appointed administratrix, January 6, 1695-6.

Thomas Low 2, son of Thomas 1, had a share in Plum
Island, &c., 1664; voter in town affairs, 1679 ; Overseer of
the Poor, 1698. He purchased land in Chebacco of Daniel

Ringe, December 22, 1664. He was Deacon of the Church in Chebacco, and died April 12, 1712, aged eighty years. His will, dated June 17, 1708, and proved May 5, 1712, represents him as "being crazy and infirm in body." He left a wife,—Martha Borman,—to whom he was married, July 4, 1660. His children:

> Thomas, born April 14, 1661
> Samuel,
> Jonathan, born July 7, 1665
> David, born August 14, 1667
> Martha, married Dodge
> Joanna, married Dodge
> Nathaniel, born June 1, 1673
> Abigail, married Goodhue

Thomas Low 3, son of Thomas 2, married Sarah Symonds, December 2, 1687. Children:

> Symonds, born November 21, 1689
> Thomas, born October 3, 1692

He died February 8, 1692

Madam Rebekah Symonds, widow of the Honourable Samuel Symonds, in her will, proved August 19, 1695, mentions a grandaughter, Sarah Lowe, to whom she bequeathes a silver porringer.

John Low, Jr., had:

> John born February 22, 1690
> Thomas, born March 5, 1691
> Hannah, born February 1, 1693
> Nathaniel, born Nov. 5, 1695

Nathaniel Low, joined the Church by taking the Covenant, March 8, 1673. Died July 30, 1692.

John Low, died November 29, 1692.

Jonathan Low, had:

> Mary, born February 1, 1693
> Martha, born March 11, 1695

John Lowe, sen'r had a seat among the elderly people in the Meeting-house, 1700.

1705-6, January 28. Elizabeth Low, Daniel Low, Joseph Low, renounce administration on ye estate of my late Husband, Jn. Low, dec'd. Thorndike Low app'd

administrator of the estate of his father, Jn. Low.   The
estate consisted of personal property amounting to £26 12.

Daniel and Susannah Low lost a son Daniel, August
24, 1721, aged one year and four months.

LOVERILL, John.   Was a commoner, 1707.   With
his wife Hannah, he had a son Joseph, born Sept. 23, 1691.
He had a seat assigned to him in the Meeting-house, 1700.
He married Love Parsons, March 19, 1701-2.

LAKE.   Mrs. Margaret Lake.   The sister of Mrs. John
Winthrop, jr., and Mrs. Dep. Gov. Samuel Symonds.   She
possessed land in Ipswich, Connecticut, Maine.   Several
of her letters are preserved in the archives of the American
Antiquarian Society, Worcester, Mass., together with letters written to Rebekah Symonds from her son in England.

The Will of Margaret Lake, of Ipswich, widow :

—————— I give unto my daughter, Hannah Gallop, and
her children, all my land at New London : and also my
best gonne, and my red cloth petticoat, and my enameled
ring.   And after her decease, my will is, that my grand
daughter, Hannah Gallop, shall have the said ring.

Also, I give unto my grandaughter, Hannah Gallop, a
pair of sheets, and one of my best pewter platters, and one
of the next.

Item.   I give unto my daughter, Martha Harris, my
tapestry coverlet, and all my other apparell which are not
disposed of to others particularly.   Also, I give unto her
my mantle ; and after her decease to all of her children, as
they need it.

Also, the coverlet of tapestry, after my daughter Martha
decease, I give it to my grandson Thomas Harris : and he
dying without issue, to his brother John, and so the rest of
the children.

Also, I give to my daughter Martha, my gold ring.
And my will is that after her decease, that my Grandaughter, Martha Harris, shall have it.

Item.   I give to my grandaughter, Martha Harris, my
bed, and bedstead, and one boulster, two blankets, two

pillows, and one coverlet.

Item.   I give to my grandaughter Elizabeth Harris, one heyfer at my cozen Eppes.

Item.   I give to my grandaughter, Margaret Harris, my carved box, and one damask table cloth, and six damask napkins.

Item.   My will is that all my brass and pewter, with the rest of my household stuffe undisposed, be equally disposed and· divided amongst my daughter Harris's children.

Item.   I give and bequeath unto my sonne Thomas Harris, all the rest of my estate, viz : my part of the vessell, and all my debt,—only my Bible excepted, which I give to my grandson John Harris : and a pair of frenged gloves.

I appoint my sonne Thomas Harris and my daughter Martha Harris, to be my executor and executrix of this my last will and testament, this thirtieth day of August, the Year of Grace, sixteen hundred and seventy two. 1672.

These being wit-                MARGARET LAKE
    nesses                            hir   mark
Thomas Knowlton, sen'r
James Chute

In the inventory of Mrs. Margaret Lake's effects, appraised by John Dane, Thomas Knowlton, John Laighton, are the following items :

| | | | |
|---|---:|---:|---:|
| one tapstre coverlet | $\mathcal{J}$ 4 | 10 | 0 |
| one bedstead, a feather bed, and a flocked bed and three down pillows | 17 | 0 | 0 |
| a sarge sute and a crimson petticoat | 2 | 10 | 0 |
| three carved boxes | 1 | 10 | 0 |
| one scarlet mantle | 4 | 0 | 0 |
| four payer of holon sheets and three payer and one sheete of others | 11 | 0 | 0 |
| a damask table cloth and five napkins | 4 | 0 | 0 |
| four holon pilobers and two others | 1 | 8 | 0 |
| four shifts | 1 | 16 | 0 |
| her weading shift | 1 | 0 | 0 |
| a great Bible | 0 | 12 | 0 |

| | | | |
|---|---|---|---|
| a pare of gloves | o | 8 | o |
| part of the barke | 12 | o | o |
| debts due from Mathew peary | 4 | o | o |
| William Quarles | 5 | o | o |
| Mr. Ipse | 4 | o | o |
| Joseph Lee | 5 | o | o |
| Debts to be paid ; | | | |
| to Marchant Wanrite | 2 | 19 | 7 |
| To decon Goodhue | 1 | 20 | o |

J. Wingate Thornton, Esq., has a fragment of a letter written at London, ye 5th Sept. 1672, by Lidia Bankes to her Dear Cousin. But the name of the cousin is wanting. That which is legible reads :

"I have received yours by your Brother Symonds.—— Your children having attained unto learning.——I doe not remember I ever saw you above once, which was at your mother's house in New England. But I very well remember you from a child & when you were in Holland, you and your cousin John Lake with us, and rejoyce you were under soe worthy a person for tuition as your grandfather.

"Besides I well remember your family of ye Eppes, for I was brought up with them from my youth —— while your mother lived we constantly corresponded —— and she always gave me an account of her children and ye blessed condition of your Sister En——, who was a pretious christian. And of your Sister m——. I desire my affectionate love to your wife and all your children ; not forgetting ould mr. Bourman, Mr. Rogers; and their wives, if alive, my great respects to them. My service to your father Symonds, my Cousin ——

"I have most dear respect for your Aunt Lake, but just as I was writing I heard of her death. If there be any of her children, remember me to them.——My sister Reade and Cousin Samuel present them servise ——"

Additional : Mrs. Margaret Lake was the daughter of Edmand Reade, of Wickford, County Essex, England. An ancient copy of her father's will was found among the Winthrop Papers, and was printed in the "Proceedings of

the Massachusetts Historical Society," 1862-3. John Ward
Dean said of this Will : " One of the daughters of the tes-
tator, named in the will, afterwards became the second
wife of John Winthrop, Jr., and the mother of all his
children.   Before her marriage her father had died and her
mother had become the wife of the celebrated Hugh Peter.
Mrs. Margaret Lake, who was at Connecticut and Ipswich,
we see by the will was an older sister of Elizabeth ; and
the other sister, Martha, is named in the will as the wife of
Daniel Epps.   We afterwards find Martha in New England, the wife of Samuel Symonds."

One of our local papers give another glimpse of Mrs.
Margaret Lake and her children :

"The earliest Harris in Ipswich, was Thomas who
married Martha Lake, November 15, 1647.   His name
does not appear in any of the shipping lists, and it cannot
be determined when he came to New England or where he
came from.   He was evidently a man of quality, or he
could not have mrrried Martha Lake, a young woman
allied to the Winthrops ; her aunt Elizabeth being the
wife of John Winthrop, Jr., who settled Ipswich, and who
had horselots on East street, High street, and at Rocky
Hill extending to Turkey Shore.

Martha Lake Harris was the daughter of John and Margaret Lake.   John Lake was of the Lake Family of Nor-
manton, Yorkshire, who claimed descent from William the
Conqueror.   Mrs. Margaret Lake was the daughter of
Edmund Reade, Wickford, County Essex.   She lived many
years in Ipswich ; and her will, on file, and dated 1672,
gives a quaint idea of ancient elegancies.

Hannah Lake, another daughter of John and Margaret,
married John Gallop, Jr., who was a bold and famous
soldier in days of early Indian warfare.

Thomas and Martha (Lake) Harris had four sons and
three daughters.   Serg't John, their son, married Grace
Searle.   Margaret, their daughter, married John Staniford, and was remembered, for her name; in her grandmother Lake's will."

LOVELL — Louel, Louewell, Louell, Lowell, — are the various spelling of the same name on our Town books.

Thomas Lovell 1, had a share and a half in Plum Island &c., 1664, the lots of which, he with others was appointed to lay out. He was a voter in town affairs, 1679. Selectman, 1680, at which date he is recorded as Thomas Louewell. He was in the same office in 1692, at which time, it is written, "1682, Nov. 27. Upon information that Thomas Louell hath been with Mr. Masson about compliance, & being one of the Select men, & it hath been made appear that he hath sugested to some as if it were best to comply with him, wch is as, hath been declared, a betrayal trust committed to him. The Town generally voted to lay the sd Thomas Louell asyd & exclude him for being a select man. And Capt. John Appleton was chosen to be a select man in his room.

He had horses on the common in 1697. He possessed land adjoining a lot which Cornelius Waldo sold to John Caldwell, August 31, 1654.

The will of Thomas Louell was proved Jan. 2, 1709-10. He speaks of himself as being aged. The will enumerates his living children ; two others had died in infancy.

He bequeathes to his son John, the eldest, and his wife Elizabeth, the house and land my son Allixander Louell bought of Moses Day.

To his son Thomas, that hath been ye greatest help and support to my Family, my dwelling house and homestead, excepting my son Allixander's shop, with three rods of land in ye Front, from ye upper end of sd Allixander's shop next my dwelling house, unto ye land of Samuel Graves, lying by ye street on ye southeast.

He left daughters, Elizabeth Perkins, Margaret Edwards, Hannah Dutch, Mary Dounton.

His will was witnessed by Nathaniel Knowlton, Edmund Heard, Nehemiah Jewett.

Thomas Lovell 2 son of Thomas 1. His grave is in the yard on the hill:

> Here lies Mr. Thomas Louell
> who was born the
> 2nd of February, 1649
> & Died August ye
> 11th, 1718, aged 68
> years 6 monthes
> and 9 days

He was a sealer of leather in 1697-8, at which time he had the addition of "Junior."
John Lovell 2, son of Thomas 1, was born in 1647.

> Here lies Mr.
> John Louell who
> died February the
> 15th 1718-19 in the
> 71 year of
> his age

He married Elizabeth Pindar, Sept. 12, 1689, and had·
    John, born December 6, 1690
In recording the birth the name is spelled " Lowell."
    David, born February 7, 1694
Alexander Lovell 2, son of Thomas 1, born May 29, 1657 ; married July 20, 1696, Elizabeth Sanford. Had
    Elizabeth, born February 28, 1696
He had horses on the Common in 1697.
    Thomas, sen'r, and Thomas, jun'r, had seats assigned them in the Meeting-house, 1700.

LUMAS, or Lomas, Edward. Came to New England in the ship Susan and Ellen, 1635, being then twenty-four years of age.
    1641. He was commoner.
    1648. One of Denison's subscribers, name spelled Lomas
    1661. Constable.
    1661. Liberty to fall two white oak trees.

1664. He had a share and a half in Plum Island, &c.

1679. Was a voter in Town affairs.

February 11, 1667. Edward Lomas, being a soldier against the Pequit Indians, and not having any land granted him as others had, the Town now granted unto him, the said Edward Lomas, six acres of land.

According to Farmer, who quotes the Life of Aaron Lummas, Edward of Ipswich came from Wales, and had four sons :

    Jonathan, lived in Ipswich
    Edward, settled in New Jersey
    Samuel, lived at the Hamlet
    Nathaniel, lived at Dover

Edward 1, died about 1682, in which year, Robert Lord charges Jonathan Lummas for "recording your father's will and inventory, 6 shillings."

Jonathan Lummus 2, son of Edward 1, was one of ten members of the young generation who joined the church by taking the covenant, January 18, 1673.

With wife Elizabeth, he had :

    Edward, born November 29, 1683,
        died in four days   •
    Jonathan, born October 25, 1684
        died November 15

With wife Mary, he had

    Mary, born January 4, 1685

He died August 20, 1728, aged eighty-five years.

Samuel Lummas 2, son of Edward 1, married Sarah Smith, November 18, 1664, and had :

    Edward, born October 12, 1665
    Samuel, born February 14, 1667
    Mary, born January 10, 1669

He died February 24, 1720, aged eighty years.

LULL, Thomas. Was a voter in Town affairs, in 1679. Freeman, October 8, 1672 ; Constable, 1683 ; Tythingman, December 15, 1679.

March 1, 1673. Goodman Lull and wife came into full communion with the church.

His will is dated January 1, 1717-18. It was proved July 7, 1719. He left a widow named Elizabeth.

> Here lies Mr.
> Thomas Lull who
> died December ye
> 31, 1719, aged 82
> years, 2 months
> & 14 days.

His children were : John, Simon, born May 28, 1672, Elizabeth, Lydia.

He mentions in his will grandchildren: .Thomas John; Mary, Elizabeth, Rebekah, Hannah, Siberas, Sarah ; children of his son Thomas, deceased.

In 1699, February, he subscribed six shilling towards procuring "ye bigger bell, for ye good of ye town."

Thomas Lull, 2, son of Thomas 1, married Jan. 21, 1689, Rebekah Kimball. Of their children, Mary was born Oct. 12, 1690 ; Elizabeth, August 28, 1692 ; Rebekah, Nov. 26, 1694 ; Hannah, November 26, 1696.

> Here lieth ye
> Body of Tho
> mas Lull, who
> died February
> ye 11, 1713-14, &
> iu ye 53 year
> of his age.

LEACH, Ambrose. [See page 205, Thomas Lee.]

LINKHORN, William, 1694, December 6, purchases of the Town a lot on the common; for the use of which he engages to pay eight shillings per annum.

He became dependant, and the Town paid John Brewer, in 1729, 'for keeping William Linkham one year, £27 10.'

In 1800, he had a seat appointed to him on the tenth seat in the Meeting-house.

William Linkham was born in 1643.

MANNING, John.  Had a houselot in 1637, three rod
of ground, more or less, bounded on ye East by a house
lot of Thomas Howlett, on the west by a highway leading
to the river; at the South by a houselot of Thomas Hardy
on the crossway leading towards the Mill.

He probably died soon after this date, (1637,) and left a
widow Susan, who had a grant, February 15, 1638, of a
house lot , one acre of ground, lyeing in the Swamp near
the Mill Street, having an acre of ground of Hugh Sker-
ritt's on the north East, and a high way on the South west.

John Manning had a lot of six acres on a neck of land,
probably Manning's Neck, January 26, 1634.

Thomas Manning.  2d day of first month, 1639.  Agreed
with Robert Wallis and Thomas Manning, they shall keep
four score hogs upon Plum Island from the 10th day of
April next, until harvest be got in, and that one of them
shall be constantly there night and day all the time.

He was a commoner, 1641.

In 1653, he sold to John Appleton and Samuel Appleton
a dwelling house situated in Ipswich near the Meeting
House, having the Meeting-house green towards the north
west, and the river towards the south East ; the land of
John Woodman towards the north east, and the land of
Mr. Symonds towards the South.

In 1647, March 15, he sold to Robert Whitman, husbandman, a house and lot.

In 1661, he was employed to keep the flock of sheep on
the north side of the River.

He died Dec. 19, 1668.  Administration was granted on
his estate, at a Court held in January, 1668-9, to his sons,
Thomas and John.  He is said by Farmer to have been
seventy-four years of age at his death.

Estate, £38, 8, 2d.  Ap'd by John Brewer, and James
Saward.

Thomas Manning 2.  1675, September.  Thomas Manning being slain in ye warr, ad'r granted to his brother,
Daniel Manning.

1675, Sept. 30·  Inventory of the estate of Thomas Manning ; amount, £107.  Appraised by John Appleton and

John Whipple.  Rendered by Daniel Manning.

Thomas Manning 3, had horses on the common, 1697.

In 1684, Upon motion of Thomas Manning of Salem, Gunsmith, with respect of his being an inhabitant here amongst us :  The Town voted for his encouragement that he shall have liberty for wood for the management of his trade.

1696.  Thomas Manning was a Surveyor of highways.

1707.  He was a commoner.

1719.  He, with eight others, objects to a vote of the Town for selling the old Meeting house, "because of their rights in pews and seats."  He and Mrs Manning, probably his wife, have seats assigned to them in the Meeting house, 1719.

> Here lyes buried
> the body of Mr.
> Thomas Manning
> who departed this life
> May ye 14th, 1737, in
> the 73d year of his age.

He married Mary Giddings, daughter of Thomas Giddings, who died June 19, 1681.  In 1690, he was guardian to Dorothy Giddings, sister of his wife.  He is styled Gunsmith.

MARSHALL, William, sen'r, and John Marshall: each had a share in Plum Island, &c.

Thomas Marshall, and Anna, his wife, had

Thomas, born Dec. 26, 1678

Anna, born August 17, 1680

Abial, born July 3, 1682

Benjamin Marshall, had horses on the common, 1697.

Was commoner, 1707.

He married Prudence Woodward, November 2, 1677. They had :

Benjamin, born November 15, 1684

Sarah, born December 2, 1693

Rachel, born December 28, 1695

Peter Marshall and Abigail his wife, had
 Elizabeth, born Oct. 29, 1684
 John, born November, 1685
Joseph Marshall had :
 Joseph, born May 18, 1690
 Thomas, born March 28, 1692
 Abiezar, born September 28, 1695

MARTIN, Abraham, died December 2, 1793. His estate, consisting of house, lands, and other property, amounted in value to £178, 11, 6. It was divided, July 8, 1700, among his heirs : Hannah Marshall, his widow, one third ; Abraham, his eldest son ; Hannah, John, Sarah, Samuel, Mehitable, Thomas.

1701, November 7. Humphrey Clarke appointed guardian of Mehitable Martin, aged ten years, and Thomas Martin aged eight years,—children of Abraham Martin deceased. Abraham Martin and Jeremiah Lambe sureties.

George Martin, had horses on the common, 1697 ; had
 John, born October 6, 1686
 Mary, born August 7, 1692
 Joseph, born December 26, 1694
 Ebenezer, born April 20, 1697
He was commoner, 1707, when he has the addition of senior.

Henry Martin had Elizabeth, born Sept. 12, 1682.

MARBLES, Nicholas, had a share in Plum Island, &c. 1664. He possessed a farm in 1667. Desires to exchange land, October, 1683.

MACE, Robert. Had a seat assigned to him in the Meeting house, 1700.

MERCHANT, William, had share in Plum Island, &c. 1664. He died September 4, 1668, and left a widow, Mary, who administered on his estate. Mary Merchant was dead in 1697, and Henry Osborne administered on her estate. Her will is dated June 25, 1697. She mentions daughter Mary Osborne, and bequeaths her property to be equally divided among Mary Osborne's children.

1697, July 29. William Goodhue and Mary his wife, release to Henry Osborne claims to estate of Mary Marchant. John Osborn, Henry Osborn the same.

METCALF, Medcalf, Joseph 1. Took the freeman's oath, in Boston, May 6, 1635. Was Representative, 1635. Commoner, 1641. One of Denison's subscribers, 1648-1661.

He may have lived in the south part of the town, for it is recorded : Thomas Gilven had granted to him 9th, 2mo. 1639, a houselot of one acre on the south side of town river having the houselot of Joseph Medcalf on the north and north east.

He died July 21, 1665, aged sixty years. He left a widow, Elizabeth Metcalf, son Thomas 2, grandson Joseph 3. His estate was £370, 10.

Thomas Metcalf 2, son of Joseph 1, was one of Denison's subscribers, 1648. Had a share in Plum Island, &c., 1664. Freeman, May 27, 1674. Voter in Town affairs, 1679. Came into full communion with the Church, March 2, 1673. He had :

>    Mary, born June 23, 1658
>    Joseph, born June 27, 1660
>    Thomas, born December 4, 1667

Abigail Metcalf, his wife, died December 6, 1668.

Elizabeth, his second wife, survived him, and died May 5, 1727, aged 85 years.

In the Meeting house built 1700, a place was assigned to old Good'n Mettcalf in one of the short seats near the pulpit.

Joseph Metcalf 3, had a seat assigned him in the Meeting house of 1700. With his wife Rebekah, he had

>    Jacob, born June 8, 1685.

He died before his wife, who deceased October 20, 1723.

Thomas Metcalf 3, being a widower, married Liddia Davis, widow, February 27, 1685.

MOSES, Samuel, and Grace, his wife, had:
Samuel, born November 30, 1675
Samuel, born February 12, 1681
Mary, born January 12, 1684
Samuel Moses settled an account with Robert Lord,
April 10, 1676.

1706, April 12. Grace Stevens of Ipswich, Relict widow
of Caleb Stevens of Ipswich, deceased, and former widow of
Samuel Moses of Ipswich, affors'd, and John Allen of
Marblehead and Hannah his wife, and Mary Moses of
Ips'h, only surviving children of sd Samuel Moses,
agree, &c.

MILLER, William. Was a Soldier to the Indians,
1643. One of Denison's subscribers, 1648. He probably
went to Northampton, where William Miller was one of
the earliest inhabitants.

MORE, or Mouer, William. Had a share in Plum
Island, &c., 1664. He conveys to his daughter, Mary
Powell, wife of Robert Powell of Ipswich, ten acres of
land in Exeter, January 20, 1660.
He died May 21, 1671. His will is dated August 14,
1660, and was proved September 26, 1671. Children:—
William, the eldest son ; Thomas, Mary Powell, Elizabeth,
Ruth Tobye. In the will the name is spelled—More.

MORSE, Joseph 1. Died 1646. His will is dated April
24, 1646. His wife, Dorothy, he appointed sole executrix.
His children were : Joseph 2, John 2, Hannah.
He possessed a house which he bought of Thomas Dorman ; six acres of land which he bought of widow Perkins;
and lands which he bought of Francis Jordan.
Joseph Morse 2, took the freeman's oath at Boston, 1635.
He was a commoner at Ipswich, 1641 ; had a house in
Brook street, 1646.
John Morse 2, was one of the Denison subscribers, 1648 ;
was admitted freeman, 1654. He possessed land in Brook
street, 1656, which probably had been his father's. He
sold to Thomas Jordan, September 24, 1664, property

which is described as "land that formerly was my father's
Joseph Morse's."

In 1647 it was " Agreed with William Symonds and
John Moss to keep the herd of cows on the north side of
the river ;" "to attend at Mr. Robert Paynes and Goodman Scotts lane, at half an hour after sunrise."  " The
herdmen to wind a horn before their going out."

In 1659, Agreed with John Morse and Samuel Taylor to
keep the herd on the north side of the river, * one of them
to go out at Mill street constantly, and the other the  other
way. * The cows to be brought to the corner by Mr. Robert Paynes; and the Mill end cows to be brought to the
end of Scott's Lane.

Children : Elisabeth, born March 29, 1657, died June 27
1659 ; Mary, born June 15, 1660.

MERRILL, John.  Took the freeman's oath, May  13,
1640.  He had a houselot granted to him on the south side
of the river before 1636.

MUSSEY, Robert.  Took the freeman's oath, Sept. 3,
1634.  Had granted to him, 1635, a houselot in Mill street
between Thomas French and Richard Jacob.  He also had
a houselot at "the west end," on the east of John Dane.
In 1639, he had a houselot granted to him on Bridge street

His will is dated January 5, 1642.  He left a wife,
Bridget Mussey, and children : John, the eldest, to whom
he gave his farm ; Benjamin, Mary, Ellen.  He appoints
Mr. Dummer, Mr. Rogers, Mr. Bradstreet, Mr. Norton,
overseers of his will.

Benjamin Mussey 2, son of Robert 1, spells his name
Muzzey, in a deed dated July 22, 1651, by which he conveys to Joseph Muzzey 2, a house and land given him by
his father, twenty acres on both sides the river call the
North River.

NELAND, Edward.  Had a share in Plum Island, &c.
1664.  He subscribed towards the bell in 1699 ; had a seat
assigned him in the Meeting house, 1700, when he has the

addition of senior.   With his wife Martha, he had :
  John, born September 30, 1673
  Martha, born January 1, 1675
  Edward, born December 30, 1677
  Philip

Edward Neland, April 22, 1691, being presented for disturbing Isaac ffoster, sen'r, in his lawful employment by threatening of sd ffoster to shoot him & to cut of his head.
Will of Edward Nailand dated January 5, 1711 ; proved February 25, 1712. Sons, Edward, Philip, Benjamin ; grandson Edward not of age.   Daughter Martha MacKentire ; brother Joseph Fowler of Wenham ; son Edward's wife Mary; grandaughters Mary Nailand, Lidiah Nailand, Martha Graves.  Son Edward, executor.  Witness :  William Howlett, Daniel Warner.

Jeremy Newland was a soldier to the Indians, 1643.
Goody Noland joined the church by taking the covenant March 8, 1673.

NASON, William, had a seat assigned to him in the Meeting house, 1700.

Margaret Nason, daughter of William, died May 22, 1716, aged twenty-two years.

Willoby Nason, was a commoner, 1707. Died November 27, 1724. In the record of his death his christian name is spelled Willoughby.

NEWMAN, Thomas, was a commoner, 1641 ; one of Major Denison's subscribers, 1648. Had a share and a half in Plum Island, &c. 1664. Was Surveyor of Highways, 1662-3. He had the addition of senior.

His will was proved November, 1673. Left property am't to £81 to his wife, Alice, during her life, to dispose of ten pounds when she would, and what she left to be returned amongst his own kindred. Witness : James Chute, Robert Peirce, John Wooddman. Appraiser, Francis Jordan.

Widow Alice Newman died November 19, 1679.

John Newman and John Newman, Jun'r, each had a share in Plum Island, &c., 1664.

John Newman had horses on the common, 1697 ; a seat in the Meeting-house, 1700.

John Newman, husbandman, sold to William Goodhue, weaver, April 3, 1646, a house in Brook street, between the dwelling house of Francis Jordan and Joseph Morse. He possessed a lot of land on the Town Hill, 1657.

John Newman married Sarah Smith, November 9, 1664. Their children :

> Sarah, born August 23, 1665
> Thomas, born March 3, 1666
> Mary, born February 15, 1668
> Abigail, born March 11, 1670
> John, born October 8, 1672
> Rebecca, born June 29, 1673
> John, born August 28, 1676
> Benjamin, born April 4, 1681

Thomas Newman married Hannah Morse, June 8, 1665. They had :

> Hannah, born February 18, 1666
> Sara, born Sept 21, 1668
> Thomas, born Novem. 13, 1670, m. Rose Sparke
> John, born March 28, 1675

1691, March 25. Administration granted on the estate of Thomas Newman to John Safford, jun'r, and his wife, Hannah Safford.  Inventory, £264, 37.

Thomas Newman and Rose Spark married June 1, 1692. The will of Mary Spark, mother of Rose Newman, dated Dec. 9. 1711, proved July 26, 1712, bequeaths to her daughters Sarah Annable and Rose Newman, twenty shillings when it shall be due, given by my brother, John Hooper, in consideration yt I am & am like to be more chargeable to my Son Thomas Newman & my daughter Rose Newman with whom I now live.  Rose Newman's father was John Sparke, Innkeeper or Ordinary, whose house was on the grounds now known as the site of the Female Academy

[See Franklin, for a Newman reference.]

NEWMARCH, John. Was a subscriber to Major Denison, 1648. A voter in Town affairs, 1679. His will is dated February 15, 1095, and was proved April 26, 1697. He left a wife, Martha; and children :

John, Thomas, Zaccheus, Martha Baulch,

Phebe Penniwell, Sarah Berry, born July 16, 1659 1699-700, Sarah Berry, widow, and phebe penewell, widow, receipt to their mother and brother Thomas Newmarch, for legacies from their father, John Newmarch.

The will of Martha Newmarch, widow, is dated Feb. 15, 1697, and was proved Dec. 14, 1699. She mentions sons Thomas and Zaccheus, and daughters Martha and Sarah ; and a grandchild, Martha Balch.

Thomas Newmarch, son of John and Martha, was appointed, March 4, 1699-700, administrator, *de bonir non*, on the estate of his father, John Newmarch. The heirs were Zaccheus Newmarch, Samuel Balch yt married Martha Newmarch, Phebe Pennuell, Sarah Berry, Thomas Hovey yt married Martha Balch, Thomas Newmarch, jun'r, John Balch, jun'r.

Zaccheus Newmarch 2, son of John 1, died Aug. 13, 1731 aged seventy-eight years. He had a seat assigned to him in the Meeting-house, 1700.

Thomas Newmarch, jun'r, had a seat in the Meeting-house, 1702.

The Rev. John Newmarch, Harvard College, an early Minister and Schoolmaster of Kittery, Maine, was born in Ipswich.

The REV. JOHN NORTON. Born at Starford, Co. Hertford, May 6, 1606. Was educated at the University of Cambridge. He came to Plymouth, October, 1635. Took the freeman's oath at Boston, May 17, 1637. Was ordained Teacher of the Church at Ipswich, February 20, 1637-8. Mr. NATHANIEL ROGERS was at the same time ordained Pastor.

Mr. Norton continued in Ipswich till 1653, when he removed to Boston, were he died, April 5, 1663, aged fifty-seven years, leaving a wife, MARY NORTON, but no children.

1641.  He was a commoner.

1648.  He was one of Major Denison's subscribers.

1638.  He purchased a house in High street, of Thomas Firmin.

1638.  There was granted to him three acres of land lying on the lower side of the Mill street, having the said street on the south west, on the north east a houselot of Christopher Osgood ; on the north west a house lot of John Wyatt, on the south east by the several houselots of Richard Lumpkin, Robert Crane, and a third lot not granted.

1640.  It was ordered that the herdsmen receive the cattle into their charge at Mr. Norton's gate, and to deliver them there again at night.

1662, October 14.  He purchased of John Payne and Sarah his wife, of Boston, son and heir of the late William Payne,—a farm, two hundred and fifty acres, with the mansion house, &c., bounded by John Norton, southeast and south ; south west and west by a great ditch,—one hundred acres or thereabouts being meadow.

William Norton, brother of the Rev. John Norton, took the freeman's oath at Boston, March 3, 1635-6.  He died April 30, 1694.  His will is dated April 28, and was proved May 15, 1694.  His children :

John,     Bonus,     Elizabeth,

William, born February 12, 1660

Lucy, born January 25, 1662

At his death, 1694, he left two sons : John, the eldest, and Bonus ; and one daughter, Elizabeth, wife of Collo. John Wainwright.

Lucy Norton, his widow, died February 5, 1697-8.

He had one and a half shares in Plum Island, 1664 ; was a voter in Town affairs, 1679.  He possessed land on High street, 1659.

John Norton 2, son of William 1, was graduated at Harvard College, 1671 ; and was ordained, November 27, 1678, minister of Hingham.  He died October 3, 1716, aged sixty-six years.

Bonus Norton 2, son of William 1, with Mary his wife, had William 3, born May 9, 1691.

George Norton, married Sarah Hart, October 7, 1669. They had:

> Sarah, born July 12, 1670
> George, born November 10, 1671
> Nathaniel, born June 30, 1675

1651, 13th February. At a meeting of the Seven men : Agreed with George Norton to Ground sell the Meeting house.

1653, 25th March. At a meeting of the seven men : Agreed with George Norton to lay four gutters to the Meeting-house of large pine trees,—to cover the ground sells about the house ; Make a shut for the turret window, and cover for the upper shuttle hole, for which he is to have eighteen pounds out of his next rate, to be paid in as good pay as come in the work, to be finished by the third of Nov'm.

1655, 30th of 6th mo. Mr. Wilson is desired to speak to Goodman Norton to fulfill his bargain in make the Me'tinghouse tight, where shingles were removed by him, occasioned by the putting in of the gutters ; and also the making good his other bargain about the ground selling the Meeting house ; and in case he doth not forth with make them good, hath order by this meeting of the select men to sue him in the Town's name.

Deacon Thomas Norton, son of George Norton, died in 1744. His gravestone :

> Deacon THOMAS NORTON :
> who departed this Life
> July ye 13th, Anno Domni, 1744
> in ye 71 Year of His Age

Soundness of Judgment, Steadiness of Mind
Plainness of Heart, Friendship to Human Kind,
Courtesie, Patience, Humility,
A strict and unaffected Piety,
Zeal for the Publick Good, the Church's Peace,
A beauteous Order did, whilst living, grace

The worthy Gentleman whose dear Remains
This Sepulcre in Darkness now Contains.

Dea. Thomas had a sister, Alice Norton, who married,
October 25, 1699, Robert Kimball, who died in England,
June 27, 1703. Alice continued a widow till her decease,
in 1733.

Dea. Thomas Norton married Mercy Russ, or Ross,
November 14, 1700. She died January 6, 1728.

Thomas Norton, their son, was graduated at Harvard
College, Class of 1725. He became Master of the Ipswich
Grammar School, 1729.

Widow Mary Norton entered into a contract of marriage
with Philip Fowler, February 27, 1659.

Freegrace Norton, dying intestate, being slaine in ye
warr, March 28, 1676.

1667, June 1. Freegrace Norton to hue timber for the
Meeting-house.

1673, November. Complaint against miller Freegrace
Norton for bad grinding.

George Norton removes to Springfield, 1675.

NICHOLS, Richard. Was one of Major Denison's subscribers in 1648. He purchased of Edward Bragg, March
21, 1658, one acre and half of land on the south side of the
river, having the highway leading to Chebacco south ;
land sometime Humphrey Griffin's, now Abraham Fitt,
towards the East ; other land of sd Richard Nicolls north
and west.

Farmer thinks Richard Nichols removed to Reading
and died there November 22, 1674.

His children born at Ipswich were :

James, born July 25, 1658
Joanna, born November 26, 1660

NORTH, John. Was an inhabitant in 1637. He sold
to Robert Kinsman, July 7, 1642, a house and lot on the
south side of the river ; also a planting lot on the Neck,
near Labor-in-vain. He possessed land at Reedy Marsh,
in 1638.

NELSON, William. Had:
> William, born March 1, 1659
> Robert, born December 12, 1661

1677, December. Complaint against William Nelsen, jr. for falling trees near the house that was Tho: Wells his house.

1673. Ordered that the Constables shall give notice unto William Nellson and Abner Ordway and an Irish or Germ'y man that married Rachell, Q'r M'r Perkins mayd, that the town will not allow them to inhabit house in this Town, unless, &c.

And Quartermaster Perkins affirmed that he "would save the town harmless," as far as the "Jersie man" was concerned, by "taking him as a tenant."

OSGOOD, Christopher. Took the freeman's oath at Boston, May 6, 1635.

1635. He had granted to him an house lot, having John Proctor's houselot on the south, John Robinson on the north, William Fuller east, and a swamp west.

1641. He was a commoner.

1645. He possessed a lot on the Town Hill.

1650. His will is dated April 19, and was proved by the oath of Daniell Rolfe, October 10, 1650.

He bequeaths to his eldest daughter, Mary Osgood, ten pounds. To three other daughters, Abigail, Elizabeth, and Deborah, five pounds each.

[Mary Osgood, his daughter, and John Lovejoy of Andover, were married at Ipswich, June 1, 1651, by Mr. Symonds.]

To his son Christopher Osgood, he bequeaths house and lands. He makes provision for Margery (Fowler) Osgood his wife. He appoints Mr. John Norton and his "father, Philip ffowler," the overseers.

Capt Christopher Osgood 2, son of Christopher 1, removed from Ipswich to Andover after 1673.

1675. He was admitted freeman.

1690. Representative at the December session.

Died at the age of eighty years, in 1723, leaving a mem-

ory in Ipswich as well as in Andover.   He is alluded to on
the church records, March 1, 1673, "Tho : Osgood, the
sonne of our brother Christopher Osgood," took the
covenant.

This "sonne Tho :" also removed to Andover, and he is
later mentioned as "Tho : Osgood of Andover;" but his
daughter, Mary, was born in Ipswich, February 1, 1675.

[A most pleasant fellowship existed between the Andover Osgoods and Ipswich relatives, continuously for a
century.]

Capt. Christopher Osgood 2, had an account with Robert Lord, June 25, 1681, as did Thomas Osgood his son.

[To Mr. Hammatt's gleanings, we add a newspaper
clipping of 1879 :]

"A venerable Powder Horn belongs to Mr. Clark
Osgood, of Cape Elizabeth, Maine.   It is covered all over
with inscriptions.   It appears that Old Buck, the original
proprietor, parted with this branching horn in 1601.

"Christopher Osgood, of Orrell, England, came to
America, Feb. ye 14, 1634."
He brought Old Buck's horn with him.   The remaining
inscriptions run as follows :

Ezekiel Osgood 3, born 1712, Andover.
Ezekiel Osgood 4, born June ye 12, 1747, died 1816
Isaac Osgood, born September 16, 1775
died November 30, 1853
Clark Osgood, born Aug. 18, 1803, Bluehill, Me.

The eighth family that settled in Bluehill, was Ezekiel
Osgood, of Andover, Mass., November 6, 1765.   He died
in 1798, aged eighty-six.   In 1810, his descendants numbered five children, forty-two grandchildren, fifteen great
grandchildren.

ORDWAY, Samuel.   had a shop on the south side of
the river, near where the south end of the Cotton Factory
mill-dam and footbridge now is.   With Sarah Ordway,
his first wife, he had

Sarah, born January 20, 1681
Ann, died April 13, 1688

He married (2) February 25, 1690, Sarah Ordway, dau. of James Ordway of Newbury.

1691, March 10.   Granted to Samuel Ardway, liberty to set up a shop on ye Town Comon, to follow his trade of a smith for ye Town benefit.

[If Mr. Hammatt's quotation refers to the "Town Comon" in front of the South Meeting-house,—as it evidently must,—then the blacksmith shop of Ordway, 1691, was the beginning of the ancient shop, which for a century was near the corner of County and Poplar streets. The old Smithy, and the quaint Balances or Scales built by Dr. Calef, were remembered by the aged folks of fifty years ago.   The last blacksmith of this ancient corner was Mr. Aaron Smith.]

1694, Nov. 5.   Adminis'n Granted to Sarah Ardway, widow, widow, on estate of Samuel Ardway.   The Widow Ardway is referred to in records, 1698.

1673.   Abner Ordway sought residence in Ipswich.

OSBORNE, Osburne, Henry.   Married Mary Marchant May 1, 1661, and had:

John, born April 6, 1662

Henry,

Elizabeth, born March 28, 1676

Mary, married William Goodhue

He administered on the estate of his mother-in-law, Mary Marchant, who died December 6, 1679; and receives an acquitance from his sons and sons-in-law, who were her heirs, July 29, 1679.

Mary Osborne, his wife, died November 19, 1679.

John Osborne, son of Henry, and Mehitable Addams were married October 11, 1685.   They had:

William, born January 20, 1686

Henry Ossbourne, 1681, 27, 7: in such a condition that I can not attend my calling, nor carry on family affairs: requests that Simon Stace and Thomas Lull be appo: guardians.

PARKER, Rev. Thomas. The first minister of Ipswich. He took the freemen's oath, in Boston, September
3, 1634. In Governor Winthrop's Journal, under the date
May 15, 1634, we read: "Mr. Parker, a .minister, and a
company with him, being about one hundred, went to sit
down at Agawam, and divers others of the new comers."

He was a learned theologian, pupil of the great Arch-
bishop Usher. Savage says : He was a bachelor, but
stood in place of a father to many divines of the succeeding generations.

He was from Wiltshire, England, born 1596, the only son
of the Rev. Robert Parker.

He remained at Ipswich about one year, when he, together with many of his people, commenced the settlement
of Newbury, of which town he was minister, until his decease, April 24, 1677, in the eighty-second year of his age.

PARISH, John, of Chebacco, had—
    Sarah, born January 16, 1692
    William, born February 11, 1694
    Isaac, born March 17, 1697
    Rachell, born February 14, 1699

PATCH, Edmund, died before May 6, when administration on his estate is granted to Benjamin Patch, his
grandson.

James Patch had horses on the common, 1697, and was
a commoner, 1707.

Abraham Patch, married Eunice Fraile, March 13, 1670,
and had, Abraham, born May 17, 1672.

PAYNE, William 1. Took the freeman's oath at
Boston, May 13, 1640.

1638, February 18. It is referred to Mr. Hubbard, Mr.
Payne, Mr. Whittingham, to view the Highway leading
from the High street to the Bridge street; and to add unto
Henry Archer and any other lots adjoining, so much out
of it as may encourage them to make Ditches to draw the
way the parties named to see the highway be drained.

William Payne had granted to him, January 20, 1647,

ten acres joining to his marsh bought of Mr. John Dillingham ; also twenty-five acres beyond Muddy River.

He subscribed six shillings towards Major Denison's allowance, 1648.

He was one of the original Feoffees of the Grammar School, to which he bequeathed Little Neck, which yet remains the property of that institution.

November 19, 1646. The Town appoint the Constables to pay the forty pounds to Mr. William Payne, John Whipple, and Richard Jacob, for the building of the Bridge.

His name is one of the twenty-three of "such as promise carting voluntary toward the cart bridge, besides the rate a day work a piece."

This bridge was where the stone bridge now is, and was the first cart bridge built in Ipswich.

1637. He possessed a farm adjoining Mr. Symonds' Argilla estate.

In 1652, Nov. 4, with Hannah Payne, his wife, he sold sundry parcels of land to Zathneul Gould of Rowley, in consideration of £100.

1656. He removed to Boston, and died October 10, 1660.

He left a wife, Hannah, and had lost a daughter Hannah, wife of Samuel Appleton.

He bequeathed £20 to Harvard College.

John Payne 2, with Sarah his wife, of Boston, sold to Rev. John Norton the farm of 250 acres, which had belonged to his father, William Payne, October 14, 1662.

ROBERT PAYNE 1. Took the freeman's oath at Boston, June 2, 1641.

Representative three years, 1647-8-9.

He subscribed ten shillings towards Major Denison's allowance, 1648.

He was one of twenty-seven, out of two hundred and thirty free holders, who were entitled to a double share in Plum Island, &c., in 1664. He then has the appellation Elder Payne.

He was County Treasurer from 1665 to 1683, when he resigned the office. He may be considered as the

FOUNDER OF THE GRAMMAR SCHOOL

He gave a lot of about two acres, on which he built a School House and a Dwelling House for the Master.

This lot Mr. William Hubbard enlarged by giving one acre of land adjoining.

The Barn builded by Mr. Chevers ye first school master imployed in ye school, and ye orchard planted by him, was afterwards, upon his removal, purchased by ye Feoffees of ye said School.

He gave a day carting, besides the rate, toward the east bridge, 1646.

He had the grant of a houselot in the northerly end of High street, where he resided.

Dorcas Payne, his wife, died February 23, 1681.

He died about 1684, aged eighty-three years.

He left two sons : John and Robert.

Robert Payne 2, son of Robert 1, was graduated at Harvard College, in 1656. He became a preacher but does not appear to have been settled in the ministry.

He married Elizabeth Reiner, July 10, 1666. They had:

>    John, born October 24, 1684
>    Elizabeth, born June 16, 1677, married Daniel
>             Smith, died in 1717
>    Robert, died December 24, 1693

After the death of the Hon. Samuel Payne in 1678, he was appointed Feoffee of the Grammar School.

John Payne 2, son of Robert 1, was appointed Feoffee of the Grammar School, February 10, 1661-2. He was Constable, 1662. He had liberty to set up a brew house by the water side, near John Taylor's house, 1664. He died July 13, 1677.

1677, November. Mr. John Payne late of Boston, deceased. Elizabeth, his wife, representing the estate insolvent. Capt. John Whipple, Capt. John Appleton, Deacon Goodhue, to examine claims.

PERKINS, William, was one of twelve men who came with John Winthrop, the younger, and commenced the settlement of Ipswich, then called Agawam, March, 1632-3 He took the freeman's oath at Boston, Sept. 3, 1634.

He was the son of William and Catharine Perkins, of London, born August 36, 1607.

According to Mr. Felt, he removed to Roxbury in 1634, where he married Elizabeth Wooton, August 30, 1636 ; he was of Weymouth, 1643; of Gloucester, 1651, where he preached ; and of Topsfield, 1655.

He died May 21, 1682, and left a widow, Elizabeth, and sons John and Wllliam.  The inventory of his estate was taken June 15, 1682, by John Gould, sen'r, and Thomas Perkin's, sen'r.

Among his effects were a parcel of Books prized by Mr. Samuel Phillips and Mr. Edward Payson, £2, 10, 11.

Another parcel of books prized by Mr. Hubbard, o, 5, o.

Another parcel of books prized by Mr. Joseph Capen, £1, 5, 5.

Other chattels, making a total of £103, 1, 10.

The General Court granted to Mr. Will : Perkins one hundred acres of country land.

William Perkins 2, died as early as 1695.  He left a widow, Elizabeth Perkins, and sons William, John, Timothy, Nathan ; daughters, Elizabeth Perkins, Mary Smith, Dorothy and Rebekah.

Administration was granted to Elizabeth Perkins, widow Of the property, William and John were to have £42 a piece.  The other children £25 a piece.  Which several sums amount to the whole estate according as it is appraised, excepting the widow's thirds of the movables, and about £20, which we all agree to allow to our mother, for the bringing up of three children.

Nathan and Rebekah were minors, under the guardianship of their mother.  Elizabeth, the mother, Mary Smith and Dorothy, sign the agreement.

William 3, son of William 2, died in 1698, unmarried.  Administration is granted on his estate to Elizabeth, his mother, February 6, 1698-9.

Isaac Perkins, was an inhabitant of Ipswich, and died before 1639; for in that year it is recorded that Alice Perkins, widow of Isaac Perkins, is possessed of a parcel of land, granted to the said Isaac, lying in Brook street.

JOHN PERKINS 1. He is usually distinguished as the Elder, on the records, and he styles himself Elder in his will.

He took the freeman's oath at Boston, May 18, 1631.

Under the date, 1634, " Giuen and granted unto John Perkins, the Elder, forty acres of land, more or less, bounded on the East by Mr. Robert Coles, his land ; on the South by a small creek ; in the west unto the Town side ; unto him and his heirs or assigns." This tract of land is now known as Manning's Neck. He sold this land in 1637 to Thomas Howlett, for £7, 10.

He was commoner, 1641.

His will is dated "ye 28th of ye first mo, called March, 1654 ;" and was proved 26, 7, 1654. The following are extracts :

" I do give and bequeath unto my eldest sonn John Perkins, a foal of my young mare, being now with foal, if it please the Lord to foal it well.

" Also, I give and bequeath unto my sonn John's two sonnes, John and Abraham :

" Also I giue·and bequeath to my sonn Thomas Perkins one cow and one heyfer.

" Also I give and bequeath to his sonn, John Perkins, one ewe.

" Also, I give and bequeath to my daughter, Elizabeth Sarjeant one cow and one heyfer, to be to her and her children after her decease, if it may please the Lord, &c.

" Also I do give to my daughter Anna Bradbury, one cow and one heyfer or a young steere, to remain to her and her children, &c.

" Also, I give and bequeath to my daughter, Lidia Bennitt, one cow and one heyfer or steere, to be equally divided to her children, &c.

"I do give to my grandson, Thomas Bradbury, one cow. I do give and bequeath unto my sonn Jacob Perkins, my dwelling house, together with all ye out houses, with all my lands of every kind, & according to a former instrument, after the decease of my wife and not before, and so to remain to him and to his heirs forever.

All the rest of my estate of one kind or other, I doe bequeath to my dear wife, Judeth Perkins, appointing and ordaining my said wife the sole executrix of this my last will and testament, desiring my said wife to dispose of ye chattels above mentioned, according to her discretion."

Witnessed by William Bartholmew, Thomas Harris.

The inventory of his estate presents curious examples of the relative value of property at that time :

His dwelling house and land and out houses are valued at £40 ; Land about the house about eight acres, £12 ; Land, about fourteen acres £21 ; Marsh, about forty acres, £20 ; one mare with a mare foal £25 ; Six milch cows £30 ; Four yearling heyfers and a steere, £11, 10. Other effects making a total of £250, 5.

He died at the age of sixty-four years.

John Perkins 2, son of John 1, an inhabitant, 1634.

Took the freeman's oath at Boston, May 17, 1637.

Commoner, 1641.

Subscribed five shillings towards Major Denison's allowance, 1648.

The inventory of his estate, not including land, amounting to £103, 8, 3, was taken by William Goodhue and John Dane, March 25, 1659.

In 1635, he purchased of John Cogswell a lot of land containing six acres, bounded by the river on south east.

In 1637, he is possessed of an Island, having on the south side thereof the great river, called Chebacco river ; on the north side an arm of the same river, running between the said island and another island called Hog Island ; bounded on the east by the great bay of Chebacco ; on the west by the meeting of many creeks coming out of the marshes.

He had a house lot in High street, near Mr. Bartholmew in 1641.

I have found no record of his children, excepting that in the will of his father, who mentions his sons John (Quartermaster) and Abraham.

John 3, son of John 2, has the title of Quartermaster in 1663 and 1665.

1673, June 5, he acknowledged himself to stand bound to the Treasurer of the Countye in the sum of £100, &c., he shall save the town harmless, by his entertaining Matthew Hooker, a Jersie man, to be inhabitant, by taking him for a tenant into a farm of his.

He agrees, November, 1673, to lay down to the town half the thatch bank at his island, viz., the thatch bank next the Town river, the remainder confirmed to him, &c.

1663, he was Selectman.     1664, he was commoner.

1679, voter in town affairs.

1668, March 30. Quartermaster John Perkins is licensed to keep an Ordinary. 1677, March. Quarter M'r Perkins his license is renewed for a year : alsoe his license to draw liquor. 1678-84, renewed the same.

Elizabeth Perkins, wife of Q'r master John Perkins, died September 27, 1684.

1686, March. Abraham Perkins of Ipswich—his Brother—Attorney to Quarter master John Perkins his father unto sd Luke according as he, sd Luke, is engaged by sd articles of agree't, bearing date, November 18, 1684, made betwixt Abraham Perkins, Jacob Perkins, attornies to the sd father & Luke Perkins.

Abraham Perkins 3. son of John 2, was born 1640. He married Hannah Bemseley, October 16, 1661. Children :

    Hannah, born March 7, 1662

    Abraham, born August 15, 1665

    John, born February 25, 1667

1669, April 20. Ordered that the constable shall destrain of Abrm Perkins forty shillings for felling or carrying away two trees—he being no commoner.

1672, February. Abraham Perkins complained against Wm Story, sen'r, for taking of a load of green timber about December last, oke timber, which he drew over my farme of the south side Chebacco river, either off the commons or my farme.

1673, Nov. Ordered—to distrain 20 shillings of Abraham Perkins for entertaining John Laveritt one week at his farme.

1688, May. Paid Corn't Abraham Perkins for entertaining ye Justices when ye rate was made £5. 11, 1.

Abraham Perkins inherited from John 2, the Island already described at Chebacco river, as it appears from a Town record, that, in 1697, he complains of the want of a way laid out to the island ; and in 1698 it is recorded that he "hath a high way laid out to his Island through Labor-in-vain fields."

He was a voter in Town affairs in 1679 ; and had horses on the common in 1697, when he has the appelation Mr.

Cornet Abraham Perkins sworn constable of Ipswich, March, 1691.

The Committee appointed to allot the seats and pews in ye new Meeting house, January 16, 1700, assign to Mr. Abraham Perkins the first seat on ye so-west of ye great door, for his wife and family ; one ye heads of sd family to sit in ye pew.

To himself was appointed the seat No. 2, with ten others who, with one exception, have the title of Mr;—Thomas Hart being styled Ensign.

Mr. Abraham Perkins died April 28, 1722, "being run over by a Trumbull, which broke many bones across his breast."

Here lyes ye body of
Mr. Abraham Perkins
aged 82 years
Died April ye
28th 1722

His will is dated April 5, and was proved June 11, 1722. He mentions Hannah, his wife ; and his sons John and Stephen. His sons Beamsley, Nathaniel, Abraham, had died before him.

His wife, Hannah Perkins, survived him until October 16, 1732, when she died at the age of ninety-one years.

Her will is dated February 1, 1732, by which she gives the house her husband purchased of Deacon Jacob Foster of Ipswich, dec'd, unto the three children of her son Abraham Perkins, deceased, namely, Joseph, Nathaniel, Abraham. She provides that if "either of them should die before they arrive at the age of twenty-one years."

She bequeathes legacies to her son Stephen and Dr. John Perkins.

To Sarah, Hannah, Martha, daughters of her son Beamsley Perkins, deceased.

To Abraham and Sarah, children of her son Nathaniel.

To Hannah Staniford, daughter of her daughter Hannah, the late wife of Daniel Ringe, deceased.

To John and Mary, children of her daughter Brewer.

To Joseph and Elizabeth, children of daughter Elizabeth Eveleth.

To her grandson, Samuel Ingalls, son of Martha, my daughter.

Stephen Perkins executor.

In 1676, Twyford West payd for his daughter, the wife of Abra : Perkins, upon hir pr'st'ment, 3s & fees, 2s 6d. [Probably for wearing silk.]

November 14, 1698. At a legal meeting of the Inhabitants of Ipswich, the Committee appointed to consider the building and the builder of a new Meeting-house, reported a design of the house, and the sum for which Abraham Tilton would build it. " And Mr. Abraham Perkins stood up and said that he would build it for £900, five hundred to be paid in money, and four hundred to be paid in pay as money ; and the meeting thereupon unanimously consented to his proposal."

[At this point Mr. Hammatt, gives a History of the edifices of worship on our Meeting-house Green. It will be printed with "Miscellaneous Papers."

Bemsley Perkins 4, son of Abraham Perkins 3, born April 7, 1673, and died July 23, 1720.

Here Lyes ye Body of
Capt. Bemsley Perkins who
Died July ye 23, 1720 in
ye 45 year of his age

The above inscription on the gravestone is probably erroneous respecting his age. The Town record gives it forty-seven years three months and sixteen days,—which may be inferred to be correct from being so very particular The gravestone had imbedded in it a tablet which probably represented the Family Coat of Arms, which, unfortunately, being secured by lead, did not escape the vandalism of the eighteenth century, which would not scruple to unplumb a father for the sake of procuring the means of killing a brace of ducks.

By his will, dated February 7, 1718-9, and proved July 29, 1720, Bemsley Perkins gave all his property to his wife Hannah, to be distributed to her children at her discretion. His children were 3 daughters: Sarah, Hannah, Martha.

Here lies ye
Body of Lucy
Perkins, Daugh
ter of Capt
Behmsly Per
kins & Mrs
Hannah his
wife who
Died Nouem'r
ye 3, 1712 be
ing 25 days
old

Doctor John Perkins 4, son of Abraham 3, was graduated at Harvard College, 1695. He had ye 4th pew next Mr. Boreman's, on ye west side, for his wife.

Nathaniel Perkins 4, son of Abraham 3, with Judith his wife had Nathaniel, born March 31, 1685, who probably died early.   At the time of his mother's decease in 1732, there were living of his children, Abraham and Sarah.

Capt. Stephen Perkins 4, son of Abraham 3, was born in June, 1683.   He was published with his first wife, Mary Eveleth, July 12, 1706.   She was born October 15, 1683, and died January 17, 1718-19.

> Here lies ye body of
> Mrs. Mary Perkins, wife
> of Mr. Stephen Perkins
> aged 35 years 3 months
> & 2 days Died Januy
> ye 17th 1718-19

Capt. Stephen Perkins was published with his second wife, Margaret Blish, Sept. 25, 1719, who survived him. He died May 15, 1733.

By his will, dated April 23, 1733, he bequeaths to his wife, Margaret, £340, having received so much of her money when he married her.   He styles himself shop keeper, and possessed considerable wealth.   His mansion house and homestead, containing about nine acres are appraised at £750.

He left one son, Francis Perkins, a minor, and two daughters, Mary Norton, and Elizabeth, who married Capt. Elias Lowater, November 10, 1731.

Francis Perkins 5, son of Capt. Stephen 4, had Francis born Sept. 4, 1748.

Abraham Perkins 4, son of Abraham 3, was born in December, 1685, and died in 1718.

> Here lyes buried ye
> body of Abraham
> Perkins son of Mr
> Abraham Perkiens
> who died February
> ye 14 1718 aged
> 32 years

He married July 12, 1707, Esther Perkins, probably daughter of Matthew and Esther Perkins, who was born July 17, 1690. She married a second husband named Porter, before 1727. She was appointed the guardian of her son, Joseph Perkins, a minor, Feb. 27, 1726-7. The older children were Nathaniel Perkins and Abraham.

Thomas Perkins 2, son John 1, was one of the soldiers who served to the Indians, December 14, 1643.

1648. He subscribed four shillings towards Major Denison's compensation.

At the time of his father's decease, 1654, he had a son,— John Perkins.

Jacob Perkins 2, son of John 1, subscribed four shillings towards Major Denison's allowance, 1648.

He was confirmed a Serjeant of the Ipswich Company, 1664. Was Tythingman, 1679.

1664, Feb. 14. Agreed with Jacob Perkins in behalf of the widow Roberts to keep the sheep, &c.

1666. August. Serj't Jacob Perkins, Surveyor.

1678, Feb. 15, commoner. 1664, 1679, voter.

1691. Juryman.

His wife died February 12, 1685.

He died February 5, 1699, and left sons Jacob and Matthew. His estate was inventoried £15, 16, 9.

His Children :

Mary, born May 14, 1658
Jacob, born 1662, married Elisabeth Sparks
Matthew, born June 23, 1665
Hannah, born November 11, 1670
Joseph, born June 20, 1674
Sarah, born May 18, 1677
Javis, born May 15, 1678

Jacob Perkins 3, son of Jacob 2, was born 1662, married Elisabeth Sparks, December 25, 1684.

Jacob Perkins
Died November
ye 12, 1705
in ye 44 year
of his age

His will dated November 10, two days before his decease, mentions his wife, Sarah Perkins, and sons Jacob, born Feb. 15, 1685, and John whose wife was Elizabeth ; daughter Elizabeth born March 18, 1691 ; brothers Matthew Perkins and Thomas Treadwell ; wives children, Elisha, Sarah, Mary, Hannah, Judith.

His sons were minors at the time of his decease, under the guardianship of Isaac Ringe, March 4, 1705-6.

Jacob Perkins, Tail'r, probably Jacob 3, subscribed six shillings towards the bell, 1699.

John Perkins 4, son of Jacob 3, was born October 17, 1693; was published with Anna Perkins, January 2, 1711.

Matthew Perkins 3, son of Jacob 2, was born June 23, 1665.   His epitaph :

> Here lies the
> Body of Cap
> Mathew Pirkins
> Decest April
> ye 9, 1738, in
> the 73 year
> of his age

His will was proved July 27, 1738.   He had buried wife Esther ; wife Mary survived him.   His children :

Matthew, of wife Esther, born April 14, 1687
Esther, of wife Esther, born July 17, 1690
Joseph, born June 15, 1695, died young
John,          Abraham,
Martha Dodge,      Hannah Woodbury,      Ruth

Matthew Perkins 4, son of Matthew 3, was published with Martha Rogers, daughter of John Rogers, and grand daughter of Samuel Rogers.   She died young :

> Mrs. Martha Perkins
> wife of Mr.
> Mathew Perkins
> died Sept ye 30
> 1720, aged 29 years

He was published with Mary Smith, widow, January 14
1720-1.  They had children :

Abraham, baptized April 5, 1735
Stephen, baptized February 12, 1736

Jacob Perkins, jun'r, 3, son of John 2.  I assume him
to have been of the third generation, although I have not
been able to trace his parentage.  He was probably son of
John 2, son of John 1, and being but nine years old at
the time of the decease of his grandfather, was not.
mentioned in his will.  His epitaph :

Here lies Mr.
Jacob Perkins
who died
November ye 26th
1719 in ye
74th year of
his age

He left a wife Sarah, probably his second wife.  His
first wife was also named Sarah, for :
Jacob Perkins and Sarah Wainwright married, 1667.
Sarah, wife of Jacob Perkins, jr. died Feb. 3, 1688.
The children of Jacob and the two Sarahs are :

John, born Jan 31, 1668, died April 6, 1669
Phillis, born January 28, 1669, died early
Phillis, born November 28, 1670
Francis, born December 16, 1672
Mehetable, born July 12, 1681
Mary, born August 2, 1685
Elizabeth b. May 8, 1687, m. Wm Leatherland 1708.
Jacob, born January 3, 1690
Unice, born May 1, 1691, married Robert Choate
John, born October 17, 1693
Robert, born October 21, 1695
Sarah, born Dec. 26, 1666, m. John Laighton
Westley, born December 3, 1697
Joseph, born October 9, 1699
Jeremiah, born December 1, 1701

Here Lyes ye Body
of Sarah Laigh
ton, Daughter
of Mr. Jacob Per-
kins & wife
to John
Laighton
Died March
ye 1 1716 aged
19 years 2
months &
5 days

Jacob Perkins, jun'r voter in Town affairs, 1679.

Corp'll Jacob Perkins had assigned to him a place on seat No. 3, in the Meeting-house, 1700.

His son Francis, born 1672, married, and died when a young man, leaving children.

The will of Jacob Perkins 3, is dated December 13, 1718, a year before his decease.   Extracts :

" To my dearly and well beloved wife, Sarah, one room, ye parlour room, in my dwelling house ; one third the cellar.   Also I give to my said wife during her widowhood, annually, to be paid equally between my two sons, Jacob and John Perkins, ye keeping of a good riding horse, and a person suitable to ride before her to meeting, or elsewhere, as she may have occasion, and ye keeping of two good milch cows, summer and winter on ye farm ; and eight cord of wood layd at ye door ; one hundred & twenty pound of good Beef ; & ye same weight of good pork ; fifteen bushels of Indian Corn ; five bush'l of Malt ; two bush'l of Rye & one bush'l of Wheat ; ten pounds of sheep wool ; six pounds of Flax ; and forty shillings in money.

And if my said wife should see cause to marry again, Then I will and order that my said two sons pay yearly to their mother, five pounds in or as money, equally between them during her natural life.

Also, household goods, within doors, during her natural life, & to dispose of ye same in her life or att her death among my children as she shall see cause.

Having given to my daughters Phillys, Sarah & Unis, their full proportions, I give them but five shillings.

I give to my daughter Mehetable, four pounds, in or as money, to make up her portion.

I give to my daughter Mary, eighteen pounds.

I give to my daughter Eliz'h, five pounds, in or as money.

Having given a deed of land to ye children of my son Francis, dec'd, which I intended for his portion, &c.

I give and bequeath to my four sons, namely, Robert, Westley, Joseph, Jeremiah Perkins, to each of them one acre of upland & one acre of marsh ground att fox point, so called, as may be convenient for house lot, and high-way thro' my farm to & from said land, as they may have occasion, & my will is that neither of them, my four sons, shall sell the said land given them, without giving their brothers the refusal of ye same.

I also give to my afforesaid four sons twenty pounds a piece.

I give to my eldest son Jacob ye half of ye wood lot wch he and I bought in partnership of Edward Webber.

Jacob and John residuary legatees and executors. Witnesses, Daniel Rindge, Robert Caleff, Dan'l Rogers.

Jacob Perkins 4, son of the above Jacob 3, married Elizabeth Kinsman. Their publishment is dated March 6, 1713-4. Her death as inscribed upon the stone :

Here lies ye Body of
Elisebeth Pearkins
ye wife of Mr. Jacob
Pearkins, who died
September ye 26, 1732
in ye 43 year of her
age

John Perkins 4, son of 'Jacob 3, married Elisabeth Endicott, of Boxford. Their publishment is dated March 15, 1718.

Robert Perkins 4, son of Jacob 3, married Elizabeth Dunton, published October 25, 1718.

Westley Perkins 4, son of Jacob 3, m. Abigail Rindge, November 27, 1725.

Joseph Perkins 4, son of Jacob 3, married (1) Elizabeth Fellows, November 2, 1729 ; he married (2) Elizabeth Choate, January 1, 1743-4. He died August, 1752, and Elizabeth (Choate) Perkins married John Kinsman, August 9, 1753.

Children of Joseph 4 and Elisabeth (Fellows) Perkins :
Isaac, born October 29, 1738
John, born May 10, 1741, died of small pox, 1773
Susannah, born September 11, 1743,
married Ephraim Kendall, Aug. 6, 1764
Children of Joseph 4, and Elisabeth (Choate) Perkins:
Ephraim, born November 9, 1746 died April 5, 1779
James, a minor in 1753
Jonathan, died before 1779
Elizabeth, married Deacon John Crocker, she died, January 12, 1803. (see gravestones.)

Ephraim Perkins 5, above named, who died April 5, 1779, left estate which was divided as follows : To Elizabeth (Choate) Kinsman, his mother, £163, 8, 2. And the same sum to the heirs of John and James Perkins, to Elizabeth Crocker and to Susanna Kendall.

Jeremiah Perkins 4, son of Jacob 2, married Novem. 7, 1730, Joanna Smith, who died May 25, 1782. He died January 13, 1790. Their children were :
Daniel, born January 14, 1738
Joanna, born January 1, 1741
Aaron, born September 29, 1744
Martha, born February 1, 1746

Aaron Perkins 5, son of Jeremiah 4, married Novem. 14, 1767, Hannah, daughter of Jabez Treadwell, who was born February 15, 1744, and died Feb. 16, 1822. Children :
Hannah, born October 9, 1768
Lucy, born October 1, 1769
Sarah, born October 28, 1770

Besides the foregoing branches of the family of Perkins, whose genealogy has been traced, there are many of the name whose line of descent I have not traced :

Samuel Perkins, died 1700, left a son John born May 12, 1692 ; daughter Elizabeth, born June 13, 1685, under the guardianship of his widow, Hannah (West) Perkins, whom he married, 1677, and had :

 Samuel, born November 26, 1679
 Ebenezer, born February 3, 1681
Widow Hannah Perkins died August 21, 1732

Nathaniel Perkins and Judith his wife, lived at Chebacco, and had :

 Nathaniel, born March 31, 1685
 Jemima, born June 29, 1686

Isaac Perkins and Hannah his wife, lived at Chebacco. In his will dated October 6, 1725, he mentions his being aged and infirm.  His sons were :

 John, born July 1, 1670
 Abraham, born September 15, 1671
 Hannah Woodward, born January 31, 1673
 Isaac, born May 23, 1676
 Jacob, born November 9, 1678
 Elizabeth, born May 26, 1680
 Sarah Marshall, born March 28, 1684
 Mary, born March 27, 1687

### PUBLISHMENTS

John Perkins and Anna Perkins, January 2, 1711
Jacob Perkins and Mary Cogswell, September 8, 1716
Nath'l Perkins    Elizabeth Decker of Rowley June 9, 1711
Matthew Perkins, jr.    Mary Smith, widow, Jan 14, 1720-1
Mark Perkins and Dorothy Whipple, January 4, 1721-2
Elisha Perkins and Margaret Newmarch, August 4, 1722
James Perkins and Margaret Andrews, Decem. 14, 1732
Jacob Perkins and Susanna Butler, widow, Feb. 12, 1738
Jacob Perkins jun'r and Elizabeth Story, July 28, 1743
Jacob Perkins, at the hill, and Mary Dresser, Oct. 27, 1733

Luke  Perkins  and  Elizabeth  Jaye  were  married,  April
26,  1677

Luke  Perkins  and  Sarah  his  wife  had:

    John,  born  May  14,  1693

    Sarah,  born  January  22,  1694

Mr.  John  Perkins  and  Mary,  his  wife,  had:

    Hannah,  born  June  9,  1699

Susannah  Perkins  in  her  will,  dated  July  1,  1763,  mentions  her  son  Francis  Perkins;  and  grandchildren  Jacob
and  Mary,  children  of  her  son  Jacob  Perkins.

Joseph  Perkins,  sen'r,  died  in  1746.

Jacob  Perkins  and  Mary  had  children  baptized:

    Marie,  December  29,  1734

    Mehitable,  February  29,  1735

    Eunice,  April  19,  1839

    William,  December  28,  1740

    Samuel,  May  7,  1748

Jacob,  the  father,  died  December  1,  1758

Nathaniel  Perkins  and  Elizabeth  had  children  baptized:

    Nathaniel,  April  6,  1735

    Beamsley,  February  5,  1736

Nathaniel  Perkins  and  Anna,  had  baptized:

    Anna,  July  10,  1738

    Elizabeth,  December  2,  1739

    Mary,  March  14,  1741

    Nathaniel,  April  15,  1744

    Esther,  August  4,  1745

    Abraham,  June  14,  1747

    Abigail,  January  15,  1748

    Sarah,  December  1,  1751

    Lucy,  May  25,  1755

    Joseph,  July  24,  1757

    Stephen,  March  1,  1758

John  Perkins  and  Elizabeth  had  Mary,  bap.  Oct  26,  1735

James  and  Margaret,  of  Chebacco,  had  Lucy  bap.  December  27,  1735

Elihu  Perkins  and  Abigail  had  Abigail,  bap.  Feb.  8,  1735

William Perkins and Elizabeth, had baptized :
William, September 9, 1750
Nathaniel, August 2, 1752
Elizabeth, June 2, 1754
Hannah, August 24, 1755
Nathaniel, January 30, 1757
Hannah, August 27, 1758
Robert Perkins and Elizabeth had baptized :
John, April 7, 1754
Elizabeth, June 1, 1755
Robert Perkins and Lucy had bap. Sarah, April 27, 1760
Robert Perkins and Sarah had bap. John, Sept. 26, 1761
Rob't Perkins and Elizabeth had bap. Rob't, May 15, 1763
James Perkins and Hannah had baptized :
James, August 14, 1763
Joseph, August 25, 1765
Joseph, February 17, 1768
Isaac, September 23, 1770
Francis Perkins and Martha (Low) had baptized :
Francis, September 4, 1748
Martha, October 22, 1758
Esther Perkins in her will, dated June 5, 1743, mentions
four sons of her son Matthew ; a grandson Matthew ; children of her daughter, Mary (Perkins) Smith ; her daughter Hubin.
Jacob Perkins, son of Isaac, paid twelve shillings for
cutting wood, 1699.

PERLEY, Allen.  Possessed land on Heartbreak Hill,
in 1635 ; and a houselot in Mill street, 1642.
According to Coffin and Farmer, he came from Wales,
and landed at Charlestown, July 12, 1634.
1641, he was a commoner. 1644, was admitted freeman.
1664, he had a share and a half in Plum Island, &c.
He died December 28, 1675, and left a widow, Susannah.
Widow Susannah Perley died February 11, 1691.
It is recorded that Abraham Perley and wife came into
full communion with the church, August 12, 1674.  It is
not improbable that this is a mistake of name—Abraham
for Allen.

The inventory of Alyn Perly, rendered February 3, 1675, by John Kimball and Nehemiah Abbot, exhibits a total of property of £330, 2, 6, of which was: "half of land as was Nathaniel Perley's—£201."

Samuel Perley, married Ruth Trumbull, July 15, 1664, and had:

Samuel, born May 28, 1667
Sarah, born June 7, 1665
John, born September 28, 1669
Hannah, June 8, 1670
Ruth, born June 4, 1675
Hepsebeth, September 12, 1679

He was a voter in Town affairs, 1679; had seat No. 3, assigned him in the Meeting-house, 1700.

Timothy Perley was a commoner, 1707. With wife Deborah, he had:

Patience, born March 28, 1682
Stephen, born January 15, 1684, died Sept. 4, 1725
Joseph, born June 3, 1685

Timothy Perley died January 25, 1707, aged 65 years.

Nicholas Perley married Elisabeth Bosworth, October 25, 1686, and had:

John, born July 17, 1692
Elizabeth, died June 24, 1702

John Perley and Jane, had Hannah, born Sept. 1, 1699.

PEARPOYNTE, Robert, was a subscriber to Major Denison's allowance, 1648.

John Pierpont purchased of William Fellows, Nov. 15, 1649, fifteen acres of land, butting upon the land of John Brown on the south, and upon land of Thomas Howlett on the west, upon the Great Brook towards the north.

Farmer, on the authority of Sarah Pierpont's deposition, 1724, says: James Pierpont came from England, and died at Ipswich, leaving two sons,—John and Robert.

John Pierpont, Robert Pierpont, the two sons of Robert, removed from Ipswich to Roxbury, where John was admitted freeman, 1652; Representative, 1672; died December 30, 1690.

John Pierpont had sons :
John, born October 22, 1652
James of New Haven
Ebenezer, died December 17, 1696
Joseph
Benjamin, Harvard College, 1689, a minister, Charleston, S. C. Died, 1697
Robert Pierpont was admitted freeman, 1675 ; died May 16, 1694, leaving a widow Sarah, living in 1724, aged 83.

1639-40. Agreed with James Pearpoynt to keep the herd on the South side of the river,—for himself and son.

PETERS, Andrew, was commoner, and had a share in Plum Island, &c., 1664. Farmer thinks he was the same who died at Andover, 1713, aged seventy-seven. He had :
John, born February 28, 1659
Elizabeth, born August 1662
William, born February 7, 1663
Mary, born June 12, 1668
Mercy, born January 27, 1670
1671, October 22. The select men of Ipswich, doe concieve that Andrew Peeters (upon consideration of carriage at mile brook, his miscarriage at quarter masters ; his miscarriage to the constable & before the selectmen,) is not fitt for to have any license for to sell liquors.

1673, November. Upon petition of Andrew Peeters about Sarah Roes living at his house, the Select men gave him liberty to entertain her till eleven weeks be expired from her coming to town from Boston ; she declaring some inclination to live with her husband as a wife, and to go to him when he comes to town.

John Peters married Susan Roberts, February 28, 1666 ; and (2) Mary Edwards, 1680.

PERRIN, Thomas. 1699, November, married Susanna, widow of Robert Roberts of Ipswich. He had horses on the common, 1697 ; was commoner, 1707 ; he kept the sheep at the Neck, 1667 ; was constable, 1703 ; had a seat assigned to him in the Meeting-house, 1700; when he is designated as "Good'm Perrin, Sen'r." He had the second lot, 24 feet front, near the Town Bridge, 1692.

PENGRY, Moses. Born, 1610.

1641, 12th day, 1st mo. Barnabas Norton of Ipswich, baker, sold unto Moses Pengry, six acres of land within the common fence, Richard Bisgood on the south east.

1642, November 25. John Tuttell, yeoman, sold to him, land lately purchased of Richard Lumpkin, deceased.

1646, February 4. William Whitred sold to Moses Pengry, Saltmaker, a dwelling house and lot.

1641, he was commoner.

1648, subscriber to Denison.

1664, had one and a half shares in Plum Island as tenant of Mr. Payne.

With the title of Deacon he is on the list of those that by law are allowed to have their votes in Town affairs, 1679. Selectman, 1661, Tithingman, 1677, Selectman, 1718.

Of his children, Thomas died January 25, 1662 ; Abigail was born January 30, 1666.

Moses Pengry died January 2, 1695, aged eighty-six years ; and Lydia Pengry, his wife, died Jan. 16, 1675.

Aaron Pengry, was an inhabitant in 1648. He had one share and a half in Plum Island, &c., 1664. Was a voter in Town affairs, 1679 ; had privileges of commonage granted February, 1667. Moses Pengry, sen'r and Aaron Pengry, sen'r, were witnesses to the will of widow Mary Marchant, June 25, 1679. Aaron was Tythingman, 1679.

His will, is dated May 4, 1684, and proved Nov. 17, 1666 He bequeathes to his wife, his estate during her life. Fifty shillings unto my wife her son Jno : Starkweather ; and forty shillings to Sarah Branscomb. To the three sons of my brother Moses Pengry, viz., to my cousin Moses, Aaron, John, Thirty Pounds each ; and to my brother Moses his daughters, twenty pounds each—six persous.

Moses, Aaron, John Pengry were of ten of the members of the young generation, who "took the covenant," Janunry 10, 1673.

Moses Pengry, jun'r, married Sarah Converse, June 29, 1680. She died February 20, 1691. They had a son Moses born November 17, 1682, 8 February following.

The will of Moses Pengry dated December 6, 1699, was proved May 16, 1709 : Being by God's providence bound to Carolina :- Wife, Abigail, in Carolina ; Brother John Pengry ; child Abigail Pengry ; daughter Ann who lives with her uncle Philemon Dane, all the household stuff and goods yt was her mother's ; son Moses, lands in Haverhill; brother Philemon Dane, Executor.

Aaron Pengry married Ann Pickard, March 22, 1681. He resided on the High street next to John Brown.   Had :

Ann, born February 8, 1685
Jane, born January 24, 1691

John Pengry, born 1653, married Fayth Jewett, May 20, 1678.   Had :

Lydia, born March 16, 1679, died August 12 1693

He had a seat, No 3, in the Meeting-house, 1700 ; gave 12 shillings towards the bell, 1699 ; he had the title, Mr.

He died January 15, 1723.

Ensign John Pengry has a tombstone :

Here lyes buried
the body of
Ensign John Pengry
Dec'd Aug't 22d 1732
in the 49th year
of his age

PEIRCE, Robert.   Had a share and a half in Plum Island, &c..   He, with Serj't Thomas Clarke, had liberty to build a wharf in 1661.

His will is dated March 8, 1664. Proved April 1, 1679.

He left a wife Abigail, daugh'r of Joanna Symonds, who died June 28, 1680 ; and children :

Samuel, the eldest
John, born May 23, 1657
Robert, born November 7, 1661

Mary, born May 30, 1664, died May 18, 1666

Moses, born June 11, 1666

Mary, born March, 1667

Abigail Lyndall

Joanna, born October 13, 1659

He appoints his loving friends Deacon Knowlton, Jacob Foster, John Staniford, overseers.

The will of his widow, Abigail Pearse, [as she spells her name,] is dated June 24, 1680, and proved September 28.

She bequeaths to her son Samuel the house and land on the other side of the way, which I purchased of Thomas Lord; the shop only excepted, and yt I give to my son John. She mentions sons Robert and Moses; daughters Joanna, Mary, Abigail Linden, and son-in-law, John Linden.

Robert Peirce the elder possessed land adjoining Deacon Thomas Knowlton on the north side of the river, 1657.

Robert Peirce in his will, mentions "that piece of land that now lies fenced out from ye orchard next ye street syd, that was formerly the land of Thomas Lord." The inventory of his estate amounted to £574, 5, 8, of which was "the housing, barn, land, on both sides of ye way, £160. Farm at Rowley Villidge, £100.

Moses Pearce made a will, dated April 8, 1690, which was proved March 31, 1691. He prefaces it thus : "Being by God's providence bound out to expose myself to a potent Enemy." He mentions brothers Samuel Pearce and Samuel Graves; sister Mary Pearce, and cousin Abigail Lindall.

Samuel Pearce, with Mary his wife had Mary, born July 11, 1685.

Here lyes ye Bodys
of Thomas & Sarah
Pears the children
Mr. Thomas & Mrs.
Sarah Pears who
died october ye
16, 1736 Sarah
in ye 10 Thomas
in ye 5 year of
there age

PERRY, Thomas.  Commoner, 1641.

1642, March 17.  Agreed to pay six bushels of Indian corn to Mr. William Payne, for Ambrose Leach ; and also to pay him £7 more in Corn or Cattle, in full discharge of a six acre lot, which the Town did purchase of Thomas Perry ; and the said Perry did assign the debt to Thomas Lee, and the said Thomas Lee to Ambrose Leach.

1677, Sept.  Ordered that the widow of Thomas Perry shall have thirty shillings in such things as may answer her present necessity.

Matthew Perry m. Elizabeth Blake, March 27, 1665, had
    Matthew, born July 16, 1666
    Samuel, born April 5, 1668
    John, born August 15, 1669
    Waitstill, born May, 1674
    Elizabeth, born December 13, 1675
    Eliphalet, bern May 9, 1677
    Deborah, born May 1, 1678
    William, born June 24, 1679

PHILBRICK, PHILBROOK.  See Filbrick.

PINDER, Henry.  Was commoner, 1641.

He sold commonage to Twiford West, Jan. 26, 1657

He had a house in High street in 1659, near the house which Richard Dummer purchased of John Andrews.

He died February 6, 1661.

John Pinder was one of Major Denison's subscribers, 1648.  Share in Plum Island, &c. 1664.  He had :
    Elizabeth, born August 16, 1658
    Thomas, born August 26, 1665
    Theophilus, born June 28, 1668

Thomas Pinder, had horses on the common, 1697.  A seat in the Meeting-house 1700.

John Pinder was a soldier in his country's service; and died 1700.  Joseph Hunt was appointed adm'r; Jan. 29, 1700-1.  His effects were £1, 2, 2, wages received.  Wages due, £1, 2, 2.

Simon Pinder, died April 5, 1725.

PICKERING, John, "the elder," possessed a planting lot at the cove of the river, the easterly termination of what was called "the Town," in 1634. According to Farmer he was a carpenter, and came to New England, 1630. Admitted an inhabitant of Salem, Feb. 7, 1637, died 1657.

PICKARD, John. Possessed a farm in 1650, lying toward the southeast of the farm which Thomas Emerson sold to Joseph Jewett, near the line of Rowley. He was Representative of Rowley, 1660; died in 1697.

Here is interred
what was mor
tal of David
Pickerd (son of
Mr. John & Mrs Jo
anna Pickerd)
Died March ye 2
1713-14, aged 20
years 10 Months
& 26 days

PETTIS, Pettice, Pittis, John. Commoner, 1641. Subcriber to Major Denison's allowance, 1648. "Died lately," May 20, 1653. Sarah Pettis, died August 12, 1667.

PIPER, Nathaniel. Had a share and an half in Plum Island, 1664. Purchased Marsh lands of Andrew Hodges, March 18, 1664. His will is dated March 17, 1675; proved Sept. 26, 1676. He left wife Sarah. Children:
Nathaniel, born June 25, 1658
Josyah, born December 18, 1661
John
Thomas, born November 16, 1666
Samuel, born June 12, 1670
Jonathan,
William, died June 18, 1674
Sarah,
Mary, born Nov. 5, 1660, died next Feb. 18
Mary born December 15, 1664
Margaret

His will was witnessed by Francis Wainwright and James Chute, sen'r.

Jonathan Piper. His wife, Sarah Piper, died May 6, 1700. He was published with Alse Darbey of Beverly, September 21, 1700.

He had house and lands at Hog Island.

Jonathan Piper, Nath'l Treadwell, Ezekiel Woodward, have liberty to build a gallery, 1666.

POWELL, Robert. Married Mary Moore, (Mouer,) daughter of William Moore, who conveys to her, January 20, 1660, ten acres of land in Exeter.

POTTER, Antonye. Was one of the subscribers to Major Denison's compensation, 1648. Had a share and a half in Plum, &c., 1664. Voter in Town affairs, 1679.

His will is dated Dec. 28, 1689. Proved March 26, following. He left wife, Elizabeth (Whipple) Potter, sole executrix. Sons, John, Edmund, Samuel, Thomas, Anthony. The two last named were residuary legatees.

His daughters were, Elizabeth Kimball, Lydia Putnam.

His "cousin," Mr. John Whipple, and Mr. Nathaniel Rust, Mr. Joseph Goodhue, were appointed overseers.

He purchased of John Burnham, June 1, 1648, a house lot, late of Humphrey Griffin, situate near the water mill.

1647, January 19. Daniel Denison conveys to Humphrey Griffin a Dwelling house near the Mill.

1648, 1st of 4th mo. John Burnham conveys to Anthony Potter a house lot late of Humphrey Griffin, Situate near the Water Mill.

1661, January 19. Anthony Potter and Elizabeth his wife, convey to John Safford Dwelling House and land three acres, north side of river, near the mill with high way round.

Anthony Potter purchased also a houselot containing three acres, lying next the houselot of Serjeant Jacobs.

April 4, 1660. Anthony Potter with Edmund Bridges, sold to Elder John Whipple, a six acre lot, which was sometime Henry Kingsbury's.

The Court Records of the County of Essex contain the following : " 1653, 7mo. Anthony Potter discharged of his wife's presentment being proved to be worth £200. This "presentment" was for wearing silk.

Elizabeth (Whipple) Potter, widow of Anthony, died at the advanced age of eighty-three years.

Here lys buried
Mrs. Elizabeth Potter
who died March
ye 10, 1712 aged
83 years
a tender mother
a prudent wife
at GOD'S command
resigned her LIFE

Among the plate belonging to the First Church, is a silver cup, inscribed :

P
A * E
THE GIFT OF ELIZABETH POTTER
TO THE CHURCH OF IPSWICH
1699

John Potter 2, son of Anthony 1, with Sarah his wife, had

    John, born May 11, 1680
    Sarah, born December, 1685
    Elizabeth, born April 23, 1695

He subscribed six shillings towards the bigger bell, 1700. And his mother, Elizabeth Potter, subscribed 3 shillings.

Edmund Potter 2, son of Anthony 1, with Abigail his wife, had :

    Elizabeth, born April 14, 1681
    Edmund, born June 14, 1683
    Elizabeth, born November 17, 1694

In 1702, April 13, Nathaniel Wells was appointed guardian of Edmund Potter, aged nineteen years.

Samnel Potter 2, son of Anthony 1, was four times married : (1) Joanna ; (2) Ruth Dunton, April 28, 1692 ;

(3) widow Hannah Tuttle, alias Pickard of Rowley, Nov. 20, 1701 ; (4) Sarah.

With Joanna, his wife, he had :
    David, born March 27, 1685
    Joanna, born June 16, 1686
    Thomas, born April 13, 1691
With Ruth, his wife :
    Anthony, born October 2, 1696
His will give names of other children. The will is dated July 7, proved Aug. 2, 1714. Wife Sarah ; three youngest daughters; Hester, Lydia, Abigail; also Johannah, and Elizabeth Lord. Sons : Samuel, Thomas, David, Anthony Witnessed by Isaac Foster, jun'r, John Sherwin, Abraham How.

Thomas 2, son of Anthony 2, married Mary Kimball, June 16, 1696 ; and had :
    Mary, born April 14, 1697
    Thomas; born August 17, 1698
Anthony 2, son of Anthony 1, married Martha Dresser, July 11, 1695 ; and had :
    Martha, born Jan. 10th, died 21st, 1697
John 2, son of Anthony 1. Wife Sarah. Their son, John 3, died October 13, 1724, aged 45 years.    John 2 :

    Here lyes ye body
    of Mr. John Potter
    Died June 13, 1724
    in ye 66th year
    of his age

Edmund Potter and Nathaniel Potter, commoners, 1707.

Christopher Potter, tanner, married Hannah Graves, daughter of Samuel Graves, sen'r, March 12, 1693-4.

Anthony Potter and Samuel Potter had seats assigned to them in the Meeting- house, 1700 ; and John, Sarah, Mary, had seats assigned, 1702.

PODD, John. Commoner, 1641; subscriber to Major Denison's compensation, 1648 ; share and a half in Plum Island, 1664 ; he was one of the 24 inhabitants who promised voluntary carting toward the cart bridge, besides the rate a day work apiece, 1646; voter in town affairs, 1679.

His will is dated November 2, 1687; and was proved December 24, 1694. Grace Podd, his widow and executrix, is represented as "aged and sick, and not able to come abroad." His estate amounted to £62, 9.

Grace Podd, his widow, died May 31, 1695.

In the ship *Susan and Ellen*, which came to New England, 1635, was Samuel Podd, passenger, aged 25 years.

POLAND, Samuel. Had horses on the common, 1697. Was a commoner, 1707.

James Poland, married April 12, 1694, Rebecca, daugh'r of Richard Kimball of Wenham.

John Poland, prosecuted for felling trees, 1669.

PRESTON, Roger. Subscribed towards Major Denison's allowance, 1648.

With Martha Preston, his wife, he sold to Reginald Foster, March 11, 1657-8, two houses and lots containing two acres, which he purchased of Robert Wallis on the north side of the river, having the highway next the river towards the south; and Thomas Knowlton's land and Robert Peirse's land towards the north; and the land of Thomas Clark east. Also a planting lot of three acres on the north side of Town Hill.

He possessed a houselot on the south side of the river, and a planting lot at Sagamore Hill, 1639.

PRITCHETT William, was a subscriber to Major Denison, 1648; and, as Richard Jacob's farmer, had two shares on Plum Island, 1664. He possessed lands in "a flat or field, called Pequitt Lotts," in 1655. He had a house and lot near the Meeting House, adjoining Thophilus Wilson's, 1654. He possessed a houselot and other land on the south side of the river, April 9, 1639.

John Pritched had: Elisabeth, born July 29, 1675

Sarah, born December 5, 1677

John, born February 29, 1680

PROCTOR, John. Came to New England in the ship *Susan and Ellen*, 1635, aged forty years; Martha Proctor, aged 28 years; John, 3 years; Marie, one year. John Proctor was a commoner, 1641; was one of the 27 richest inhabitants who had two shares in Plum Is. 1664. He had a houselot adjoining Christopher Osgood; and another, where he had his house, on the south side of the river, 1635, it being the lot nearest the bridge. This last mentioned lot, with the dwelling house, he sold to Thomas Firman, May 1, 1647, in exchange for a farm.

In 1635, he had a planting lot, "on the east side of the great hill called Heartbreak." This planting lot adjoined lots of Mr. Samuel Dudley, Thomas Wells, and "the way leading to Mr. Saltonstall's Farm."

His will is dated August 28, and proved Nov. 28, 1672. In it he speaks of himself as aged and infirm.

His first wife, Martha, died June 13, 1659. He left a wife, Martha. His sons were: John, Joseph, Benjamin. His daughters: Martha White; Abigail Varney; Sarah Dodge; Hannah Widden.

Benjamin 2, son of John 1, married Deborah Hart, Feb. 1673. He was commoner, 1678.

John 2, son of John 1, born 1632, married Elizabeth Thorndike, December, 1662. They had born in Ipswich: Mary, born Jan. 1, 1657; Benjamin, born June 10, 1659; Martha, born April 1, 1665.

He removed to Salem, where, in 1692, he was hanged as a witch. A petition for a reprieve, signed by thirty-two of his Ipswich neighbors, testifying to the goodness of his character, availed nothing. His will, made in prison after his conviction, August 2, 1692, directs his property to be equally divided among his children. It amounted to £17, 6, 8, for each: Benjamin, Martha, Mary, William, Joseph, Samuel, John, Elizabeth Verry, Thorndike, Sarah, Elizabeth Proctor, Abigail.

It appears from the following that his wife, Elizabeth, was also convicted. Sir William Phipps prevented her execution by pardon:

Essex, Ss.   By ye Hon'bl Barth'o Gedney, Esq., Judge of Wills, &c., for said County, April 19th, 1697 :

Whereas Elizabeth Proctor Producing from under the hand & seal of Sr William Phips, late Gov'en'r, a Repreve after her being Indicted, arraigned, convict and sentenced of & for the detestable crime of Witchcraft : and the said Gov'en'r in the names of their most Gracious Maj'es Wm & Mary, by ye Grace of God of England, Holland & France & Ireland, King & Queen, defenders of the faith, freely, clearly & absolutely Pardon the said Elisa'h Proctor of the sd Crime of Witchcraft of & for wch she stood convict & sentenced as afores'd, so as she may Injoy her life & liberty in as free & full manner as before, as in & by sd Pardon at large may appear : & whereas the sd Eliza'h being looked upon as dead in law & left out ye will of her Hus'd, John Proctor, & nothing given her ye'in, nor ordered her upon the distributiou of the Estate of the said Proctor, but since which producing the aforesaid pardon she becomes alive in law, whereby to Recover her right of Dowry, and upon her Request a citation went forth to the Ex'r of her dec'd Husb'ns Will, &c.

PENGILLEY, John.   Joined the church by taking the covenant, March 1, 1673.   Full communion, April 12, 1674.   He took the freeman's oath October 8, 1678.

PURRION William.   Had a houselot on High street near the Burying place, 1638.

PULSIFER, Bennet, Benedict, Benedictus,—had share in Plum Island, 1664.   Under the appellation of Goodm'n he is among those who have horses on the common, 1697 ; and has assigned to him a place on one of ye short seats among the elderly people, in the Meeting-house, 1700.

Benedict Pulsifer's wife died, July 16, 1673.

He married (2) Susannah Wallis, in the following February.

The children of Benedict and Susannah (Wallis) Pulsifer, were :—

Richard, born May 31, 1675
William, born December 12, 1676
Susanna, born September 5, 1678
Joseph, born November 30, 1680
Benjamin, born March 19, 1683
David, born September 27, 1685
Elizabeth, born December 4, 1789
Margaret, born February 14, 1693

1689. Benedict Pulsifer gave the Mastif [Indian] a blow with the edge of his broad-axe upon the shoulder ; upon which they fell to it with a vengeance, and fired their guns on both sides, till some of each partey were slain.—*Magnalia.*

1675. Benedict Pulsifer's wife upon pr'st'ment for wearing silk hood & scarf, fined 10s and costs.

PYKE Mr. Probably Robert Pike, son of John Pike of Newbury. He possessed a six acre planting lot at Rabbit hill, before 1639. He probably settled first at Ipswich, whence he removed to Newbury, and then to Salisbury as one of its original settlers. Of the sixty-eight first inhabitants of Salisbury, ten went from Ipswich.

This useful and respectable man,—Robert Pyke,—died 12 December, 1706, aged ninety years. We gather a few facts from Farmer and elsewhere, concerning him :

He was born about 1616 ; came to New England with his father before 1635.

In Salisbury : A rate made 18th 5th mo, 1652, for the Rev. Mr. Worcester's half year due, 24 : 4 : mo, Leift. Pike is rated £1, 10, 0, the highest rate on the list. He Represented Salisbury, 1648, and the 7 following years.

Lieutenant, 1647, Captain, 1663, Major, 1668 Assistant, 1682-86 ; one of the Council of Safety, 1689, Of the first Council nnder the Charter of William and Mary, 1692.

QUILTER Mark, was a commoner, 1641 ; subscribed
to Major Denison's allowance, 1648 ; had a share in Plum
Island, 1664.  He died before November, 1657, and left a
widow, Thamar Quilter.  She died July 2, 1694.  She resided, November 14, 1659, on High street, on the lot adjoining the one which Richard Dummer bought of John
Andrews.

The will of Mark Quilter 1, is dated February 7, 1653,
and was proved March 28 following.  He bequeaths his
house and lands to his wife, with reversion to son Joseph.
He gives legacies of £5 to each of his other children,—
Mark, the eldest son, Mary, Rebekah, Sarah.

He bequeathed to Mark 2, his son, a planting lot, which
was formerly purchased of John Johnson, of Ipswich,
Schoolmaster, containing six acres ; and lyeth upon ye
Town hill.  This lot Mark 2 sold to John Woodam,
November 30, 1657.

Mark Quilter 2, son of Mark 1, married Frances Swan,
daughter of Richard Swan of Rowley.  She is mentioned
in her father's will.  Mark left no children at his death ; a
daughter, Dorothy, died January 21, 1662.  His will is
dated November 4, and proved November 6, 1678.  He
bequeaths to Myhill Cresy ten pounds ; to Mary Cresy
five pounds ; to Richard Sutton ten pounds.  All the rest
of his property he gave to his brother, Joseph 2.  He desires that Joseph, and Edward Lumas and Simon Stace be
overseers.  [See Gen. Ct. Records, May 28, 1679.]

Corporal Joseph Quilter 2, son of Mark 1, was a voter
in Town affairs in 1679 ; had horses on the common, 1697 ;
was commoner, 1707.

He died February 8, 1723.  In the record of his death
he is entitled "Corporal," and with the same title he had
a place assigned to him on seat No. 4, in the Meeting
house, 1700.

Among the plate belonging to the First Church, is a silver cup : " The Gift of Joseph Quilter to the First Church
in Ipswich, 1724."

Rebekah Quilter 2, dau. of Mark 1, died Aug. 10, 1723.

QUARLES, William.  Married Martha Dickinson,—
December 9, 1669.  Children:

> William, born November 9, 1670
> Martha, born October 11, 1672
> Ann, born October 20, 1679

REDDING Joseph.  Took the freeman's oath at Boston, May 14, 1634.  He was a commoner, 1641 ; a subscriber to Denison, 1648 ; a share in Plum Island, &c., 1664.  He possessed a planting lot near Labor-in-vain, 1639.  He died February 19, 1674.

1673, December.  The will of Joseph Redding, written on parchment, of which the greater part has been destroyed by mice.  He left a wife, and daughter Hunt.  The estate amounted to £351.  Appraised by Jonathan Wade and John Dane.

1693, March 29.  Francis Palmer of Rowley sheweth : Joseph Reding of Ipswich, deceased, gave his whole estate to Agnes, his wife, during her life ; and after her decease to be equally divided amongst ye children of his daughter ye wife of Samuel Hunt,—the names of which were Samuel, William, Joseph, Elizabeth and peeter Hunt Elizabeth ye complainant, married and had two children.  Before our marriage sd Samuel her father made great promises what he would give his daughter, as much as any man in Ipswich should (except five) give theirs for portion.  Some estate I have rec'd, which the sd Samuel saith now his daughter is dead, is part of sd Joseph Reding's legacy to his daughter, who I married; but it was inconsiderable to what he promist with his daughter when he engaged my Father palmer to give me half his lands in Rowley, &c.

REYNOR William.  Was born 1623.  Married Elizabeth Gilbert, Sept. 24, 1658.  Had :

> Susanna, born June 18, 1659
> Elizabeth, born July 29, 1661

He was employed with Mr. Richard Hubbard, Cornet Whipple, Edw : Coburn, to "run the line between Wenham and us," 1665.

Humphrey Reynor of Rowley, died in 1660, and left an estate appraised at £865, 1, 2.  His will is dated Sept. 10, 1660, by which he provides for his wife, Mary, with reversion to his daughters Whipple and Hobson.  He bequeaths to his son Wigglesworth, for the use of his grandchild Mercy Wigglesworth, £100.  He bequeaths a legacy to his son John Whipple, jun'r, of Ipswich.  To Ezekiel Rogers, Pastor of the Church at Rowley, ten pounds.  To Mr. Samuel Phillips, ten pounds.  To his grandchildren, Umphry Hobson, John Hobson, William Hobson, ten pound a piece.

There was £300 due to him from John Whipple and John Whipple, jun'r.

I request my dear brother, Mr. John Raynor, Pastor of Dover, and Deacon Jewett of Rowley, to be overseers; and do give to each of them twenty shillings.

The Rev. John Reynor is included in Dr. Cotton Mather's " First Classes;" i.e. "such as were in the actual exercise of their ministry, when they left England."

Mr. Raynor was minister of the Church at Plymouth, about eighteen years, 1636–54.  The church records at Plymouth say:

" The unhappy differences that fell out in the Church at Barnstable, had such ill influence upon the Church at Plymouth, that, together with the unsettledness of the Church and the going away of divers members, yea, of the most eminent of them, it was the means of the unsettlement of this holy man of God."

He left Plymouth in November, 1654, and the next summer was invited to preach at Dover, N. H., where he settled in the ministry and spent the remainder of his life.  He died April 21, 1669.

He left a son John, who was graduated at Harvard College, 1663; ordained successor to his father, minister of Dover, 1671, died at Braintree, Dec 21, 1676, aged 34 yrs.

He had also a daughter, Elizabeth, who married Capt. Thomas Southworth, of Plymouth, and had one child, Elizabeth, who married, Nov. 7, 1664, Joseph Howland, son of John Howland the Pilgrim, and died in 1717.

RINDGE, Daniel. Was one of Major Denison's subscribers, 1648. He died February, 1661. His will is dated February 3, and was proved March 25, of that year. He left a widow, Mary Rindge, to whom he bequeathed one third of his property during her life. Also, " House and lands now in possession of Thomas Wayt, until my youngest two daughters be of age ; and if they desire it, they may have the same for their portion."

He had a farm in the hands of Daniel Davison.

He left three sons :

Daniel, born 1654

Roger, born June 19, 1657

Isaac

The eldest son, Daniel, to have double part, and to take possession at twenty-one years of age.

To his three daughters :

Mary

Susanna

Sarah, born August 7, 1659

he bequeaths thirty pounds to each, to have possession at the age of sixteen, or at the time of marriage.

Deacon William Goodhue, Daniel Hovey, sen'r, and his wife, are appointed executors ; Richard Hubbard, John Dane, Sen'r, overseers ; Robert Kinsman and Richard Jacob, witnesses.

His wife, Mary Rindge, was the daughter of Robert Kinsman.

He purchased of John Davis, February 8, 1648, a six acre lot on Heartbreak Hill, bounded on the west by William Knowlton.

He purchased of Thomas Emerson, February 14, 1648, a dwelling house and six acres of land, lying next the dwelling house of John Dane towards the south.

He purchased of Thomas Bishop and Margaret his wife, March 5, 1670, for the consideration of £180, a farm lately bought of Mr. Woodmansy, containing one hundred and ten acres, bounded east by the Mile Brook, south by land of Matthew Whipple, north and west by Richard Jacob.

He was licensed as an Inn Keeper in Ipswich, May, 1661 ; and was "to keepe the herd on the south side of the River," May 9, 1655.

Daniel Rindge 2, son of Daniel 1, has a grave stone :

> Here lyes buried
> the body of
> Mr. Daniel Rindge
> Aged 84 years.   Dec'd
> Nov'r ye 30th, 1738

He was one of eight "of the young generation," who joined the church by taking ye covenant, Jan. 25, 1673-4.

His first wife was Hannah Perkins, daughter of Abraham Perkins, by whom he had :

> Hannah, born June 30, 1684, married Thomas Staniford, published Dec. 27, 1707
> Daniel, died June 6,  1688
> [See " Additional."]

Hannah (Perkins) Rindge died July 9, 1684.

He was published with Sarah Knowlton, Mch 22, 1711-12

He sold lands in Chebacco to Thomas Low, jr., December 22, 1644.

When in 1698, it was " Voted that a new Meeting-house be forthwith built," a committee consisting of ten of the most considerable of the parishioners was appointed to carry the vote into effect.   One of this committee was Capt. Daniel Rindge.

He was one of the purchasers of the old Meeting-house in 1703, after the new one was built.

He was appointed with James Fuller, sen'r, on ye south side of ye river to see to the due observance of ye laws relating to horses, &c.

In the new Meeting-house in 1700, there was allotted to Capt. Daniel Rindge and Mr. Francis Crompton, ye 4th pew on ye so-east side of ye great door for their wives and families.   To himself was appointed a place on the third seat.   He gave one pound in 1699 towards procuring of a bigger bell for ye good of ye Town.

Roger Rindge 2, son of Daniel I, born June 19, 1657, married Sarah Shatswell, June 9, 1784.   Children :

Sarah, born June 28, 1685

Daniel, born February 4, 1686

Isaac Rindge 2, son of Daniel 1. Wife Elizabeth, who died May 3, 1700. He married (2) Elizabeth Kinsman, with whom he was published July 21, 1700. Of his children : John, born June 5, 1695

Isaac, born May 28, 1698

He had horses on the Common 1697.

————o————

Additional.

## THE RINDGE FAMILY.

Augustine Caldwell.

Daniel Rindge was in Ipswich in 1648. He married Mary Kinsman, and had six children.

Mary Kinsman Rindge was the daughter of Robert Kinsman who came to New England in the *Mary and John*, 1634, and came to Ipswich in 1635. His homestead was very near the present South Meeting house and the Cove ; and his lands are now possessed by Mrs. John Heard.

Daniel Rindge died February 6, 1661 ; his will is on file :

" The last will and testament of Daniel Rtndge of Ipswich, this 5th day of february, 1661. In the name of God, amen, I Daniel Rindge, being of pfect memory and understanding do dispose of what outward estate that God hath given me, and in the manner as followeth :

In the first place I commit my soul to almighty God and my body to decent buryall :

I give unto Mary, my beloved wife, one third part of my ffarme now in the hands of Daniel Davison, during the terme of her natural life ; and after her decease to be divided amongst my three sonnes,—the eldest to have a double share thereoff.

I give and bequeathe unto my three sonnes, Daniel, Roger and Isaack, my ffarme above Sd, to bee divided amongst them : the eldest to have a double part; then the two youngest to be equal, and they to take possession therof at the age of one-and-twenty : my wives third part being reserved for her, during her life ; and then her third part to be divided according to ye proportion above sayd.

I give and bequeathe unto my three daughters, Mary, Susanna, and Sarah, thirty pounds to each of them, and they to have possession thereof, at the age of sixteen, or at the time of their marriage.

I leave my house and lands now in ye possession of Thomas Wayt, unto my wife, * * and I will when my youngest two daughters shall bee of age, that if they desire it, they may have the same for their portions : allowing the overplus of their portions to my other Daughter, as part of her portion; or if they so desire it not, to be left to ye executors to dispose of for ye discharge of my daughters portions.

My mind and will is that if my eldest son shall dye without children, that his portion shall be left to the two younger Brothers, the elder of them two to have a double share thereof, provided that he allow to each of his sisters five pounds : and if both the eldest dye childless, the youngest to inherit their portions, allowing to each of my Daughters ten pounds, or if the youngest leave no children, the two eldest inherit his portion, the eldest having a double share: and if the two youngest leave no children the eldest to inherit their portions, paying to each of my Daughters Ten pounds.

If my wife marryeth, my mind is, her husband shall give sufficient security for what estate he is possessed of by my wife, for the discharge of my children's portions.

The remainder of my estate I leave to my wife to dispose of at her decease equally amongst all my children.

My mind is that if my wife marryeth, my children shall have liberty if they desire it, to be disposed of to good services, if they shall think meet to whom they are * * which so confirmed, I have here unto set my hand, this third day of February, 1661.          DANIELL RINGE.

I constitute and appoint my loving friends, Deacon William Goodhue, and Daniel Hovey, sen'r, of Ipswich, and my wife, executors and executrix of this my Last will and

Testament, and Rich'd Hubbard and John Dane, sen'r, overseers. In ye presence of Robert Kinsman, jun'r, and Richard Jacob.

Proved in Court, held at Ipswich, the 25th March, 1662, by the oath of Robert Kinsman and John Dane to be the will and testament of Daniel Ringe to the best of your knowledge,—by me      ROBERT LORD, Clerk.

The estate was appraised at £563, 11. The house was described as having parlor, hall and chambers ; and was furnished with chairs, cushions, carpet, tapestries, chests.

The farm of 110 acres was at Mile Brook, at the Hamlet, and his home was on Turkey Shore, [Prospect street,] and the house is now called variously : Emerson house, Rindge house, Howard house, &c.

The children of Daniel and Mary (Kinsman) Rindge, were six in number :

i. Mary, evidently the oldest. She married soon after her father's death, Uzziel Wardwell.

ii. Daniel, the oldest of the boys, early had the title of " Captain ;" he was a soldier at Narraganset, 1675

iii. Roger, born June 19, 1657, married Sarah Shatswell.

iv. Susanna, chose her uncle, Robert Kinsman, as her guardian, in 1669. Essex Deeds, 3 : 129.

v. Isaac, may have been a military officer, as he disposed of his sword by will.

vi. Sarah, the youngest of the daughters, born August 7, 1659, married Joseph Andrews, Feb. 16, 1680.

Capt. Daniel Rindge 2, son of Daniel 1, seems to have taken his place among the gentlemen of the town. He was twice married :

(1) Hannah Perkins, born August 7, 1662. She was the daughter of Abraham and Hannah (Beamsley-Bushnell) Perkins. She died July, 1684. She was the mother of Capt. Rindge's children.

(2) Hannah Rust, daughter of Nathaniel and Mary Rust. Her brother, Nathaniel 2, is the first recorded Schoolmaster of Essex.

Children of Capt. Daniel and Hannah Perkins Rindge :
Daniel, died in infancy
Daniel, Harvard College, Class 1709
Hannah, married Thomas Staniford, 1707
Mary, married Ammi Ruhami Wise, 1713
The Class of Daniel, (H. C. 1709,) had another conspicuous Ipswich name : Col. John Wainwright. And among his College associates were John Denison, Francis Wainwright, and the John Rogers who became the first Minister of Eliot, Maine. Daniel Rindge after his graduation passed most of his brief days in Portsmouth. He was buried early and with many tears.

Ammi Ruhami Wise, was the son of the Rev'd John Wise of Chebacco. He built the house which stood upon the site of the South Meeting-house. Mary, daughter of Ammi Ruhami and Mary (Rindge) Wise married Doctor Samuel Rogers. She lived in this home of her father. It was bought by Dr. Rogers. It is now [1885] the home of Mrs. Rhoda Brown Potter.

The old slate slab in the High street yard gives the date of the departure of Capt. Daniel Rindge 2, Nov. 30, 1738. He had a long and busy life. At the age of seventeen he was a soldier of the Narraganset war, and ever onward he was intimate with military and town duties.

His estate was appraised at £2462. At his death his branch of the family ceased in name. The Rindges of Ipswich were descendants of his brothers, Roger and Isaac. Deeds, Vol. xxiii, leaf 176.

Roger Rindge 2, son of Daniel 1, was born June 19, 1657, and married Sarah Shatswell, June 9, 1684.

Sarah Shatswell Rindge was born August 19, 1658, and was the daughter of Richard 2 and Rebekah Tuttle Shatswell, and granddaughter of John 1 and Joanna Shatswell.
Children of Roger Rindge :
Daniel 3, married Sarah Knowlton, 1712.
Richard, married Sarah Brown, 1716.
Sarah, married Philip Amme, 1729.
Rebekah, married Archelaus Lakeman, 1710.

Isaac Rindge 2, son of Daniel 1, died in 1714. He married (1) Elisabeth Dutch, daughter of John and Mary (Roper) Dutch; she died May 3, 1700.

He married (2) widow Elisabeth (Burnham) Kinsman, daughter of Dea. John Burnham.

At the death of Isaac Rindge in 1714, he gave to his son John Rindge his negro, Jack; and to his son Isaac he gave his sword.

His estate was valued at £202 o6. Two of his sons, John and Isaac, "upwards of 14," chose for their guardian their "uncle Francis Crompton." John, while yet in his youth, migrated to Portsmouth.

The children of Isaac Rindge :

John 3, born June 1, 1695, married at Portsmouth, Anne Odiorne

Isaac, born May 28, 1698, married Mercy Quarles, 1749. No further record.

Elisabeth, born Sept. 2, 1701, married Caleb Kimball.

Abigail, born Dec. 26, 1703.

Daniel, born August 24, 1705.

Samuel, born December 27, 1709, married (1) Mary Appleton, (2) widow Martha (Potter) Quarles.

Mary Rindge 2, daughter of Daniel 1, married Uzziel Wardwell, May 3, 1664. He was the son of William and Alice Wardwell, of Boston. Uzziel is styled "Carpenter." His brother, Elihu Wardwell married Elisabeth Wade, May 26, 1665.

The children of Uzziel and Mary (Rindge) Wardwell :

Abigail, born October 27, 1665

Alice, born December 27, 1670

Hannah, Mary, twins, born September 1, 1677

The Hon'ble John Rindge 3, son of Isaac 2, Daniel 1. Went to Portsmouth shortly after his father's death. He became a man of wealth and social altitude. He married Anne Odiorne, a lady five years younger than he. She was the daughter of Jotham and Mary (Johnson) Odiorne of Newcastle.

John Rindge was "one of the King's Council," 1740.
He was born June 1, 1695, and died November 6, 1740,
aged forty-five years.  His eight children were:

Elisabeth, married Mark Hunking Wentworth, and
was the mother of the last Gov. Wentworth.

Anne, married Counsellor Daniel Pierce.

Mehitable, married Hon. Daniel Rogers, of "the
King's Council."

John

Jotham, married Sarah Vaughan

Daniel    Isaac    William

Of the Hon. Daniel Rogers, the husband of Mehitable, it
is printed: "Son of Hon. Nathaniel Rogers, Esq., of
Portsmouth ; son of Rev. Nathaniel Rogers, minister of the
Portsmouth First Church ; Son of President John Rogers,
of Harvard College ; Son of Rev. Nathaniel Rogers of
Ipswich, 1636."

A portrait of Elisabeth Rindge Wentworth is yet extant.

Historical Sketches of Portsmouth tell us that William
H. Rindge, a direct descendant of Hon'ble John Rindge 3,
was the hero of Mrs. Sigourney's pretty verses, " The
Noble Sailor."  The said William died in 1840, aged 23.
In his last sickness he quietly told the story, and confessed
that he was "The Noble Tar," of the New York fire.

### The Noble Sailor.

Mrs. Lydia H. Sigourney.

It was a fearful night,
  The strong flames onward spread
From street to street, from spire to spire,
  And on their treasures tread.

Hark ! 'tis a mother's cry,
  High o'er the tumult wild,
As rushing toward the flame wrapped home
  She shrieked : "My child, my child !"

A wanderer from the sea,
  A stranger, marked her woe ;

And in his noble bosom woke
The sympathetic glow.

Swift up the burning stair,
With daring feet he flew ;
While sable clouds of stifling smoke
Concealed him from the view.

Fast fell the burning beams
Across the dangerous road,
Till the far chamber where he groped
Like fiery oven glowed.

But what a pealing shout,
When from the wreck he came,
And in his arms a smiling babe
Still toying with the flame.

The mother's raptured tears
Forth like a torrent sped ;
But ere the crowd could learn his name,
The noble tar had fled.

Not for the praise of men,
Did he this deed of Love ;
But on the bright, unfading page,
'Tis registered above.

Samuel Rindge 3, son of Isaac 2, Daniel 1, was born
August 24, 1709, and died February 25, 1769.

His mother was Elisabeth (Burnham) Kinsman, the
second wife of Isaac Rindge 2, and the daughter of Dea.
John Burnham.

Samuel Rindge 3, was twice married :

(1) to Mary Appleton, the mother of his children.

She was the daughter of—John and Mary (Allen) Appleton ; Grandaughter of Samuel and Mary (Woodbridge)
Appleton ; great-grandaughter of John and Priscilla (Glover) Appleton.

She was born in 1714 ; married 1739 ; died December 28,

1746, leaving four babes motherless.

He married (2) widow Martha Potter Quarles.

She was born October 19, 1700; and was the daughter of Anthony and Martha (Dresser) Potter; married John Quarles, 1720; died May 4, 1795, aged ninety-five years.

Samuel Rindge died at the age of sixty years, 1769; and his son Daniel administered on his estate.

He united with the South Church, [Dr. Dana,] April 10, 1756. In 1725, he was sixteen years old, and his father was dead; he made choice of John Choate as his guardian and advisor. It was a wise choice.

The children of Samuel Rindge 3 :

Daniel , baptized November 30, 1740 ; married Elizabeth Caldwell, 1764

Mary, bap. Oct. 24, 1742, m. Andrew Dodge, 1769

Lucy, bap. Sept. 16, 1744, m. Ebenezer Caldwell, she died 1772, leaving two sons, Ebenezer, Samuel

Elizabeth, baptized August 31, 1746


Daniel Rindge 4, Samuel 3, Isaac 2, Daniel 1, baptized November 30, 1740 ; married Elisabeth, daughter of John and Abigail Hovey Caldwell, 1764; he was lost at sea, April 5, 1795. His children were:

Daniel, baptized Feb. 23, 1766, went south

Elisabeth, bap. Sept. 20, 1767, m. Abraham Seward

Samuel, bap. Jan. 14, 1770, went south

John, baptized July 12, 1772

Lucy, baptized February 12, 1775


Elisabeth Rindge 4, Samuel 3, Isaac 2, Daniel 1, bap. September 20, 1767, married Abraham Seward, lived in a large and ancient house which stood on the land adjoining (north) the Emerson house, Turkey Shore. There was but a cart-road between the two homes. Abraham Seward died October 23, 1841. The children were:

Huldah

Daniel Rindge

John

Lydia  Caldwell

Elizabeth, married Elisha Glover
Mary Caldwell

Daniel Rindge 3, Roger 2, Daniel 1, married :
(1) Sarah Knowlton, March 22, 1711-12 ; she died April 4, 1714.
(2) Martha (Caldwell) Ayres.
Widow Martha (Caldwell) Rindge married John Wood February 11, 1729.
Daniel and Martha (Caldwell) Rindge had :
  Daniel, born June 26, 1721, died August 9, 1800
  Anna, born June 16, 1723 ; died April 5, 1730, aet. six years ten months

Daniel Rindge 4, Daniel 3, Roger 2, Daniel 1, married Mary Kimball, January, 1745 ; she died October 10, 1801. Their children :
  Anna, born 1746 ; married Elisha Newman, 1786 ; had daughter, Mary, who married Nathaniel Caldwell
  Mary, baptized December 7, 1749
  Daniel, born 1752, died May 16, 1773
  Margaret Woods, born 1755, married Benjamin Caldwell, died December 24, 1788
  John, born Sept. 28, 1759, married Sarah Baker, May 18, 1786 ; she died Oct. 17, 1824 ; he died October 18, 1801

Richard Rindge 3, Roger 2, Daniel 1, and Sarah Brown, were married May 9, 1716. He was drowned in Ipswich River, March 2, 1730. 2 h : A. M. Estate, £257. Children :
  Sarah, baptized September 13, 1719
  John bap. April 2, 1722, died early.
  Daniel, bap. July 26, 1726 ; died 1729
  John, 1727, was fourteen years old, 1741
  Daniel, bap. Aug. 17, 1729, died early

John Rindge 4, Richard 3, Roger 2, Daniel 1, married Elisabeth Storey, December, 1745 ; she died August 14, 1796. They had : Elisabeth, born 1747
              Sarah, born 1748
              John, born 1749

RING, John. Had a share in Plum Island, &c. as tenant of Edmund Bragg, 1664.

His wife was Mary Bray, whom he married Nov. 18, 1664. He had sons David and Thomas; and John, the oldest, was born October 18, and died the 21st, 1665.

He made a noncupative will, August 20, 1684, witnessed by Samuel Rogers, Nathaniel Emerson, John Low, by which he gave "all his property to his wife, for herself and children." He died the next day, August 21, 1684.

James Ring, had son John, born March 1, 1675

ROBERTS, Robert. Was a soldier to the Indians, 1643. He witnessed a deed, Feb. 1648. He had :

Abigail, born March 27, 1658

Patience, born February 20, 1660

1658, Dec. 24. Liberty granted to Robert Roberts to fence in half an acre of land by the Spring near the Little Neck, the propriety to remain to the Town.

1661. Agreed with Robert Roberts to keep a flock of sheep at Jeffry's Neck.

1669, November. Thomas Perrin of Ipswich, married Susanna, widow of Robert Roberts, of the same town.

Richard Roberts was entitled to horse commonage, 1697 ; seat No 12, in the Meeting-house, 1700.

Goodwife Roberts agreed with, to keep the sheep at the Neck, 1664, 1666.

RAWLINSON, (Rolison, Rowlinson, Rolandson,) Thomas. Was commoner, 1641. He was appointed, with the addition of Sen'r, one of the executors of the Will of Thomas Scott, March 8, 1653-4.

He possessed a house and eleven acres of land, having the Common on the northwest ; which he sold to Jeremy Belcher, and which Belcher sold to Mr. John Appleton, 1657, when Rawlinson is styled, "late of Ipswich."

He possessed land adjoining William Warner, 1637.

He took the freeman's oath at Boston, May 2, 1638.

He removed to Lancaster, where he died, Nov. 17, 1657, leaving several sons.

Thomas Rawlinson 2, son of Thomas 1, was slain by the Indians at Lancaster, February 10, 1676.

Joseph 2, whose name is spelt Rowlandson, was the first Minister of Lancaster. He is said by Joseph B. Felt to have been the son of Thomas 1, of Ipswich. He was graduated at Harvard College, 1652.

He was in Lancaster, 1654; was ordained, 1660; and went to Weathersfield when Lancaster was destroyed by the Indians, February 10, 1676. He died at Weathersfield, November 24, 1678.

Mary, his wife, was the daughter of John White. She published a narrative of her captivity, and various removes while a prisoner. This has been frequently reprinted; and the sixth edition contains a piece of satirical poetry which Joseph, her husband, wrote while in College. It seems that he posted his poem on the Meeting-house, with additions in prose. The Court pronounced it to be "a scandalous libel;" and he was sentenced, September 20, 1651, "to be whipped or pay £5 and charges, thirty shillings, for thus writing prose and verse against the government and certain individuals of the town."

In describing one of the characters, he wrote : " When he lived in our country, a wet eele's tayle and his word were something worth ye taking hold of." He made an humble submission to the Court for the offence; and it is also printed in Mrs. Rowlandson's narrative : "and his punishment was remitted by the Court, March 25, 1656."

Thomas Rolandson, died at Ipswich, July, 1682. The inventory of his estate by Samuel Fellows and Richard Hubbard is dated July 27, 1682. It consisted of a House lott & house, att £24; ten acre planting lott, £10; three commonages, £8.

Dorothy Rolandson, his wife, survived him.

ROLFE, Ezra. Possessed a lot of land on the Town Hill, between the lots of William Whitred and Christopher Osgood, Dec. 20, 1645.

He subscribed to Major Denison, 1648, 1s, 6d.

Daniel Rolfe testified to the will of Christopher Osgood, October 10, 1650 ;

Subscribed to Major Denison, 1648, four shillings.

Thomas Rolfe, his will dated 1657, August 12, proved September 29. " For that little outward estate the Lord hath given me, I leave unto my dear wife, conceiving it little enough and too little to maintayne her in the condition she is in." Witness: Robert Lord, Hannah Day.

John Rolfe, had Abigail, born October 14, 1672.

Ezra Rolfe, had Daniel, born December, 1679.

ROWELL, Jacob, married (1) Mary Younglove, April 29, 1690. She died in April, 1691.

He m. (2) Elizabeth Wardwell, Sept. 29, 1691, and had :
   Elizabeth, born November 3, 1695
   Mary, born June 25, 1698.

He died February 18, 1700.

He had a shop lot granted to him on the south side of river, 28 feet front on the street, being the ninth lot from the bridge, 1692-3.

Thomas Rowell, 1658.

ROGERS, NATHANIEL. (Rev'd.) Born in Haverhill England, in 1598. He was the second son of the Rev'd John Rogers, a distinguished minister, afterwards of Dedham, England, who was grandson of the noted martyr, John Rogers, and died October 18, 1639, aged 67 years.

Nathaniel Rogers was educated at Emmanuel College, which he entered when about fourteen years of age. He began his ministry as Chaplain in a nobleman's family; and afterwards became a curate in the established Church, at Bocking, Essex.

After serving there four or five years, he was dismissed in consequence of his entertaining scruples respecting the wearing of the surplice.

The next four or five years were spent at Assington, Suffolk; and again his scruples threatened persecution, and he determined to embark for America.

He married Margaret Crane, daughter of Robert Crane, of Coggshall, or Coxhall, Essex.

He arrived at Boston, after a singularly long and distressful voyage, November, 1636.

He was ordained Pastor of the Church at Ipswich, February 20, 1638. At the same time the Rev'd John Norton was ordained Teacher. Their predecessor was the Rev. Nathaniel Ward. Mr. Ward and Mr. Rogers were related by marriage. Richard Rogers, the uncle of Nathaniel Rogers, married the widow of John Ward, the father of Nathaniel Ward. [Hist. Gen. Reg. vol. iv, p. 179.]

On 6 Sept. 1638, the Magistrates of Ipswich had order to give Mr. Nath : Rogers the Oath of freedom.

He died July 3, 1655, aged fifty-seven years, [and was embalmed with the loves and the tears of his Parish.]

A nuncupative will was proved September 25, 1655, by the oaths of Mr. Ezekiel Cheever and Deacon John Whipple. It is in the hand writing of Mr. Cheever, who was the First Master of the Grammar School, and is a very neat specimen of the chirography of the age :

The last will and testament of Mr. Nathaniel
Rogers Pastor of the church of Christ
at Ipswich, as was taken from his
own mouth, July 3, Anno Dom
1655

Concerning my outward estate : To one of the brethren I have left a peculiar charge which he shall have power in himself to doe and not to suspend.

[This probably related to a manuscript Diary which he ordered to be destroyed.]

The summe of my estate both in old England and new, seems to amount to about ye value of twelve hundred pound ; of which summe, four hundred pound is expected from my father, Mr. Robert Crane, in England.

[Mr. Rogers estate had been at the expense of a liberal education to the eldest son, John, and later to the son, Ezekiel, therefore the father dictates :]

To my sonne John, to prevent expectations of a double portion, I have not so bequeathed : he hath never been by any labor serviceable to his brethren, but hath been upheld by their labour and paine, while he hath been determining his way. Therefore I give and bequeath to him an equal portion with his other brethren, viz., ye summe of one hundred pound of my estate in Old England and one hundred pound of my estate in New England.

[He makes like bequests to his sons, Nathaniel, Samuel and Timothy.]

To his son Ezekiel :

Twenty pounds which he shall have liberty to take in my books if he please.

To my daughter, I have already given her at least two hundred pound.

The time of ye children receiving their portions either in whole or in part, shall be according to ye mutual advice of my executors, with those godly friends named, viz. my cousin, Mr. Ezekiel Rogers, Mathew Boyes, Ezekiel Cheever, who are entreated to advise and counsel in this and all other case as need shall require.

He bequeathes legacies to his three grandchildren, John, Nathaniel, Margaret Hubbard.

To his cousin John Rogers, to children of John Harris of Rowley, viz., Elizabeth, Nathaniel, John, Mary; to Mary Quilter and Sarah Fillebrown, domestics ; to '' Harbert College,'' and to the poor he gives the summe of three pound.

To my dear wife, Mrs Margaret Rogers, the remainder, during her life. And he appoints his wife with his trusty and well-beloved friends, Mr. Robert Payne and John Whipple, executors.

1676, March 28. Mrs. Margaret Rogers, dying intestate, the Court appoint Mr. John Rogers, her eldest son, adm'r. Mrs. Rogers death is recorded January 23, 1675.

John Rogers 2, son of Nathaniel 1, was born in England about 1630, and came to New England with his father in 1636. He was graduated at Harvard College in 1649, and studied both physic and divinity. He commenced preaching as colleague to Mr. Hubbard, July 4, 1656.

1656, July 4. At a Town meeting. It was voted that the Town did declare their desire to enjoy the gifts and labors of Mr. Hubbard and Mr. Rogers amongst us ; and also their real purpose to contribute yearly £120 for their encouragement as long as they shall continue with us, or Providence dispose us to a nearer union or relation.

Mr. John Rogers continued to preach occasionally and to practice medicine, until 1683, when, on the decease of Urian Oakes, President of Harvard College, he was chosen to succeed him, and was installed August 12, 1683.

He died July 28, 1684, the day succeeding the first Commencement after his installation.

He married Elizabeth, daughter of General Daniel Denison, November 14. 1660.  Her epitaph is :

> Here lyes interred
> ye body of Mrs. Eliza
> beth Rogers, Relict
> of Mr. John Rogers
> (sometime) President
> of Harvard College
> and Daughter of Major
> General Daniel Denison
> of Ipswich, who decd July
> the 13th, 1723, in ye 82nd year
> of her age

The children of Pres't John 2, and Elizabeth Denison Rogers were :

Elizabeth, born February 3, 1661, married the
> Hon. John Appleton
Margaret, born February 18, 1664, married
> Thomas Berry of Boston, Dec. 28, 1686
> (2) Hon. John Leverett.
John, minister of First Church, Ipswich, married
> Martha Whittingham
Daniel
Nathaniel, born Feb. 21, 1669, Minister of
> the Church at Portsmouth
Patience, born May 13, 1676

The inventory of Mr. John Rogers estate exhibits an amount of £2133, 13.  It includes wearing cloaths, linen and woolen, £27, 5 : hats, gloves, shoes, £4, 5; watch, rings, and other small things found in his pockets, £6 ; plate, £27 ; ready money, £36 ; books, £94, 5.

Nathaniel Rogers 2, son of Nathaniel 1, died June 14, 1680; concerning whom we have the following Deposition of Walter Roper, aged 68 years, 1676. Mr. Nathaniel Rogers being ordered to go forth a trooper against the Indians, in the year 1676, just before his going from his brother, Mr. John Rogers' house, he would not be satisfied till he had declared his will, bequeathed to his kinsman, John Rogers, eldest son of his brother John Rogers, all his houses and lands in Ipswich.

Samuel Belcher, aged about 40 years, deposes to the same, Sept. 23, 1680.

Samuel Rogers 2, Nathaniel 1, married
(1) Judith Appleton, April 8, 1657 ; she d. July, 1659
(2) Sarah, dau. Jona. Wade, Nov. 13, 1661. They had :
   Sarah, born Oct. 14, 1664, died Sept. 30, 1682
   John, born April 29, 1667
   Susanna, born March 17, 1668
   Jonathan, born March 24, 1671
   Mary, born September 10, 1672
   Margaret, born October 24, 1675
   Elisabeth, born October 11, 1678
   Abigail, born July 5, 1681
He was Town Clerk and Register of Probate many years. He died December 24, 1693.

His widow, Sarah (Wade) Rogers, who administered on his estate, married before April 15, 1695, a second husband, Mr. Henry Woodis.

The estate amounting to £274, 9, was then divided among the four Rogers daughters,—Susanna, Mary, Elizabeth, Abigail, a minor under the guardianship of her mother, Sarah Woodis, who seem to have been his only surviving heirs.

1695, Oct. 7. Mrs. Sarah Roggers, alias Woodis, appointed guardian of her daughters, Abigail Roggers, aged 14 years ; Elizabeth Roggers, age 16 years and upwards.

1696, Oct. 28. Rec'd of my daughter, Martha Rogers,

£27, for the use of my children,—part of estate of my son John Rogers, dec'd, I being ad'r of my husband, Mr. Samuel Rogers.  Sarah Woodis of Concord.
In 1694, Nov. 21, there is the record of an " Additional Inventory of Mr. John Rogers' estate." Debts due, To Mrs. Woodis, alias Rogers, £128, 19.
To Mrs. Woodis, alias Rogers, during her natural life, £10 per Annu :

1695, April 15. Sarah Woodis alias Rogers, exhibits her account of administration on ye estate of Samuel Rogers :

| | | |
|---|---|---|
| Personal estate, as per inventory, | £150 | 14 |
| Due the estate in pay from est. John Rogers dec'd | 200 | 8 |
| The estate Dr. | 76 | 13 |
| Clear estate | 224 | 9 |

Distributed thus : To the widow but Fifty pound, because of a anuity due from Jno : Rogers estate payable to her.

The balance £224 9, divided into four equal parts amongst ye four daughters of Samuel Rogers dec'd, viz, Susanna, Elizabeth, Mary Abigail.

To Mrs. Sarah Woodis, Living in Concord,
These present :
Hon'rd mother : Duty & Respects by these psented to yr self & Hon'rd Father, hoping you & yrs are in good measure of health, as through God's mercy we are.

You may Remember yt when my dear Husband was living you gave him an acquittance bearing date June 24, 1694, for several debts wch he payd & took upon his acct to pay, thereby discharging your self as administratrix to Mr. Samuel Rogers, our Hon'd Father, of the Sum of Three hundred pounds : the Debts in that discharge & acquittance with ye names of the psons which w'r creditors I have herein exprest, not knowing whether you kept an acc't thereof : viz.

[Here follow the items amounting to £300.]

I find also several others w'h my husband hath payd, in his book that you were indebted unto : which I have sent the acc't of, some of which are mony & others pay.

The debts in pay are as hereafter mentioned :

[Items amounting to £33, 18, 3.]

The debts in money are as hereafter mentioned :

[Items amounting to £15, 9, 5.]

Also, I find a distinct acc't in my husband's book, thus charged, to money lent and payd for you :

[Items amounting to £12, 3, 2.]

The Sums in pay yt are demanded by the pticular psons on the other side amount to thirty & three pound, Eighteen shillings, & 3d. The sums in money & money pay, amount to Twenty six pounds & ten shillings.

If there be any just objection wch you can make why I should not pay the several sums, I would entreat you to send me word ; for psons will hardly be satisfied to stay any longer : they would have me engage to pay them : I must therefore have your order if I pay them :

If the Sums in money be payd, I had need to have more than one third advance : for this year I shall loose considerable els.

I pray you send me word how much my husband is behind of paym't of the last year rent.

Not further to trouble you at p'sent, I take my leave, committing all our concerns to ye wise dispose of him who is able to help a poor helpless widow, who am yr dutifull daughter                    MARTHA ROGERS.

Ips. ye 7th Feb'ry, 1694.

In the Records of Concord it appears that Mr. Henry Woodist, with Elen Woodist his wife, sign a deed, 24 : 10 mo : 69 : Mrs. Elen Woodis, wife to Mr. Henry Woodis, died September 4, 1693.

Mr. Henry Woodis ye husband of Sarah his wife died June 16, 1700. Sarah Woodis, relict of Mr. Henry Woodis died Jan'y 19, 1717.

Elizabeth Rogers, daughter of Mr Samuel Rogers of Ipswich and Sarah his wife, died January 23, 1717.

Ezekiel Rogers 2, son of Nathaniel 1, was graduated at Harvard College, 1659. He married Margaret, daughter of Mr. William Hubbard, who survived him and died January 23, 1679. He died July 5, 1674. Children :

Martha

Nathaniel, born August 14, 1664

John, born June 12, 1666, died

Ezekiel, born June 4, 1667

Timothy

Samuel,

Ezekiel Rogers 2, of Ipswich, gives receipt dated Jan. 6, 1662, to the Town and Church of Rowley, for £160 bequeathed to him by Mr. Ezekiel Rogers of Rowley

[Rev. Ezekiel Rogers of Rowley, died January 23, 1661, aged seventy years. His will is dated April 17, 1660, in which he mentions with gratitude that his father was the Rev. Richard Rogers of Wethersfield, Essex, in Old England.

He left a wife Mary, but no children.

He mentions the Rev. Nathaniel Rogers of Ipswich, as his cousin. This appellation was used in that age in a more enlarged sense than at present. It was usually applied to nephews, nieces and yet more distant relatives.

He bequeathes to Ezekiel, son of his cousin Nathaniel, eight score pounds to be paid by the town and church of Rowley under certain conditions ; and appoints Mr. John Whipple of Ipswich, the Ruling Elder, to be guardian to receive the same, which, as appears by the foregoing receipt, was paid punctually. He also alludes to his nephew, Mr. Nathaniel Stone of Connecticut.]

1677, Nov. Martha Rogers, aged about sixteen years, made choice of her mother, Mrs. Margaret Rogers, guardian. The other children of Mr. Ezekiel Rogers being under age, viz., Nathaniel, Timothy, Ezekiel, Samuel, the Court appoint sd Margaret guardian.

1679. April. Nathaniel and Martha chose th'r uncle Wm. Hubbard.

Rev. John Rogers 3, son of Pres't John 2, was born July 7, 1666; was graduated at Harvard College, 1684. He began to preach in our First Parish, March, 1685-6 ; but in consequence of a misunderstanding with the people

respecting a grant of land, he was not ordained until
October 12, 1692.

1689, October 22.   Att a legal Town meeting in order to
giving Mr. John Rogers a further invitation to ye work in
ye ministry here in this place—

Voted, by ye inhabitants as to Mr. Rogers' incurrag-
ment that in case Mr. Rogers do accept to return hither
and help carry on ye work of ye ministry, They will give
him yearly the sum of eighty pounds according to former
custome & usage here in this place, so long as he carry on
half ye work of ye ministry.

Mr. Rogers continued in the ministry at Ipswich nearly
sixty years,—until his death, December 28, 1745.

He married Martha, dau. of William Whittingham,
March 4, 1690

The children of Rev, John and Martha (Whittingham)
Rogers were :

> John, born January 27, 1692, married Susanna Whip-
> ple, the First Minister of Eliot, Maine
> Martha, born November 2, 1694
> William, born June 19, 1699
> Nathaniel, born March 4, 1702, Minister of First
> Church, Ipswich
> Richard, born December 2, 1703
> Daniel, Elizabeth, born July 28, 1707
> Daniel was a Minister of Exeter
> Samuel, born August 31, 1709
> Mary

Mrs. Martha (Whittingham) Rogers, died March 9,
1759, æ 89 years.

Rev. John Rogers was a subscriber toward the bigger
Bell of 1699.

August 2, 1702.   The Rev'd Mr. Habbard ditained the
Brethren of the Church and then signified and declared his
inability (thro age) to carry on the work of the ministry
any longer among them, and desired that they would take
care and carry on sd work.

W'upon a church meeting was warned on the tuesday
following.

On ye 4th of August, 1702, The Church having met & considered what might be needful to be done for the calling of some suitable & meet help for ye carring on ye Reverend Teacher Mr. William Hubbard's part of ye publick Worship of God in this place—

It was Voted yt our reverend Pastour, Mr. John Rogers, should be desired to take upon him the whole work of ye publick ministry for ye present.

Voted, yt Coll'n John Appleton, Coll'n John Wainwright, Deacon Foster, & Deacon Knowlton should be the persons to treat with the Rev'd Mr. Rogers, to know his mind therein, and to make report thereof to the Town.

Voted, that a Town meeting be warned to know their minds, so yt y'er may be a Christian mutual agreement & carrying on together so great & necessary a work.

On August 13, The Gentl'n yt heard Mr. Rogers give in his answer to the Town on yt Day, in manner following—

That Mr. Rogers would take care & supply Mr. Hubbard's part of the Sabbath for the present while they were in the way of duty, to proceed with as much speed as might be settled help in that work.

And the Town signified their approbation in that matter

Upon which the Brethren of the Church, appointed Thursday, ye 27 of this instant to be kept as a day of fasting & prayer, to seek God's direction & blessing in so weighty a concern, and desire the concurrence of ye inhabitants of our Town in carrying on ye work of sd Day.—Church Records.

January 16, 1700. The two pews at the end of the men's and women's short seats, fronting the alleys, shall be for ministers' pews. On the East side to Mr. Hubbard and his successors ; On ye nor west side to Mr. John Rogers and his successors.

October 6, 1726. Mr. Rogers writes to his people that he had served them thirty-seven years ; had lost by having his salary in depreciated bills ; had sold one portion and another of his estate, and mortgaged the remainder to make up the deficiency of maintenance for his family ; had said nothing to his Parish about his Condition, and wish'd to live in love with them and die in peace.

The parish immediately vote him £100, to clear his property from incumbrance.

October 6, 1726. Voted that the Parish do unanimously, freely, cheerfully promise and engage to cancel and dis-charge the mortgage the said Mr. Rogers has given to the Town of Ipswich, for the sum of one hundred pounds, part of the Towns proportion of the last fifty thousand pounds loan.

March 15, 1733. Grant Mr. Rogers £40 to repair his house.

Rev. John Rogers 4, son of Rev. John and Martha (Whittingham) Rogers 3, was a Minister of Kittery, Me., now Eliot.

[In addition to Mr. Hammatt's record, we copy from the *William Fogg* (*of Eliot*) *Papers*, now in possession of Dr. J. L. M. Willis, of that Town, the following geneal-ogical facts. After a glance at the honored ancestry of the Rev. John Rogers 4, (of both father and mother,) he proceeds :

The Rev. John Rogers 4, of Eliot, was born at Ipswich, January 27, 1692. He was graduated at H. C. 1711. He married Susannah Whipple, of Ipswich, the youngest daughter of Major John Whipple, Esq., October 16, 1718. She was the niece of Sarah (Whipple) Goodhue, whose "Valedictory and Monitory Writing," "found after her Decease," was printed and reprinted, and is read even now

The Rev'd John Rogers 4, was ordained as the First Minister of the Church in Eliot, then a Parish of Kittery, October 25, 1721. He had preached several years at this Parish before his ordination ; and he continued his minis-try till his death, October 16, 1773.

Mrs Susannah (Whipple) Rogers, died October 22, 1779. Their children, nine in number, were :

John, born at his grandfather Whipples, in Ipswich, August 7, 1719 ; H. C. 1739 ; Minister at Glou-cester, Mass.; died October, 1780, æ 61 years

Timothy born at Eliot, Sept. 8, 1721 ; died June,
1765, aged 44 years
William, born October 1, 1723, died June 1, 1747,
aged 24 years. His uncle, Rev. Daniel Rogers,
"preach't at yt Solemnity," [funeral.]
Catherine, born Dec. 2, 1725, married Dea. William
Leighton, Nov. 17, 1747, died March 17, 1750 :
one child, d. e.
Nathaniel, born in April died August 7, 1728
Nathaniel, b. August 2, 1729; m. Abigail Hammond
Martha, born Jan. 14, 1731-2, married John Hill,
d Nov. 1788, æ 55 yrs ; left son and daughters
Daniel, born October 6, 1734, between nine and ten at
night ; was a merchant of Gloucester, Mass.,
died Jan. 5, 1800, aged 66 years
Mary, born Jan. 4, 1738, at ten o'clock at night, mar-
ried Capt. Thomas Hammond, died June, 1819,
aged 81 years ; two children, Mary, married
William Jones, of Portsmouth ; Joseph, mar-
Mary Staples ; he was of a public spirit and life
Nathaniel Rogers 5, son of Rev. John and Susannah
(Whipple) Rogers 4, married Abigail Hammond, April
30, 1756. She was born Sept. 2, 1734. She was the sister
of Capt. Thomas Hammond, who married Mary Rogers.
Nathaniel 5, died March 25, 1803, in the seventieth year
of his age. Children of Nathaniel and Abigail (Ham-
mond) Rogers :
Lucy, born 1759, died July 19, 1835, aged 76 yrs, unm.
Nathaniel, born October 13, 1660; m. Lucy Moody.
Nathaniel Rogers 6, son of Nathaniel 5 and Abigail
(Hammond) Rogers, married Lucy Moody of York, 1786
She was born June 19, 1768 ; died of dropsy, March 22,
1819, aged fifty-one years. Their children :
Abigail, born August 20, 1786
Daniel, born 1788
Martha, born Jan 18, 1790
Sarah
John, born August 25, 1795
Shubael G. born July 12, 1799
Nathaniel, born February 23, 1803
William D. M., born Sept. 4, 1809

The Rev. Nathaniel Rogers 4, son of Rev. John 3, and Martha (Whittingham) Rogers, was born 4 March, 1701-2, graduated at Harvard College 1721.

He began to preach at Ipswich when Mr. Fitch left for Portsmouth, in 1724.

August 16, 1726. At a Church meeting, 35 votes of the Brethren were given for Mr. Nathaniel Rogers; 8 votes for Mr. Will'm Welstead, one for Mr. Charles Chauncey, for Minister.

Parish concurred, provided he be settled upon Congregational principles, agreeably to the Platform of Church Government.

This condition occasioned some difficulty and delay in the settlement, the elder Mr. Rogers objecting to it, as unprecedented. The objection seems to have proceeded from a wish on the part of the clergy to put down the office of Ruling Elder; which was fully recognized by the Cambridge Platform. The parish persevered, and Mr. Rogers was ordained, with the condition, October 18, 1727.

December 23, 1726. Voted, that the sum of one hundred and thirty pounds in Bills of Credit be paid to Mr. Nathaniel Rogers annually, for the space of three years, and afterwards the Sum of one hundred and fifty pounds in Bills of Credit, or in lieu thereof, the like sum in silver money, accounting it at fifteen shillings per ounce: and so to rise or fall in proportion to the value of silver: or pay two thirds of said sum in Barley Malt at six shillings per bushel: Indian Corn at five shillings: Pork at sixpence per pound: Butter at twelve pence.

In 1746, Mr. Rogers declines to have Mr. John Walley as his colleague, because he was unwilling to exchange with a preacher who had officiated for a new Church in Boston, which had seceded from other orthodox churches. This produced considerable excitement against Mr Rogers and led to a division of the Parish, and the settlement of Mr. Walley in the south parish.

Rev. Nathaniel Rogers 4, married (1) Mrs. Mary Denison, widow of Coll'n John Denison, and the daughter of Rev. John Leverett, President of Harvard College:

Here lyes ye body of Mrs.
Mary Rogers ye Excellent
Consort to ye Rev'd Mr. Nathaniel
Rogers, and daugh'r of the Hon'bl
and Rev'd Mr. John Leverett, Esq.,
who died June ye 25th, 1757, Aetat's 55

John xi, 25 : JESUS said unto her
I am the Resurrection & ye Life : he
that believeth on me tho he were
Dead yet shall he live.

He married (2) Mary Staniford, widow of Daniel Staniford, May 4, 1759. She died, 1780. Mr. Rogers died five
years earlier, 1775, [and the Rev'd Joseph Dana, D. D.,
wrote the epitaph inscribed upon the slab at his grave :]

In            Memory of
The Rev. NATHANIEL ROGERS: who was
more than 47 years, a faithful & beloved
Pastor of the first Church & congregation in
this place : Colleague the first 18 years with
his venerable Father, the Rev. John Rogers of
precious memory, whose dust lies near : Alone
in office after, until death translated him to
the high reward of his labours. He slept in
JESUS, May 10th, A. D. 1775, Æt 74

A mind profoundly great, a heart that felt
The ties of nature, friendship and humanity;
Distinguished wisdom, dignity of manners,
Those marked the man :—but with superior grace
The Christian shone in faith and heavenly zeal
Sweet peace, true greatness, and prevailing prayer.
    Dear man of God ! with what strong agonies
He wrestled for his flock and for the world :
And, like Apollos, mighty in the Scriptures,
Opened the mysteries of love divine,
And the great name of JESUS.

Warm from his lips the heavenly doctrine fell,
And numbers rescued from the jaws of hell,
Shall hail him blest in realms of light unknown,
And add immortal lustre to his crown.

His children were :
Margaret,
Sarah, died 1772
Elizabeth, b. 1735, m. Daniel Rogers, d. Sept. 23, 1774
Lucy, born 1739, died 1747, buried Sept. 9, aged 9 yrs
Lucy, married Jabez Farley, died July 24 1788
Martha,
Nathaniel,

Rev. Daniel Rogers 4, son of Rev. John 3 and Martha (Whittingham) Rogers, was graduated at H. C. 1725; became a Tutor in the College ; preached by invitation "at the Farms," in Ipswich ; he was invited to Exeter, and Sept. 3, 1747, he "rec'd a Call fm ye New gathered Chh at Exeter," was ordained July 13, 1748, and died Dec. 9, 1785, aged 79 years.

[In 1899, we received the loan of an Interleaved Almanac, 1747, from Mr. H. F. Bryant, Secretary of the Maine Historical Society, with permission to copy its memoranda. It was an Almanac of the Rev. Daniel Rogers, and the inter-leaves were his notes for 1747 : his services at Candlewood and the Farms ; his attendance upon Whitefield ; his call to Exeter. We quote from the Diary, as a supplement to Mr. Hammatt :]

DIARY OF REV. DANIEL ROGERS, 1747.

memo : in ye year 1746, I found by an Epitaph upon Mr. Jno. Rogers, of Dedham, in Essex, Old England, Minister, That He died October 18, in ye Year 1636. my Great, Great Grand Father.

January, 1747.

2. I pr. at Deacon Haskell: gt Snow.
3. Went up to ye Farms.    4. pr. at ye Farms.
8. Br. Nath'l pr. Lecture
11, 18, 25, I pr. at ye Farms, 18, had but one Meeting.
15. I pr. ye Lecture. 20. Mr. Parsons of Newberry
    pr ye Lecture
23. rode Over to Rowley, returned in Evening.
30. a Healthy Time in Gen'll, Tho the Small Pox is at Salem, Beverly, Whenham.

February. 1747.

Sunday, 1. I was detained fm going to ye Farms by Depth of ye Snow.

8, 15, 22, I pr at ye Farms.

5. Mr. Jewet of Rowley pr the Lecture.

10. Visited Old Mr. Burnham.

11. Was at Chebacco. Took Rockwell Horse.

12. Mr. Cleavland pr the Lecture.

13. a Total Eclipse of ye moon 11 'Clock night.

17. pr at Mr. Burroughs at ye Farms.

19. Br Nath'l pr Lec. 24. went to Chebacco.

25. Wednesday, mr Cleveland Ordained Chebacco

26. Mr Croswel pr ye Weekly Lecture.

27. Friday. I went to Exeter. 28. I went to see Robert Gilman Sick of a Consumption.

March, 1747.

1. 8. I preach't at Exeter.

9. I pr at Stratham.

This Day Mr. Jno Walley was Chose Pastor of ye Chh at Ipswich.

11. Went to Portsmo. pr at Mr. Sherborne's House in ye evening.

12. Went up to Kittery, ·[now Eliot.]

15. pr at Exeter. Mr Prince pr for me at ye Farms.

19. Went Stretham. 20. Mr Joseph Adams Ordained here

21. returned to Ipswich. 22. pr at Ipswich Farms.

26. Thursday. Mr. Emerson of Topsfield pr Lecture.

27. I pr at Robert Potters. 29. pr at ye Farms. fine Pleast Weath'r. Warm Spring Comes-on Early.

April.

5. Sunday. Mr. Walley came to preach here.

7. I pr up at Mr Ayers's : in ye Evening at Abel Bordman's after Mr Fitts' Funeral.

9. Gen'l Fast. pr at ye Farms

17. pr at Chebacco

20, 22. Mr. Wade plowed here Homestead

23. pr ye Weekly Lecture.

5, 12, 19, 26, I pr at ye Farms.

30. Gen'lly cold y' month. a Time of Gude Health.

May, 1747.

3. Sunday. I pr at ye Farms.

5. Set out for Newberry : a Fast for ye out pouring of ye Spirit Kept in Mr Parsons Congregation : I pr part of ye Day.

6. Came to Rowley: pr in ye School House.

7. Returned to Newberry : Mr Cleveland pr Lec :

10. Sunday. the Sacrament was administered in Mr. Parsons Chh : I pr P M

11. I went to Exeter, pr yr in the Evening.

12. went to Portmo : Mr Moody prea'd in ye meeting-House. 13, in ye Evening I pr at Mr Shoreburne's. 14, Mr Shurtleff's Funeral. Bro John [of Eliot] preached.

16. returned to Exeter. 17, pr there. 18, went to [Eliot.]

19. tarried there. 20. went to Portmo : in ye Evening I pr at Mr Sherburne's. 21. attended a Fast at the bereaved church. 22. went up to [Eliot] pr there.

23. Returned to Exeter : 24. pr there.

25. pr at Hampton Falls : returned to Ipswich.

27. pr in ye Evening at Abel Bordmans : 28, pr the Weekly Lecture : 29. pr at Moses Wells's.

31. I pr at yr Farms. Mr. Leavitt of Salem pr for me in ye forenoon.

June.

2. Br Nathaniel buried his Negro Woman.

3. Went to Newberry with Cozen Jno Rogers.

4. to Portsmouth. Visited vid'm.

5. to [Eliot.] attended Cozen Wm Rogers Funeral: pr at yt Solemnity. returned to Portsmouth. [William, son of Rev. John and Susannah (Whipple) Rogers, of Eliot, died June 1, 1747, aged 24 years.]

6. Came to Newberry : pr at Newberry : Mr. Roberts supplied my Place. 8. returned to Ipswich in good Health.

10. pr at Old Mr. Wallis's. 11. Mr. Taylor pr ye Weekly Lecture. 12. attended a Fast at Chebacco.

14. I pr at Chebacco : Mr Cleavl'd pr for me at ye Farms

17. pr at Neighb'r Ayres : 18. Mr Cleaveland pr ye Weekly Lecture.

19. with Bro'r Nath'l Sett out for Exeter. P. M. Bro Nath'l pr at Exeter. 20. P. M. Bro Nath'l pr here again. 21. Bro'r Nath'l pr and Administered ye Sacrament. 22. I came with Bro'r Nath'l to Portmo' 23. went to [Eliot] 24 Bro'r in ye eve'g pr at Portsmouth. 25. in ye Evening Mr Cleaveland pr yr. 26. at [Eliot] again. Bro'r Nath'l pr Lecture. 27. Broth'r Nath'l went Home. 28. I pr at [Eliot] at Bro Jno's. 30. pr at ye Upper End of Kittery: (probably at Unity parish, now Berwick.)

### July.

1. I pr at Mr. Walton's in Newington: in the evening gave a Word at Mr. Sherburnes. 2. Continued at ye Bank. 3. returned to (Eliot.) 5. pr at Newington. 7. at Berwick 8. very hot day: I stay'd at Broth'r Jno's. (Eliot.) 9. went to Portsmouth. 10. in ye Evening Bro'r Jno. pr yr wth Power. 11. went to York. 12. A. M. pr there, and in the Evening pr at a private meeting in York. 14. returned to (Eliot.) pr at Sturgeon Creek. 15. Very Hott. Continued at Bro'r Jno's. 16. Went down Portsmouth. Hott. 17. went up ye River again to (Eliot,) and Newington with Mr. Moody. 18. Returned to Portsmo: went to Exeter. 19. pr at Exeter for Mr. Phillips. 20. Returned to Ipswich. 21. A New Church gathered in Ipswich. 23. Mr. Whitefield came to Ipswich. 25. I went to Newbury. 26. pr at Newberry P. M. 27. went with Mr. Parsons to Portsmouth. 28. Mr. Whitefield pr his farewell sermon at Portsmouth. 29. I came to Newberry with him 30. He preach't at Newberry, P. M. went to Exeter. 31. He p't at Exeter P. M. went to Durham.

### August.

1. Mr. Whitef'd pr at Durham, P. M. we returned to Newberry. Went to Ipswich. 2. Mr. Whitef'd pr at Newberry in ye evening.

3. Mr. Whitefield pr at Ipswich, A. M.  I went to Mr. Royal's at Charlestown.

4. went to Boston.  Mr Whitefield pr at ye Evening Lecture at Dr. Colman's.  5. at Mr. Webb's.  6. at Mr. Gee's.  7. at Mr. Webb's.

8. at Mr. Gee's.  P. M. I went down to Nantasket

9. I pr at Nantaskett.

10. Returned from Nantaskett to Boston.  P : M : Mr Whitef'd pr at Mr Bound's.  11.  A. M. at Mr. Webbs.

12. He pr at Copps Hill to ab't 10.000. and took his Leave of Boston.

13. at Cambridge to ye Condemned Malefactor.

14. at Salem.

15. at Reading.  I was there.  P. M. Went to Concord

16. Mr. Whitefield pr Here.

17. Mr. Whitefield took leave of me at Mr. Royal's.  I returned to Boston.  18. evening I heard Mr. Bruce preach.

19. I came to Salem : lodged at Mr. Bartons.

20. came to Ipswich.

23. Sunday. Sacrament day.  P. M. I pr for Br. Nath'l. New Church met in ye Town House first.

26. Kept as a Day of Fasting & Prayer in ye 1st Parish upon acco' of mortal sickness.

28. Mr. Denison deceased, Æ 25.  His birthday.  ab't two o'clock.  [See John Denison 5, page 74.]

30. I pr at Chebacco.

30. Attended Mr. Denison's Funeral.  Ye great number of People in Town attended.

31. I visit Dec'n Haskell.

N : B : a Time of Sore Sickness and mortality in Ipswich this month.

### September, 1747.

3. I rec'd a Call fm ye New gathered Chh at Exeter.

4. preached at a Fast at Chebacco.

6. pr at Ipswich A. M. & P. M.

9. Br. Nath'l buried his Daughter Lucy Æ 9 years.

13. A : M : I pr at Exeter.

P: M: Mr. Phillips pr.

14. Attended Deacon Moors funeral & Capt. Daniel Childs. [Exeter.]
24. pr ye Weekly Lecture at Ipswich. 27. at Newberry

October, 1747.

4. Sunday. I pr at Ipswich. Bro Nath'l Confin'd by Sickness.
8. A woman executed at Cambridge for Murder.
18. Sunday. I pr at Exeter. A : M : 145 Ps 10. P: M : Isa. 51 : 7.
20. pr in ye Evening at ye New Meeting House.
29. The great Earthquake twenty years ago.

November, 1747.

1. 8, 15, 22, 29. I pr at Exeter.
2. went to [Eliot.]
3. Fasting & Prayer for ye outpouring of ye Spirit in Concert at th' Xtian Societys in Scotland. Bro Jno preac'd A. M. I pr P. M.
4. Mr. Walley ordained at Ipswich.
9. Exeter. Went to see a Sick man at Copyhold.
13. Hard Clap of thunder.
18. last Saturday, 14th, deceas'd Dear Old Mr. Moody, and was interred Yesterday. Mr. Wise of Berwick p'd a Sermon at ye Funeral.
21. last evening I pr at ye House of Josiah Ladd.
22. Sunday. Exeter. A: M: Eph. ii, 13. P : M : 2 Kings ii, 9. latter part upon Occasion of old Mr. Moody's Death.

December.

2. was an ordination at Keenborough.
3. This morning An Earthquake was heard.
6, 13, 20, 27. I pr at Exeter.

memo : rec'd at Several Times of the People at ye Farms before y'y were made a Parish, for preaching, beginning Feb'y 16,—22 Sabbaths at £3 00 p Diem    Tot : £54 17 2

Feb. 23d, new Tenour, Recd of Mr Abraham
    Howe, The Sum of                        £10 18 4
March 23, 1746-7, New Tenour, Rec'd of Mr
    Abraham How                             10 00 0

| | | | |
|---|---|---|---|
| March 29, rec'd of Decon Ladd of Exeter, old Tenour | 12 | 00 | 0 |
| rec'd of Xtian Friends threabt | 10 | 00 | 0 |
| at Hampton Falls | 2 | 00 | 0 |
| June 15, recd of Mr Abr How, old Tenour | 21 | 00 | 0 |
| Aug 10, rec'd of ye p'le of Hull | 4 | 00 | |
| Sept 8, rec'd of Mr Abr How old Tenor | 11 | 00 | 0 |
| Jan 28, 1747-8 | 9 | 00 | 0 |
| Octo'r rec d of Dea Lord | 11 | 00 | 0 |
| Nov'r recd of Dea Lord | 16 | 13 | 0 |
| Dec'r recd Elsewhere | 3 | 00 | 0 |

Jan'y 29 To Eben'r Smith for mending my surtout £2 10 0
pd Mr Warner for cutting Wood    16s
To Mr Warner cutting wood, Carting Board and a  load of
wood and work done at ye field    £1.

memo : March 31.  Mr Cogswell Carted Dung for me.
Richard  Potter  Splitting  Posts.
Apr 2, Richard Potter,  Spreading  Dung.
April & May, Mr Burrows 2 days work about ye Homest'd
Mr Burroughs Weeding Corn.
June 9, Mr Timo: Wade ploughed corn.
June 13, Burroughs molding half a day.
June 17, expense tow'd fitting ye chain.
To Cloth & lace for lining,  £3 8 0
To Mr. Joseph Appleton for his work  £4
Nov'r 29 pd Mr. Wilson of Cheshire for linen cloth  £15 4
Due to  Him  2 months  16s.
Dec 12, pd sd Wilson on Bro Jno acco'  £13.

Daniel Rogers 3, son of John 2 and Elisabeth (Denison)
Rogers, was born Sept. 25, 1667 ; graduated at H. C. 1686 ;
was Master of the Grammar School from 1687 to 1715 ;
and was chosen Feoffee of this institution a few months
before his death.  He was Town Clerk and Clerk of the
Commons from 1710 ; Register of Probate from 1708 to the
time of his decease.  He subscribed 12 shillings toward
the bell, 1699.

Here lyes buried
ye Body of
Daniel Rogers, Esq'r
who Dec'd Decemb'r ye 1st
1722, Æ tatis 56

Turbidos ad Læto Solari Lumine Portus
Sollicitus Nautus per mare fert Aquilo ;
Me Borealis Agens Nitidum super Ætheris Axem
Fustitiæ Solis Luce beavit Hyems

The following town record renders intelligible the otherwise obscure Latin epitaph :

" Daniel Rogers, Esq., was frozen to death, ye 1st day of December, 1722, in ye 56th year of his age, as he was comeing home from Hampton, looseing his way on Salisbury Marshes."

[Mr. Hammatt's usually most kindly pen writes more about Daniel 3 :]

" He has the unenviable distinction of being the clumsiest Clerk that ever had the custody of our Records. He was careless, incorrect, illegible. The wearied and vexed searchers into these abused volumes, feels quite relieved when he comes to the end of this good man's labors, and is not disposed to quarrel with the "Borealis Hyems" that translated him "super Ætheris Axem."

He left a widow Sarah, and children :

John, born Sept. 16, 1708
Daniel, H. C. Class 1725 ; ordained minister of
      Littleton, March 15, 1732 ; died Nov. 1782
      aged seventy-six years.
Sarah, born May 29, 1795, m. John Watson of
      Plymouth, January 26, 1715
Elisabeth, born Feb. 21, 1697, m. Peleg Wiswell of
      Boston ; pub. November 21, 1719
Priscilla, married Rev. Nath'l Leonard of Plymouth,
      pub. Oct. 22, 1724
Patience, m Joshua Freeman, Plymouth, Sept 11, 1728

Margaret, born January 8, 1698, m. Rev. Robert
Ward, Wenham
Mary, died at 21 years of age :

> Here lyes ye Body
> of Mrs. Mary
> Rgers        Daugh'r
> of Daniel Rogers
> Esq'r & Mrs. Sarah
> His Wife who Dec'd
> Octo'br ye 9th 1723
> Ætatis 21

In the Meeting-house of 1700, the third pew  next  Maj'r
Wainwright's was for the wife and family of Daniel Rogers

Richard Rogers 4, son of John 3, born Dec 2, 1703,  died
November 26, 1742 :

> Here lies buried ye body of
> Richard Rogers of Ipswich, Esq.,
> son of ye Rev'd Mr. John Rogers
> of Ipswich, who departed this life
> Nov'r 26th, 1742, Ætatis 39.

He was of Harvard College, Class 1725.   Became a merchant and acquired wealth.   He married Mary Crompton,
published June 11, 1726.   Her portrait in oil is carefully
preserved by the Misses Martha and Mary Ann Rogers,
Poplar street. [1847.]

Samuel Rogers 4, son of John 5, born August 31,  1709,
and died December 21, 1772.   Harvard College, 1725.   He
became a physician and practiced this profession in Ipswich.   He married Hannah Wise, January 1, 1735.

[His early married home was the  northerly  part of the
house successively occupied by Rev.  John  Walley  and
Rev. Joseph Dana, D. D.   Dr. Dana built the  southerly
extension.   Dr. Rogers' later home was the  house  which
stood on the site of the  present  South Meeting house ;
built by Ammi Ruhamah Wise, and then possessed by
Doctor Rogers.   After the Death of the Doctor, Mrs. Rog-

ers received into this house young ladies from other towns, as pupils ; her school was regarded as a public interest.]

John Rogers 3, (Samuel 2, Nath,1 1) and Martha Smith married January 12, 1687. See pp 294-6. He had:

Martha, born October 12, 1691

Jonathan, born May 1, 1694

He is designated as " John Rogers, farmer," to distinguish him from the Rev. John, his cousin.

He died August 20, 1694. Martha, his widow, was appointed adm'x, October 22, 1694. A letter of Martha Rogers as adm'x, is given p. 295-6. His estate amounted to real, £860 ; personal, £293 11 6. He possessed lands near " Haffils bridge."

[While Mr. Hammatt's gleanings of the Ipswich Families of Rogers are in press, we cut from a newspaper the Will of the Rev. John Rogers, of Dedham, England ; father of the Rev. Nathaniel 1, of Ipswich. It belongs, surely, to these Papers. A copy of his portrait is in the Public Library. The will is prefaced : " Copied from Court files, 1863, and printed in the Genealogical Reg."]

THE WILL OF REV. JOHN ROGERS, DEDHAM, ENGLAND.

Oct. the 14th, 1636. In the name of God, Amen. I, John Rogers, Minister of God's word in Dedham, doe ordaine this to be my last will and testament, hereby revoking all my former wills by me made:

ffirst I bequeath my soul into the hand of Almightie God my merciful ffather in Jesus Christ ; and my body to be buried att my executrix her discretion.

And for my worldly goods that God of his mercie hath given me, I dispose them thus :

ffirst for the house I dwell in, with the orchards and gardens, and twoe acres of land thereto belonging, with an ould cottage and an orchard belonging to that, I give to Dorathie, my wife, during her life, and then to John Rogers, my grandchilde, sonne of my eldest sonne John Rogers of Colchester, deceased, and to his heirs ; and for default of such heirs, I give to his mother, my daughter-in-lawe, for tearme of her naturall life, then I give it after her decease to my sonne Nathaniell and to his heire male, and ffor default of such I give it to my sonne Samuel and to his heire male, and if he have noe such, then I give it to my sonne Daniell and his heirs forever.

Item: I will that my daughter-in-lawe shall keep the house in good and sufflcient rep'ac'ous, till her sonne, my grandchild, shall come of age, and during the time that she shall enjoy it if she come to have it, requesting that if any of my children, especially of my sonnes, shall desire to hire it, that they may have it before another, giveing for the same as another would give.

Item : I give to my beloved wife all my corne in the chambers att home of all sorts ; the wood and broome in or about the yards, and the horse I ride on, the best cowe, and the hogg, and all the fruite, and half my hey, and the fowles in the yard, and tenn pounds of money.

Item : I give to my sonnes Nathaniell and Samuell all my bookes to be equally divided, excepting some englishe bookes that I have given to some other of my children, as appeareth in a paper annexed hereto.

Item: I give to the poore of Dedham in present five pounds ; and to the worke house I give ffiffteene pounds, to be imployed by the appointment of the governours for the benefitt of such poore folkes as shall be in the house.

Item: I give to my sister Garood and her children twenty pounds to be disosed of as my wife shall think fittinge.

Item : I give to Sam, Hanna, and Marke twenty pounds

Item : I give to my cossen Webb of Colchester, tenn pounds, and to John, her sonn, tenn pounds.

Item : I give to my sonne Angers' children, ffiefty pound

Item : I give to my sonne Nathanills children 40 pounds

Item : I give to my son Samuel his son thirty pounds.

Item : I give to my son Pecks children tenn pounds.

Item : to my daughter Marthaes child five pounds.

Item : to these poore men, Abraham Ham, Robert Ham, John Ham, John Cannon, Simon Cowper, widdow ffrench, John Shinglewood, John Weed, Edmund Spinke, William Wood, to each of them five shillings.

Item : to my servants, to Martin Garood tenn shillings ; to George Havill twenty shillings ; to Tameson Princett tenn shillings ; Goodman Allen of Santoosey twenty shillings : to Elisabeth present my maide twoe pounds.

Item : To my cossens Elizabeth Rogers tenn pounds and to her brother Sadler five pounds.

Item : I will that all my other goods not bequeathed, within doors and without be given and equally divided between all my children in old England, my funeral expenses deducted.

All my legacies given, I will be paid into their own or their parents hand within six months after my death.

I appointe my lovinge wife to be my sole executrix of this my last will and testament, praying her in all love to see my will discharged faithfully.

[Proved in the Prerogative Court of Canterbury, February 20th, 1637, by Dorothee Rogers, relict etc.]

ROGERS, John.    Sadler and Innholder.    Had a seat assigned to him in the Meeting-house, 1700.    He had a house near the present Female Academy, 1715.    Martha, his wife, died October 15, 1721.

In 1694, he kept Tavern with the sign of " The Black Horse."    It was near the Female Academy.

ROPER, Walter.    Took freeman's oath, 1642.    Had a share in Plum Island, &c., 1644 ; and horses on the common, 1697.

In a deposition respecting the will of Nathaniel Rogers, given in 1676, he represents himself as being sixty-eight years of age.    He was a voter in Town affairs, 1679.    He died July 15, and his will was proved September 28, 1680. He left a son John.

John Roper 2, (Walter 1,) married Anna Caldwell, daughter of John and Sarah (Dillingham) Caldwell.

He had horses on the common, 1697.

He had sisters and a brother Nathaniel who died before him.

Anna, his wife, survived him.  The graves of both are
marked by stones :

> Here lies what
> was mortal of
> John Roper who
> Died Noumber ye
> 27, 1709, & in ye
> 60th year of his
> age

According to the inscription on her tombstone, Mrs.
Anna (Caldwell) Roper survived her husband 12 years :

> Here lies Mrs.
> Anne Roper
> wife   of   Mr
> John  Roper
> Died     Septem
> ber  ye  4  1721
> aged 60 years

Of a sister of John Roper 2, it is recorded : " The widow
of John Dutch, sister of John Roper, died of small pox.
She possessed housing and lands  appraised at £120 ;  and
other property, making a total of £157 15 6."

Another  recorded  as  sister  of  John  Roper,  is Mary
Spark.  The  will  of  Mary  Spark,  December  9,  1711,
alludes to "the  twenty  shillings  given  by  my  brother,
John  Rooper."

The will of John Roper, dated November 22, 1709, was
proved December 12.  He bequeaths to his wife Anna, his
whole estate during her widowhood ; and gives her leave
to sell, should it be needful for her maintenance, a salt
marsh which his father purchased of Mr. Jewett, and til-
lage land which he bought of Thomas and Jeremiah Dow.
She was to seek advice of Serg't Samuel  Hart, Nathaniel
Knowlton, and Dillingham Caldwell her brother.

He bexueaths to his cousin, Benja : Dutch, the salt
marsh he bo't of John Pengry ;

To sister Sparks, and cousins Susanna (Spark) Annable Margaret White, Rose (Spark) Newman, Susannah Kinsman, each £20.  To Hannah Fellows, $25.

He also gives legacies to "two cousins," Sarah Caldwell, daughter of John Caldwell, and Mary Foster, dau. of Jacob Foster,—forty shillings each.  These "two cousins," were his wife's neices.

1680, March.  Walter Roper releast from training without pay for the future.

1675, September 19.  Benjamin Roper, slain in war.

Nathaniel Roper 2, Walter 1 :  September 29, 1685.  Was on board a sloop in Ipswich harbour, about the middle of March last :  bound for the barbadoes :  Capt. Thomas Bishop.

Samuel Bishop, aged 40 years ;  Jacob Perkins, aged 23 years :—Nathaniel Roper affirmed, " My brother, John Bishop should have my estate, pay my debts, give to my cozen Nath'l Dutch, (John Dutch his son) ten pounds."

ROSS, Killicross.  Had a share in Plum Island, &c., as tenant of Mr. Symonds, 1664.

He married Mary Gally, May 9, 1661, daughter of John and Florence Gally.

His will is dated June 11, and the inventory rendered February 20, 1683.

His wife, Mary (Gally) Ross, died February 1, 1720, aged eighty years.  Children of Killicross and Mary :

John, born May 9, 1662
Elizabeth, born December 13, 1668, died early
William, born February 11, 1670
Samuel, born May 25, 1673, died 1696, and his bro.
John appointed administrator of his estate.
Jonathan, born July 14, 1681
Daniel, born July 1679
Mary, born M 31, 1664, m. Abraham Fitts
Sarah, born January 22, 1666
Elizabeth, July 27, 1667
Jean [Jane] born May 15, 1675, d July 30, 1736, unm
Abigail, born June 20, 1677, m. Philemon Wood

His widow, Mary, and his son John, were the executors of his estate.  To his children he gives ten pounds each. The whole estate was £330, 7.

Mrs. Rebekah Symoods, in her will, proved August 19, 1695, bequeaths a legacy to her maid,—Elisabeth Ross.

Mary (Gally) Ross came into full communion with the church, December, 1673.

Jane Ross and Abigail Ross had seats in the Meeting House, 1702.

[We have gleanings from the Town Records of later generations of Ross, to be soon printed with ten or more Ipswich names.]

Others by the name of Ross in Ipswich 1655–66 :

Thomas Ross, died M 1, 1657

Fennel Ross.  Tenant on the farm of John Whipple. Daughter Susannah, born October 2, 1666.  Died and left a widow, 1683.  Inventory, February 12, 1683.

John Ross, tenant of Mr. Wardwell, had a share in Plum Island (as a tenant,) 1664;  had horses on the Common, 1697.  The children of John Ross were :

John, born April 9, 1664
Mary, born April 16, 1665
Sarah, born February 16, 1667, married ——— Hoar
Hannah, born February 1, 1669
Abigail, born 1670, died at the Hamlet 1749, æ 79
Joseph
Susannah, born December 14, 1674
Elisabeth
Daniel, born January 6, 1678
Jonathan, born December 1, 1680
Isaac and Benja. March 10, 1682

1704, Nov. 13.  The estate of Jonathan Ross amounting to £21, 3, divided among his brothers and sisters : Mary, Sarah Hoar alias Ross, Abigail, Daniel, Susannah, Hannah, Joseph, Elisabeth.

ROGERTALL, Peter.  Servant to John Sparks.  Died November 22, 1684.

RUST, Russ, Nathaniel. Had a share in Plum Island, 1664 ; voter in Town affairs, 1679. He was a glover by trade. Freeman, May 27, 1674; Tithingman, 1677 ; had a seat in the Meeting house, "short seat near pulpit, 1700." He was dead in 1713. His widow, Mary Rust, died Jan. 16, 1720. Children of Nathaniel 1, and Mary Rust :

Mary, born June 1664
Hannah, married Captain Daniel Rindge
Nathaniel, born March 16, 1667, m. Joanna Rinsman
Margaret, born February 7, 1669, married Samuel
    Williams of Salem, October 24, 1694
Elizabeth, married William Fellows, Dec. 7, 1693
Mercy, married Thomas Norton, Nov. 14, 1700
Dorothy, died November 10, 1684
John, born July 9, 1684, married Sarah Potter
Sarah, married Nathaniel Hart, 1706-7

Nathaniel Rust 2, son of Nathaniel 1, born March 16, 1667 ; married Joanna, daughter of Quartermaster Robert Kinsman, 1694. She died at Chebacco, January 28, 1733. He was School Master at Chebacco, 1696, and many succeeding years. Children of Nathaniel 2, and Joanna Rust :

Ebenezer, Harvard College, 1707, lived at Stratham
Joseph. born March 23, 1696, died at Chebacco, Feb.
    3, 1734, aged 39 years ; wife Rachel
Benjamin, born May 4, 1698
Dorothy, born July 14, 1700

John Rust 2, son of Nathaniel I, born July 9, 1684, and died 1713. He married Sarah Potter, Septemper 26, 1705. He was a commoner, 1707. Widow Sarah Potter Rust married Jonathan Fellows, 1716. Children of John and Sarah Rust :

John, born March 18, 1707, married Sarah Foster
Daniel, born October 2, 1708, died August 17, 1724
Sarah, b June 28, 1710, m Thomas Hovey Dec 17, 1729
Nathaniel, (Posthumous) ) born March 29, 1713; he
was Captain ; married Sarah Wallis.

RUSSELL, Henry. Came from Marblehead to Ipswich ; purchased of Richard Wattles a dwelling house and
land in High street, April 18, 1663 ; about one acre ; Mr.
Richard Dummer on the south east, the street north east,
Mr. William Norton north west, Mr. Dummer south west.
He purchased marsh and other lands of the said Wattles
at the same time.

He had a share in Plum Island, 1664.

His children were Andrew and Henry, also, born here,
    Tryphosa, July 9, 1664
    John, September 8, 1667
Mr. Russell and his sons Henry and Andrew were appointed Shepherds, north side the river, May, 1670.

Noadiah Russell was Master of the Grammar School
from October 31, 1683 to February 28, 1686-7, when he
removed to Cambridge.

December 15, 1685, Paid Mr. Russell, Schoolmaster,
for what is for the mending the school house, dwelling
house and barn, £30.

SAFFORD, Thomas 1, was commoner, 1641; subscriber to Denison's allowance, 1648; had a share and a half in Plum Island, &c., 1664. His will is dated February 20, 1666. He died in February. He left a wife Elisabeth, who died March 4, 1679; and a son Joseph, and three daughters. He gave a day's work, besides the rate, "towards the East Bridge," in 1646. He purchased of Henry Kingsbury, Feb. 8, 1648, a farm of 32 acres.

1667, March. Thomas Safourd dying intestate * * lands given by his father unto his mother * * the Court conceived her children to be her heires and the eldest son to have a double portion.

Joseph Safford 2, son of Thomas 1, was born about 1631 and died August 29, 1701 æ 70 years. He was one of the Selectmen, 1697. With eight others he objected to the selling of the old Meeting-house in 1699, "because of their pews and seats." He had a seat appointed to him "in ye short seats" in the new Meeting-house in 1700. He then had the designation of Mr. He married Mary Baker, March 6, 1660. He had :

Mary, born February 20, 1661
Joseph, born August 11, 1664
Sarah, born M 20, 1666
Thomas, died June, 1678
Elisabeth, born August 3, 1670
Samuel, born July, 1678
Hannah, born January 11, 1681

John Safford had a share in Plum Island, &c., 1664.— He purchnsed of Anthony Potter and Elisabeth (Whipple) his wife, January 19, 1761, a dwelling house and three acres of land. This land is designated in deeds, thus :

1641, Jan. 19. Daniel Denison conveys to Humphrey Griffin a Dwelling House, &c., near the Mill ;

1648, 1st, 4th mo. John Burnham conveys to Anthony Potter a houselot late of Hnmphrey Griffin, near the Water Mill.

1661, January 19. Anthony Potter and Elisabeth his wife convey to John Safford Dwelling House and Land, three acres, north side the River, near the Mill, bounded by high ways round.

Children of John and Sarah Safford :

Sarah, born July 14, 1664 [see epitaph]
Margaret, born February 28, 1665
Rebekah, born August 30, 1667
Mercy, born February 26, 1668
Elisabeth, born February 27, 1670
Thomas, born October 16, 1672
Joseph, born March 12, 1674

Sara Safford dau
ghter of John &
Sara Safford
died July ye 21, 1712
aged 47 years
Read consider
& stand in aw
Doe not sin
Keep Gods law

Samuel Safford and Hannah his wife had seats appointed to them in the Meeting-house in 1702. He was a commoner, 1707.

Thomas Safford married Eleanor Satchwell, October 7, 1648. She died December 22, 1724.

John Safford, Jun'r, married Hannah Newman, September 15, 1685, daughter of Thomas Newman.

1691, March 25. Administration granted on the estate of Thomas Newman to John Safford, Jun'r, and his wife Hannah. Inventory, £266, 3, 7.

John Safford, Jun'r and Abigail Martin were published June 28, 1702.

SALTER, Theophilus, subscribed three shillings to Major Denison's allowance, 1648. He soon after removed to Salem. [See note Mass. Col. Rec., about 1680.]

RICHARD SALTONSTALL. He was son of Sir Richard Saltonstall, and came to New England with his father in 1630.

1631, May 18, he took the freeman's oath.

1635-6. He was Deputy to General Court; Assistant from 1637 to 1649, and 1664.

1635. He built the first Grist-mill in Ipswich.

1635. A planting lot of six acres was granted to Thomas Wells on the east side of the great hill called Heartbreak hill, "butting at the east end upon the way leading to Mr. Saltonstall's farm."

He had a house and garden on the north side of the river, near the Mill, in 1635.

In 1637 he possessed lands near Labour-in-vain Creek.

1638. 27th day of July. John Tuttle bought a house and lot. The house was built by Richard Brown, who when he moved to Newbury, sold it to Mr. Richard Saltonstall, and Mr. Saltonstall sold to Richard Lumkin, and said Richard Lumkin sold it to John Tuttle. This house lot "lies near the great cove of the town river, having a house lot now in the possession of William Avery on the south west; Robert Kinsman's house lot on the north west; the town river on the south east; a houselot now in possession of Samuel Hall on the east.

In 1641 lhe was Serj. Maj. of Col. John Endicot's regiment.

Mr. Saltonstall was commoner in 1641; a subscriber to Gen. Denison's allowance in 1648.

He was on a committee in 1645, authorized to grant lots to the inhabitants.

1659. He had a lot on the south side of the river, called "the forty acres."

He went to England in 1672, and returned in 1680.

He was again chosen Assistant, 1680-82.

He returned to England in 1683, and died at Hulme, April 29, 1694, aged eighty-four years.

He had three daughters married in England; and a son, Rev. Nathaniel Saltonstall, minister of Haverhill.

Mr. Richard Saltonstall has the honor of being the

FIRST TO PROTEST AGAINST THE SLAVE TRADE;

and to use his influence to bring some gross offenders in this business to justice. The following are extracts from Savage's Winthrop, vol ii, p. 243-4 :

"Mr. James Smith, (who was a member of the Church of Boston,) with his mate, Thomas Keyser, were bound to Guinea to trade for negroes. But when they arrived there, they met with some Londoners, with whom they consorted, and the Londoners having been formerly injured by the natives, (or at least pretending the same,) they invited them aboard one of their ships upon the Lord's Day; and such as came they kept prisoners; then they landed men, and assaulted one of their towns, and killed many of the people; but the country coming down, they were forced to retire without any booty; divers of these men being wounded with the negroes arrows, and one killed.

* * For the matter of the negroes, whereof two were brought home in the ship, and near one hundred slain, by the confession of some of the mariners, the magistrates took order to have these two set at liberty, and to be sent home; but for the slaughter committed they were in great doubt what to do in it, seeing it was in another country, and the Londoners pretend a just revenge."

The following from the pen of Mr. Saltonstall, was written about October, 1645:

To the Honoured General Court:

The oath I took this yeare att my enterance vpon the place of assistants was to this effect: That I would truly endeavour the advancement of the gospell and the good of the people of this plantation, (to the best of my skill,) dispensing justice equally and impartially, (according to the laws of God and this land,) in all cases wherein I act by virtue of my place.

I conceive myselfe called by virtue of my place to act (according to this oath,) in the case concerning the Negérs taken by Captain Smith and Mr. Keser: wherein it is apparent that Mr. Keser upon a Sabboth day gave chase to certain Negers, and upon the same day tooke divers of them ; and at another time killed others ; and burned one of their townes.

Omitting several misdeminours which accompanied these acts above mentioned, I conceive the acts themselves to bee directly contrary to these following laws, (all which are capitall by the word of God ; and 2 of them by the laws of this jurisdiction.)

The act (or acts) of murder whether by force or fraude,) are expressly contrary both to the law of God and the law of this Country.

The act of stealing Negers, or taking them by force, (whether it be considered as theft or robbery,) is, as I believe, expressly contrary both to the law of God, and the law of this country.

The act of chaceing the Negers, (as afore sayde,) upon the Sabboth day, (being servile worke, and such as cannot be considered under any other heade,) is expressly capitall by the law of God.

These acts and outrages being committed where there was noe civill government which might call them to accompt, and the persons by whom they were committed being of our jurisdiction, I would conceive this Court to be the Ministers of God in this case ; and therefore my humble request is that the several offenders may be imprisoned by the order of this Court, and brought into their deserved censure in convenient time ; and this I humbly crave, that soe the sinn they have committed may be upon theire owne heads, and not upon ourselves, as otherwise it will.    Yrs in all Christian observance,

RICHARD SALTONSTALL."

"Upon a petition of Richard Saltonstall, Esq., for justice to be done on Captain Smith and Mr. Keyser, for their injurious dealing with the negroes at Guinea, the petition was granted, and ordered that Captain Smith and Mr. Keyser be laid hold on and committed to give answer in convenient time thereabouts."

The same year, 1645, he protests against the interference in the controversy between De la Tour and D'Aulney, the rival French claimants of the government of Nova Scotia. He writes these names, "Monsieur Delatore," and "Monsieur Dony."

In 1672 he gave £50 to Walley and Goffe, the Regicides.

[See Ancestry and Descendants of Sir Richard Saltonstall. Privately printed, 1897. Presented to Ipswich Public Library, by Richard M. Saltonstall, Esq.]

SARGENT, William. Was one of the twelve who, with John Winthrop the younger, in March, 1632, commenced the settlement of Agawam. He removed to Newbury, thence to Salisbury, later to Amesbury, where he died, 1670.

Andrew Sargent, was an inhabitant in 1685, when he was granted liberty to build a wharf.

He left a widow named Mary, who exhibited an inventory of his estate, amounting to £216, 4, March 31, 1691.

Administration is granted, May 10, 1691, to Andrew Dyamond.

SAUNDERS, John. Possessed a houselot in Mill St., between Mr. Sewall's house lot and Mr. Saltonstalls garden at the Mill, which he sold to William Fuller, 1635.

He possessed land in the Meadows, 1639.

He removed to Salisbury, of which he was one of the sixty-eight first inhabitants, 1640.

SAWYER, Samuel, hatter. Purchased of Theophilus and Elizabeth Wilson, Dec. 1, 1654, "a dwelling house and about one half an acre of land, which was the house of Jane Kenning, lately deceased, being near the Meeting-house, having John Knowlton southwest end of it; Goodman Pritchett northwest side; John Wyatt northeast end of it."

Mary Sayer, wife of Joseph, Esq'r, died 1738 :

> Here lyes the body of
> Mrs Mary Sayer wife
> to Joseph Sayer, Esq'r
> Died Sep ye 6 1738
> in the 32 year
> of her age

SCOT, Thomas.   Was a Commoner in 1641.

One of Denison's subscribers, 1648.

He took the freeman's oath at Boston, March 4, 1634-5.

He had a houselot on Mill street in 1635, adjoining Thomas French.

There was granted to him in 1639, "about one acre of ground for a houselot lying in the Lane called Bridge Lane, near the Meeting-house, having a houselot granted to Philip Fowler on the southeast, and a houselot formerly granted to Humphrey Bradstreet on the northeast."

In the grant to Philip Fowler, in 1636, the lot is described as being "in the Cross street called the Meeting-house lane."

Under the date of 1647, " Good man Scott's Lane" is mentioned.   The same is called Scott's Lane to this day.

Winthrop : One Scott and Eliot of Ipswich were lost in their way home, and wandered up and down six days, and eat nothing.   At length they were found by an Indian, being almost senseless for want of rest.

Thomas Scott's will is dated March 8, and was proved March 28, 1653-4.   He gives to his daughters Elisabeth, Abigail, Hannah, Mary, £25 each.   The same to his dau. Sarah, one half to be paid at her marriage, the other half when she is 21 years old.

He makes Thomas, his son, residuary legatee; and appoints his brother, Richard Kimball, Thomas Rowlinson, sen'r, and Edward Bridges, executors.

Estate consisted of house, barn and land, £129 ;

Cattle, £111 ;   Personal made the total, 318, 19, 11.

Thomas Scott 2, son of Thomas 1.   Subscriber towards Major Denison's allowance, 1648.

1649, September.   Joseph Fowler, Thomas Scott, John Kimball, Thomas Kimball, for their presentment had a legal admonition.

1650, 1st mo.   Thomas Scott fined unless he learn Mr. Norton's Catechism, by next Court.

7th mo. 1650.   Thomas Scott not appearing to make known that he hath learned Mr. Norton's Catechism, his fine is to be taken.

He died September 6, 1657. The following extract contains all that is further known of the family :

"1694, January 14. William Rogers, showeth : Thomas Scott, my grandfather, died in Ipswich about thirty-eight years ago, and made no will. Left my grandmother with only two children, viz., Margaret Scott my mother, and Thomas Scott.

My sd uncle Thomas Scott went into old England and died there."

1684, March. Thomas Patch and Abigail Bosworth petition Sept. 25, 1683, for ad'n of estate of their brother, Thomas Scott, dec'd.

SCOFIELD, Richard. Commoner, 1641.
Subscriber to Denison, 1648.

He purchased of Humphrey Griffin, Jan. 1641, a house and lot containing two acres, having Robert Andrews towards the east, a high way leading to the Meeting house towards the South, a house lot of Mr. Bartholmew towards the west, and a houselot of John Perkins the younger, and a piece of land of Thomas Boreman towards the north.

SEARLE, William. Was a carpenter, and worked on the Meeting-house, 1683. He had a share in Plum Island, &c., 1664.

He died August 16, 1667. By a noncupative will, proved September 24, 1667, he gave all his property to his wife.

He had a son William, born November 22, 1665.

Samuel Searle and Deborah his wife, had a son born October 15, 1685, who died December 22.

Deborah Searle died at Rowley, March 25, 1703.

SEWALL, Henry i.   Son of Henry, a linen draper, in the city of Coventry, in Great Britain ; out of dislike to the English hierarchy, sent over his only son Henry, to New England, in the year 1634, with net cattle and provisions suitable for a new plantation.  He settled in Newbury, according to Judge Samuel Sewall, his son ; whither, continues the Judge, "my grandfather soon followed him."  It is manifest that he resided a considerable time in Ipswich before he removed to Newbury.

In 1634, there was given and granted unto Mr. Henry Sewall forty acres lying next south of Spencer and Easton, with right of road through them."  These lots were on the south side of the river.

March, 1637-8, Samuel Symonds records his title to "a Town house and house lot containing by estimation three acres more or less.  Which houselot on the north side there off abutting on the Meeting house green ; upon the north east end there off it abutteth upon the house lot of William White ; upon the south east side thereoff it abuteth ypon Ipswich River and William Fuller's lot ; and upon the south west end thereoff it abutteth upon the highway leading to the Meeting-house, which houselot the Town of Ipswich, viz : the freemen thereoff, granted to Henry Sewall the elder : which he sold to Samuel Symonds, 6th day of 5th month, 1637."  This house stood near where the Female Academy now is.

Nov. 18, 1634.  About this time an open pinnace of one Mr. Sewall of Ipswich, going deep laden from Boston, was cast away upon the rocks at the head of Cape Ann in a northeast storm ; but all the men were saved.—Winthrop

January 5, 1634.  A well in question of difference between Mr. Henry Sewall and Mr. White was ended by Henry Short, Robert Mussey, John Perkins, John Gage, who were "a committee appointed for that end."

It would seem from the foregoing that Mr. Sewall the elder, must have resided in Ipswich nearly three years. He removed first to Newbury then to Rowley, where he died in March, 1656, aged eighty years.

Henry Sewall 2, son of Henry 1, was born about 1614. Came to New England in 1634; took the freeman's oath at Boston, May 17, 1637; probably resided first at Ipswich, afterwards at Newbury.

On the 25th of March, 1646, Richard Saltonstall, Esq., joined him in marriage with Jane Dummer, eldest child of Mr. Stephen and Mrs. Alice Dummer, then of Newbury.

The next winter, Henry and Jane, together with Mr. and Mrs. Dummer, returned to England, and resided in Warwick and Hampshire until 1659, when he came back to New England and settled at Newbury.

Henry Sewall died May 16, 1700. Jane Dummer Sewall his wife, died Jan. 13, 1701. Their children were :

Hannah, born at Tunworth, Eng. May 10, 1649,
married Jacob Tappan, Newbury,
died Nov. 12, 1699

Samuel, (the Judge,) born at Bishop Stoke,
March 28, 1652

John, born Oct. 10, 1654, died Aug. 8, 1699

Stephen, born Aug. 9, 1657, d. Oct. 17, 1725

Jane, born Oct. 25, 1659, m. Moses Gerrish Sept.
24, 1677, died January 29, 1717

Ann, first of the family born in New England
Sept. 3, 1662, married William Longfellow

Mehitable, born May 8, 1665, m. William
Moody, died Aug. 8, 1702.

Dorothy, born Oct. 29, 1668, m. Ezekiel Northend
of Rowley, Sept. 10, 1691

SHATSWELL, John.   Was a commoner, 1641.

He was a Deacon of the Church.

His will is dated Feb. 11, 1646, and was proved the ensuing 30 March.

He left wife Johan, who died April 17, 1673; and son Richard, who is mentioned as having an intention of marriage with Rebecca Tuttle.

He mentions a brother Theophilus Satchwell and sister Webster.

He possessed a planting lot on Town Hill, which he

sold before 1638, to John Baker.

He had granted in 1636, "about six acres of ground, upon part of which the said John Shatswell hath built an house, being between Mr. Wade's houselot on the east, and Mr. Firman's on the West, having Goodman Webster on the northeast." In 1634, there was given unto him "a portion of land lying next unto Henry Short northward, in sixty rod broad and unto the path leading toward Merrimac River, in equal length with Henry Short and others." A part of this grant has descended by inheritance to the present possessors.

Theophilus Shatswell, brother of John 1, was a soldier against the Indians, 1643. He subscribed towards Denison's allowance, 1648. He removed to Haverhill, and died, 1663.

Richard Shatswell 2, son of John 1, was a subscriber to Denison's compensation, 1648 ; had one and a half shares in Plum Island, &c., 1664. He died July 15, 1694. His wife was Rebecca Tuttle. Their children :

    Mary, died September, 1657
    Sarah, born August 19, 1658, m. Roger Ringe
    Richard, died January 28, 1662
    Johannah, also called Hannah, born Feb. 21, 1664
        died "an antient maid" Aug. 1720
    Richard, married Eleanor Cheney ; died 1698
    John, m. (1) Sarah Younglove; (2) Lydia

Richard Shattswell 3, Richard 2, left a will dated May 16, proved July 4, 1698. He bequeaths the use of his estate to his wife for the bringing up of his son Richard. He mentions his brother John and his sisters Hannah Shattswell and Sarah Rindge ; his wife's brothers, James Cheney and Joseph Cheney ; and his "beloved friends" William Baker and Kaleb Kimball.

John Shatswell 3, Richard 2, married June 20, 1684, Sarah Younglove; and had :

John, born 17 March, 1685, died April 31
John, born 3 April, 1688, died Feb. 6, 1694
He married (2) Lydia ———, and had :
John, born 25 October, 1701
Jonathan, born 14 July, 1704
John Shatswell had horses on the common, 1697 ; was a commoner, 1707.

Richard Shatswell 4, petitions the Town, March 3, 1723-4, setting forth that a highway was laid out to Green's Point Creek, in 1667, which took up about an acre of land, of his grandfather, Richard Shatswell.

SHERWIN, John. Married Frances Lomas, Nov. 25, 1667. They both joined with the Church in full communion, April 12, 1674. He had granted to him trees for fencing,—300 rayles,—January 13, 1667. Seat in the Meeting-house, 1700 ; commoner, 1707.

He married (2) Mary Chandler, Sept. 30, 1691, and he then had the designation of "sen'r." Children :
Mary, born August, 1679
Frances, born January 27, 1681
Sarah, born October 8, 1683
Alice, born February 3, 1693
Abigail, born May 4, 1695
Eleanor, born June 28, 1696
William, born June 27, 1698
Jacob, October 17, 1700

SKILTON, Benjamin and Susanna, had Elisabeth, born December 25, 1693.

SHORT, Henry. Had a sixty acre lot in 1634, "on the path leading towards the Merrimac." He took the freeman's oath at Boston, September 3, 1634 ; was elected Representative, March, 1635, but did not hold his seat.

He removed to Newbury, which he represented, in March, 1644.

Elisabeth Short, his wife, died March 22, 1647.
He married (2) Sarah Glover, October 9, 1648.
He died May 5, 1673.
His chlidren were Henry and Sarah.

Henry Short 2, died October 23, 1706.

May 23, 1677. This may signify to whom it may Concern, yt Mr. Richard Dummer & Mr. Henry Shorte are members in full communion wth ye Churche of Newbury: as affirms                    Jno : Richardson, Minister.

SHERRATT, Hugh. Took the freeman's oath at Boston, March 4, 1634-5.

1635. He possessed a houselot, having a houselot of John Covington southeast ; William Fuller southwest.

He possessed an acre of land near High street, Feb. 15, 1638.

He removed to Haverhill, where he died, Sept. 5, 1678, aged One Hundred Years.

SMITH. Richard Smith 1, and Thomas Smith 1, were commoners, 1641.

George Smith I, and Robert Smith 1, were subscribers to Major Denison's allowance, 1648.

[The records of the Smiths, and several other families, as gathered from the Ipswich books, will be printed in a few weeks, giving dates to 1800, and later.]

Richard Smith I, came from Shropham, Co. Norfolk, England. His children were :

Richard, born 1642, m. Hannah Cheney, Newbury

Elisabeth, m. Edward Gilman of Exeter

Mary, m. (1) Philip Call ; (2) John Burr ; (3) Henry Bennett. She died in Ipswich, Jan. 12, 1707-8

Martha, m. Mr. John Rogers, farmer.

Richard Smith was born about 1629. He died in Ipswich, 1714 :

Here lyes ye Body
of Mr. Richard
Smith * aged 85
Years * died
Sept. the 24 1714

Richard Smith 2, was a voter in town affairs in 1679. He had horses on the common, 1697, and with the title of Mr. had a place on the second seat in the Meeting-house assigned to him in 1700. He subscribed six shillings towards the bell in 1699.

Richard Smith 2, married Hannah Cheney of Newbury, in November, 1660, when he was about nineteen years old. The names of nine children can be gleaned from records and references :

Richard, died July 22, 1700 ; left a widow who married ——— Wood.

Daniel, died June 8, 1725, aged eighty-two years ; he was published with Elisabeth Payne, May 10, 1700 ; he m. (2) Deborah Wicom, Rowley.

Nathaniel, married Elisabeth Fuller.

John married Mercy Adams, Dec. 4, 1702 ; died at the early age of thirty-six years. [See epitaph.]

Joseph, born July, 1685, m. Joanna Fellows, 1710.

Hannah, m. ——— Chadwell, lived in Lynn ; her three daughters are mentioned in a will : Margaret, Eunice, Mary.

Martha, married Jacob Boardman.

Dorothy, m. Robert Rogers, December 4, 1702.

Elisabeth, died 1747 ; unmarried.

The epitaph of John Smith 3, son of Richard 2 :

> Here lyes ye body of John
> Smith son of Mr. Rich-
> ard Smith who died
> May ye 2oh æ tates 36

> For this departed soul and all ye rest
> that christ has purchased they shall be blest

> those must transgress
> the rules of charity
> who do object
> or in the least deny
> that this immortal soul
> is now conveyed
> to heavens glory
> by the Angels aid

Thomas Smith 1. Had a share in Plum Island, 1664. He died in 1666.

Granted to Thomas Smith a house lot one acre, on the street called West End, having a house lot granted to John Cooley, south east ; common near the common fence gate north west. 9th 2 mo, 1639.

George Smith and Mary (French) Smith, his wife, 1648.
1648. One of Denison's subscribers.
1664. Share in Plum Island, &c.
His will is dated August 13, 1674, proved March 30,
1675. Children :

Samuel, born 1647, married Martha Smith, Nov. 13,
1678, died May 31, 1727, aged eighty years.
Elisabeth, married (the same day as Samuel) to John
Smith, Nov. 13, 1678.
Thomas, married Joanna Smith October 25, 1671.
Mary, married (the same day) Obadiah Bridges,
'October 25, 1671
Sarah, married John Newman, Nov. 9, 1664.
Rebeccca, married John Chapman, Sept. 30, 1675.
Joanna, born April 14, 1660, married John Yell,
July 27, 1690.

Samuel Smith 2, George 1. Horses on the common, 1678
Had seats appointed to him in the Meeting house, 1700,
and 1702. He subscribed three shillings towards the bell,
1699. Married Martha Smith, Nov. 13, 1678. He m. (2)
Widow Priscilla Gould, of Topsfield; she died Oct. 16,
1732, aged eighty-six. He died May 31, 1727, aged
eighty years. Children :

Mary, born August 24, 1679
Samuel, born Sept. 28, 1680, died April 20, 1744
Mary, born Oct. 26, 1684, m. Wm. Manning, 1702
George, born Sept. 20, 1687
John, married Meriah Emins
Sarah, born Nov. 23, 1690, m. Joseph Goodhue
Elisabeth, born Nov. 20, 1692

Robert Smith 1. Is mentioned in 1648.
He had Mary, born Oct. 28, 1658.
He died 1674.

John Smith 1, as tenant of Mr. Appleton, had a share in
Plum Island, &c., 1664. He was a commoner in 1707.
His son John was one of the eight of the young generation
who took the covenant, in the church, 1673, and his dau.
Elisabeth took the covenant April 12, 1674. Children :

John, born October 29, 1654
  married Elisabeth, dau. Geo. Smith
Elisabeth, m. William Chapman, March 30, 1682
William, born April 28, 1659; Narraganset Ex.
  1676; Topsfield, 1675.
Thomas, born June 7, 1661
Moriah, born February 28, 1664
Ruth born October 6, 1666
Mary and Prudence, twins, born June 11, 1670
Mary, spinster, died June 24, 1739

Thomas Smith and Esther,—children :
Thomas, born 1677
George, born March 29, 1683, m. Abigail Kirke
Joseph, born Sept. 21, 1685, m. Elisabeth Moses
Benjamin,
Mary, born 1687, m. —————— Kimball
Anthony, m. (1) Elisabeth Damarell, (2) Margaret
  Harris.  He died October 14, 1732, aged 42 ;
  Margaret died December, 1744

Thomas Smith and wife Mary, had :
Sarah, born December, 1685

Thomas Smith and wife Martha, had ;
Thomas, born January 24, 1688
Ebenezer, born July 31, 1680, wife Mary
Ephraim, born August 12, 1692, died Sept. 1720
Mary, Sept. 10, 1694

Jacob (son of John and Elisabeth) and his wife Lydia :
                In Memory of
                Mr. Jacob Smith
                who died March 4th
                1789, Aged 92 years
                Also Mrs. Lydia his Wife
                who died March 17th
                1772 aged 76 years
        Happy exchange to part with all
                            (below
        For worlds of bliss where joy's
                            (unceasing flow

Prudence Smith, daughter of Samuel Howard, and wife of Stephen Smith, died July 14, 1721.

Stephen Smith in 1751 is designated as tailor.

Elisabeth Smith, wife of Corp'l Joseph, d. May 7 1725.

Thomas Smith, Innholder, and son of Robert Smith of Boxford, died February 25, 1725.

William Smith, voter in Town affairs, 1679.

Mr. Ralph Smith occupied a piece of land belonging to Thomas Betham near ye meeting house green, March 10, 1652.

The epitaph of Elisabeth Payne Smith (see page 334 :)

Here Lies the body of Mrs.
Elisebeth Smith, the wife
of Mr. Daniel Smith who
Deceased May the 14
1717 in the 40 year of
her age. They that dye
in the Lord are blest
From all there sorrows
They do rest & are of
Endless Joys possest.

An early Smith grave has the infant history :

Gilburt Smi
th son of
Ebenezer
& Mary
Smith died
April ye 9th
1716, aged
28 days

Philip Fowler, appointed administrator of the estate of Thomas Smith, blacksmith, April 8, 1706, and on the 27th of the same month was appointed guardian of Richard Smith, son of Richard, dec'd.

1681, 5, 10. Agreed with Richard Kimball of Bradford for his keeping and providing for his grandfather, Thomas Smith, for the year ensuing, thirteen pounds.—T. R.

SNELLING, Jeffrey.    Possessed a house in Brook street, 1655.

SPENCER, Mr. John.    Took the freeman's oath at Boston, Sept. 3, 1634.    He received a grant of 20 acres of land in 1634; and another lot of six acres, with other grants, all of which he relinquished and removed to Newbury.  He represented Ipswich, 1635; Newbury, 1636; returned to England, 1638 ; died, 1648.

SPARK, John.    As tenant of Thomas Bishop, he has a share in Plum Island, 1664.

Mr. Spark has horses on the Common, 1697.

John Spark had :

Margaret, born March 2, 1670
Rose, born April 18, 1673
Sarah, born February 17, 1675
John, born September 15, 1678

Sarah Spark has a seat in the Meeting-house, 1702.

John Brown app'd adm'r of estate of Thomas Sparke, January 18, 1700-1.

1671, June 8.    The Town allow John Sparke to draw beer at 1d a quart, if he entertain no inhabitants in the night, nor suffer any person to bring drink in his house, or wine.

The house where he kept was near the site of the Female Academy ; and was, in 1693, kept by John Rogers, sadler, and had "the sign of the Black Hor ;e."

1680, March.    By desire of the Select men, of Ipswich, that John Spark, his license for an ordinary be enlarged— for retailing wine.

1692, March.    Mr. John Spark, his license renewed, provided he pay his excise duely as the law requires.

1712.    The will of Mary Spark, dated December 9, 1711, and proved July 26, 1712.  She bequeaths to her daughters Susannah Annable and Sarah Newman, twenty shillings, "when it shall be due, given by my brother, John Rooper.'  " My son Thomas Newman and my danghter Rose Newman with whom I now live."

STANIFORD, John. Married Margaret Harris, (born August 6, 1657,) daughter of Thomas and Martha Harris, and had :

    John, eldest son, born October 21, 1678

    Thomas, born Nov. 21, 1680

    William, born April 6, 1685

    Ebenezer, born June 27, 1686, died early

    Samuel, baptized August 27, 1688

    Tryphena, baptized March 21, 1690, married
          Philip, son of Nathaniel Lord

    Jeremiah, baptized Sept. 1, 1693

    Margaret, born November 29, 1695, died Oct.
        7, 1727 : married Robert Calef

John Staniford, Ipswich, 18 Dec. 1692, bo't of John Honewell, Conecticot, a prcell of land at Winter Harbor, Mayne, called Honewell's Neck, forty acres more or less. Dillingham Caldwell, Caleb Stevens, witnesses.

John Staniford was born about 1648, and died :

    Here lyes buried
    ye body of Deacon
    John Staniford
    aged 82 years
    Decd May ye 27
    1730

His wife, Margaret (Harris) Staniford, born August 6, 1657, died Feb. 25, 1752, aged ninety-five years.

Deacon John Staniford by his will made March 10, 1726-7, gives to Margaret, his wife, all his estate real and personal, to enjoy the "use and improvement during her natural life."

"Whereas a considerable part of my estate is out in debts, and being uncertain what may be recovered, my will is that my executors, hereafter named, do annually give an account thereof to their mother, during her life."

He directs that after the decease of his wife, his property be divided thus: "I give and bequeath unto my eldest son Jno : a double portion aboue ye rest of his brethren and sisters, to him and his heirs." All the rest he directs to be equally divided among Thomas, William, Samuel, Jeremiah, Tryphena Lord.

He adds : " Whereas it hath pleased God to take to himself that mirrour of filial love and duty, my daughter Margaret, who hath left two children, my will is, that if what I have given upon marriage doth not amount in value to ye rest of my children, that her two children shall have one part."

" Whereas I have bestowed ye bringing up of my grand-child, Benjamin, ye son of my son William," nothing is to be deducted from William's portion on that account.

He appoints John, sole executor. The witnesses were John Harris, William Harris, Jun'r., Hannah Newman.

Widow Margaret Staniford survived her husband 20 yrs. After her decease, February 25, 1752, the heirs enter into an agreement for the distribution of the property.

The names and additions of the heirs were as follows :

John Staniford, Gent. of Boston ;
William, Gent. of Hampton ;
Thomas, Gent., Daniel, Gent., Jeremiah, mariner, of Ipswich ;
Children of Thomas, of Ipswich, Gent., deceased, and Hannah his wife ;
Samuel, cordwainer, Philip Lord, Gent., and Tryphena his wife ; John Calef, Physician, all of Ipswich.

Doctor Calef was Margaret's son.

The mansion house and lot were assigned to John of Boston and William of Hampton. It was bounded south by the highway, west by Samuel Baker, northeast by Brook street and Abraham Caldwell's.

He was a Deacon of the First Church; and in 1697 is entitled "Mr."

In the Meeting-house built 1699, there is assigned to Mr John Staniford and Marshall Harris, the two last pews, next Mr. Wardwell. Marsh' Harris having taken up one half of ye upper pew, Mr. Staniford hath liberty to take his whole share in ye middle, till further order. Marshall

Harris is " John Harris, under Sheriff," brother to Mar
garet, Dea. Stanifords wife :

> Here lyeth ye body
> of Mr. John Harris
> Under Sheriff
> who died Sept ye 15
> 1714, d in ye 64
> Year of his age

Rebecca Symonds, relict of the Hon. Samuel Symonds,
in her will, August 19, 1695, bequeaths "to my cousin
John Staniford, a gold ring and three pounds in money."

John Staniford 2, son of John 1 ; wife Mary ; he died
March 4, 1752.

Thomas Staniford 2, son of John 1 ; has the title of
Ensign, 1727 ; his intention of marriage with Hannah
Rindge, daughter of Daniel Rindge, was published Dec.
27, 1707. They had :

> John, born April, 1709 ; his tombstone says : John
> Stanford, son to Mr. Thomas & Mrs. Han-
> nah Stanford, aged 18 years & 2 Mo Decd
> June ye 29, 1727
> Thomas, born 1710
> Daniel, baptized March 17, 1717
> Jeremiah

> Here lyes buried
> the body ot
> Mr. Thomas Staniford
> who departed this life
> Augt ye 23d 1740 in the 60
> year of his age

Daniel Staniford 3, son of Thomas 2, John 1, was graduated at Harvard College, 1738. He was Master of the
Grammar School, 1740-46, seven years. He then became
a merchant, and was Representative of the Town, 1755-6-7.
He married Mary Burnham, who survived him, and married Rev'd Nathaniel Rogers, May 4, 1759, and died 1780.
His children were :

Daniel, H. C. 1772

Mary, born Jan. 1744-5, m. Rev. Joseph Dana, (see
    epitaph)

Hannah, married Thomas Dodge, Esq.,

Margaret, married Dr. Josiah Smith, Newburyport,
    February 9, 1779

Sarah, married the Hon. and Col. John Heard

Abigail, married Doct. Joshua Fisher

Martha, unm; her home was in the family of Col.
    John Heard

The tombstone of Mary Staniford Dana :

Here lie the remains of
Mrs. Mary Dana, Consort of
the Rev. Mr. Joseph Dana,
the eldest daughter of ye late
Mr. Daniel Staniford.
She departed this life
May the 14, 1772
Aged 27 years & 4 Months

Samuel Staniford 2, son of John 1, published with Mary
Chadwell, August 15, 1715.

Walter Staniford and widow Sarah Whipple, published
intentions of marriage April 14, 1711.

Capt. Thomas Staniford 3, son of Thomas 2, married
Sarah Burnham, December 28, 1732. They had :

John,     Thomas,     James.

The parents died 1778 :

In Memory of
Capt. Thomas Staniford &
Mrs. Sarah Staniford his
Consort : who lived esteemed
died lamented, and in their
death were but a short time
divided. He departed Aug
13th, A. D. 1778, Æ 68. She five
weeks after, Sep'r 18th, Æ 63.

STACYE, Stace, Stacey,—Simon. Was a commoner in 1641. He died before 1649. We find [under date of "Feb. 22, 1649, granted unto Widow Stace, one half of a parcel of meadow lying by Mr. Saltonstall's farm."

The will of Elizabeth Stace, probably the above named widow, was proved March 29, 1670, as "rec'd from her own mouth," by Simon Stace, Sarah Stace, Ann Stace.

She directs her body to be buryed in Ipswich burying place; and gives her son Simon "a bullock for the burial of me." She gives her son Thomas a great Bible and a damask napkin. She bequeaths legacies to her daughters Sarah Buswell, Susannah French, and daughter Meoers. " To my daughter Ann, in consideration of her staying with me in my old age, all my other household stuff."

Thomas Stace 2, son of Simon 1, married Susanna, dau. of the Rev. William Worcester of Salisbury. He was a subscriber to the Cart Bridge in 1646; and to Maj. Denison's allowance, 1648. He came into full communion with the church, March 1, 1673-4. His will is dated Feb. 9, 1698-9, in which he mentions his wife Susannah. His children :

Thomas
William
Elisabeth, born April 16, 1659
Joseph, born June 27, 1660
Mary, born November 7, 1661
Simon, born December 25, 1664,
John, born March 16, 1666
Susannah, born January 16, 1668
Sarah, born December, 1670
Nimphas, born May, 1673
Rebecca, married James Burley, May 25, 1685

Thomas Stace 2, died about November, 1690

Simon Stace 2, son of Simon 1, was born about 1636. He was freeman, April 29, 1668.
Selectman, 1675-80.
He married Sarah Wallis, April 19, 1659. She was the daughter of Robert Wallis. She died November 21, 1711,

aged seventy-four years. In 1699, she subscribed six shillings towards the new bell.

Simon Stace is designated as Ensign, in 1684; and Lieut. in 1696; and Capt. in 1699.

In 1679 he was a Tythingman. In 1695 he was one of a Committee to consider the proper and suitable dimensions of a new Meeting-house, and of the most easy way to make payment of the same.

He was Representative 1685-86, 1689-90.

It does not appear that he left any children. The tombstones of himself and wife are inscribed :

Here lyes buried
ye body of Capt.
Simon Stace
aged about 63 years
Dec'd Oœober ye
27 * 1699

Here lyes ye body
of Mrs. Sarah Stace
wife of Capt. Simon
Stace who died ye
21 of November, 1711
aged 74 years

The will of Simon Stace is dated October 20, 1699. He bequeathed all his estate to his wife during her widowhood, and in case she see cause to marry, sixty pounds in money, and twenty pounds in household stuff, and silver tankard.

"If it so happen that my sd wife die in widowhood, I give unto my sd wife ye sums and sd Tankard and household stuff, to be disposed of at her death."

He gives in reversion, to his cousin Simon Adams, house and land I bought of John Pingree.

To Simon Adams, eldest son of sd Simon, five acres of land lying in reedy marsh.

To Josiah Perry and George Frink forty shillings each.

To my servants Symon Eams five pounds; Deliverance Doak four pounds; when their apprenticeship has expired, if they demean themselves dutyfully towards my wife.

He gives all the rest of his estate, after the decease of his wife, to be divided equally to Thomas Stacy, William Stacy, John Stacy, Elisabeth Woodwell, Mary Conner, Susannah Martin, Samuel Mears, Elizabeth Adams, Simon French, Ann Mudgett, John Adams brother to Simon Adams.

He appointed his wife Sarah, and good friends Cornett John Whipple, William Baker, John Staniford, his ex's.

After the decease of his widow, March 21, 1711-12, the estate was divided into twelve lotts, and drawn by ye legal heirs of Capt. Simon Stace, as given in his will.

A silver cup belonging to the communion service of the First Church, has this inscription: "Ex Dono Capt. Simon Stace, to the Church of Ipswich, 1697."

The estate of Simon 2, was appraised at £722, 4, 4d.

The will of Sarah Stace, widow of Simon, is dated April 1, 1710. She bequeaths her property to her cousins, Saml Wallis, Robert Wallis, Sarah Perkins, Samuel Wallis, Jr. son of Samuel.

Ann Stace, daughter of Simon 1 and Elisabeth Stace, left a will dated Feb. 13, 1681-2. She died Feb. 21. In it she mentions her brother Simon, sisters Sarah Burrell, Susan French, Mary Fitch; cousins Simon Adams, Rebecca Stace, Ann French, Elisabeth Mears, Wm. Adams.

John Stace 3, son of Thomas 2, left a wife named Eleanor and an estate of £144, 9, 5, the inventory of which was rendered Feb. 28, 1671.

Samuel Stace 3, and Margaret his wife, lost a son :

Here lies
William Stacy
ye son of
Mr. Samuel & Mrs.
Margaret Stacy
who died the
29th March,
1726

Samuel was a clothier ; had a lot granted him by the town, March 7, 1726, near the Mill : Beginning at an Elm tree nigh the highway, and so by the high way on a straight line forty-eight feet to Mr. Farley's warehouse, then twenty one feet by said house to a stake at the lower corner of said ware house, then on a straight line fifty feet to a stake nigh the great rock, then nine feet to the Elm tree first mentioned.

Thomas Stacy 3, son of Thomas 2, with his wife and nine children removed to Salem, where they were received by the First Church, April 20, 1676. In his will dated Feb. 9, 1689-90, proved November 25, he mentions a farm in Ipswich, worth £200. He left a wife, Susannah, and children : Thomas, William, Joseph, Simon, John, Elisabeth, Mary, Susannah.

He was a miller.

SHERMAN, Samuel. June, 1636, Samuel Shoreman is possessed of one hundred acres of land, lying from the town to the north beyond a small River commonly called Egypt river.

He was disarmed November 20, for favoring Mrs. Hutchinson's views.

Granted to Thomas Shareman four acres, further end of common next Egypt river, January 4, 1678.

Thomas Sherman received a wound in the neck, in a battle with the Pequod Indians, July, 1637.

STEWART, William. A merchant, died Aug. 3, 1693.

> Here lyeth ye body
> of William Stewart
> aged about 44 years
> dyed August ye 3, 1693

He left a widow, Ann Stewart, and one child, Margaret, ten years old. His house and land were valued at £300. His whole estate £1447, 6, 4d. A silver cup belonging to the communion service of the First Church has this inscription ; " Mr. William Stewart's Gift to ye Church of Ipswich, June, 1693."

Widow Ann Stewart married Col. Bartholmew Gedney

of Salem ; and on a visit to Ipswich, died October 15, 1697. [See page 118.]

Duncan Stuart, had Katherine, born June 8, 1658.

SPILLER, Henry, and wife Sarah : had
    John, born May 3, 1693.
Sarah Spiller, wife of John, died Sept. 12, 1723.

STARKWEATHER, John, wife Ann ; had
    John, born Sept. 16, 1680
    Robert, born Novem 12, 1684
As tenant of John Appleton, he had rights of commonage, 1678.

1673. Nov : Robert Starkweather desired to have liberty to hold the house of Tho : Perrin & little neck for seven years. Granted.

March. Agreed with Robert Starkweather to keep ye sheep at ye neck.

1688. John Starkweather app'd keeper ot the Pound.

1673. Nov. Edward Bragg, bound to keep the town from any charge by his entertaining Robert Starkweather and his family.

1664. Aaron Pingry's will : " Fifty shillings, unto my wife, her son Jno : Starkweather.

STEVENS, Edward, and wife Martha, had
    Samuel, born May 17, 1688
    Thomas, born August 31, 1690
    Edward, born March 2, 1692
1706, April 12. Grace Stevens of Ipswich, Relict Widow of Caleb Stevens of Ipswich, deceased, and former widow of Samuel Moses.

STONE, Nathaniel. Subscribed four shillings to Maj. Denison, 1648.

With Elisabeth his wife, sells to Joseph Jewett of Rowley, June 12, 1656, a house and land, having the house and land of Henry Archer towards the northwest ; the street north east ; John Woodam, south east ; Henry Pindar south west.

Thomas Knowlton and Susanna his wife, February 26, 1655, sell to Sarah Stone wife of Dea. Simon Stone of Watertown, land lying in a flat or field called pequitt Lotts, having Sargeant French's on the west, William Pritchett east, the town river south, the town common north.

In 1660, June 20, the same Sarah sold to Daniel Hovey, with consent of husband, seventy acres in Topsfield, being the land that Townsmen of Ipswich did grant unto Richard Lumpkin, at that place called pye-brook. See Lumpkin, Richard.

William and Ester Stone had William born September 13, 1699.

Robert and Sarah Stone of Ipswich and Salem. Three sons: Robert, Benjamin, Samuel.

Robert Stone married Hannah Eager in 1685, and were both dead 1689, leaving two babes: Elisabeth and Robert. Benjamin Stone, brother of Robert, died about 1704.

Samuel Stone was in Salem in 1692, and had: Samuel, Robert, Elizabeth, Katherine, Mary.

May 29, 1693, Phebe Stone married Daniel Larcom.

1734. Benjamin Stone was at the Hamlet, and his wife died there, January, 1738.

### Additional.
## THE STONE FAMILY, IPSWICH.
#### Augustin Caldwell

William Stone married (1) Esther Cross, widow, pub. October 22, 1698.

He married (2) Elizabeth Bulley, pub. April 19, 1718. William and Esther had:

William, born September 13, 1699.

William 2, son of William 1, married Elizabeth Downs, pub. June 11, 1717. He died, September 25, 1746; she died December 14, 1752.

Their children were:

John, born October 26, 1718
William, born Aug. 6, 1719, m. Abigail Hodgkins
Elizabeth, bap. September 18, 1720, died early
Samuel, born December, 1721, m. Elizabeth Bergen
Esther, bap. Sept. 20, 1724, m. Benja. Brown, 1748
Mary, bap. March 14, 1725, m. —— Severance, 1745
Sarah, married William Dean, 1748
Anna, baptized September 3, 1727
John, baptized May 12, 1728
Edward, bap. July 4, 1731,
    m. (1) Lucy Hodgkins, Feb. 16, 1754
    m. (2) Hannah Lampson, 1778
James, bap. July 21, 1734
Elizabeth, born 1737

William Stone 3, (William 2, William 1,) m. Abigail
Hodgkins, published October 30, 1741. Children:
Daniel and Samuel, twins, born 1744: Samuel mar-
    ried (1) Esther Perkins, 1767; (2), Eliza'h
    Hodgkins, 1785. He died Dec. 18, 1834.
    She died Nov. 18, 1834, aged 86 years.
Abigail, born 1746, died 1788
Elizabeth, born 1747, married Joseph Wise
Esther, baptized November 24, 1751
Mary, baptized August 4, 1754
Hannah, married Job Smith, 1788
Sarah, married Abram Patch, 1789
Dorcas, married William Smith, 1796

Samuel Stone 3, (William 2, William 1,) married Eliz'h
Bergen, published November 10, 1744. Children:
Elizabeth, born 1742, married Nath'l Treadwell
Samuel, born 1747, William, born 1750, both d. e.
William, bap. Sept. 22, 1751, m. Sarah Mansfield
Susannah, born 1757, married Benjamin Kimball
Robert Bergen, born 1759; Patience, born 1752
Esther, born 1764, m. William Cressey, Jun'r
Lucy, m. Winthrop Runnels, Lee, N. H., 1783
Samuel, born Sept 5, 1768, m. Abigail Spiller, 1792

William Stone 4, (Samuel 3, William 2, William 1,) married Sarah Mansfield, 1774. She died Dec. 3, 1832, aged seventy-seven years.

He was a Soldier of the Revolution, and was killed by the explosion of the magazine during the engagement of the Wasp and Frolic.

The children of William and Sarah :
  Robert, married Mary Harris
  William, born Jan. 26, 1778, m. Polly Hovey

William Stone 6, (William 4, Samuel 3, William 2, William 1,) married Polly Hovey, September 12, 1801. Their children :
  William, married Mary L. Lord, 1831
  Mary J. married Amos Dixon, 1831
  Elizabeth P. married Isaac D. Buzzel, 1831
  Almira, married Perley Scott, 1839
  John B. married (1) Sarah Stanly, 1847
              (2) Sophronia A. Burnham (3) Mary Pace
  Caroline, married John Gilbert

Robert Stone 5, (William 4, Samuel 3, William 2, William 1,) m. Mary Harris, March 13, 1796, and had :
  Robert, born 1797, died 1825, aged 28 years.
  Mary, born Aug. 23, 1798, m. John Raines 1815

Robert Stone 6, (Robert 5, William 4, Samuel 3, William 2, William 1,) married (1) Anna Hodgkins, 1818; she died February 8, 1820, aged twenty years. He m. (2) Hannah Shatswell, 1821. He died April 7, 1825, aged 28. He had :
  Robert Stone, born November 23, 1823

Others of the name on the Ipswich Records :
Josiah Stone and Dorothy Fuller, pub. July, 1715
Benjamin Stone, at the Hamlet, and Elizabeth Annable, pub. October, 1721 ; she died January, 1738.
  He m. Mary Edwards, Wenham, pub. Nov. 1739.
  Remember Stone and Benj. Allen, married 1725, both of Beverly.

David Stone and Elisabeth Corning, m. 1726, Beverly.
Mary Stone and Nathan Jackson, m. 1726.
Susannah Stone and John Barrow, m. 1733.
Dorothy Stone of Gloucester and Thomas Varney of
Ipswich, married 1751.
Martha Stone and Ambrose Dodge, married 1762.
Benjamin Stone and Lucy Roberts, m. Jan. 25, 1766.
Hannah Stone and Edmund Potter, of Sutton, married
July 28, 1770.
Elizabeth B. Stone and Simon Kinsman, m. 1829.
Widow Susannah Stone died May 8, 1800.

———o———

STOCKWELL, William.   Had a seat in the Meeting-
house in 1700.   Married Sarah Lambert, April 14, 1685.

STINSON, Stimson, George and Alice his wife, had :
   George, born June 10, died July, 1677
   Richard, born March 10, 1678
   Elizabeth, born January 1, 1680
   Allis, born February 18, 1684
   Sarah, born June 14, 1691
   George, born August 27, 1693
   Mary, born March 24, 1695

STORY, William.   Was a subscriber to Major Denison
1648.   Had a share and a half in Plum Island, 1664.
   In 1679 he was a voter in Town affairs, with the addition
of "senior."
   Mary Story, his daughter, joined the Church by taking
the Covenant, April 12, 1674.
   He sold a lot of land to William Knowlton, previous to
February 12, 1643.
   He purchased, Jan. 1, 1655, of William Symonds, Gent.
and John West, yeoman, two lots of land, adjoining other
land which he had bought of Robert Kinsman, seven acres
of which was granted by the town of Ipswich to John
Wedgewood.
   He was Surveyor of Highways, 1662.   He then had the
addition of "carpenter."

He possessed lands in Chebacco, Nov. 10, 1652, adjoining on the northwest, land of John Webster.

He purchased, May 8, 1649, of Henry Archer and Elisabeth his wife, a farm of ninety acres, granted unto Archer by the Town of Ipswich, beyond Chebacco Falls.

He had permission to have a Mill, 1671, Chebacco river.

In February, 1672, Abr'hm Perkins complained against William Story, sen'r, for taking of a load of green timber about Dec'r last; oke timber, which he drew over my farme of the south side Chebacco river; either off the commons or my farme.

Andrew Story. 1638. Granted to Andrew Story five acres planting ground upon Sagamore Hill.

1639. Andrew Story had two acres of land granted to him in consideration of his services as one of the Pequit soldiers.

[Additions.] William Story, carpenter; came 1637, from Norwich, Norfolk co.; servant of Samuel Dix. Embarked April 8, 1637; 23 years old. His children:

William, m. Susannah Fuller, October 25, 1671
Mary
Hannah
Seth, deacon, born 1646, died Oct. 9, 1732, aged 86.

Dea. Seth Story 2, died October 9, 1732, aged 86 years. With wife Elizabeth he had:

Zechariah, born March 14, 1684
        pub. Rachel Andrews, July 14, 1714
Sarah, married ——— Jewett
Elizabeth, married ——— Andrews
Martha, born Sept. 28, 1691
        pub. Thomas Butler, 16 January, 1719
Seth, born April 14, 1694, m. Martha Low, d. 1786
Damaris, born January 26, 1696
        pub. Joseph Martin, March 17, 1722

Dea. Zechariah Story 3, (Dea. Seth 2, William 1) and Rachel Andrews, pub. May 4, 1714 ; he died February 16, 1774, aged ninety years.    Their children :

Jeremy, born May 21, 1715
>pub. Margaret Harris, May 20, 1737
Lucy, born Jan. 5, 1716 m. Wm. Butler, Apr 7, 1737
Rachel, born March 13, 1718,
>pub. Joseph Goodhue, March 20, 1740
Nehemiah, born Sept. 29, 1720, pub. Sarah Gould
>Nov. 7, 1741, died July 4, 1802, aged 81.
Deborah, born August 6, 1723 ; pub. Wesley Burnham, August 20, 1743 ; she died Nov. 24, 1821, aged 98 years; he died June 28, 1797, aged 78 years
Isaac, b. Jan. 23, 1724, m. Deborah Foster,Mch 14, 1761
Nathan, b. April 21, 1727 ;
Jesse, b. Mch 12, 1730, m. Ruhami Burnham, 1753
>Their son Jesse killed at Bunker Hill
Jerusha, born Sept. 29, 1732, m. Caleb Norwood, 1770
Lois, born March 11, 1734
>married Francis Poole, October 19, 1752

Seth Story 3, (Dea. Seth 2, William 1,) married Martha Low ; pub. Nov. 30, 1717 ; he died August 11, 1786, aged ninety-three years.    Their children :

Elizabeth, born March 3, 1718, m. Jacob Perkins
Amos, born Nov. 16, 1720 ; in French War, 1755
Martha, born Dec. 16, 1721 ; m. Samuel Burnham 1743
Johannah, b. Oct. 13, 1723, m. Jacob Goodhue, 1744
Sarah, b. Sept. 28, 1725, m. Joshua Martin, 1744
Anna, born September 1, 1727
Lydia, b. Mch 18, 1728-9; m. Nath'l Lufkin, 1783
John, m. Hannah Perkins, 1760
Ebenezer, died October, 1803

STANWOOD, Philip.    Jane Stainwood, now Jane Pearce, made report Sept. 30, 1673, of administration on the estate of her late husband, Philip Stainwood.

The two eldest sons, Philip and John, were to take the

land, and pay the other children five pounds a piece, as they come of age.

[See History of the Stanwood Family, in America. By Ethel Stanwood Bolton: 1899.]

SUTTON, Richard, of Roxbury, husbandman, bought land in Andover of Simon Bradstreet, March 10, 1658.

At the Court held at Salem, March, 1666, he is "bound to good behavior."

He was a field-driver, 1698-9.

With Susannah, his wife he had :

Richard, born February 9, 1697
William, born April 5, 1699

William Sutton 2, son of Richard 1, was published with Susanna Kimball, Jan. 8, 1725. She was a widow 1746.

They had : Ebenezer, bap. Dec. 25, 1728.

Ebenezer Sutton 3, (William 2, Richard 1,) was published with Katherine Low, November 23, 1754.

William Sutton was surveyor of highways, 1730.

In the High street burying ground are two memorials of later dates :

Sacred
To the Memory of
Mr. Richard Sutton
who died
Dec. 12, 1825
aged 89 years.

In Memory of
Mrs. Elisabeth Sutton
wife of Mr. Richard
Sutton, who died
Oct'r 29, 1806
Æt 69

My Children and friends when
This you see remember me.

SYMONDS. Births of the children of Samuel and Dorothy Symonds, copied fram the Register of the Parish of Toppesfield, Co. Essex, England : copied by T. Cleavland :

Anne, born April 25, 1622
Margaret
Samuel, born October 29, 1623
Elizabeth, born December 22, 1624
Samuel, born January 3, 1625
Samuel, born April 17, 1627
John, born July 15, 1628
Robert, born August 13, 1629
William, born June 22, 1632
Roger, born December 5, 1633

SAMUEL SYMONDS, was among the most distinguished of the First Settlers of Ipswich.

He was descended from an ancient and honourable family in Yieldham, Essex, where he had good estate.

He was born in 1595. He married (1) Dorothea Harlackenden in 1620. The children he brought with him to New England :

William,
Harlackenden,
Samuel,
Dorothea and Elisabeth

His second wife was Martha Eppes, widow ; daughter Edmund ' Reade, of Wicksford, Kent ; married 1659.— Their children were :

Martha,
Ruth, married John Emerson
Priscilla, married Baker
Samuel, (probably)

Mr. Symonds married for his third wife, Rebekah Swayne. He was her fourth husband, and she outlived him. She died July 21, 1695, aged 78.

Mr. Symonds took the freeman's oath at Boston, March 1637-8.

He had previously, viz., Sept. 3, 1637, purchased of Mr.

Henry Sewall, a dwelling house which stood near where the Female Academy now stands. The lot contained three acres, on the north side thereoff abutting on the Meeting-house Green : upon the northeast end thereof abutting on the houselot of William White ; upon the south east side thereoff it abutteth upon Ipswich River ; upon the south west end thereoff it abutteth upon the highway leading to the Meeting-house.

This house and lot descended from Mr. Symonds to his grandson, Major Symonds Eppes, who sold the property to Mr. Edward Eveleth, Jan. 9, 1715. (Eveleth married Elizabeth, the daughter of Eppes.)

Under the marginal date, 1637, is recorded : Granted by the freemen of the Town of Ipswich to Samuel Symonds, Ipswich, in New England, Gent, a farm of five hundred acres of ground, upland and meadow, which farm was laid out accordingly, and is since called Argilla ; bounded, viz. that end thereof toward the northeast, abutting on the now common ground of the Town of Ipswich, beyond part of the West meadows ; that part thereof toward the south east, abutting upon the farm grounds of Mr. William Payne ; that end thereof toward the south west, abutting upon a little Brook called Dry Brook ; that side thereof toward the north west abutting partly upon the ground of Thomas Dorman, partly upon common grounds, and part-ly upon fhe farm now or lately of Mr. John Winthrop the younger.

Also, a planting lot of six acres abutting upon the south west end of Mr. Richard Saltonstall's meadow, lying near a creek called Labour-in-vain,—the north end upon the land of Mr. Nathaniel Rogers, pastor of the church at Ipswich.

Also, all that parcel of ground both upland and marsh, lying at the hithermost side of Saggamore hill, not exceeding forty acres.

The date of giving out these copies is the 5th day of December, 1745, by order of Court : Signed, Richard Saltonstall, Daniel Denison, Samuell Appleton.

" Said Symonds is also possessed of a farm containing about three hundred and twenty acres more or less, which lyeth upon and beyond ye creek called labour in vain—towards the south in a place called Shebacco, which farm was granted by ye freemen of ye Town (divers years since) to John Winthrop ye younger,—which said farm said Winthrop sold to said Symonds, 8, 12mo, 1637."

" Also, one acre and half abutting on the east side thereof on lower end of Mr. William Hubbard's shop; before the town house, and the rest of said parcel of land is surrounded by highways, which parcel of ground was part of Mr. John Winthrop's six acre lot, which the freemen of the town of Ipswich granted him, and which said Winthrop granted to said Symonds, 24 October, 1638.

1665, January 1. Samuel Symonds conveys to Daniel Eppes, "all my farm called Castle hill, containing two hundred acres."

" Also, the Islands containing one hundred acres, divided from Castle hill by a small creek."

" Also, Dec. 1, 1664, four hundred acres betweeu Mr. Saltonstall and Mr. William Hubbard."

Mr. Hubbard was Town Clerk from 1639 to 1645 ; and a Feoffee of the Grammar School, the earliest records of which institution are in his hand writing.

1667, Sept. 24. The Judges of the Court were : Mr. Samuell Symonds, Mr. Symon Bradstreet, Maj. Gen. Denison, Maj. William Hathorne.

Mr. Symonds was Representative from 1638 to 1643 ; when he was elected one of the Magistrates or Assistants, which office he sustained thirty years. In 1673 he was chosen Deputy Governor, in which office he remained until his decease, October, 1678.

He left wife Rebekah ; sons Harlakinden and William ; daughters, Elisabeth, wife of Daniel Eppes ; Martha, widow of John Denison, who afterwards married Richard Martyn of Portsmouth; Ruth, wife of Rev. John Emerson of Gloucester ; Priscilla, wife of Thomas Baker of Topsfield ; also, Susannah, his grandaughter, who married Dec. 18, 1690, Joseph Jacobs.

His will is dated Feb. 16, 1673, and proved Nov. 6, 1678. By a codicil, dated Nov. 8, 1677, he bequeaths certain property to his son Harlakinden, "provided, that if in the life time of my son Harlakindin, my loving brother, Mr. Richard Fitts Symonds decease in the interim, and be bountifull unto my son Harlakinden (which I believe he will,) and bequeath him more than the value of five pounds per annum, then my will and mind is, &c.

He bequeaths to his wife Rebecca, all the property he had with her, "as by a note of particulars, bearing date the last day of November A. D. 1669, under my hand and seal."

" Also, I give to my wife a good breeding mare, or one of my riding horses, which she shall choose."

" Also twelve pound per annum, to be paid her out of my 'farm called Argilla, during her natural life ; to be paid, one half in wheat and malt, at the price current among the merchants of Ipswich ; the other half in pork and Indian corn."

" She shall have liberty to make use of my town house in town, with my children, as formerly, and to take what apples, pears, and plums, and what ground she pleases for her garden,"—at Argilla.

" I give to my dear wife my feather bed and bolster, which we usually lye upon."

" I give to my wives grand daughter one Cow, viz : Rebeckah Stacy, because of her diligent attendance on me.

" I give to my grand daughter Sarah Symonds, land which was her father's in Coxall." [Coxall, Maine.]

" To sonne and daughter Eppes, one hundred pounds promised before marriage, to be paid in one year or two, after my decease ; and if she still desire to have the suit of damask which was the Lady Cheynies, her grandmother, let her have it upon appraisement."

" Whereas I promised to give to my daughter Martha one hundred pounds as a portion upon her marriage with her husband,—Mr. John Denison,—it being desired by the Major and herself so to do, according to the bond I entered into, I do by this my last will confirm the same."

"Son and daughter Emerson, four score pounds. * * Having paid son Baker forty pounds. * Daughter Hale, twenty shillings. Sonne Chewte, twenty shilling. Daughter Dunkin 20s. * Rev. Mr. Cobbett our pastor, 40s.

"My mind and meaning is that the legacies here given to my children shall be paid, not in money, according to money, but in such pay as they usually pass from man to man, which is called the current pricc."

Mr. Symonds gives his real estate to his two sons Harlakinden and William; except the Argilla farm, which seems not to have been disposed of.

He appoints his son William to be his executor; and his loving friends Captain John Appleton, Levtenant Samuel Appleton, and sonne John Hale, to be overseers.

This "sonne John Hale," was the first minister of Beverly. He married December 15, 1664, Rebecca Byley, daughter of Mr. Symonds last wife, by her first husband, Henry Byley of Salisbary.

The "daughter Dunkin" was probably the wife of Peter Duncan of Gloucester; how she became the daughter of Mr. Symonds does not appear. Neither can I discover who was the "sonne Chewte."

In a deed dated June 11, 1662, Peter Duncan, of Gloucester, Merchant, styles Daniell Epps of Ipswich, his brother.

Mr. Symonds had lost three sons: Samuel, died 1653; another Samuel who was graduated at H. C. in 1663, and died November, 1669; and John.

The will of Samuel, jun'r, is dated November 22, 1653. By it he gives to his brother Harlakinden Symonds all his lands in Wenham; to brother John Symonds, £2, 10; to brother Samuel Symonds, sisters Martha, Ruth, Priscilla, and nephew Samuel Epps, twenty shillings a piece;

To sister Mary Epps, a little piece of new Holland cloth;
To Killicross Ross, his chest with lock;
To brother Samuel, all his books;
To Rebecca Ward, five shillings;
To brother William all his lands at Chebacco.

Madam Rebecca Symonds, the last and surviving wife
of Dep. Gov. Symonds, was, first, the wife of Henry Byley,
who came from Sarum, England, and settled at Salisbury
as early as 1640. By him she had a daughter Rebecca,
who married the Rev. John Hale. The record reads :
" Mr. John Hale, son of Robert Hale late Deacon of ye
Church of Charles Town, and Rebecca Byley, late of Salisbury in England, Gent'n, were married Dec. 15, 1664, at
Ipswich, before me : Samuel Symonds." John and Rebecca Hale had a son Robert who graduated at H. C. 1686.
Of this son Robert it is written : "Many years Magistrate
in Beverly." A letter of attorney, written to his father,
dated September 16, 1695, ˙styles him "Minister of the
Gospel in Preston, Con't., grandson of Mrs. Rebecca
Symonds."

Mad. Symond's second husband was Mr. John Hall, of
Salisbury, who left property for her in Salisbury.

In 1682, Mr. Samuel Hall, sometime a resident in Massachusetts, had died at Langford, near Malden, Essex,
England. He bequeathed £100 to those who lost by the
great fire in Boston and by Indian Wars in this colony.
Mr. John Hall of Islington, near London, was his executor, who sent an order to his mother, Mrs. Rebecca Symonds of Ipswich, to dispose of the bequest.

Mrs. Symonds married for a third husband, August 22,
1650, the Rev'd William Worcester, the first minister of
Salisbury, who lost his first wife, Sarah, April 23, of the
same year. He died October 28, 1662. In his will dated
ten days previous to his decease, are these bequests :

" My will is that my beloved wife shall have that bond
of fifty pound wh is due unto mee from Thomas Clark of
Boston, Iron monger ; she securing my daughter in law,
Rebeckah Bilie of wt remains due to her out of yt bond."

" Also my will is that my wife shall have the use of my
dwelling house, orchard, &c., during the time of her
widowhood."

" Also, that my wife shall have wt moneys soever are
due in England for rent ; for wt lands and housings belong unto her, or any otherwise due."

After several bequests to his children he adds :
"All ways provided that the marsh lott that was formerly my wife's by her former husband, Mr. John Hall : remayne to the use of my said wife hir heirs and assigns forever."

He had a daughter Susanna by a former wife, who married Thomas Stacey of Ipswich, and had Rebecca, who married May 25, 1681, James Burleigh, and died before 1695. She is the grandaughter, Rebecca Stacey, mentioned in the will of Mr. Symonds.

Mr. Worcester furher bequeaths "to my daughter Rebecka Bylie my brass chafindish : and also I give unto her a book of Mr. Anthony Burgases conserning the tryals of grace, as a small token of my special love unto her.

" To my grand child, Rebecka Stacy, five pounds in household stuff such as her grandmother may think meet."

Seven years after the decease of Mr. Worcester, Mrs. Rebecca, his widow, entered into a covenant of marriage with the Houourable Samuel Symonds. In his will Mr. Symonds directs to be returned to his wife, according to the covenant, various pieces of property, among which are : land in Salisbury, being six acres of meadow ; seventy acres of land in Salisbury, now called Amesbury ; £62, 12s, New England money which I received of Mr. Clark, Iron monger, of Boston.

Mrs Rebeckah Symonds died in the summer of 1695 :

MEMENTO MORI
The Relict of Samuel Symonds
Esquire, Mrs. Rebeckah Symonds
Dec'd July ye 21, 1695, in ye 79th year
of her age
A Memory blest thou hast & shalt tho here in dust
The matron, pious, prudent, grave & just

From her will are made the following extracts :
I give unto my Kinsman, Bennett Swaine, in England, three pounds, if he have so much in hand ;
To grandaughter Elisabeth Rogers, twenty shillings and the gold ring wh was my mothers ;

Son, Mr. John Hale, my horse ;

Son, Mr. John Emerson, my ffrench history ;

To the two ministers of Ipswich, twenty shillings each ;

Son Hierlackendine Symonds, one good cowe ;

To daughter Baker, my Grogram Gown and coul'd silk petticoat ;

To daughter Emerson one silk petticoat ;

To grandson Daniel Epps, one Jacke ;

To grandson Symonds Epps ye Bedstead in ye parlour;

To cousin Martha Harris, a good new scarf ;

To cousin John Staniford, a gold ring and £3 ;

To daughter Elisabeth Symonds all my wearing linen, excepting the value of twenty shillings out of it, which I give unto my maid, Elisabeth Ross ;

To grandaughter Sarah Low [wife of Thomas Low of Gloucester,] one silver poringer ;

To daughter Hale, my black cloth gown and peticoat ;

To grandson Robert Hale all the rest of my estate.

Rebecca Hale, the daughter of Mrs. Symonds had died, and Mr. Hale had married, March 31, 1684, Sarah Noyes.

Martha Harris was widow of Thomas Harris who died in 1687 ; she was the daughter of Mrs. Margaret Lake, and mother of Margaret, wife of Dea. John Staniford.

Sarah Low : 1709, Nov. 14. Sarah Loe, ad'x of the estate of Thomas Loe late of Glocester, who left a widow, and Simonds Loe, his eldest son ; other children, Thomas Elizabeth, John.

Mrs. Symonds appointed her two sons Jno : Hale and Thomas Baker and cousin Jno : Staniford overseers of her will, to each of whom she bequeathed a gold ring.

The will was witnessed by Jn : Staniford, James Fuller, Margarett Pynchon.

The appraisers were Robert Kinsman and John Harris.

The estate of Mr. Symonds was appraised at £2534. The Argilla farm, containing 300 acres. £1500 ; houses, barns, &c., on the farm, £220.

The house and two acres of land at Town, £50.

1652, 1st of 2d mo.   Samuel Symonds and Martha his

wife, convey to Isaac Cummings, in consideration of £30 paid to my sons Harlakinden, John and William, 150 acres of land butting on land of Daniel Clark.

Harlakinden Symonds 2, Samuel 1, was living in 1695, aged sixty years. He was of Ipswich in May, 1666, when he was fined by the Essex county Court for driving cattle on ye Sabboth. He remained in Ipswich until the division of the Argilla farm in 1694; soon after which he removed to Maine. He had purchased, April 24, 1664, of Thomas Kemble, merchant, of Boston, five hundred acres of land on the west side of Damara Cotta River, which Kemble bought of an Indian, Sagamore Witta Noies.

June 12, 1688, he sold Coxhall, which he inheritted from his father, being six miles long and four miles broad, lying at the head of Wells and Arundel, York county, Maine, to Roger Haskins and thirty-five others.

[An examination of the York Deeds confirms Mr. Hammat's statement, and also reveals the fact that more than the "thirty-three" were proprietors by previous purchase. The Ipswich Land-owners in Maine would make an interesting chapter. We copy the thirty-three names from the Deeds:]

12 June 1688.
The sale of Coxall, County of
Yorkshiere in the Province of Maine

Harlackenden Symonds, Gentleman, of Ipswich, Haue Giuen, Granted, bargained, sold, Enfeoffeed and Confirmed and by these presents Doe fully, Clearly and absolutely Giue, Grant, bargain, sell, Alienate, and Infeoff and confirme vnto

| | | |
|---|---|---|
| Roger Haskins | Thomas Shepherd | John Gitting, s'r |
| Edwrd Bishop | William Goodhew | Paull Thorndike |
| William Baker | Samuel Gittings | Isack Fellows |
| George Herrick | Barnett Thorne | Richard Walker |
| Thomas Edwards | Michell farlo | John Brown farmer |
| Samuell Ingalls jr | Mesheck farlo | Nathaniel Brown |
| John Low, Jn'er | Moses Bradstreete | Zachary Herrick |
| William Dixey | Mathew Perkens | Thomas Higginson |

| John Staniford | Nicho: Woodberry | John Harris |
| Thomas Low, senr | Marke Haskell | John Burnham |
| Samuell Ingalls sr | William Cleeves | Nath'l Rust, sen'r |
| Robert Lord, jr. | William Haskell | Andrew Elliot, jr. |
| Robert Bradford | | |

to them and their heires and Assignes for ever, a Certaine Tract of land, six miles in length and foure Miles in breadth, known by the name of Cokshall in the County of Yorkshiere, in the Province of Maine : and is bounded as followeth, viz : at the South east end partly vpon the line of the township of Wells, and partly vpon the line of the Township of Cape porpus, and on the north east side partly bounded by the line of the land formerly Majr Wm Phillips his land, and partly uppon the Coman land ; and on the north west end the said land is bounded on the common land, and bounded on the south west side with the land of the sd Symonds.  Acknowledged in Boston :

Symonds "Did make Delivery by Turff and Twig."

William Symonds 2, Samuel 1, was born in England. He has the title of Gentleman, Jan. 4, 1655, under which date he conveys a lot of land to William Story, carpenter.

He and Elisabeth his wife, Nov. 19, 1656, convey to Jno: Woodam a house and about an acre of land in the street called Brook street.

June 29, 1657, hs styles himself of Preston, alias Wells, gentleman, when he sells to Thomas Wells of Ipswich, a farm of 200 acres, and other lands.

He was admitted freeman in 1670, and was the Representative of Wells in 1676.  He had the rights of Commonage, 1678.  He died May 22, 1679.

He married Mary, daughter of Jonathan Wade, Esq., and had :

Susanna, born Jan 3, 1668, m. Jos. Jacob Dec. 18, 1690
Dorothy, b. Oct. 4, 1670, m Cyprian Whipple Dec. 19, 1695
Mary, b. Jan. 6, 1673, m. Joseph Whipple, Dec. 10, 1697
Elizabeth, born July 20, 1678

The two last were minors in 1694, and under the guardianship of their uncle, Col. Thomas Wade.

There was an agreement entered into by the heirs of Mr. Symonds (1) for the division of the Argilla farm, dated April 10, 1694. They divided it into two equal parts, one of which was assigned to the children of William 2: Susanna, Dorothy, Mary, Elizabeth. The other half to:— John and Ruth Emerson of Gloucester; Thomas and Priscilla Baker of Topsfield; Daniel Eppes of Salem, Symonds Eppes of Ipswich, sons of Daniel and Elisabeth Eppes both deceased.

MARK SYMONDS. Took the freeman's oath at Boston, May 2, 1638; was commoner of Ipswich, 1641.

He died April 28, 1659, aged 75 years. At the time of his decease he possessed a house and twelve acres of land lying in ye common fields on ye north side ye river, and a planting lot at Reedy Marsh. Inventory, dated May 16, 1659, £257, 6, 9.

Joanna Symonds, died April 29, 1666. Her will was dated April 6, proved May 9. She left two daughters:
   Priscilla, married John Warner
   Abigail, married Robert Pearce

John Symonds made a will August 16, 1671. Wife Elisabeth. Their children:
   James,        Samuel,
   Katherine, married ——— Downe
   Ruth
His property, consisting of house, orchard, land, was valued at £230, 14. Personal £100. He is styled John Symonds carpenter.

William Symonds, [also spelled Simmons,] was an inhabitant in 1635.

December 28, 1647. William Symonds, laborer, sells to Simon Bradstreet a planting lot containing seven acres, being on the hill in Ipswich, on the north side of the river. He lived at the upper end of High street, near the Burying Ground, and was for many years herdsman of the town. Several contracts made with him as herdsman are recorded. His signature is invariably an arrowhead, so uniform that it may be testified to with confidence.

1645. William Symonds purchased of William Whitred a five acre lott of planting ground, which the said Whittred bought of John Whittingham on the north side of the town.

1638, Feb. 15. Granted to William Simmons a house-lot half an acre at the farther end of High street.

1647. Agreed with William Symonds and John Moss to keep the heard of Cows on the north side of the river. To attend at Mr. Robert Paynes and Goodman Scott's lane at half an hour after sunrise. The herdsmen to wind a horn before going out.

SEVERANCE, John. Had a grant of a six acre planting lot on the far side of the brook and on this side of Mr. Andrews farm. He removed to Salisbury in 1640, where he died, April 9, 1682.

SEABORN, John. Possessed a lot of planting ground near Labour-in-vain, 1636. He exchanged lands with Thomas Wells, March 22, 1637.

SHEFFIELD, Mary. Had a daughter, born Feb. 19, 1661, died December, 1662.

SILSBEE, Henry. Had six acres of Marsh by the Hundreds: granted 1644.

TILTON, Abraham sen'r and Abraham, jun'r. Both were inhabitants in 1679.
Abraham, sen'r, was freeman, May 11, 1681.
The children of Abr. Sen'r and Mary, his wife:
Abigail, born 1679
Samuel, born April 14, 1681
Mary, born August 8, 1683
Rebecca, born March 8, 1692
Isaac, born May 2, 1695
Daniel, born April 2, 1697
Abraham Tilton, sen'r, was one of the committee ap-

pointed in 1698, to Consider of a New Meeting-house ; and he and Abraham, jun'r, made a proposal for building the house ; but they were under bid by Mr. Abr. Perkins. He was, however, associated with Mr. Perkins in the work :

" 1702-3, March 3. Whereas Abraham Tilton, jun'r, petitioned the Town to consider his loss in the building of the Meeting-house, and more especially for the communion table which was not comp'd for in his covenant.

Voted, to give the said Abm. Tilton, jun'r, six pounds for said work of the table, if it be not in his covenant in-dentured for."

When the Meeting-house was completed in 1700, the committee appointed for that purpose, assigned to Mr. Abraham Tilton, sen'r, and Abraham Tilton, jun'r, ye 1st pew on ye east of ye pulpit for their wives and families ; a passage to be allowed thro sd pew to Mr. Wardwell's pew.

To Mr. Tilton, sen'r, was appointed a place on ye first of ye short seats, near the pulpit, among the most elderly men.

Abraham Tilton, sen'r, and Samuel, his son, were com-moners, 1707.

It is supposed that Abraham Tilton, jun'r, Isaac Tilton, (who died, 1695,) and Lieut. Jacob Tilton, are sons of Abraham, sen'r, born at an earlier period than those re-corded from 1679 to 1697. Mary Tilton was probably his second wife.

1695, April 2. Abraham Tilton, sen'r, appointed adm'r on the estate of his son, Isaac Tilton.

The N. E. Hist. Gen. Reg. July 1848, has a curious article entitled " The Hostile Actions of some Pagan In-dians towards Lieut. Jacob Tilton and his brother Daniel.'

THORNDIKE, Mr. John, was one of the twelve who came with John Winthrop the younger, and commenced the settlement at Aggawam, March, 1632-3. Died in London. Buried in Westminster Abbey.

TAYLOR, Samuel. Was one of Major Denison's sub-scribers, in 1648.

1659. It was agreed with John Morse and Samuel Taylor to keep the herd on the north side of the river : one of them to go out at the Mill street constantly, and the other the other way : The cows to be brought to the corner by Mr. Robert Paynes ; and the Mill end Cows to be brought to the end of Scott's lane.

He was granted liberty to fell trees, 1666.

His will is dated June 20, and was proved June 29, 1695. He bequeaths to his cousins, Thomas Wilson, Seaborn Wilson, Thomas Treadwell, Nathaniel Treadwell, Mary Gaines, Ester Hofe, [Esther Hovey,] and Martha Cross, my will is to give to every one of those my cousins, twenty shillings in money; to Thomas Sparcks for his care in tending of me, ten pounds in money ; to Samuel Treadwell all my house and ground.

He appoints Nathaniel Treadwell, Executor.

His property consisted of a house and three fourths of an acre of land, valued at £45 : cash and bills, £35 : with other effects, making a total of £94, 9, 5. He was eighty-one years old.

TINGLEY, Palmer. A Pequot Soldier. Had eight acres of land granted to him for that service in 1639.

THORNE, Barnard. Was an inhabitant in 1673. In December, 1673, the wife of Bernard Thorne came into full communion with the Church.

He was Surveyor of Highways in 1675 and 1697.

Had a seat assigned to him in the Meeting-house, 1760.

John Thorne. Seat in the Meeting-house, 1700. Commoner, 1707. With the title of Mr. was Assessor, 1727.

TOWSEY, Thomas, and wife Arminell, had

Thomas, born December 22, 1680
John, died September 19, 1684
Arminell, died August 1, 1686

6th of novbr, 1685. Mrs. Towsey for sugar, ten shillings : for use at Mr. Cobbitts funerell.

TOMPSON, Symon.  Born 1610.  An inhabitant of Ipswich, 1642. when it was agreed with him to keep the cow herd on the south side of the river ; which is to be the third part of the whole number on both sides.

1648.  One of Major Denison's subscribers.

1664.  Had a share and a half in Plum Island.

1647, September.  Witnessed the will of Luke Heard.

1648, Dec. 11.  Sold to John Ward, house and land bounded north by John Lee ; north west by John Browne and myself; in the south by the highway leading unto Heartbreak hill.

By a deed, in which he styles himself Ropemaker, dated August 5, 1658, he conveys to Abraham Fitts, a house and land which he bought of Humphrey Griffin, three acres, having Rocky Hill toward the west; John Fuller south ; the highway east and north east.

Abraham Fitts married the daughter of Symon Tompson Symon Tompson died March 1, 1675.  His will. was proved in March, 1676.  In it he mentions his wife, Rachel ; grandchild Simon Wood ; his brothers Samuel and William Wood ; sister Joanna ; cousin Sarah Fitts.

He appoints his friend Mr. William Hubbard, Mr. John Rogers, Deacon William Goodhue, overseers.  His seal is the same as that on the will of John Lee, probably Mr. Hubbard's.

In 1636, he had a house lot on the south side of the river having a lot granted to Humphrey Wyeth on the south.

He was admitted commoner by vote of the Town, February 28, 1644.

Rachel Tompson, his widow, died August 19, 1700. William Hunt, glazier, administered on her estate.

Alexander Tompson, made a will, dated Nov. 21, 1693; proved April, 1696.  He left a wife, Deliverance Haggett, to whom he was married Sept. 19, 1662.  Children :

David, born May 19, 1664

John,    Mary,    Elisabeth,    Hannah

William, married Mary Graves

Alexander,    Henry,    Sarah,    Matthew

David Tompson, 2. Alexander 1, wife Mary, had :
    Mary, born September 27, 1694
    David, born November 11, 1696
    John, born February 10, 1698
    Hannah, born July 23, 1700
    Jacob, born April 30, 1703
    Martha, born January 16, 1704-5
Widow Mary Tompson was a commoner in 1707.

William Tompson 2, Alexander 1, and Mary Graves were married October 3, 1673. He was a Tythingman in 1679. He had a seat in the Meeting-house, 1700. With the addition of "sen'r," his name is in a list of commoners made att ye Genl Town-meeting, ye 9th of March, 1707-8

William Tompson and Dorothy his wife, had :
    Hannah, married Col. William Stanwood of Revolutionary memory, and lived in Brunswick, Me., and their daughter Dorothy, born April 3, 1786, married James Jones ; and their son, Justin Jones, was the proprietor and editor of the Yankee Blade, Boston.
    Joanna, married (1) David Stanwood, of Brunswick, (2) Philip Owen.

TREADWELL, Thomas 1. Came to New England in 1635, in the Hopewell. He was thirty years old. His wife Mary was thirty-and-three. Their son Thomas was one year.

1638, April 16. He possessed a house lot in High St. having the planting lot of Mr. John Norton north west.

1635. He had land towards the Neck, adjoining Mr. John Tuttle's ten acres.

1639-40, March 12. In an agreement respecting cattle, he has the designation of Mr.

1648. He is one of Major Denison's subscribers.

1684. Mr. Treadwell has two shares in Plum Island.

1638, Sept. 7. He took the freeman's oath, at Boston.

He died June 8, 1671. His will is dated June 1, and was proved Sept 26, 1671. In it is mentioned his wife Mary, and his children :

Thomas, born in England, 1634

Mary, born in Ipswich, September 29, 1636
        married John Gaines, 1659

Martha, born March 16, 1643-4
        married Robert Cross, 1664

Esther, married October 8, 1665, Daniel Hovey: her
        death is recorded : "Esther, widow of Daniel
        Hovey and daughter of Thomas Treadwell,
        died Jan. 4, 1730, aged ninety years.

Widow Mary Treadwell survived Thomas eleven years.
Her will is dated October 28, 1682, and was proved April
20, 1686.  She mentions grandchildren :

Mary, Abigail, Hannah   Treadwell ;

Martha, Esther, Sarah   Gaines ;

Esther Hovey ;      Martha Cross.

She appointed Nathaniel Treadwell and Daniel Hovey
her executors.  She died Dec. 1, 1685, aged eighty years.

Thomas Treadwell 2, (Thomas 1,) came to New England with his parents in the Hopewell, being then one
year old.

He was freeman May 24, 1682.

He complains to the town, May 23, 1696, of having no
highway laid out to his Island.  This Island lies between
the Heard Farm and Jeffreys Neck: and continued in the
Treadwell Family until 1848, more than two centuries.

The date of his death I have not ascertained.  Children :

Thomas, born M 3, 1665

John, born November 28, 1670

Elisha, on whose estate adm. was granted, Mch. 1691

Sarah, born January 10, 1673

Mary, born August 19, 1675

John Treadwell 3, son of Thomas 2, died :

> Here lies ye body
> of. Mr. John
> Treadwell who
> died December
> ye      16      1727
> in ye 58
> year of his
> age

His will is dated November 28, 1727.  His children :
Elisha,
John, wife Priscilla
Jonathan, aged 18 in 1727
Mary, born June 8, 1694
Elisabeth, born July 16, 1699
Sarah
Martha, died 1727, aged 22 years

Here lies ye body of Mrs Martha Treadwell, ye dafter
of Mr. John Treadwl, who died October ye 27 : 1727 : in
ye 22 : year of her age.

John Treadwell 4. (John 3, Thomas 2.)  Died, 1752.
His will is dated March 9, proved May 7, 1752.

To his wife Priscilla, he gives during her life, "the use
of one half of the new house and the lot of land I purchased of Madam Elisabeth Appleton." This lot of 15
acres, he purchased in 1765, £520.

To his son, John 5, he gives one half of his Island, lying
on the south side of Ipswich River, which he purchased of
Capt. Jacob Tilton and Thomas Cross.

To his son Elisha, he gives his upland and salt marsh,
lying on the north side of the river, near Jeffrey's Neck,
"which was given to me by my Hon'd father, John
Treadwell." His children were :
Elisha,   John,   Martha Jewett,   Sarah Wilcomb,
Priscilla Kinsman,   Margaret, unmarried,
Elisabeth unmarried.
He mentions a grandaughter, Hannah Treadwell Rust.

Thomas Treadwell 3, son of Thomas 2.  Will dated
December 13, 1743, and proved Jan. 23, following.  Wife
Frances ; daughter Leighton,   son Thomas 4.

Thomas Treadwell 4, (Thomas 3,  Thomas 2,) died
about March, 1744-5.  Wife, Sarah Goodhue, a sister of
Benjamin Goodhue.  His children were :
Joseph,   Thomas, died April, 1757,   Mary
Elisabeth, married Aaron Cogswell,   Sarah
His estate : Real, £376, 7, 6. Personal, £148, 15, 6.  To
Joseph Treadwell, the eldest son, is assigned by the Court

the houses and land, he paying to the other children £47, 7, 2 each. All the aforesaid in bills of the emission of forty-one."

Nathaniel Treadwell 2, son of Thomas 1, married (1) Abigail, daughter of Thomas Wells, June 19, 1661 (2) Rebecca Titcomb, March 25, 1678

He was freeman, May 24, 1682.

Selectman, 1680.  Voter in Town affairs, 1679.

Horses on the common, 1697.

Place assigned to him on the second seat in the Meeting house, 1700.

1660, May. Fined for smoking on the street on the Sabbath Day.

His children were :

Abigail, born February 2, 1662

Mary, born October 22, 1665

Nathaniel, born Jan. 15, 1667 died June 3, 1672

Hannah, born February 7, 1669

Thomas, died July 11, 1672

Thomas, born May 25, 1673

Sarah, born Aug. 15, 1674

Nathaniel, born June 13, 1677

Elizabeth, born January 10, 1678

Thomas, born April 6, 1686

He died in 1726-7.  His epitaph :

Here lyes ye body of Mr. Nathaniel Treadwell, Aged 88 years.  Decd Janry ye 11th, 1726-7.

Nathaniel Treadwell 4, (Nath'l 2, Thomas 1,) born June 13, 1677, and died at 47 years :

Here lies ye Body of Mr. Nathaniel Treadwell who Died August ye 17, 1723, in ye 47th Year of his age.

He was Constable, 1697 ; Surveyor of Highways, 1699.

His wife, Hannah, administered on his estate, which amounted to: Real, £563, 10.  Personal, £139, 17, 6.

Among his "effects" were: one negro boy slave five yrs old, £20 ; one ditto garl, £30.

His children mentioned in 1723, were :

Jacob, born Jan. 24, 1698-9, lived at Portmouth

Nathaniel, born Sept. 10, 1700

Jabez, ten years old

Charles, 18 years, Jacob his guardian

Hannah, fourteen years old

Nathaniel Treadwell 4, (Nathaniel 3, Nath. 2, Thos. 1,) was born Sept. 10, 1700, and died March, 1777. He left a wife Hannah, and children:

Moses,    Aaron,    Jacob,    Mary Fellows

Grandsons: Nath'l Treadwell Fellows, Sam'l Fellows

Jabez Treadwell 4, (Nath'l 3, Nath'l 2, Thomas 1,) born about 1718. Wife Lucy. His will is dated Nov. 30, 1780, proved Jan. 1, 1781. His children:

Jabez,    Samuel,    Nathaniel,    William

Hannah Perkins,    Sarah Kinsman

He gives to Jabez all the real estate on the south side of the river;

To William the house in which I now live;

To Samuel and Nathaniel the new barn and the land at Timber Hill;

To Hannah Perkins land at Tuttle's Point;

To Sarah Kinsman one hundred and seventy-eight spanish milled Dollars;

To Jabez and Hannah one of my pews; the other pew to the other children;

Grandaughter Hannah Perkins one good Cow.

At the first sale of pews in the Meeting-house which was built, 1749, Capt. Nathaniel Treadwell purchased the second pew on the right hand side of the front door, No. 29; and Mr. John Treadwell purchased the corresponding pew on the left hand side, No. 2. These were the highest priced pews in the house, excepting the two nearest the door, Nos. 1 and 30, which were purchased, No. 30, by the Rev. Nath'l Rogers, and No. 1, by Maj. Samuel Rogers.

Jabez Treadwell purchased No. 50, the second pew from the broad aisle in the second row; he afterwards purchased the pew between that and the broad aisle. These were the two pews bequeathed in his will.

Edward Treadwell. The name of Edward Treadwell appears on the Ipswich Record in 1638. He possessed at that date, a house lot on the lower side of the High street. And John Hanchet had a six acre grant of planting ground towards Reedy Marsh, adjoining the planting lot of Edw: Tredwell, 19 Nov'r, 1638.

TUTTLE, JOHN. Had a grant in 1635, of a houselot on the south side the river, about one acre and twenty rod, lying between Mr. Rogers and Mr. Ward and Mr. Winthrop and the highway.

In 1643, there was granted to him one hundred acres lying on the south side of the river near Mr. Hubbard's farm, adjoining upon the line there.

July 27, 1638. He purchased of Richard Lumpkin a house lot lying near the great cove of the town river, having a house lot of William Avery on the south west, the houselot of Robert Kinsman on the north west, the town river south east, and a house lot of Samuel Hall on the east. Upon the said lot is one dwelling house formerly built by Richard Brown, now of Newbury, and by him sold unto Mr. Richard Saltonstall, by whom it was sold unto Richard Lumpkin.

1635. There was granted to Mr. John Tuttle, ten acres towards the Neck, having Mr. Bracy his land west; Mr. Treadwell east; Philip Fowler north, and a Creek south.

Also a planting lot on Heartbreak hill, 1635, having Mr. Dudley west, Michæl Williamson, John Johnson, and the marshes east; and two little swamps north and south.

1640. The Committee for furthering trade amongst us are Mr. Bradstreet, Mr. Robert Payne, Capt. Denison, Mr. Tuttle, Matthew Whipple, John Whipple, Mr. Saltonstall.

1642. The parcel of land late Mr. Tuttle's, between Mr Wade's and Goodman Webster's is granted to Mr. Rogers, so far as concerns the town.

1641. A commoner, with the title "Mr."

1648. Subscribed to Maj. Denison's allowance.

1642, Nov. 25. He sold to Moses Pengry the land purchased of Richard Lumpkin, deceased. In the deed Mr. Tuttle is styled yeoman.

Symon Tuttle 2, born 1631.

1674, April 4. Symon Tuttle, aged forty-three years, the only child living of Mr. John Tuttle and Joannah his wife, who are deceased.

[Margin : Joannah, daughter of Thomas Burnham.]

1664. Symon had a share and a half in Plum Island.

1663. Surveyor of Highways.

1679. Voter in Town affairs.

He died in January, 1691-2, was interred the 11th day.

Sarah Tuttle, wife of Symon, died January 24, 1731, aged eighty-six years.

At the death of her husband she administered on the estate, which was appraised £863, 1, 6.

The chlidren of Symon and Sarah: (age at father's death is given.)

John, born April 22, 1666
Symon, aged 24; born Sept. 17, 1667
Joanna, eldest daughter, married ——— Pickard
Elisabeth, aged 20; born Nov. 24, 1670
Sarah, aged 18; born Sept. 3, 1673
Abigail, aged 17; born Oct. 7, 1674
Susanna, aged 16; born May 7, 1675
William, aged 15; b. May 7, 1677, d. Dec. 10, 1726
Charles, aged 13; born March 31, 1679
Mary, aged 11 years
Jonathan, born June 11, 1682
Ruth, born August 16, 1685

John Tuttle 3, son of Symon 2, was born April 22, 1666. He married Martha Ward, December 3, 1689.

1702. He was one of the seven purchasers of the old Meeting-house.

1707. Was a commoner.

Children of John and Martha : Martha, b. Nov. 23, 1690 Mary, born July 7, 1696.

Here lyes ye body of Mr. John Tuttle who died February ye 27, 1715-16 aged 49 years 10 Monthes & 5 days

When ye Messenger was sent of God
He soone submitted to His rod

Symon Tuttle 3, son of Symon 2,  married Mary Rogers,
January 16, 1696.  Children :
    Sarah, born October 11, 1697
    Margaret, born August 24, 1699
    1707.  He was a commoner.
    1719-20.  He had appointed to him a seat in the meeting
house on the men's second seat.
    Mrs. Tuthill appointed to sit in the women's front  seat.
    Chareles Tuttle 3, (Symon 2) commoner, 1707.

TUCKERMAN, Nathaniel.    Commoner, 1707.    Wife
'Martha.   Children :
    Nathaniel, born September 9, 1684
    Martha, born June 27, 1686

THURRILL.  "Old Mr. Thurrill" died Nov. 7, 1685.

TURNER.  Capt. Turner.  1638.  " Capt. Turner's hill,"
so called in 1638, and still called Turner's Hill.

URAN, Francis, and Ann his wife, had :
    Francis, born August 16, 1685
    John, born Sept. 29, 1687
    Joseph, born February 23, 1691
    Peter, born May 15, 1694
William and Marah Uran :
Here lies ye body of Mary Uran,  daughter of William
    & Marah Uran, died January ye 7, 1713, aged one
                  year & 5 months

VARNEY.  Thomas Varney, May, 1670.  Represents
* * controversy about a piece of land containing four or
five acres, upon part of which his house and barne and
orchard is sett, being allways pursuaded in  himself, by
divers others, that it was within that tract of land,  bought
of goodman Tompson, accordingly have possessed it this
twenty years and upwards.
    Corporal Thomas Varney, had a share in  Plum  Island,
1664.  Voter in Town affairs, 1679.

He is called Corporal Varney of Chebacco. His wife was named Abigail.  Children:

Thomas, born December 24, 1682

Martha Smith

Mary Chote

Rachell Fellows

In 1692, three children of daughter Abigail Burnham, deceased, are mentioned.

His will is dated November 25, 1692. He died at Chebacco, December 4, 1692. His will was proved March 28, 1693. The witnesses were John Staniford and Joseph Proctor. His estate by inventory made by Thomas Low and Abraham Martin, amounted to £736, 7, 6, of which, buildings, orchard, 60 acres of upland and meadows, were appraised at £500.

His wife, Abigail Varney, and his son Thomas Chote, were appointed executors.

Thomas Varney, son of Corp'l Thomas, was Constable in 1729.

VARNUM, George.  Had a houselot in 1635, adjoining the lot of Reginald Foster.  He died about 1649.

Ralph Varnum, was "agreed with, June 11, 1640, for ringing the Bell, keeping clean the Meeting-house, and publishing such things as the town shall appoint: shall have for his paines for every man, for the year past, whose estate is rated under £100, sixpence; from £100 to £500, twelve pence; and upwards, eighteen pence. The like for this year to come."

Samuel Varnum, one of the Denison subscribers, 1648. Had a share and a half in Plum Island, 1664.

He removed to Dracutt, where he had two sons killed by the Indians, 1676.

He came from Wales; married Sarah Langton, and had five sons:

Abraham, born April 3, 1659

Thomas, born in Ipswich, Nov. 19, 1662, married a Jewett, and had Samuel, Thomas, and a daughter

John, married Dolly Prescott of Groton, and had :
    John, Abraham, Jonas, James, and three
    daughters
Joseph, had Joseph, Samuel, John

VINCENT, Humphrey.   Was one of Major Denison's
subscribers in 1648.   He received a grant of land  in  1638.
He was of Cambridge, 1634.
    He died December 5, 1664.   His will is dated  February
1, 1660.   He bequeaths to Mrs. Martha Symonds, daughter
of Mr. Samuel Symonds, one of our honoured Magistrates,
twenty  pounds.   To  Thomas Davis ten pounds.    To
Samuel Symonds aforesaid all my houses and lands.
    Joanna, wife of Humphrey Vincent, died July 17, 1657.
No record of children.

WADE.   Col. Jonathan Wade was probably born in
the parish of Denver, Co. Norfolk, England.   He owned
large lands there.
    Came to Charlestown, 1632 ; Ipswich, 1635.   Died 1683.
Left estate valued at £7859, 5s, 3d.
    He was a member of the Grand Jury, 1637 ;
    Representative, 1669, 1681, 1682;
    Lieutenant, 1663.
                                    Boston Transcript, August, 1899.

Jonathan Wade.   Took  the  freeman's  oath at Boston,
May 14, 1634.
    1639.   Granted Mr. Jonathan Wade at Chebacco, 200
acres, southwest of Mr. Samuel Dudley, southeast of Mr.
John Winthrop, northwest of Chebacco Creek.
    1641, he was commoner.
    1662, he was Selectman.
    1664, with the appellation of Mr. he had two shares in
Plum Island.
    1679.   Voter in Town affairs.
    1667, March 26.   Mr. Jonathan Wade has his license
renewed to sell strong waters for one year.
    He died in 1683.   His will is dated May 22, 1669, ''being
to go a voyage to sea.''   Proved Nov. 27, 1684.
    1683, Sept. 25.   It is  recorded :  The  will of Jonathan

Wade being disallowed, Thomas Wade, third son of deceased, app'd adm'r.

In the will is mentioned wife Susanna, who died Nov. 29, 1678. [Mr. Wade had two wives previous to Susanna. He married, December 9, 1660, Mrs. Dorothy Buckley. His son Thomas was born 1650, consequently must have been the fruit of a yet earlier marriage.]

The will mentions his children :
    Jonathan,
    Nathaniel,
    Prudence, wife of Anthony Crosby
    Elisabeth, wife of Elihu Wardwell
    Mary, wife William Symonds
    Sarah, wife of Samuel Rogers

He gives to Thomas Crosby, Nathaniel Crosby, Jonathan Crosby, fifty pounds a piece, for the use of Prudence Crosby, their mother ;

    To William Crosby, my son, £200

    To Elihu Wardwell, my son, £200, for the use of his wife Elisabeth and her two children.

In the inventory of his estate, is returned among debts due to the estate "what appeared upon book charges to children," as follows ;

    Mr. Anthony Crosby, £290, 7, 7 1-2
    Mr. Samuel Rogers, £225, 2, 1,
    Mr. William Simons, £223, 17, 6
        ditto and his widow  49, 14, 9
    Elihu Wardwell, £323, 0, 6 1-2

He lived with his son, Coll : Thomas Wade, and held, as appears by the inventory, considerable property jointly with him: of which was the homestead, consisting of buildings, orchard, and plow land and pasture land, with privilege on ye common : 'the said homestead valued at £160 ; a wind mill ; salt marsh and other small pieces of real estate ; with cattle, farming utensils and other chattels, among which were two negro slaves : the whole amounting to £783, 5, 11.

Among his property were lands at Mistick, valued at

£3560 ; land at Osburn, seventy-seven acres, £77 ; lands in England cost £1500. The estate amounted to a total of £7859, 5, 3.

With Susannah his wife he sold to Henry Bennet, April 1, 1661, "his farm known by the name of said Wade his farm," given him by the Town of Ipswich ; land of Mr. Samuel Symonds on the north; Mr. Saltonstall east ; Mr. Rogers west ; a brook on the south. Two hundred acres or thereabouts. Consideration, £237.

1674, 16 April. The agreement about repairing the Meeting-house the committee propounded to the Town, was approved, and the Town chose Mr. Wade, Capt. Appleton, Merchant Wainwright, Cornet Whipple to see it carried on with speed.

The epitaph of Thomas Wade 2, son of Jonathan 1 :

> Here lyeth interred
> ye body of * L * t
> Col'nl Thomas Wade
> Esq'r Dec'd ye 4th of
> Oactober, 1696
> in ye 46 year
> of his age

Col. Thomas Wade by his will, dated October 3, 1696, gives all his lands, houses, mills, to his two sons, Jonathan and Thomas, they giving to their mother, (for her comfort and bringing up of ye Young Children,) one half of the produce. To the rest of his children, William, Elisabeth, Nathaniel, Edward, Samuel, Susanna, he gives sixty pounds each.

To his son Jonathan in consideration of his being the oldest son, besides his other legacies, he gives the six acre lot at Labour-in-vain.

To his son John he gives "but twenty pounds in consideration of his education."

To Capt. Wade was granted March 23, 1692-3, the tenth lot of 36 feet front by ye River side, between Samuel Ordway's shop and ye Town Bridge.

Col. Thomas Wade married Elisabeth Cogswell, daughter of William Cogswell, Feb. 22, 1670. She survived her husband and reached the age of 76 years :

> Here lyes ye body of Mrs. Eljzabeth Wade who died January ye 3, 1726, aged 76 years.

1680. Col. Wade was Selectman.

1684, July 17. Chosen Clerk of the Writts, (approved by the Town, August 1, 1684.)

The children of Thomas and Elisabeth Wade :

> Jonathan, born May 15, 1672
> Thomas, born December 16, 1673
> John, born February 15, 1674. H. C. 1693
> Minister of Berwick, Maine
> William, born April 20, 1677, "killed in a fight at sea by a Frenchman," April 3, 1697
> Nathaniel, born Dec. 15, 1678
> lost at sea, August, 1702
> Elisabeth, born August 7, 1681
> Edward, born May 15, 1683
> Samuel, born December, 1685
> Susannah, born Feb. 20, 1691,
> married John Shepherd, Boston

Jonathan Wade 3, son of Thomas 2, married Jane Diamond ; publishment is dated March 11, 1709.

He had a seat appointed to him in the second seat in Meeting-house, 1700.

The committee of 1700, "to appoint seats and allot pews in ye new meeting house," allot to Mr. Wade's family ye third pew between ye east doors next Mr. Appleton's : Mr. Thomas Wade having liberty to sit in ye sd seat when straitened for room in sd pew. Inscriptions :

> Here lies buried the body of Jonathan Wade, Esq'r, who departed this life Feb'y 9th, 1749, aged 77 years.

> Here lies buried the body of Mrs. Jane Wade, the wife of Jonathan Wade, Esq., who departed this life March 2, 1752, aged 77 years.

Thomas Wade 3, son of Thomas 2, married, April 4, 1700, Elizabeth Thornton, of Boston. He died in 1737.

> Here lies the body of Capt. Thomas Wade desest January ye 5, 1737, aged 64 years

Elisabeth Thornton Wade died January 5, 1753. The children of Thomas and Elizabeth were :

Thomas, born May 27, 1705, d. e.

Elizabeth, married (1) Benj. Appleton, Feb. 23, 1722
                he died Feb. 12, 1731
                (2) William Cogswell of Rowley,
                    March 13, 1734

Sarah, born May 20, 1711, m. Capt. Thomas Baker,
        of Topsfield

Timothy, born Sept. 7, 1712, married Ruth Wood-
        bury, daughter of Beverly, April,
        1737, died April 16, 1763; Ruth died
        January 23, 1802, aged 87 years

Priscilla, born April 10, 1715, died early

Thomas, born Feb. 14, 1717, lived at Boston, one son

William, born August 2, 1719, died early

Mary, married Henry Wise of Ipswich

Timothy Wade 4, son of Thomas 3 and Elizabeth, with Ruth Woodbury his wife, had :

Thomas, born March 24, 1738, died in the West In-
        dies, July 21, 1761

Elisabeth, born Augnst 1, 1740, m. Nath'l Heard

William, born July 29, 1742, died early

Mary, born September 8, 1744

John, born June 24, 1746, died September 17, 1771

Nathaniel, born February 27, 1750

Samuel, born August 24, 1752, died Dec. 30, 1771

Nathaniel Wade 5, son of Timothy 4, was born Feb. 27, 1750. He married July 17, 1777, Mary Foster, daughter of Col. Joseph Foster, of Gloucesier, and died Oct. 26, 1826. He was a distinguished officer in the U. S. A. under Gen. Washington, in which he attained the rank of Colonel.

After the Declaration of Peace, 1783, he was for many years Representative of the Town of Ipswich in the Legislature of Massachusetts.

Mary Foster, his first wife, died Dec. 25, 1785, aged 28 years. Their children were:

Nathaniel, born May 3, 1778
William Foster, born January 3, 1780
Mary, born February 2, 1782
Timothy, born September 3, 1785, d. e.

Col. Nathaniel Wade married (2) Hannah Treadwell, daughter of Jacob and Martha Treadwell, Oct. 29, 1788.

Nathaniel Wade 2, son of Jonathan 1, married Mercy, daughter of Gov. Simon Bradstreet, October 31, 1672. He resided in Medford, and died November 28, 1707.

WAINWRIGHT, Francis: was among the earliest settlers of Ipswich. He came with Alexander Knight, with whom he had lived at Chelmsford, England.

1637. He was a soldier in the war against the Pequod Indians.

The following extract from P. Vincent's "Relation," gives a glimpse of the energy which distinguished him through life: "July ·13, 1637. Francis Wainwright, a young man of Ipswich, pursues some Pequods, expends his ammunition, and they turn upon him. He breaks his gun over them, and brings two of their heads to camp."

1639. The committee for the Pequitt Soldiers, did grant as followeth : To Francis Wainwright, Eight acres.

1648. He was one of Major Denison's subscribers.

1664. He is appointed Corporal of the Ipsw'h company.

1664. Had a share and a half in Plum Island, which indicates that he was already among the wealthier inhabitants.    1671, Oct. 31.  Freeman.

1674. He is entitled "Merchant Wainwright."

1675, March 29. Granted liberty to Francis Wainwright to set up a pew six foot square, or so much as amounts to it, between the two seats and the stairs on the south side of the house.

In the list of those that by law are allowed to have their votes in Town affairs, he is entitled : Mr. Wainwright, senior.

His first wife, Phillis Wainwright, died Oct. 6, 1669.

He died suddenly while on business at Salem, May 19, 1692, and his tombstone is in the ancient Charter street burying yard.

He left a wife Hannah Wainwright, who married Daniel Eppes of Salem. His children were :

John, born 1649, died Aug. 3, 1708, aged 60 years
Jacob, killed by Indians at Northfield
Martha, born January 24, 1658
Simon, b. Nov. 20, 1660, killed by Indians, Haverhill
Mehitable, born Dec. 4, 1662
Benjamin, born September 16, 1666

John Wainwright 2, son of Francis 1, died August 3, 1708, in the 60th year of his age.

1679. He was Tythingman.

1698. He was one of a committee of the principle inhabitants, appointed to build a new Meeting-house.

1700, April 18. Voted that the money that was procured for the Bell that was sold to Marblehead, which was £37, 10, be Committed to Coll : John Wainwright, to procure a new Bell of about 5 or 6 100lb weight. Then was raised by subscription towards the new bell, £50, 18, of which Coll : John Wainwright gave £6 ; and his brother Francis gave £3. The new bell cost £72, the " Clapper," £1, 6, 8.

1707. He was Colonel of the Regiment, and went on an expedition against Nova Scotia.

1675, March 10. He married Elizabeth Norton, daughter of William Norton, who survived him. She married Nov. 19, 1713, the Hon. Isaac Addington, and died at Roxbury, Nov. 22, 1742, æ 88 years.

The children of Col. John and Elizabeth Wainwright :

A daughter born Nov. 30, 1675
John, born June 10, 1677
Francis, H. C. 1707, died at Boston Sept. 4, 1722
Elizabeth, born December 5, 1679
        m. Addington Davenport, Nov. 16, 1698
Ann, born May 25, 1682,
        married Adam Winthrop, Nov 7, 1700

Lucy, born December 13, 1684
        married Paul Dudley, Sept. 15, 1703
John, born April 30, 1687, died early
John, born June 14, 1691, H. C. 1709
Samuel, born Aug 31, 1693

He was a Feoffee of the Grammar School from 1700 to 1708, the year of his death.

After giving liberal portions to his daughters, he left an estate of nearly £20,000.

In the new Meeting-house, 1700, there were assigned to Coll: John Wainwright and Lt. Coll: Jno: Appleton, the two pewes that were designed for Elders Pewes at ye going of each side door, nearest the pulpit.

In the Meeting-house which was built 1749, John Wainwright purchased pew No. 4, and Samuel Wainwright, pew No. 41. These pews were for the wives and families ; the gentlemen themselves were appointed to sit on the seat numbered One.

John Wainwright 3, son of John 2, died Sept. 1, 1739, aged 48 years. He was graduated at H. C. 1709; married Christiana Newton. of Boston, February 11, 1723; was for many years Town Clerk; and Representative in the General Court, eighteen years, 1720-38; Clerk of the House twelve years, 1724-36; member of the Artillery Co. 1714; and Colonel of a Regiment.

His wife and two sons, John and Francis, survived him.

Samuel Wainwright 3, son of John 2. Wife Mary. He died July 19, 1773, æ 66 years.

Francis Wainwright 2, son of Francis 1. Born August 25, 1664. His tomb has the Coat of arms :
Here lies entombed the
Body of
Colonel Francis Wainwright, Esq.
who died August ye 3, 1711, Ætatis 47
& his vertuous consort Mrs. Sarah
Wainwright who died March ye 16
1709, aetatis 38
with three of their youngest children,
John, Francis, John, who died in infancy

He married March 12, 1690, Sarah Whipple. She died
as above inscribed in 1709.

He was Town Clerk ; Representative to General Court ;
Feoffee of the Grammar School.

He was graduated at Harvard College, 1686 ; Member
of the Artillery Company, 1709 ; Colonel of a Regiment ;
Justice of the Sessions Court ; Commissioner and Collec-
tor of Excise for the county. He left three daughters :

Sarah, born February 26, 1692
      pub. with Stephen Minott, Boston, Sept 16, 1710
Lucy, pub. with Sam'l Waldo, Boston, June 9, 1712
Elizabeth, born July 19, 1668
      m. Dr. Parker Clark, Newburyport

His will is dated August 2, 1711. He gives to Elizabeth
Hirst of Salem, a lady with whom he was published June
23, 1711, one hundred pounds money. He bequeaths legacies to his kinswoman Mary Whipple ; to his good friend
Daniel Rogers, Schoolmaster; and to his mother Eppes a
mourning suit.

August 11, 1696. John Cobbett of Ipswich, Gentleman,
sells to Francis Wainwright, in consideration of seventy
pounds : a houselot and tract of land containing three
acres more or less, bounded by land of John Baker, north-
north-east ; by said Baker east ; and south-east by the
highway ; on the south-south-west by said Wainwright ;
and by Mr. Robert Payne west and north west; "with ye
House upon said land." John Cobbett and wife Elisabeth.

1704-5, March 12. Maj'r Francis Wainwright may set
his fence so far as to make ye street four rods wide at
Goodman Lovell's corner of his orchard wall ; and said
fence to range away towards his Barn to ye wall yt fences
ye house yt sd Wainwright bought of Mr. Cobbett.

Two silver cups belonging to the communion service of
the First Church have these inscriptions: Mr. John
Wainwright's Gift to ye Church of Ipswich, June, 1693.

The gift of Col" Francis Wainwright To the church
of Ipswich :

WALDO, Cornelius : sold to John Caldwell August 31, 1654, his house which he purchased of Richard Betts, bounded by land of Edward Browne south east, Robert Collins north west, Thomas Lovell north east.

In 1664 he had a share and a half in Plum Island, as tenant of Mr. Cogswell.

He removed to Chelmsford ; was a Deacon of the church. He died June 3, 1701.

He married Hannah Cogswell, daughter of Mr. John Cogswell, and had :

 Daniel, born August 19, 1657
 Martha, born February 27, 1658
 Twin sons, February 24, 1659
 Deborah, born June 14, 1661
 Rebekah, born January 28, 1662
 Judith, born July 12, 1664
 Mary, born Sept. 9, 1665

WAITE, Serj't Thomas : 1667, March. Granted to Sergeant Waite the privilege of commonage.

1664. Share in Plum Island. Tho : Wayte had a share also, as tenant of Mr. Osgood.

There is no one of the name in the list of voters, 1679.

1695, June 26. Jonadab Waite is burning lime at Pemaquid with Isaac Tilton.

1696, June 26. Mary wife of Thomas Waite, aged 34 years ; Thomas Waite, jun'r, aged 42 years.

Thomas Waite had :

 John, born December 11, 1658
 Sarah, born November 21, 1661
 Mary, born August 9, 1664, died Sept. 4, 1665
 Jonadab, born September 8, 1667

Thomas Wayte and Susan Ayres m. Nov. 21, 1677

 Mary, born September 9, 1678
 Susannah, born April 7, 1681
 Hannah, born January 17, 1681
 William

1683, February 7. The selectmen agreed with Thomas
Waite, jun'r, and Nath'l Lord, to build two seats upon
the north side of the Meeting-house, from Gallery to Gallery, and to provide everything for them. * They are to
receive eight pounds half, when the work is done, and the
other four pounds in the fall of the year following, when
the rates are laid; all in such pay as the Town usually
pay their rates in.

John Waite died December, 1665.

John Waite married Catherine Carrol, August 14, 1685.
Children :

Samuel, born October 20, 1686
Jonadab, born February 20, 1690
Joseph, born May 25, 1692
Katherine, born July 27, 1695

Thomas Waite and John Waite had seats in the Meeting-house, 1720.

Here lies ye body  of John Wait,  ye son of Mr.   John &
Mrs Sar   ah Wait who    Died October 22    1786 aged 3
years   1 month 14 days

Here  lies John Waite ye son of Mr John and Sarah  Wait
died December ye 27 1721 in ye 5th year of his age

Here  lies  John   Waite  ye son of Mr John & Sarah Waite
who died August ye 8 1717 aged  14 Months & 25 days

WALLIS, Robert : was an Inhabitant in 1639, when he
had  granted  to him an acre of ground for an houselot, be-
neath  the  High  street,  having  a  small parcll of ground
granted to John Hassell on the north west, and a  houslot
formerly granted to Robert Lord on the north  east, and a
house lot of Susan Manning on the south  west.

He also possessed a lot of land containing two  acres on
the north side of the river, having the highway next the
river toward the south, which he sold to Roger Preston
before March, 1657.

He was one of Maj. Denison's subscribers, 1648.

In 1664 he had a share in Plum Island.

He, with  Nicholas  Wallis his son, sold to  William

Goodhue in January, 1661, the land which he purchased of Joseph Bigsbee, being a three score-and twelve part of village land, which the said Joseph also purchased of Mr. Joseph Jewett, being within the limits of Rowley.

April 2, 1674. Nicholas Wallis and Simon Stace, enter into an an agreement "consarning the Estate of our father, Robert Wallis, dec'd." In it they stipulate for the maintenance of their mother.

Nicholas Wallis 2, son of Robert 1.  Epitaph :

Here lyes ye bo  dy of Jnsign  Nicholas Wallis  who
died Febru  ary ye 1, 1710 : 11  & in ye 78
year of his  age

He was Freeman May 27, 1674; Rep. to Gen. Ct. 1691.

He was three times married : (1) Sarah Bradstreet, April 13, 1657.  They had :

Sarah, born July 24, 1658
Hannah, born February 11, 1659
Robert, born M 12, 1661
Samuel, born June 11, 1664

He married (2) widow Rebekah Somerby of Newburyport, April 28, 1691. He m. (3) Sarah ———.  And Sarah widow of Nicholas Wallis, died October 21, 1721.

He joined the church in full communion, Aug. 12, 1674.

January 20, 1701-2, liberty is granted to Ensign Walls and his two sons to build a shed for their horses, next to one granted to be built by Corn't Matthew Whipple and others, of forty feet in length and not exceeding ten foot wide, about twenty feet from ye Watch House, southerly towards ye old Meeting-house.  The two sons were Robert and Samuel.

He subscribed 12 shillings towards the bell, 1699.

Was a voter in Town affairs, 1679.

Robert Wallis 3, son of Ensign Nicholas 2, born March 12, 1661.

1697.  Surveyor of highways ; horses on the common.

1699.  He subscribed six shillings towards the bell.

March 8, 1719-20.  He has the title of Sargeant ; and is chosen Selectman.

1719-20.   Seats are appointed to him and his wife in the Meeting-house.

Samuel Wallis 3, born June 11, 1664, son of Nicholas 2, married Dec. 30, 1690, Sarah Watson, daughter of William Watson, born November 2, 1672.   They had :

Samuel, born September 23, 1691

He married (2) July 7, 1696, Anna Potter, who died Feb. 15, 1726, aged 61 years.

He married (3) Allis, who died Sept. 15, 1733, æ 57 yrs.

He had horses on the common, 1697.

Seats appointed in the Meeting-house, 1719-20.

He died August 8, 1737, aged seventy-four years.

Samuel Wallis 4, son of Samuel 3 and Sarah (Watson) was a Physician.   He had wife Sarah, and lost an infant daughter: Sarah, D'r To Doc'r Samuel & Sarah Wallis, Who Died October ye 4, 1715, Aged 7 Months.

He died in the strength of manhood :

> Here Lyes Buried
> ye Body of Doct'r
> Samuel Wallis
> Who Dec'd Octob'r 16
> Anno Dom'i 1728 in ye
> 38 year of his Age

WARR, Abraham: was one of Major Denison's sub-scribers in 1648.   He possessed land in Brook street, and in November, 1656, it is spoken of as 'lately Abra'm Warr's.'

NATHANIEL WARD, distinguished as the author of THE SIMPLE COBBLER OF AGGAWAM,

was a son of the Rev. John Ward, and was born at Haver-hill, England, 1570.   He was educated at the Cambridge University, and came to New England in June, 1634, and soon after became the minister of Ipswich.

His health becoming impaired he resigned the pastoral office, February 20, 1637.   He continued, however, to preach occasionally, until his return to England in 1647.

He died at Shenfield, Essex, 1653, aged 83 years.

He had a grant of six hundred acres of land near Pen-tucket, (Haverhill.)

The place of his residence in Ipswich is not certainly known. Tradition fixes it on the south side of the river, near the house of Deacon William Foster Wade. In 1664, his houselot was on the south side the river, near Mr. Rogers and Mr. Winthrop.

In 1636 "Mr. Ward's Farme," is referred to, near Maj. Denison's, near the Creek called labour in vain.

He resided at first in Mr. Winthrop's house. Gov. Winthrop writing to his son, John the younger, Dec. 12, 1634, then at Connecticut, says : "Mr. Ward continues at your house this winter ; and Mr. Clerk (to give him content,) in his own."

John Ward 2, son of Nathaniel 1, was born, as Dr. Cotton Mather supposes, at Haverhill, England, 5 Nov. 1606. Came to New England, 1639 ; admitted freeman, 1643 ; settled at Haverhill, 1645 ; died in Haverhill, Dec. 27; 1693, æ 88 years. He continued to possess and to purchase property in Ipswich, after the period assigned for his settlement at Haverhill :

Nov. 20, 1648, he sells to Simon Tompson, House and ground, eight or nine acres, that was sold to me by Mr. John Clarke.

December 11, 1640, he purchased of Simon Tompson, House and land bounded north by John Lee ; north west by John Browne and Simon Tompson ; on the south by the highway leading into Heartbreak hill.

Major Samuel Ward made a will dated April 29, 1689, which was proved April 22, 1691. He says : "Whereas the governour and Counsell have ordered me upon an expedition to Canada by God's assistance against the common enemy," &c. He mentions goods in Boston or Charlestown which my father Ward left me ; his honoured father Bradstreet ; his wife Sarah ; his sons John and Samuel ; his daughter Mercy. The will is witnessed by Thomas Wade, Joseph Brown, Daniell Hovey.

WARDWELL, Thomas, was one of Major Denison's
subscribers, 1648.

Ursual Wardwell had a share in Plum Island, 1664.
Liberty to fell trees for furnishing house, 1668.
He married Mary Rindge, daughter of Daniel Rindge,
May 3, 1664. They had:
  Abigail, born October 27, 1665
  Hannah, born September 1667
  Alice, born December 27, 1670
  Mary, born June, 1673

Elihu Wardwell is contracted with by the Selectmen,
June 18, 1668, together with Ezekiel Woodward, for get-
ting shingles for the Meeting-house, 19s per thousand;
and with them Walter Hooper and Thomas Burnham, j'r,
for the laying of them ; each of them to do a quarter and
to have for laying 7s 6d per 1000 f.
Elihu had liberty to fell trees for fencing homestead,
June 13, 1668.
Elihu married Elisabeth, daughter of Jonathan Wade,
May 26, 1665, and had:
  A child, born Dec. 20, 1666
  Elihu, born January 2, 1668
  Prudence, born October 6, 1670
  Jonathan, born July 26, 1672
  John, died April 9, 1688
In the Meeting:house built in 1699, the committee chosen
to appoint the seats and allott the pews, allot to Mr Ward-
well ye 2d pew on ye east side of ye pulpit for his wife and
family. Mr. Wardwell himself hath liberty to sitt in ye
6th of ye men's long seats upon consideration of his son
Elihu sitt in sd pew.
Elihu subscribes ten shillings towards the bell, 1699.
1698. He is paid for work on the Town Bridge.
Elihu Wardwell, sen'r, had the seventh lot of 28 feet
front, lying by ye River side, between Samuel Ordway's
shop and ye Town Bridge, granted to him March 23, 1693.
1699. Jonathan Wade by his will, gives to Elihu Wardwell my son, £200, to be laid out in housing and land, to
be for the use of his wife Elisabeth during her life, and his
two children after.

## WARNER.

Copy of a Manuscript in the hand-writing of Daniel Warner.

Ye posterity of Mr. William Warner, formerly of Ipswich. My Great Grandfather, William Warner, Came out of England in ye year 1637, and Brought over three Children : two sons and a daughter. [the daughter, my Grandfather's sister, married with Mr. Wells.]

The oldest son was John, which went southward, which had six sons, to wit : Sam'll, John, Mark, Daniel,

Nathaniel, & Oliver.

My Grandfather had four sons and three daughters :

Daniel, John, William, Nathaniel,

Elisabeth, Abigail, & Susanna.

My father and mother married in September 23, 1668. My Mother's maiden name was Sarah Dane. Her mother's Elener Clark.

My father's five Children which lived to marry, to wit :

the first ch : Daniel, had priscilla, Caleb, joshua, mary,

Sam'll, and William & Ruth

ye 2, Sarah, Had Eight : Joseph, Eunis, Mercy, Stephen

joshua, Daniel, philemon & Dane

ye 3 philemon, which had 10 Children : philemon,

Daniel, william, Nathaniel, & jonathan

ye Daughters : Abigail, Sarah, Susanna &

Mercy

ye 4 John, wch had one son named John & Eight

daughters : Hannah, Elisabeth, Sarah,

Abigil, Susanna, Mary, Lucy & Margaret

ye fift mercy, which had six children, Israel, Daniel,

Keturah, Sarah, Hannah & priscilla

My uncle John Warner Had 4 sons, William, Daniel, John, Nathaniel : & 5 Daughters, Elisabeth, Hannah, Susanna, mary and Abigal

My uncle William Warner of wethersfield, had 3 Sons : William, Daniel & John, and 2 Daughters Hannah & Abigal

My uncle Nathaniel had 2 sons, Nathaniel and Daniel,

ye Latter was kild by a Horse, & 2 Daughters
named Hannah

Elizabeth, my ant Heard, had 3 sons : Edmund, Nathaniel & Daniel, and 3 Daughters : Elizabeth,
Sarah & Abigail

Abigail, my Ante Dane's sons, John and Nathaniel, and 3
Daughters, Abigal, Rebeka, and Elisabeth

My Grandfather deceased in September, 1683.

My Grandmother whose maiden name was Elisabeth
Denne, Deceased Long Before. [Nov. 1, 1659.]

My father Deceased ye 24 of November, 1696.

My mother, Sarah Warner, Decem. 28 : 1701.

My uncle John Warner, 10 April, 1712.

My uncle William Warner of Wethersfield, 23 february,
1713-14; and my ant ye 3 of march following ; and their
son William's son William ye 8 of march.   William's wife
ye 11 of march & john in may following.

my uncle Nathaniel about ye year 1684.

my ante Heard Deceased 1724, in ye 77 year of her age.

Daniel and Dorkas [Adams] married ye 29 february,
1699-700.   Our Children :

Dorcas, was born ye 6 of december, 1700
                who Deceased 23 january following

Daniel, was Born 15 february, 1701-2

priscilla, was Born 23 march 1703-4

Caleb was born 19 April, 1706
                who Deceased 11 may following

Caleb, 23 march, 1706-7

joshua, 16 may, 1709

mary, 14 august, 1711

Sam'll, 28 nouember, 1713

Ruth, 22 february, 1715-16

william, 4th July, 1718

In the hand of Caleb Warner, son of the Daniel who wrote what precedes:

My sister, Mary Warner, Deceased Nov'r ye 4th, 1732

my sister Priscilla Adams, Decest 6 of January 1733-4.

my Brother William Warner Decest November 3, 1736.

My sister, Ruth Curtis, Decest July 20, 1740
    her Daughter, Ruth Curtis, Decest May 21, 1744
my mother Decest May 13, 1749
my Honored Father Daniel Warner Decest on the 20th
    of January, 1754, Aged 82 years four months & 15 Days
my Brother Daniel Warner of pomphrit, Deceased the
    first of January, 1766.

In another hand.

My Honored Father, Caleb Warner, Deceased march ye
10th, 1774, aged sixty six years eleven months and seven
Days.

———

In the hand of Daniel Warner, concerning the family of Sarah Dane Warner,
his mother:

the posterity of mr. Dane, formerly of jpswich, New-
england :

my Great Grandfather Dane Had 2 sons : john and
francis, and 1 Daughter which married to mr. james How :
His son francis settled ye first minister in Andover.

my Grandfather john dane Had 2 sons, john & philemon
and 4 Daughters, Elisabeth, mary, Rebecca and Sarah.

my uncle john Dane Had 3 sons, john, Daniel & Nath'll
and 3 Daughters, Abigal, Rebeca, and Elisabeth.

my uncle philemon Dane Had 2 sons, philemon & Edward, and 2 Daughters, mary and Ruth.

my Ante foster Had 3 sons, jsaac, john & nathaniel, and
6 daughters, Elisabeth, judith, mary, sarah, neomy, &
Elenor.

my ant Chandler 3 sons : william, philemon, & thomas,
and 2 Daughters, mary and Hannah :

my ant Hovey, one son named Daniel.

Mr. Hammatt continues:

William Warner with his two sons, John and Daniel,
and one daughter who married Thomas Wells, came from
England and settled in Ipswich, in the year 1637.

The houselot granted to him in 1637, is thus described :
"One house lot one acre more or less in the Mill street,

bounded on the east by another houselot as yet ungranted; on the north west by an high way leading from the Mill street to High street; butting on the Mill street at the south west end : at the north end butting on the swamp.

John Warner 2, eldest son of William 1, "went southward." He had six sons, viz: Samuel, John, Mark, Daniel, Nathaniel, Oliver.

Samuel and John remained in Ipswich.

Daniel Warner 2, son of William 1, married Elizabeth Denne before they came to America ;

He married (2) July 1, 1660, Faith Brown, she died November 10, 1679;

He married (3) Ellen Jewett, widow, June 1, 1686.

He died September 9, 1688.

1641, he was a commoner.

1646, Feb. 4. He was one of 24 who promise carting voluntary toward the Cart Bridge, besides the rate, a day work apiece.

1648, subscriber to Major Denison's compensation.

1657. He possessed land adjoining land of Jeremy Belcher.

1662, he was Selectman.

1664. Had a share in Plum Island.

1677. Tithingman.

At his death his property was valued at £707 1 9.

His children were :

    Daniel, married Sarah Dane

    John,

    William,

    Nathaniel, married Hannah Boynton

    Elisabeth, married Edmund Heard, Sept. 26, 1672
            died 1724, aged seventy-seven years

    Abigail, married John Dane, December 27, 1671

    Susanna, married John Brewer, January, 1674

He left a will, of which his sons Daniel and John were executors : witnessed by John Appleton and Nehemiah Jewett.

Daniel Warner 3, (son of Daniel 2, William 1,) married Sarah Dane, daughter of John and Eleanor Clarke Dane, September 23, 1668.  Their children "who lived to marry" were :

>Daniel, born September 5, 1672, m. Dorcas Adams
>Sarah,
>Philemon, born Feb. 2, 1675, m. Abigail Tuttle
>John,
>Mercy,

Nathaniel Warner 3, (Daniel 2, William 1,) married November 29, 1673, Hannah Boynton.  They had :

>Nathaniel, born March 26, 1676, d. Dec. 8, 1697
>Daniel, born January 11, 1678
>John, born October 12, died November 19, 1679
>Hannah, born Feb. 13, 1680, died early.
>Hannah, born May 28, 2684

He was one of eighteen of the young generation who took the covenant January 18 and 25, 1673.

He with his wife, and his father and mother, and Daniel, jun'r, came into full communion, April 12, 1674.

Nathaniel Warner died in 1684.  His property amounted to £59 16.

His son Daniel was killed by a horse, August 2, 1686, aged eight years.

His daughter Hannah married May 19, 1703, Ephraim Fellows, son of Isaac Fellows.

John Warner 3, (John 2, William 1,) married Priscilla Symonds.  Joanna Symonds, widow of Mark Symonds, died April 29, 1666, mentions her two daughters : Priscilla wife of John Warner, and Abigail wife of Robert Pearce. They had :

>Joseph, born Aug. 15, 1657, died June 18, 1658
>Mehitable, born April 16, 1659
>Daniel, born 1661
>Eleazer, born November 13, 1662

Samuel Warner 3, (John 2, William 1,) married October 21, 1662, Mercy Swan, daughter of Richard of Rowley. It was his second marriage.  The name of his first wife is

not recorded.    By his first marriage he had :
    Abraham, born October 28, 1659
    Hannah, born May 22 1661
Children of Mercy (Swan)
    Priscilla, born September 25, 1666
    Samuel, born July 5, 1668
    John, born August 2, 1670, died July 14, 1671
    Dorothy, born June 2, 1673
    Sarah, born May 28, 1674
    Richard, August 13, 1676

Daniel Warner 4, (Daniel 3 and Sarah (Dane,) Daniel 2,
William 1,) born September 5, 1672 and died January 20,
1754; married February 29, 1699, Dorcas, daughter of
John and Dorcas Adams.    She was born March 16, 1678,
died May 13, 1749.    Their children :
    Dorcas, born December 6, 1700, died January 23.
    Daniel, born February 15, 1701-2
    removed to Pomfret, where he died Jan. 1, 1766
    Priscilla, born March 23, 1703-4
        married ——— Adams, died Jan. 6, 1733-4
    Caleb, born April 19, died May 11, 1706
    Caleb, born March 23, 1706-7
        died March 10, 1774, left a son Daniel
    Joshua, born May 16, 1709
    Mary, born August 14, 1711
    Samuel, born November 28, 1713
    Ruth Curtis, born Feb. 22, 1715-16, died July 20, 1740
    Wiliiam, born July 4, 1718, d. Nov. 3, 1736

    John Warner 4, (Daniel 3, Daniel 2, William 1,) mar-
ried (1) Hannah Bachelor, April 20, 1665; (2) Mary ———.
His children:
    Elizabeth, born June 13, 1666
    Nathaniel,
    Sarah,    Lucy,    Margaret,
    Hannah, born May 14, 1674
    Mary, born August 18, 1675
    John, died July 21, 1676
    Abigail, born April 7, 1677

By his will proved May 5, 1712, he appoints wife Mary and son Nathaniel ex'rs.

Philemon 4, (Daniel 3, Daniel 2, William 1,) born Feb. 2, 1675, married Abigail, daughter of Symon Tuttle ; she was born October 7, 1674. They had :

Philemon, born January 17, 1697

## A Chronology of Remarkable Events.

From the manuscript of Daniel Warner.  1745.

| | |
|---|---:|
| And first of all since this our world began | 5695 |
| Since it was Drowned for the sins of man | 4038 |
| Since Samson did himself and foes destroy | 2826 |
| Since noble Hector fell with ancient Troy | 2735 |
| Since Homer lived, for Poets never die | 2694 |
| Since Daniel wrote his wondrous prophesie | 2527 |
| Since ancient London was by Ludd up Reared | 2352 |
| Since Rome was built which all the world Revered | 2243 |
| Since Jesus Christ at Bethlehem was born | 1745 |
| Since Crucified with cruelty and scorn | 1712 |
| Since England first the Christian faith received | 1581 |
| Since Constantine the Great in Christ believed | 1434 |
| Since the destructive Ball by Guns was hurled | 365 |
| Since first the use of Printing blest the World | 317 |
| Since our forefathers ventured on the sea | |
| And planted first old Plimouth Colony | 125 |
| Since White was born ye first that ere had birth | |
| Of English Blood on this Newengland Earth | 125 |
| Since Harvard did the Colledge first provide | |
| Where great Apollos' learned sons Reside | 106 |
| Since Narragansett fort was Bravely fired | |
| Where many a Captain nobly expired | 70 |
| Since Philip first His cruel war Begun | |
| Which made our English blood wth rivers Run | 70 |
| Since yt last comet whose flaming tail Reach'd High | |
| And Brandished His tresses in the sky | 65 |
| Since fair Bostonia fed the Crackling flame | |
| And Phenix like new from her ashes came | 34 |
| Since the grand Congress of the superior stars | |
| When Saturn joined at once to Jove & Mars | 23 |

Since our Newengland Hero Lovel Dy'd
Whilst victory Lay bleeding By his side          20
Since the earth Received a most tremendous shock
Which made us tremble and our Houses Rock          18
Since Britans patience would no more sustain
The great abuses of affronting Spain          6
Since the long winter of prodigious ffrost
By which much sheep and cattle too were lost          5
Since in our Skys there blaz'd an awful star
Presaging Earth quake and a general war          5
Ad 5 to all the above said numbers
and it brings them to the present year 1750 : in December.

WHITTLES, Richard. Was a commoner, 1641 ; a subscriber to Major Denison's allowance, 1648. In 1679, he was a Tythingman. He was by trade a bricklayer.

He possessed a houselot on High street, adjoining the houselot of Mr. Richard Dummer, in 1659. This house and land together with marsh and other lands, he sold to Henry Russell of Marblehead, April 18, 1683.

WEBSTER, John. Came from Ipswich, England, and was admitted a freeman, at Boston, March 4, 1634-5.

Hé possessed a lot of land which was granted to Mr. Rogers, 1642.

He was admitted a commoner by vote of the Town, February 28, 1644-5.

It seems that he had been employed in some business for the Company, for we find under the date, 1664, this record : "Concerning Webster debt of £8 17 8 due to the Town, he sayth that he paid in the colonies £5 13 8, so that there remains due to the Town, £3 4 3.

He died in 1646 ! and left a widow and four sons.

John Andrews conveys to Mary Webster, widow, to the use of her and her children, all ye island lately in possession of George Carr, twenty acres more or less, bounded by the labour-in-vain creek west ; Thomas Emerson's farm southeast ; Thomas Boreman's farm on the north east ; which said island lyeth in the town of Ipswich. Acknowledged 14th 8th mo., 1652.

Widow Mary Webster married John Emery, sen'r.

The children of John and Mary Webster :

John, born 1632, married Anna Batt, 1653

Stephen,    Nathan,    Israel.    Four daughters.

John Shatswell in his will, 1646, mentions sister Webster

John Webster 2, (John 1,) was a blacksmith and settled at Newbury.

Nov. 10, 1652, he sells to Rob't Kinsman, glazier, for £35, all his farm, which John Webster, his father, bought of the assignees of Johu Fane : twenty-five acres at Chebacco, having Thomas Bishop south west, a brook south east, Samuel Symonds and Nathaniel Rogers north east, William Story, north west.    Ack. 30th 5th mo, 1654.

WELLS, Thomas'  Commoner, 1641.    He took the freeman's oath at Boston, May 17, 1637.    Two shares in Plum Island, 1664.

Under the marginal date of 1635 is granted to him a house lot one acre and a half more or less, lying on the farther side of the river, between the houselots of John Proctor and Samuel Younglove, on the east and west encompassed by the Town river.

1635, a planting lot of six acres lying on the east side of the great hill called Heartbreak hill, bounded by the lots of Mr. Dudley, John Proctor, the Town river, and the way leading to Mr. Saltonstall's farm.

1651.    He had granted to him ten acres of marsh, in full satisfaction of the land taken from him for the County Highway at the Bridge.

He died October 26, 1666.    His will is dated July 31, 18 year Charles 2d, 1666, and was proved Nov. 15.

He left a wife Abigail, who died July 22, 1671, and children :

Nathaniel, the eldest son

John, married Sarah Littlefield

Thomas, born 11 of 11 mo. 1646

married Mary Perkins, June 10, 1669

Sarah Massie of Salem

Abigail Treadwell

Elisabeth,    Hannah,    Lydia Rogers

He bequeathes to his son John, 350 acres of land in the Town of Wells, in the Province of Maine.

To Thomas he gives £250 sterling, and all the books called orthodox evangelist ; to be given at the age of 22 years. "The charges of his going to College."

He directs that Mistress Mary Rogers of Rowley, shall have the tuition and education of my daughter Hannah Wells, till she marry.

He mentions my cousin Mary Baker, alias Lowe, of Colchester.

My son John's wife Sarah, and Francis Littlefield, her father. Nathaniel, my eldest son, Lydia his wife.

The will of Abigail Wells, widow, is dated July 22, proved 26, (7) 1671. She mentions the children ; and also Mary Greely my sons maid servant. Nathaniel Wells, ex'r. Witnesses, Mary Fowler and Faith Warner.

Nathaniel Wells 2, (Thomas 1,) married Lydia Thurley, May 9, 1661. 1675, he was Selectman. 1677, he was Tithingman. 1678, he was commoner.

1676, September. Nathaniel Wells having brought up George Greeley from his birth, in recompense of his charge, he is ordered to live with the said Nath'l his heirs and assigns, until he is twenty-three years of age.

1681, January 26. Nathaniel Wells dying intestate, Lydia Wells, relict, app. adm'r.

In 1694, Aug. 6. Widow Lydia Wells, relict of Nath'l Wells, had become Mrs. Ledia Emerson.

Children of Nathaniel and Lydia :

> Abigail, born Aug. 17, 1662, m. Edmund Potter
> Martha, born January 13, 1664
> Sarah, born March, 1667, married John Day
> Ledea, born April, 1668, married Richard Kimball
> Nathaniel, born January 27, 1669
> Thomas, born June 10, 1673
> Hannah and Elisabeth, born January 7, 1676

Nathaniel Wells 3, (Nathaniel 2, Thomas 1,) wife Mary. Surveyor of Highways, 1697.

His children :

Abigail, born April 13, 1693
Mary, born May 7, 1697
Capt. Nathaniel, born April 24, 1699 d. May 27, 1790
Here lyes buried ye body of Mr Nathaniel Wells who
    died October ye 13 1717 aged 48 years
Here lies Mrs. Mary Wells wife of Mr. Nathaniel Wells
    died August ye 19, 1721, aged 52 years

WEDGEWOOD, John, was a soldier in the Peqnot war in which he was wounded. He is referred to in Mr. Hubbard's Indian Wars.

He had a grant of seven acres of land, which he sold to William Symonds, who sold the same to William Story, January 11, 1655.

In 1639, he had a planting lot at Rabbit Hill.

WEST, John: was one of Maj. Denison's subscribers, 1648. He sold his house and land to John Woodam, June 28, 1649. He sells lands to William Story, Jan. 4, 1655, adjoining the common. He is called "yeoman."

Twiford West, 1667, payd for his daughter, the wife of Abra: Perkins, upon her pr'st'ment (for wearing silk,) three shillings, and fees, 2s 6d.

He had a share and a half in Plum Island, 1664.

He purchased commonage of Henry Pindar, Jan 20, 1657

He was complained of for felling walnut trees, 1666.

His will is dated Dec. 5, proved Jan. 11, 1685. He appointed his wife Mary, ex'r.

Mary West: will dated June 22, proved Sept. 27, 1697. She confirms to her son John several parcels of land given to him June 1, 1687.

To her son Nathaniel she bequeaths lands bounded by Bull Brook.

Children of Twiford and Mary :
    John, born October 20, 1661
    Nathaniel, born January 1, 1666
    Elisabeth,        Hannah

John West, son of Twiford, with wife Sarah, had Elizabeth, born July 31, 1688. Sarah died, and he m. (2) Elizabeth, widow of Thomas Atwood. She died Aug. 20, 1720. He was Constable in 1698, and later.

WHIPPLE, John, took the freeman's oath at Boston, May 13, 1640.

1641. He was a commoner.

1648. Subscriber to Major Denison's allowance.

1640-1653. He was Representative to General Court, eight years.

1646, February 1. He was one of such as promise carting voluntary toward the Cart Bridge, besides the rate, a day work a piece.

1651-2, January 26. He was appointed together with Mr. Hubbard, Mr. Rogers, Mr. Norton, Mr. Denison, the two Mr. Paynes, and Mr. Bartholomew, to

ORGANIZE THE GRAMMAR SCHOOL

and afterwards, on the removal of Mr. Bartholomew to Boston, 1665, he was chosen a Feoffee of that Institution.

1664. Had two shares in Plum Island, &c., at which date he has the title "Elder." He was Deacon and Ruling Elder of the First Church.

He died June 30, 1669. Sarah, his wife, died June 14, 1658 ; and he left a widow, Janet. In his will he mentions his children :

John, whom he appoints ex'r
Susanna, widow of Lionel Worth
Mary Stone
Sarah Goodhue
Son-in-law Anthony Potter

John Whipple 2, son of John 1, had one and an half shares in Plum Island, 1664.

1664. Selectman.    1665. One to lay out Castle Neck.

1668, April 29. Freeman.

1668. Cornet of the Troop.

1673, Feb. 22. Came into full communion with Church

1674-1683. Representative to General Court four years.

1679. Voter in Town affairs.

He was born in Essex, Eng., and was bap. Sept 6, 1632.

He married Mary Reynor, daughter of Humphrey Reynor, of Rowley.

He died November 22, 1695, and left his wife Mary, and children :

John, born March 36, 1660
Elizabeth, born January 12, 1661
Joseph, died August, 1665
Matthew, born May 29, 1664
Joseph, born Sept. 17, 1665, died June 8, 1666
Hannah
Joseph, married Mary Symonds, died 1699
Cyprian, born January 17, 1670
Sarah, born September 2, 1671
Anna, born October 25, 1675
Mary. born May 11, 1677

John Whipple 3, (John 2,) was one of the eighteen of the members of the young generation who joined the Church by taking the covenant, January 18, and 25, 1673. He subscribed £2 towards the bell of 1699.

With his wife, Katharine Leighton, (married June 26, 1681,) he had :

Katherine, born August 15, 1685
Elisabeth, born April 9, 1688, d. e.
Sarah, born December 16, 1692
Elisabeth, born June 2, 1695
Susanna, born April 3, 1696
Mary, born February, 1697

Here lyes buried ye body of Major John Whipple who Decd June ye 12th, 1722, in ye 65th year of his age

Here lyes ye body of Mrs. Ketherine Whipple, late wife of Majr John Whipple, who Died January ye 15, 1720-21, aged 63.

Matthew Whipple 3, son of John 2, married Martha Thing, January 11, 1697. She died August 7, 1774. He died February 17, 1764.

Joseph Whipple 3, son of John 2, married, Dec. 10, 1697, Mary, daughter of William Symonds. They had :

Archelaus, born March 26, 1692
Sarah, born May 14, 1693, died May 14, 1695
Elisabeth, born December 9, 1696
Mary, born February 15, 1698

Joseph was dead in October, 1699. Mary (Symonds) his wife, died June 20, June 20, 1703.

Cyprian Whipple 3, son of John 2, married December 19, 1695, Dorothy Symonds, daughter of William Symonds.

1699, October 2. Cyprian Whipple and Dorothy his wife, Mary Whipple, widow, and Elisabeth Symonds apply for letters of administration on the estate of William Symonds, their father deceased.

Matthew Whipple, 1, was commoner in 1641. He was twice married. His second wife, Rose, he married November 13, 1646. His children were :

John, born July 15, 1657

Matthew, born December 20, 1658

Joseph,

Mary,     Ann,     Elisabeth

He had together with his brother John, 200 acres of land granted February 19, 1637, at the Hamlet, where he resided. He died October 20, 1658.

Capt. John 2, son of Matthew 1, was one of Major Denison's subscribers, 1648.

Had a share and a half in Plum Island, 1664.

Voter in Town affairs, 1679.

He was appointed Captain of the Troop, February 2, 1676 ; and in 1677 he went out against the Indians at Salisbury.

He was appointed County Treasurer, April 10, 1683.

He married (1) Elisabeth Woodman, May 5, 1659.

He married (2) Martha ——— she died Feb. 24, 1679.

He married (3) Elisabeth Payne, June 28, 1680.

His children : John,   Matthew,   Joseph,

Susan Lane, Sarah.

He died August 10, 1683, and left an estate of £3314. His will is dated August 2, 1683. Inventory Septem'r 10. Among the items were : Farm occupied by Arthur Abbott; Farm occupied by Fennel Ross ; John's house and barn and kiln ; Matthew's house and barn ; Joseph when he comes of age shall enjoy the houses, buildings, Malting Office, wth ye others. Witnesses William Hubbard, Samuel Phillips, Daniell Epps.

John Whipple 3, son of John 2, was born March 30, 1660
with Hannah his wife, he had :
  Martha, married Rev. Richard Brown, Newbury
  Susannah, wife of Rev. John Rogers of Eliot
  Mary, wife of Benjamin Crocker, Gram. Sch. Master
  Hannah, born June 30, 1692
  John, born December 16, 1695
His wife, Hannah, died October 20, 1701. He died June
11, 1722.

In 1695, he was Representative and Justice of Sessions.

January 29, 1701-2.    Liberty granted to Cornet Matthew
Whipple, Mr. John and Joseph Whipple, and Mr. Isaac
Rindge, to build a shed for their horses forty feet in length
and not exceeding ten foot wide, about twenty feet from
ye watch-house, southerly towards ye old meeting house.

To John Whipple with title of Lieut. was assigned in the
new Meeting-house, 1700, "that pew next Mr. Rogers at
ye end of ye men's short seats for his wife and family.  To
himself was appointed a place on seat Number 1.

To Lieut. Whipple was granted March 23, 1692-3, the
thirteenth lot of 22 feet front, lying by ye River side, between Samuel Ordway's shop and ye Town Bridge.

  1699.   He subscribed £2 toward the bell.

  1708.   He was commoner and had the title Capt.

Matthew 3, (John 2,) married the eldest daughter of
William Cogswell.  To him was assigned ye 2d pew on ye
so-east side of ye great door for his wife and family.  To
himself was appointed a place on seat No. 2.

  1699.   He subscribed £2 toward the bell.

  1709, May 15.   He was appointed guardian of Dorothy
and Emerson Cogwell, minor children of William Cogswell deceased.

  1697-8.   He was chosen Selectman.  He is at this date
designated as "Malster."

Matthew 3, and Joanna his wife, had :
  Matthew, born Oct. 20, 1686, died Feb. 17, 1764
  John, born July 2, 1689
  Joanna, born July 22, 1692, died August 31
  Appleton, born October 19, 1693
  Elisabeth, born March 1, 1694-5
  William, born Feb. 28, 1695-6, of Kittery, Maine
  Joseph, H. C. 1720, minister of Hampton Falls

William Whipple 4, was of Kittery, Maine, in 1730, and married Mary, daughter of Robert Cutt. They were the parents of Brigadier General William Whipple, who was a signer of the Declaration of Independence. Gen. Whipple resided in Portsmouth, N. H. His grave is in the North Cemetery, and designated by an altar stone. In an old-time burying gronnd at Kittery are the graves of Capt. William and Mary (Cutt) Whipple :

In Memory of Capt.
William Whipple
Departed this Life
Aug'st 7th 1751
In the 56 year
of his age.

Here lies interred the Remains
of Mrs. Mary Whipple, Relict
of Capt. William Whipple
late of Kittery deceased
She departed this Life
the 24th day of February, 1783
aged 84 Years
Her religion was without ostentation
And her charity unlimited.

Here Lies interred ye Remains of Mr. Robert Cutt
Whipple, who Departed this Life May ye 4th,
A. D. 1761, aged 25 years.

Joseph 2, son of Matthew 1, wife Sarah ;

1664.  Had a share in Plum Island.

1697.  Horses on the common. He is then styled, joiner.

1673.  Joseph Whipple, ex Uxor, came into full communion with the Church, February 23.

Joseph and Sarah had :

Joseph, born November 1, 1665, d. e.

Joseph, born October 31, 1666

Ruth

Margery, born August 28, 1668

Sarah, born March 29, 1670

Matthew, born November 25, 1673

Mary, born December 25, 1674

Sarah Whipple, wife of Joseph, died July 16, 1676.

Capt. John Whipple, claimed the right of commonage for Joseph Whipple's heirs, March 9, 1707-8.

Joseph Whipple, jr., subscribed £1 to the bell, 1699. He had: Ruth b. Oct. 27, 1692 ¦ Anna, b. July 29, 1695.

[Note. Joseph Foster, U. S. N., says: The John Whipples are most grievously confounded by different writers ; there is a book, however, which can be taken as authority, "Genealogy of the Whipple Family, by J. H. Boutelle."]

WELCH, Philip and Hannah Haggett, married Feb. 20, 1666, and had: Philip, born Dec. 27, 1668

John and Sarah Welch, had : John, born Sept. 6, 1693.

Moses Welch, born October 20, 1685.

Thomas Welch, born April 13, 1691.

WHITE, William.  Had a houselot at the corner of High and North Main streets, in 1635.  His residence was on a lot which he possessed in 1634, on the south easterly side of Meeting-house green, near where the Female Academy how stands. [See Henry Sewall.] He possessed another houselot in 1635, adjoining a lot of John Hassell.

1641.  He was a commoner.

1664.  Had a share in Plum Island.

1671, May 21.  He was freeman.

1679.  He was a voter in Town affairs.

In October, 1647, he mortgaged to Ralph Dix a farm of two hundred acres, for £60.

He married Katherine, widow of John Jackson who died 1648 ; and with her sold to John West before June 28, 1649, a dwelling house and land which had belonged to Jackson.  She died June 2, 1671.

1659, January 16.  He mortgaged to Samuel Ingalls ye part of my farm which I sold unto John West and purcased of him again.

His death is recorded: "William White died August 25, 1684, or thereabout."

James White, was a voter in Town affairs in 1679. Had horses on the common, 1697.

George White married Lydia Lamson, April 5, 1671, and had: Lidia, b. Jan. 5, 1672 ; Nath'l, b. Feb. 3, 1673.

WHITRED, William.    Possessed a houselot at the farther end of the High street, in 1638.

1648.    One of Major Denison's subscribers.

1664.    As tenant of John Perkins, a share in Plum Island

1667, Feb. 11.    He had granted to him to make use of five acres of land, by Nicholas Marble's farm, during life.

1640, October 17.    He mortgaged to William Tinge his houselot containing two acres.

1646, Feb. 4.    Sold Moses Pingry, saltmaker, a house.

1653, Oct. 15.    He sold conditionally one half of his farm to Richard Brabrook.

Thomas Whitred had a share in Plum Island, 1664.

His wife, Frances, died April 26, 1658.

He had son William, born March 31, 1658.

He exhibited an inventory of his father's estate, Dec. 9, 1668: House and land, £10; Cattle, £20; Total, £84, 13.

1672, September 3.    Robert Colborn appraised the estate of Thomas Whittredge ; will noncupative ; proved by his brothers, Robert Morgan and Richard Norman : "Brethren, you being most Intimate with me, and dearest, in whom we have put our Confidence : and in whom I doe Confide : of all our relatives remaining alive: I have therefore sent for you - - to committ unto you my three sonnes, which I had by your sister,—my wife now taken from me.    He said he had been very sick.    But yesterday, Mr. Newman administering phisick unto him, he was revived and something better.    Sonnes, Thomas, Richard, William.    He would send for his brother Morgan againe, he being nearest to him."    His brother Samuel Whitredge and his son-in-Law John [Twaste?]

1695, March 11.    Thomas Whitredge appointed administrator of the estate of William Whitredge, his grandfather.    Joseph Morgan and Philip Fowler sureties.

WHITMAN, Robert, was commoner, 1641 ; was employed to keep a flock of sheep south side of the river, 1661; had a share in Plum Island, 1664 ; was a voter in Town affairs, 1679.

He purchased a house and land of Thomas Manning, March 15, 1647.

Sold to John Woodam, February 18, 1647, my house situate in Ipswich near the Meeting-house ; and the house and land of John Jackson towards the north west; the land of said John Jackson towards the south east; one end abutting on the street; the other end abutting on the land now in possession of Thomas Manning toward the so. west Acknowledged 14, 1st mo. 1649. He is styled husbandman.

Susanna, his wife, died in May, 1664 ; and he married Hannah Knight, November 9, 1664.

WHITYEAR, Whitgers, John. Had a houselot adj. William White ; 1635.

WILES, Michael. Resided at Chebacco. His dau. Experience, born February 25, 1695.

WHITTINGHAM, Mr. John, of 1637.

1638. Member of the Artillery Company.

1641. Commoner.

1645. Sold a five acre planting lot on the hill on the north side of the town to William Whitred.

1646. One of the seven-men of the Town.

1649, June 27. His will was proved.

It is said that he was a son of Baruch and grandson of the Rev. William Whittingham, a famous Puritan who married a descendant of John Calvin.

Mr. John Whittingham came to New England with his mother from Lincolnshire.

He married Martha Hubbard, daughter of Mr. William Hubbard, and sister of the Rev. William Hubbard.

His will was witnessed by John Norton, William Hubbard, jun'r, James How, Hamill Bosworth. In it are mentioned his wife Martha ; his children : John, the eldest son, Richard, William, Martha, married Rev. John Rogers, Elisabeth, Judith.

He appoints his father-in-law Mr. Hubbard, brother Mr. Samuel Haugh, and his wife Martha, ex'rs: the present elders of Ipswich, Mr. Nath'l Rogers, Mr. John Norton, overseers. Inventory rendered, Sept. 1650.

WISE, Humphrey.  March 26, 1639.  Humphrey Wise
died lately at Ipswich, intestate; and Samuel Greenfield,
late of Salem, married his widow.—Essex Deeds.

JOHN WISE, son of Joseph Wise of Roxbury; baptized August 15, 1652; Harvard College, 1673; ordained
the Minister of Chebacco Parish, August 12, 1683.
At a Town Meeting, August 23, 1687, he took an active
part in the refusal of the Town to comply with Sir Edmund Andros's order for raising a Province Tax, as being
contrary to Charter rights.  For this he was tried at Boston, fined, imprisoned and deposed from his ministry.  At
the same time and for the same offence

JOHN APPLETON,
THOMAS FRENCH
ROBERT KINSMAN
WILLIAM GOODHUE

were also fined and imprisoned.
After the expulsion of Andros he prosecuted Chief Justice Dudley for refusing him the privileges of the habeas
corpus act, while he was imprisoned.
He died April 8, 1725.  He lies buried in the old burying ground of Chebacco:

Underneath Lies the Body of the
Rev. John Wise, A. M.
First Pastor of the Second Church in Ipswich
Graduated at Harvard College in 1673
Ordained Pastor of said Church in 1681
And died April 8, 1725
Aged 73
For talents, piety and learning
He shone as a Star of the
First Magnitude

Mrs. Abigail wise, his wife, survived him with their
children:

Jeremiah,
Lucy
Joseph, pub. with Mary Appleton, Feb. 5, 1708
Ammi Ruhami, married Mary Rindge
Mary, born May 12, 1685
Henry, Harvard College, 1717
John, married Mary Rogers, pub. Oct. 23, 1714

Ammi-Ruhami Wise 2, son of Rev. John 1, married
Mary, daughter of Capt. Daniel and Hannah (Perkins)
Rindge, In 1713. He was a merchant; Justice of the Court
of Sessions ; Representative at the General Court, 1739-40.
His house was in Ipswich, on the site of South Church.
He died August 14, 1749, and Mrs. Mary (Rindge) his
wife, survived him.

Henry Wise 2, son of Rev. John, was graduated at H. C.
in 1717. His wife, Mary, died early:

Here lyes ye body of Mrs. Mary Wise ye wife of Mr.
Henry Wise, Decd October ye 18th 1725, in ye 28 year
of her age.

His second wife was also Mary : and they buried a dau.
Abigail : Here lies ye body of Abigail Wise Dafter to Mr.
Henry and Mrs Mary Wise who died May 28, 1742, in ye
6th year of her age.

Mr. Wise was a merchant. For a time he resided in Boston. He was chosen Tythingman in 1732.

He was chosen in Town Meeting Grammar School Master, May 6, 1726. There was no Master of the Grammar
School appointed by the Feoffees, November, 1719, when
Mr. Benjamin Crocker's engagement ceased, until 1757,
when Mr. Wigglesworth was appointed. In that dark
age it appears that the action of the Feoffees was suspended
There is no record of any meeting from February 13, 1721-2,
when Daniel Rogers, John Denison, Esquires, were chosen
until February 10, 1749, when Jonathan Wade, the only
survivor of the Feoffees, appoints the Honb'l Thomas
Berry, Collo : Daniel Appleton. Mr. Thomas———? Maj.
Samuel Rogers and Mr. Benjamin Crocker.

WILSON, Theophilus, received a grant of land, 1638.
1641, was a commoner.
1648, was one of Major Denison's subscribers.
1653, Prison Keeper.
1664, a share and a half in Plum Island.
1677, was a Tythingman.
1679, Voter in Town affairs.

1655, 30th, 6mo.  Mr. Wilson is desired to speak to Goodman Norton to fulfil his bargain in make the Meeting house tight, where shingles were removed by him, occasioned by the putting in of the gutters.  And in case he do not forth with make them good, hath order by this meeting of the select men to sue him in the Town's name.

1655, February 19.  Agreed that Mr. Wilson shall take care to lay the floor in the turret of the Meeting-house with plank, and calk it, and daub the north east side below the floor.

1656, December 23.  Agreed with Mr. Wilson to ring the Bell at nine of the Clock : to begin the next second day, being the 12th of January, for which he is to have forty shillings a year added to the rate.

1655, 30th, 6mo.  Sold unto Theophilus Wilson for his son Thomas, the meadow that is common at ye west meadows, neare to Samuel Varnham, at £2 : 6, per acre, not exceeding six acres.

1639.  He possessed a houselot which he bought of John Saunders, bounded on the south wast by the Meeting house green, and on the north east by the stoney street, and on the south east by a house lot formerly granted to Robert Morey.  This lot must have been near the site of the Rev. D. T. Kimball's.

He sold to John Knowlton, shoemaker, January 28, 1646, land he bought of John Warner.

1642, December 20.  He purchased a farm of William Whitred.

1654, December 1, with Elisabeth, his wife, he sold to Samuel Sawer, hatter, dwelling house and about half an acre of land which was the house of Jane Kenning lately deceased, being near the Meeting-house ; having John Knowlton southwest end of it; Goodman Prichett north west side, John Wyatt northeast end of it.

1654, March 28.  He testified to the will of John Knowlton, who styles him his "brother Wilson."

Thomas Knowlton in his will dated February 14, 1653, mentions his sister Elisabeth Wilson ; his sister's children : Elizabeth Wilson, Seaborn Wilson, Thomas Wilson

And Elisabeth Wilson, his sister, died January 10, 1680.

The will of Theophilus Wilson is dated October 3, 1690. He gives the farm to his son Thomas. Legacies to his grandchildren: Elisabeth Lovel, Elisabeth Russell, and Thomas Pindar.

Thomas Wilson 2, son of Theophilus 1, had a share in Plum Island, 1664; horses on the common, 1697. His children were: William, John, Seaborn or Shoreborn.

1676.    Thomas is employed to keep a flock.

1661.    Shoreborn has liberty to fell ten oak trees.

1692-3.    John has the first and John the eighth lot between Ordway's and the Town Bridge.

1697.    William has horses on the common.

1707.    Shoreborn is commoner.

Shoreborn Wilson and Abigail Osgood m. Sept. 9, 1657. In the record Shoreborn is spelled Shone.    Children:

Joseph, born May 8, 1660
Mary, born and died August 24, 1662
Samuel, born April 4, 1664
John, born May 4, 1665
Abigail, born March 20, 1666
Christopher, born December 13, 1671
Deborah, born September 22, 1673
William, born May 14, 1675

JOHN WINTHROP, the younger, son of John, Governor of Massachusetts, was born February 12, 1605-6; his father having married 16 April preceeding, being then only seventeen years and three months old, Mary, dau. of John Forth, Esq'r, of Great Stanbridge, Essex.

He was educated at the Universities of Cambridge and Dublin; and came to New England in 1631. He took the freeman's oath, April 4, 1632.

In March 1632-3. he came with twelve others, and commenced the settlement of Ipswich. His first wife, Martha, daughter of Henry Painter, came with him, and soon died; family memoirs say she was buried in Ipswich.

All his children were born of his second wife, Elisabeth Reade, step-daughter of Hugh Peters.

He was elected Assistant from 1632 to 1649.

He went to England in the winter of 1634, and returned in October, 1635. He had a Commission from the Lords Say and Brook, and divers other great persons in England, to begin a Plantation at Connecticut ; and to be Governor. He continued in the office of Governor of Connecticut, until his death at Boston, April 5, 1676, aged 70 years.

He had several grants of land in Ipswich. He had a house lot at the south eastern end of the High street, near the Cove; a farm at the south side of the river, at or near the Burnhams ; and with respect to this location, it appears that John Tuttle had a houselot of about one acre and twenty rod lying between Mr. Rogers and Mr. Ward and Mr. Winthrop and the highway.

In 1639, there was granted to Mr. John Winthrop, Castle Hill, and the meadow and marsh lying within ye Creek, provided he lives in ye town, and ye town may have what they shall need for building a fort. This estate he sold to his "brother Samuel Symonds," August 30, 1647.

1634. Granted to John Winthrop six acres near the river on the south side.

WOOD, Daniel, was one of Major Denison's subscribers, 1648, and died the same year.

Obadiah Wood had a share in Plum Island, 1664 ; voter in Town affairs, 1679 ; liberty to sell cakes and penny beer 1677. His will is dated October 26, 1694. Children :
Obadiah, Nathaniel, Josiah, Samuel, James, Joseph
Elisabeth, Mary Boyer, Susanna Blythe, Ruth Robbins
His wife, Margaret died July 5, 1667.

His second wife had the singular name, Hazelelpony :

> Haselelpony Wood
> widow of Obadiah
> Wood died Nouem'r
> ye 27 1714, Aged 78
> years
> Wright blesed are ye dead
> Wc die in ye Lord

Obadiah was a baker ; and left property amounting to £185. His seal was a coat of arms.

Joseph Wood, son of Obadiah ; will dated July 29, 1690, proved March 31, 1691. He was 'Joseph Wood, Carpenter,' being called out by the Providence of God in the expedition of War against cannaday ; Knowing not how it may please ye Lord to dispose of me. * I doe appoint my honoured father, Obadiah Wood to be sole executor. * I desire my brother James may have my carpenter's tools, provided he larnes ye trade. * Sister Mary Bryer forty shillings. * To my brothers Samuel and Josiah Wood all that my wages due me from ye Country for my service in ye time of Sir Edmund Andros, governor, which is seven pounds sixteen shillings, * and any wages or plunder that may be due to me from ye country for my service, I doe give ye same to my honoured father.

1691, April 21. Inv'r, £157, 4, 1 deceased in ye Can-, nada voyage.

1708-9, Feb. 4. The will of James Wood, son of Obadiah, proved February 4, 1708-9. He bequeaths to his Sister Susannah Blythe, his black mare ; to his sister Robbins his youngest mare ; to his sister Elizabeth Wood his oldest mare. The rest of his property he gives to his dear and loving mother, Hazelelpony Wood.

Simon Wood, was of the young generation who joined the church by taking the covenant, Feb. 1, 1673-4. He married Elisabeth Foster: August 8, 1674. Children :

    Elisabeth, born September, 1675
    Ebenezer, died December 24, 1676
    Mary, born December 27, 1676
    Jonathan. born March 6, 1678
    Elisabeth, died August 16, 1678
    Philemon, born April 5, 1679
    Daniel, born June 12, 1685
    William, born January 3, 1689

He had horses on the common, 1697 ; with title of Sergt. he had a seat assigned him in the meeting house, No. 4, January, 1700. March 15, 1719-20, he had a seat at the communion table with the title Lieut. His wife in the women's third seats.

Thompson Wood, m. December 8, 1691, Martha Foster.
Samuel Wood, hatter, and Judith, had Samuel, born
July 15, 1685, John, died April 9, 1688.
John, married Mary Healey, May 1, 1676. They had :
Margaret, born Sept. 1679 ; Mary, born Dec. 19, 1681.
John, died August 13, 1684.
William, died Feb. 27, and Ruth, his wife, Feb 8, 1721.
Daniel, died July 22, 1722.
Joseph, m. Mary Grover, June 11, 1666, died Jan. 1700.
Ezekiel, had son Samuel, born July 20, 1659.
Anthony, had son William, born M 20, 1666.
Symon had the 15th, Samuel, saltmaker, the 23d lots,
between Ordway's and the Bridge.

Here Lies ye Body of Mr. John Wood who Died
August the 22 A. D. 1751, in the 66 year of his Age.

Here lies ye body of Mrs. Mary Wood, wife to Mr.
John Wood, Decd Sep ye 23 1726, in ye 37 yr of her age

WOODBORNE, Samuel and Mary, had Margaret, b.
March 20, 1684.

WOODBURY, Isaac, of Chebacco Parish, had horses
on the common, 1697. Children : Isaac, b. July 20, 1697;
Benjamin, born August 20, 1699.

WOODEN, Ithamah and Bethiah, had Nathan, born
October 24, 1693.

WOODMANSY. Mr. Woodmansy was a commoner,
1641. He sold a farm of 110 arcres, March 5, 1660, to
Thomas Bishop, who sold the same to Daniel Rindge. It
was bounded by the Mile Brook, land of Matthew Whipple, and Richard Jacob. He removed from Ipswich to
Boston.

WOODAM, John, purchased of John West, June 28,
1649, a dwelling house and half an acre of land which formerly belonged to John Jackson, which Woodam sold,
February 5, 1650 to Humphrey Gilbert.
He purchased of Thomas Manning, Oct. 13, 1653, a

piece of land which is for the constant maintenance of the whole fence between the houselot of Mr. Samuel Symonds and this lot.

He purchased of John Warner in 1665, March 10, a dwelling house in Brook street, having Roger Langton northeast, Jeffrey Snelling south, street west.

He purchased of Mark Quilter, November 30, 1657, the planting lot bequeathed unto me by my father, Mark Quilter, formerly purchased of John Johnson, school master, upon ye Town Hill, &c.

He purchased of William Symonds a house and an acre of land on Brook street, November 19, 1656.

With Mary his wife he sold to John Brown a house and land at the nor east end highway called the high street.

He was one of Major Denison's subscribers, 1648 ; had a share and a half in Plum Island, 1664.

He died May 29, 1678, and left a widow Mary, who died Feb. 12, 1681; an only child, Mary Eyr [Ayres.]

1683, March. Mary Woodam, dying intestate, John Ayres app't adm'r of his late mother-in-law.

WOODWARD, Ezekiel.    Had a share in Plum Island, 1664. He made a contract with the Selectmen June 18, 1668, for shingling the Meeting-house. Had liberty to cut trees, 1665. With Nath'l Pyper, Nath'l Tredwell, had liberty to build a gallery, &c., 1666. He and Free-grace Norton agree to get and hue timber for ye Meeting house, 200 feet, June 1, 1667.

He purchased a house and lot of Ralf Dix, March 20, 1661, containing two acres and a half, bounded on the north east and south east by the Mill River ; and on the north west by land of Samuel Younglove, and on the south west by the highway; consideration, £60. He had:

Martha, born May 3, 1662
Mary, born December 8, 1664
Ezekiel, born August 9, 1666
Rachell, born January 20, 1668

WYTH, Humphrey.    Had a houselot in 1636, one acre
of ground lying on the south side of the town river, having
a houselot of Symon Tompson on the north ; and a  house
lot formerly granted to John Merrill on the south.

WYATT, John.    He possessed a houselot in Mill st.,
1638, adjoing a house lot granted to Mr. John Norton.
    He was one who promised voluntary carting  toward the
Bridge.    He had land on Heartbreak hill near the way
leading to Mr. Saltonstall's farm.
    He is called Goodman Wyatt.    He was commoner, 1641.
One of Major Denison's subscribers, 1648.    A share in
Plum Island, 1664.    He was witness to the will of Luke
Heard, Sept. 28, 1647
    He purchased of Nathaniel Bishop of Boston, March 10,
1652, the house in which said  Wyatt  now dwelleth, with
the  land, and having  the  land of Thomas Botham, now
in possession of Ralph Smith toward the north east, the
Meeting house green toward the south  east, a lane  toward
the·south west, adjoining to other lands of the said John
Wiates towards the  north west.
    A houselot sold by Theophilus Wilson to Samuel Sawer
Dec. 1, 1654, is described as being near the Meeting-house,
and  having  John Wyat at the north east end of it.    John
Woodam sold to John Brown, 1663, a house in High street,
John Wyatt's pasture at the south of it.
    He died January  15,  1664-5, and left a wife Mary, and
house and lands valued at £177.

WILKINSON, Henry.    1638, August 20, reference is
made to his three acres of land at Sagamore Hill.

WALKER, Richard.    In  1679,  he is recorded as a
Tythingman.
    1677, December 20.    He  had  granted "too  pine trees,"
to use upon the house where he now lives.
    He married Sarah Storey, October 29, 1661.    Children :
        Hannah, born September 10, 1662
        Sarah, born November 29, 1666
        Richard, born February 6, 1674
        Joseph, born December 29, 1679

WATSON, William.  Had Sarah, born November 2, 1672, who married Samuel Wallis, Dec. 30, 1690.

WILLARD, Simon, had :
    Jacob, born September 17, 1680.

YELL, John, and wife Johanna, had ;
    Elisabeth, born June 15, 1691
    John, born January 20.  1693
John Yell 2, and Abigail Stewart of Rowley, published November 6, 1736.
    Jan. 29, 1700-1.  John Smith, Adm'r estate of John Yell.

YORK, Samuel.  Wife Mary died April 16, 1709, and he married (2) another Mary.

> Here lies ye body
> of Samuel Yorke
> Son of Mr. Samuel
> Mrs. Mary Yorke
> who died Nou'r 27
> 1735      in ye      15th
> year of his age

YOUNG, Francis.  Had horses on the common, 1697.
Rebecca Young had seat in the meeting house, 1702.
Francis Young and Rebecca Chapman were married December 4, 1678.  Children :
    George, born April 28, 1680
    Rebecca, born March.22, 1681

YOUNGLOVE, Samuel.  In the Hopewell, of London, Thos: Babb, Master, for New England, 1635 :
    Samuel Younglove, aged 30 years ;
    Margaret Younglove, aged 28 years ;
    Samuel Younglove, aged 1 year.
He had a houselot on the south side of the river next to the lot of Thomas Wells, 1635.
    1641.  He was a commoner.
    1648.  One of Major Denison's subscribers.
    1664.  A share in Plum Island.
    1664.  He is called, Samuel, sen'r.

1679. Voter in Town affairs.
He died in 1689.

Samuel Younglove 2, son of Samuel 1, married Sarah
Kinsman, August 1, 1660.    Children:
    Sarah, born Feb. 5, 1662
    Samuel, born Oct. 30, 1665, died March 16, 1666
    Mary, born M 17, 1667
    Samuel, born July 27, 1671
    Truman, born May 31, 1674
    Mercy, born May 25, 1676
    John, born August 29, 1679
He had a share in Plum Island, 1664.
Was a voter in Town affairs, 1679.

Samuel Younglove 3, (Samuel 2.)   Jan. 27, 1706-7.—
Mary Younglove declining adm'r of the estate of Samuel
Younglove, her husband.   John Younglove is app'd.
    1708, April 3.   Mary, widow of Samuel Younglove, by
advice of her brother Samuel Roe, sells her dower and her
child's part of the estate, excepting his right in land when
he comes of age, to John Younglove, adm'r, in consideration of 20 pounds.

Joseph Younglove died July 14, 1712, his will dated
the same day.   To wife Jane housing and land.   Seven
shillings to my sister-in-law, Susanna Hadley.   To cousin
Samuel Younglove, five shillings.   Inv: £68, 19.

The end.

# INDEX

A name may appear more than once on a page. The names appearing on the page following page 6 have been indexed as being on page 7.

INDEX 433

Frink, George, 108, 344
John, 108
Mary, 108
Frost, Edmund, 115
John, 76
Fuller, (?), 87
Daniel, 112, 113
Dorothy, 350
Elizabeth, 87, 112, 165, 334
Hannah Hovey, 163
James, 112, 113, 178, 278, 362
John, 86, 87, 103, 112, 113, 369
Joseph, 112, 113
Katherine, 145
Mary, 112, 166
Nathaniel, 112, 113, 163
Sarah, 161
Sarah Jones, 178
Susanna, 87, 112, 352
Thomas, 112, 113
William, 66, 111, 112, 113, 128, 237, 326, 329, 333
Fuzz, William, 136

Gage, Amy, 118
John, 7, 108, 117, 118, 329
Gages, John, 118
Gaines, Abigail, 117
Abyell, 117
Elizabeth, 117
Esther, 371
John, 117, 371
Martha, 117, 371
Mary, 117, 368
Mary Treadwell, 371
Sarah, 117, 371
Gallop, Elizabeth, 124
Hannah, 124, 217
Hannah Lake, 220
John, 124, 220
Galloway, Lydia, 149
Gally, Florence, 317
John, 317
Mary, 317
Gamage, John, 123
Mary, 123
Nath'l, 123
Gardiner, Edmu d, 119
Gardner, Edmund, 118
Garood, (?), 314
Martin, 315
Geddings, Joanna, 146
See also Giddings.
Gedney, Anne, 118
Barth'o, 272
Col. Bartholomew, 346
Bartholomy, 118
John, 118
Gee, (?), 308
George, Sarah, 176
Gerrish, Jane Sewall, 330
Gerrish, Rev. Joseph, 115
Moses, 330
Gibson, Mary, 157
Giddinge, Abigail, 78
Anna, 171
William, 12
Giddings, (?), 12, 121
Abigail, 83
Dorothy, 226
Elizabeth, 50
Eunice, 52
George, 73, 116

James, 12, 116
Jane, 116
Job, 12, 116
John, 34, 116
Joseph, 116
Joshua, 116
Lawrence, 116
Martha, 149
Mary, 116, 226
Samuel, 12, 116, 363
Sarah, 116
Solomon, 116
Thomas, 116, 226
William, 116
See also Geddings.
Gifford, Margaret, 61
Gilbard, Humphrey, 113
Gilbert, Abigail, 115
Benjamin, 115
Caroline Stone, 350
Daniel, 115
Elizabeth, 113, 114, 275
Hannah, 115
Humphrey, 113, 114, 115, 117, 118, 419
John, 113, 115, 350
Joseph, 115
Lydia, 115
Martha, 115
Mary, 115
Noah, 115
Sarah, 115
Thomas, 113
Giles, Elizabeth, 179
Gilman, Abigail S. Lord, 214
Daniel, 214
Edward, 115, 116, 333
Elizabeth Smith, 333
John, 115, 116
Robert, 305
Gilven, Thomas, 228
Gitting, John, 363
Glazier, Joseph, 118
Zacerias, 118
Glover, Elisha, 287
Elizabeth Rindge, 287
Rev. Jesse, 17
Priscilla, 17, 20
Sarah, 332
Goffe, (?), 326
Goodenough, David, 117
Robert, 117
Goodhew, William, 363
Goodhue, (?), 216
Deacon, 56, 108, 121, 219, 242
Aaron, 121
Abigail, 121
Abigail Low, 216
Benjamin, 120, 372
Bethiah, 121
David, 121
Ebenezer, 65, 120
Elizabeth, 121
Francis, 89, 121
Hannah, 120, 121
Jacob, 353
Johanna Story, 353
John, 121
Jonathan, 121
Joseph, 55, 96, 120, 121, 193, 201, 267, 335, 353
Margery, 121
Mary, 116, 120, 121, 228
Mary Osborne, 239
Mercy, 162
Moses, 121
Nathaniel, 12, 53, 121

Samuel, 120
Sarah, 121, 372, 405
Sarah Smith, 335
Sarah Whipple, 300
William, 12, 28, 34, 102, 117, 119, 121, 228, 232, 239, 245, 277, 280, 369, 279, 280, 413
Goodridge, Benjamin, 176
Daniel, 176
Deborah, 176
Joseph, 176
Josiah, 176
Gordan, Francis, 27
Jane, 27
Goss, Anna, 141
Richard, 123
Gott, Charles, 114
Lidia, 35
Nathaniel, 115
Gould, Henry, 117
Isaac, 117
Joanna, 117
Priscilla, 335
Sarah, 117
Gould, Sarah, 353
Zathneul, 241
Granger, Lancelot, 118
Grant, Deborah, 188
John, 123
Robert, 108, 123
Roger, 123
Graves, Abigail Hodgkins, 145
Elizabeth, 50, 123
Francis, 123, 130, 131
Hannah, 123, 269
Joanna, 123
John, 123, 130, 131, 145
Martha, 123, 131, 231
Mary, 369, 370
Samuel, 123, 221, 264, 269
Gray, Lydia Lewis, 163, 164
Greely, George, 403
Mary, 403
Green, Henry, 122
Thomas, 122
Greenfield, Samuel, 413
Greenleaf, Ruth, 37
Greenough, Daniel, 94
Robert, 94
Gregory, James, 123, 206
Jonas, 89, 123
Griffin, Elizabeth, 76, 122
Humphrey, 41, 72, 98, 103, 122, 236, 267, 321, 328, 369
Joan, 122
Lydia, 122
Samuel, 122
Groton, Damaras, 52
Grove, Hannah, 121
John, 121, 122
Mary, 122
Nathaniel, 122
Ruth, 122
Samuel, 122
Thomas, 122
William, 122
Grover, Mary, 419
Grow, Hannah, 208
John, 122, 208
Samuel, 122
Gutterson, John, 122
Mary, 122
Sarah, 122
William, 122